CRANNOG TO CASTLE

A HISTORY OF THE BURNETT FAMILY IN SCOTLAND

ADDENDA: To Acknowledgements:
Malcolm Lingen Hutton & Connie Hildebrandt.
Mrs Robert Calvert & Charles Burnett Landreth.
ERRATA:
p.80 line 24 - for College read School.
p. 80 line 27/28 - for Philips read Phillips.
p.81 line 10 - for Francia read Francis.
p.81 line29 - for 1966 read 1996.
p.81 line 32 - for Vanessa Wladyslaw Gallica read Vanessa Josephine Bronislawna Gallica.
p.81 line 36 - add to married (3) ' in 1998'.
p.82 line 1 - for 1952 read 1983.
p. 128 line 36 - for 1824 read 1624.
p.150 - ref. General Sir John T. Burnett - Stuart delete " Knight of the Thistle"

CRANNOG TO CASTLE

Edited by

Eileen A. Bailey

Foreword by

James C. A. Burnett of Leys

Leys Publishing

First published in 2000 by
Leys Publishing - St Nicholas House
Station Road - Banchory - Kincardineshire- AB31 5YJ

ISBN : 0-9538640-1-4

Printed and Bound by Thomson Press (India) Ltd.

CRATHES CASTLE

**JAMES AND FIONA BURNETT
AND FAMILY**

FOREWORD

As the present Head of the Burnett family, I am aware of the efforts of my ancestor, George Burnett, Lord Lyon, to record our family history and I have no doubt that had he lived to complete his research much more would have been included in *The Family of Burnett of Leys* which was published at the start of the last century. It is for that reason that I feel my personal contribution to the family at the commencement of the new millennium should include the publication of an expanded genealogical and other record of the various Burnett branches in Scotland.

Since I came to live at Crathes in 1965, every year has seen an increasing number of visits, letters and telephone calls from my kinsmen all over the world indicating how widespread they are and how great their interest in the Burnett ancestry. I have been invited to and most graciously received at Clan events abroad and my wife and I have been delighted to meet with so many Burnetts at the several organised visits with which we have been involved here in north-east Scotland. The House of Burnett in the USA has, in particular, done much to promote the family contact throughout that country by the production the Burnett Banner newsletter and other activities.

The research findings for this new book have highlighted to me how continuous the relationship of the Burnetts to Crathes and the Banchory area has been; how diverse the occupations of my ancestors and how far travelled they were. At the present time, the area of Scotland in which I live is regarded as a major centre of commerce, trading with almost every part of the world and yet I find members of my Burnett family were trading extensively in salmon and many other commodities with countries in Europe as early as the 1300s. I am aware that the book contains more details on the northern Burnetts than on other branches further south. This is not deliberate but simply results from the levels of accessible information that could be compiled at this time.

It is my sincere wish that *Crannog to Castle* will serve as a source of information on the family history of the Burnetts of Scotland for present and future generations and I am grateful to the various contributors for their support, interest and expertise.

James C. A. Burnett of Leys.
House of Crathes. 2000.

THE AUTHORS

BAILEY, Eileen A. (nee PROCTOR), D.M.S. Dip.M., FSA. Scot. is a Scottish genealogist and local history researcher with a special interest in the north-east of Scotland. In 1996, she was appointed the official genealogist and family history researcher to the Burnett family. To her has fallen the additional challenging task of General Editor of *Crannog to Castle.* An accomplished photographer, she has been responsible for photographs taken specifically to illustrate this book. Eileen Bailey combines her genealogy skills with interest in Scottish and local history and in archaeology to undertake an interesting array of assignments and has several publications in preparation. She is a Fellow of the Society of Antiquaries of Scotland.

BRYCE, Ian B.D, FSA. Scot., followed a career in engineering for fifteen years before spending some time as a student of Aberdeen University. In 1974 he was a founder contributor to the Aberdeen *Leopard* magazine for which he has written articles on some 30 castles, a series on Doric humour, book reviews and many other topics of local interest. Ian Bryce is well known as a prolific and enthusiastic author on things historical with articles published in *Aberdeen University Review*, *Deeside Field* and the *Transactions of the Buchan Field Club*. He contributes to the annual Proceedings of the Society of Antiquaries of Scotland of which he is a Fellow and he recently completed his first book *A Chronology of the Castles of Scotland*. With his wealth of local knowledge he is in regular demand to give talks to a wide variety of organisations.

BURNETT, Charles J., FSA. Scot., an expert in Heraldry, is Ross Herald at the Court of the Lord Lyon which is the governing body of Heraldry in Scotland. As a Fellow of the Heraldry Society of Scotland he is a well-known author and lecturer on the subject. His recent publications include *Scotland's Heraldic Heritage - The Lion Rejoicing* which he co-authored with Mark D. Dennis in 1997 as part of the Discovering Historic Scotland Series. He was Curator of the Scottish Services Museum at Edinburgh Castle before returning to his roots in north-east Scotland to take up his present appointment as Chamberlain of Duff House Country House Gallery, Banff, which exhibits part of the National Art Collection of Scotland. Charles Burnett is a Fellow of the Society of Antiquaries of Scotland to whose annual Proceedings he is a regular and valued contributor.

BURNETT, James C.A. of Leys, is Head of the Burnett Family worldwide. In 1965, he assumed his maternal surname of Burnett, at the express wish of his grandfather, and moved north to the family estates of Leys, near Banchory, Kincardineshire. The home of James Burnett and his family is now House of Crathes, built in traditional style on the estate. He is a successful landowner and active businessman with a strong interest in maintaining traditional values and community involvement. He has served as a Local Councillor and on the Council of the National Trust for Scotland. James Burnett values the links with Burnetts worldwide. He has devoted a considerable amount of time and finance to the task of ensuring that his ancestry and the accumulated archives of the Burnett family and Leys estate are recorded and preserved.

ACKNOWLEDGEMENTS

This publication could not have been achieved without the considerable work, input and support of many people. In particular, I would like to thank my fellow contributing authors, Charles J. Burnett, Ian B. D. Bryce, and Eileen A. Bailey for the time and expertise devoted to preparing their individual Chapters. David Paton, Peter Cumyn, Geordie Burnett-Stuart, Mrs. M. Bogdan, Nicholas Bogdan and David Lees provided valuable additional information about the branches of the family of which they are descendants. Jim Fina, Charles B. Rose Jnr., Jennifer Mackenzie and Annie Lee Burnett Vuillemot contributed supplementary genealogical facts, which have been included where appropriate. I appreciate the other submissions of genealogy, which I have retained in the Burnett files to help in future research. I wish to thank Mrs. Heather Bree for undertaking the proofreading and Bill Bailey for his technical expertise and support. In the production process, Bill Williams generously shared his experience in giving most helpful guidance on aspects of publishing.

Individuals and organisations gave assistance in a wide variety of ways. The National Trust for Scotland and the Administrator of Crathes Castle willingly gave access for photography at Crathes as did Dr. & Mrs. Hogan, the owners of Muchalls Castle. Jim Henderson kindly allowed me to reproduce his photograph of the opening of the Family Room at Crathes and the Gordon Highlanders Museum provided photographs from their archives. Some early photographs of Crathes Castle were reproduced with permission of The Royal Commission on the Ancient & Historical Monuments of Scotland. In support of the authors, John Mathieson undertook to research the military career of Sir James L.G. Burnett, and William Adams, David Humble, John Ross, Arthur Ruxton and other current or former tenants of the Leys estate contributed background information about the estate. Mrs Jo Edwards typed the Chapter on Heraldry, Dr. Nicola Mill skilfully translated Mottoes from Latin and Mrs C.J.W. Roads, Lyon Clerk, gave special help with locating Burnett Arms in the Lyon Records.

Burnetts from many parts of the world have shown great interest in this book and I especially thank Joseph Burnett-Stuart of Aberdeenshire; Ruth Burnett Philips of Edenton, USA; Annetta Burnett Collins of High Point, NC, USA; Gilbert H. Burnett of Wilmington, NC, USA; Marvin & Mary Holmberg of Northville, MI, USA; Mildred Burnett Jones, of Raleigh, NC, USA; and D. Byron Arneson, of Germantown, MD. USA, who all contributed towards the cost of publication.

James C.A. Burnett of Leys.

INTRODUCTION

Old parchments lay before me, old deeds of men long dead.
Who took great pains to write and thought of what they said

(From *The Legend of Birse* written Christmas 1893 by a brother of Marquis of Huntly.)

In common with most Scottish families, that of Burnett has many branches and descendants in Scotland and in most other countries of the world. To attempt to include, in this volume, expansive details of all branches and connections world-wide is understandably impossible. Nevertheless, there is much in the history of the principal Burnett families in Scotland to intrigue many whether one's interest is in a particular aspect of the genealogy, in the very early records, in the colourful heraldry or the lands and houses over the centuries. Sources indicated at appropriate points in the text will enable readers to more fully understand the background to the times in which various generations of Burnetts lived. Some descendants, especially, those whose home is outwith Scotland, will hopefully be able to identify their ancestral links.

In his genealogy of *The Family of Burnetts of Leys*, Dr. George Burnett, Lyon King of Arms, set out to record that family's succession. After his death on 23 January 1890, his uncompleted manuscript- sadly without any notes as to the intended full content of the final work - was taken over and completed by James Allardyce. The book was eventually published in 1901 by the Spalding Club of Aberdeen, on whose behalf Dr Burnett had originally agreed to write it. Of the George Burnett/James Allardyce work, surviving original copies are now almost all in reference libraries and private collections. Similarly, much of the genealogy of the Burnetts of Burnetland and Barns was diligently gathered together by Montgomery Burnet but printed privately, originally intended for members of the family only. *Crannog to Castle* understandably incorporates information, which appeared in both of these prior works. As a result of research undertaken for this publication, substantial additional facts, dates and biographical detail have been added or amended.

The history of the Burnetts in Scotland focuses around two main geographical areas - the southern counties particularly Peebles and Roxburgh and the counties of Kincardine and Aberdeen in the north-east. As one would expect, generation after generation spread further afield and soon Burnetts were to be found in the large towns and cities such as Edinburgh, Glasgow and London and in those countries overseas where they chose to pursue their profession. Professional people the Burnetts most certainly were. The children in each generation clearly set out to make their own way in the world for, although the Burnetts were landowners and upstanding in the community, the assets which supported them did not come easily and were largely the result of their own efforts. Financial crises were not unknown to several of those who inherited. From the earliest records and throughout their history we find a liberal spread of merchants, clergymen, lawyers and advocates, officers of the Crown, high ranking military men, writers, doctors and surgeons, officials of universities and those with a strong interest in genealogy and heraldry without whose influence this volume would probably never have been written. Archival material such as the Register of the Great Seal of Scotland contains evidence of a long affinity with land and property. Aware that man is simply a guardian for following generations, Burnetts throughout the centuries, with an occasional exception, appear to have made great efforts to improve the status of the family estates, residences and fortunes for the future.

This book has aimed to bring together detail of the Burnetts against the background of changing historical events and to show where they made their family homes. Many charters and other documents have been retained, deliberately or accidentally, by the families themselves or by other repositories. In the context of compiling a clearer picture of individuals, these papers are often as frustrating in what they do not tell us, as they are fascinating in their historical content. Fortunately, some of the later Burnett families took steps to have recorded a Coat of Arms for their particular branch and, in so doing, added a further dimension to research resources. Old parish records in Scotland often show only a child's father but do not record the mother. By no means have all church and other records been saved for posterity, ravaged as they have often been by the destructive forces of nature. Prominent Burnetts have had their exploits written about by others but sadly there are individuals within each family about whom little is known. This is particularly evident in the case of the second and any following sons, some of whose careers, spouses and children will never be known, and of most of the daughters. Information on daughters is occasionally to be found in recorded genealogy of other local families with whom they intermarried. Prominent people were normally active in the community and in their support of the church and so tended to have more elaborate gravestones and inscriptions raised to their memory. In the case of the Burnetts, many attended the Episcopalian church. The records, church and churchyard of St. Nicholas in Aberdeen are, in themselves, an archive of the northern Burnett family history.

Scottish estates have, in the major of cases, been quite diligently archived in terms of land charters, sasines, tenancies and the records made by employees. From those various papers it is possible for social historians, and others, to add detail and interest to the background of the lives of earlier generations, their place within, and their impact on, local communities. An example is the surviving Barony Book of the Leys Estate, which contains fascinating examples, of how the Laird of Leys in the 1600s controlled, disciplined and influenced the tenants of his lands. A chapter has, therefore, been included to show how the Laird of Leys in the 20th and 21st centuries managed the lands and the present day relationship between estate and community.

Although the contributing authors have aimed to bring the history of the Burnetts in Scotland into the new millennium, it must be appreciated that, in so doing, due respect has been paid to the privacy of living individuals and for that reason some personal information is not available or has been deliberately omitted. In addition, not all of the genealogy of all branches is totally updated and in some cases incomplete. This is because information has not yet been located or has not been established as correct. Every century produces more clues, facts and understanding of the past whether it is in the field of genealogy, archaeology or any other. It cannot be claimed that *Crannog to Castle* is the definitive book about the Burnetts but it does attempt to bring together all that we think we know about those who have gone before. Tomorrow will no doubt change today's thinking.

The search goes on.

Eileen A. Bailey.
General Editor.
2000.

CONTENTS

Crathes Castle

James & Fiona Burnett and family

Foreword

Authors

Acknowledgements

Introduction

1	**SAXON OR NORMAN?** Eileen A. Bailey The origins of the Burnet(t) surname.	**1**
2	**THE BURNETS IN SOUTHERN SCOTLAND** Eileen A. Bailey The Burnets of Farningdon, Burnetland & Barns and Ardross. The genealogy and descendancy of these Burnet families.	**6**
3	**THE BURNETTS IN NORTH-EAST SCOTLAND** Eileen A. Bailey The Burnetts of Leys and branches. The genealogy and descendancy of the Burnetts of Leys.	**26**
4	**THE BURNETTS OF CRAIGMYLE AND CRIMOND** Eileen A. Bailey Genealogy.	**89**
5	**THE BURNETTS OF KEMNAY** Eileen A. Bailey Genealogy and descendancy.	**97**
6	**THE BURNETTS OF MONBODDO** Eileen A. Bailey Genealogy and descendancy.	**111**

7 **THE BURNETTS OF CAMPHILL, ELRICK AND KIRKHILL** 128
Eileen A. Bailey
Genealogy.

8 **THE BURNETTS OF SHEDDOCKSLEY, COUNTESSWELLS, AND POWIS** 142
Eileen A. Bailey
Genealogy.

9 **THE BURNETT-STUARTS and BURNETTS OF DALADIES** 147
Eileen A. Bailey
Genealogy.

10 **THE RAMSAYS OF BALMAIN** 154
Eileen A. Bailey
The genealogy and descendancy of the Burnett-Ramsays.

11 **INDETERMINATE BURNETT CADETS** 166
Eileen A. Bailey
Burnetts of Kinchyle and Burnetts of Lethenty.

12 **THE HERALDRY OF THE BURNETT FAMILY** 176
Charles J. Burnett, Ross Herald at Arms
The Arms of members of the Burnett family.
Location of associated heraldry.
Colour illustrations of Registered Arms.

13 **THE CRANNOG OF LEYS** 225
Eileen A, Bailey
The earliest residence of the Burnetts of Leys.

14 **CASTLES AND OTHER RESIDENCES** 232
Ian B. D. Bryce
The castles of Crathes and Muchalls.
Other Burnett residences in Scotland.

15 **LEYS ESTATE AT 2000AD** 270
James C.A. Burnett of Leys
An account of the Leys Estate from 1900 to the present day.
Its relationship with the local community.
Maps and appendices.

16 **BURNETT BURIAL PLACES** 345
Eileen A. Bailey
The location of various Burnett burials and memorial inscriptions.

GENERAL INDEX 348

ILLUSTRATIONS

Crathes Castle. (Colour) i

James & Fiona Burnett and Family. (Colour) ii

Chapter 1

Fig. 1.1 The seals of Odo and Richard Burnard. 5

Chapter 3

Fig. 3.1 Leys Charter. 26
Fig. 3.2 The Horn of Leys. 27
Fig. 3.3 Sir Thomas Burnett, 1st Baronet. 48
Fig. 3.4 James L. G. Burnett. 68
Fig. 3.5 James Burnett, R. G. Forbes & J. R. F. Stanford at Spitz Kop, 1900. 69
Fig. 3.6 James Burnett at Gymkhana, Pietersburg, 1901. 70
Fig. 3.7 Officers' Pipe Band, 1901. 71
Fig. 3.8 Sir James J. G. Burnett of Leys. 77

Chapter 4

Fig. 4.1 Bishop Gilbert Burnett. 94

Chapter 6

Fig. 6.1 Thomas Burnett of Kepplestone, Advocate. 114
Fig. 6.2 Newell Burnett of Kyallachie, Advocate. 114
Fig. 6.3 Lord Monboddo. 120

Chapter 7

Fig. 7.1 Gravestone of John Burnett of Elrick (drawing). 131
Fig. 7.2 The Jameson House. 132

Chapter 10

Fig. 10.1 Fasque House, Fettercairn. 156

Chapter 12 (in Colour except Fig.12.44)

Fig. 12.1 Panel on Crathes - Arms of Burnet and Hamilton. 204
Fig. 12.2 Three heraldic panels, on Crathes Castle. 204
Fig. 12.3 Painted ceiling ingo, Crathes – Burnet & Hamilton Arms. 205
Fig. 12.4 Painted ceiling ingo, Crathes – Burnet & Gordon Arms. 205
Fig. 12.5 Pendant boss, Crathes – Hamilton Arms. 206
Fig. 12.6 Carved panel on Muchalls – Burnet and Gordon Arms. 206
Fig. 12.7 Carved panel, now on Crathes – Burnet and Moncrieffe Arms. 206
Fig. 12.8 1838 Armorial achievement, Burnett of Leys. 206
Fig. 12.9 Embroidered Pipe Banner - Burnett Arms. 207
Fig. 12.10 Armorial Achievement of current Head of House. 207
Fig. 12.11 Standard of Head of House. 208
Fig. 12.12 Pinsel of Head of House. 208
Fig. 12.13 Carved panel on Crathes – Burnett & Dalrymple. Includes badge of Baronet of Nova Scotia. 208
Fig. 12.14 Armorial device – Thomas Burnett, Woodalling, Norfolk. 209
Fig. 12.15 Armorial device – Alexander Burnett of Craigmyle. 209
Fig. 12.16 Armorial device – Thomas Burnett of Inverleith. 210
Fig. 12.17 Armorial device – Andrew Burnett of Wariston. 210
Fig. 12.18 Armorial device – Alexander Burnett, Aberdeen. 211
Fig. 12.19 Armorial device – James Burnett, Sheddocksley. 211
Fig. 12.20 Armorial device – William Burnett of Barns. 212
Fig. 12.21 Armorial device – Robert Burnett, W.S. 212
Fig. 12.22 Armorial device – John Burnett, Dalladies. 213
Fig. 12.23 Armorial device – Robert Burnett, Aberdeen. 213
Fig. 12.24 Armorial device – Dr. Thomas Burnett. 214
Fig. 12.25 Armorial device – Lord Lyon, George Burnett. 214
Fig. 12.26 Armorial device – William Tather Bridgeford Burnett. 215
Fig. 12.27 Armorial device – Charles John Burnett, Ross Herald. 215
Fig. 12.28 Armorial device – John Cameron Burnett, Oklahoma. 216
Fig. none Achievement of Arms, Sir John Burnett-Stuart of Crichie. 216
Fig. 12.29 Scottish Royal Arms of King Charles I., on Muchalls. 217
Fig. 12.30 Armorial achievement, Sir Thomas Burnett of Leys. 217
Fig. 12.31 Burnett of Leys, shield on ceiling, Muchalls. 218
Fig. 12.32 Impaled shield, Burnett & Moncrieffe, ceiling, Muchalls. 218

Fig. 12.33 Stewart Royal Arms, fireplace, Muchalls Great Hall. 218
Fig. 12.34 Achievement of Arms, Sir Thomas Burnett of Leys, on ceiling, Muchalls Great Hall. 219
Fig. 12.35 Achievement of Arms, Sir Thomas Burnett of Leys and Katherine Gordon, on ceiling, Muchalls Great Hall. 219
Fig. 12.36 Achievement of Arms, Sir Thomas Burnett of Leys and Dame Jean Moncrieffe, on ceiling, Muchalls Great Hall. 219
Fig. 12.37 Arms of Earl of Dunfermline, ceiling, Muchalls Castle. 219
Fig. 12.38 Arms of John Maitland, 1st Earl of Lauderdale, Muchalls. 220
Fig. 12.39 Arms of John, 2nd Marquess of Hamilton and 4th Earl of Arran, ceiling, Muchalls Castle. 220
Fig. 12.40 Arms of Elizabeth Forbes of Echt, ceiling ingo, Muchalls Great Hall. 220
Fig. 12.41 Arms of Janet Hamilton, ceiling ingo, Muchalls Great Hall. 220
Fig. 12.42 Arms of Katherine Arbuthnot, ceiling ingo, Muchalls Great Hall. 220
Fig. 12.43 Arms of Katherine Gordon, ceiling ingo, Muchalls Great Hall. 220
Fig. 12.44 Arms of the (former) Burgh of Banchory. 202
Fig. 12.45 Burnett of Leys tartan. 221
Fig. 12.46 Hunting version, Burnett of Leys tartan. 221
Fig. 12.47 Burnett tartan. 222
Fig. 12.48 Leys Estate tweed. 222

Chapter 13

Fig. 13.1 Map of Leys and Crathes. 226
Fig. 13.2 Surface of Crannog of Leys. 228
Fig. 13.3 The present day drained Loch of Leys. 229
Fig. 13.4 Crannog of Leys (aerial view).Colour. 223
Fig. 13.5 Crannog of Leys (aerial closeup).Colour. 224
Fig. 13.6 Various vessels recovered from the Loch of Leys. 230

Chapter 14

Fig. 14.1 Crathes Castle. 232
Fig. 14.2 Crathes Castle (drawing). 234
Fig. 14.3 Crathes Castle (ground floor plan). 236
Fig. 14.4 Crathes, Drum and other significant locations (map). 239

Fig. 14.5	Routes into Deeside showing Cairnamounth Pass (map).	239
Fig. 14.6	Early Tower of Crathes (drawing).	242
Fig. 14.7	Table of Comparative Analysis.	243
Fig. 14.8	Muchalls Castle (drawing).	246
Fig. 14.9	Profile of Muchalls Castle location (drawing).	249
Fig. 14.10	Corner detail, Muchalls.	253
Fig. 14.11	Ceiling Medallion, Muchalls Great Hall.	255

Chapter 15

Fig. 15.1	House of Crathes.	271
Fig. 15.2	Old Cairnton House.	273
Fig. 15.3	Woodend Barn Theatre - a typical improved steading.	279
Fig. 15.4	Hattonburn.	283
Fig. 15.5	Woodbine Cottage, Crathes.	284
Fig. 15.6	Neuk Smiddy.	284
Fig. 15.7	Dower House - formerly the Neuk Smiddy.	285
Fig. 15.8	Thistleycrook.	285
Fig. 15.9	Mill of Hirn.	288
Fig. 15.10a	Milton of Crathes.	288
Fig. 15.10b	Milton of Crathes.	289
Fig. 15.10c	Milton of Crathes.	289
Fig. 15.11	Craigton Quarries.	291
Fig. 15.12	Craigton Cottages.	291
Fig. 15.13	Bancon company logo.	303
Fig. 15.14	Crathes Castle – an early 20th century view.	307
Fig. 15.15	Crathes Castle – an early 21st century view.	307
Fig. 15.16	Tower Room before refurbishment.	308
Fig. 15.17	Tower Room with revealed stonework.	308
Fig. 15.18	Plaque in Crathes garden.	312
Fig. 15.19	Opening of the Family Room.	318

Chapter 16

Fig. 16.1	Burnett Family burial ground, Crathes.	345

SYMBOLS & ABBREVIATIONS

The following symbols have been used within the chapters on genealogy to define individuals within each generation.

❑ Child of the Laird

♦ Grandchild

□ Great-grandchild

➢ Great-great-grandchild

▪ Great-great-great-grandchild

◊ Great-great-great-great-grandchild

\- Great-great-great-great-great-grandchild

The following abbreviations have occasionally been used within the text:

HEICS	The Honourable East India Company Service.
PSAS	Proceedings of the Society of Antiquaries of Scotland.
RGS	Register of the Great Seal of Scotland.
RPS	Register of the Privy Seal of Scotland.
IGI	International Genealogical Index.
NTS	National Trust for Scotland.

1

SAXON OR NORMAN?

Eileen A. Bailey

Tradition pre-supposes the reality of what endures
(Igor Stravinsky, 1947)

Two questions face those with a serious interest in the history of the Burnett family. One is the origin of the surname Burnet(t) and to what extent it is a variation of, or independent to, that of Burnard(e). The other is whether the surname in either form was introduced to Britain having roots in Norman French or Anglo-Saxon stock.

The use of surnames is generally regarded as having evolved around the late eleventh century when, with increased population and mobility, there began to be a need to have some method of more clearly identifying one individual from another. In terms of the history of England, this was after the Battle of Hastings in 1066 and the conquest by the Normans. Many of those who crossed the English Channel to fight for William the Conqueror at Hastings were from northern France and brought to England a number of family names from which some modern surnames are derived.

James Coutts quotes Foxe who describes how " The day after the Battell, very early in the morning, Odo, Bishop of Baieux, sang mass for those that were departed. The Duke after that, desirous to know the estate of his Battell and what people he had therein lost and were slaine, he caused to come unto him a clerke that had written their names when they were embarked at St. Valeries and commanded him to call them all by their names, who called them that had been at the Battell and had passed the seas with Duke William ". [(1)] Not only was it important to the orderly mind of William to know the state of his support, it was also a matter for future family pride and fortune that those who fought should have their names recorded as having participated in this great event. This record was called The Roll of Battle Abbey and hung in the Abbey, which William the Conqueror built in gratitude to God for his success. To the great detriment of genealogical record, this treasure was lost without trace, thought to have perished in the fire of 1792 that totally destroyed Cowdray House, Sussex, where the document had latterly been held. Prior to its demise, several historians had already attempted to decipher the Roll of Battle Abbey with the aim of listing the names.

The Doomsday Book, which was completed by 1085-6, was a unique record of England in the 20 years after 1066. It is said to have been commissioned by William the Conqueror as a survey of all the lands which he had acquired with his victory at Hastings, along with the names of those who had previously and, or, later owned that land. Exceptions to the survey were the areas of Cumberland and the north of Westmoreland. These lands had been so laid waste by conflict as a result of resistance to William's troops that they became of little or no value. The sad fact for present day researchers is that not all of the original record was transcribed. Furthermore, parts of it lost much detail through the process of editing into the eventual two volumes. It is suggested by some historians that the Doomsday Book, as we now know it, is actually an amalgam of an earlier Inquest of land-holdings, compiled just after Hasting in order to identify all those who owed allegiance to King William, and a later inventory commissioned just prior to the king's death in 1087.

The battle of Hastings, and subsequent events, led the way for an influx of associates of the Royal Court, many of Norman origin, who were rewarded for their loyalty and support by gifts of land and titles in both England and Scotland in lieu of wages. Rowley states that by 1086 "only a handful of the 180 greater landlords or tenants-in-chief were still English and it is estimated that the new land owners replaced 4-5,000 Saxon thegns. The crown itself had acquired one-fifth of the land and much of the remainder was held by a select few of William the Conqueror's favourites who had come with him or followed him from France and the Low Countries ". (2) From those many of Scotland's titled families can trace their origins. There were, however, earlier settlers in southern England before the Conquest whose arrival had been the result of invasion and settlement by the Anglo Saxons who were Germanic from several parts of Europe. Their arrival overlapped quite peacefully, as archaeologists have deduced, with the period that marked the diminishing interest in Britain of the invading Romans. It is from from these Germanic peoples that England or Angle-land got its name. After the Anglo-Saxons adopted Christianity, oral preservation of their traditions and the genealogies of their rulers gave way to written recording by monks prior to and after the Norman Conquest by William. Family names from this period are also the origin of a number of present-day surnames.

Did the surname Burnet(t) evolve from Burnard(e), Barnard(e) and Bernard(e) or was it an individual surname in its own right? There are those who suggest that Burnet with the later addition of an additional 't' had its origin in the OFr. *burnette*, a diminutive of the French *brun* meaning dark brown. The term *burnete* was later used for a dark-brown woollen cloth. If this were the case we would have a stronger argument for promoting a French root for the present day bearers of the surname. We would also expect to see the surname Burnet used, albeit with the customary variation in spelling, throughout early documents. Instead what we find is not only a variety of spellings of Burnet and of Burnard/Bernard but also recorded instances of them being interchangeable in records of the same persons or within a family. This can be seen in the genealogy of the Burnets in southern Scotland, later in that of Leys and in local records. It has so far been generally accepted that the progenitor of the Burnet(t) surname was a Saxon family of Burnard. Beornheard was a Germanic personal name which, translated, means "bear-hard". This origin is given for all spellings of Burnard by most onomasticians. Although Burnards may have been landowners by force in England, their origins were possibly rooted in Germanic or even Viking stock. This was the view held by George Burnett [(3)] who, in describing the Southern ancestors of the Burnetts of Leys, states that " there is proof, amounting to moral certainty, that the Saxon family of Burnard which flourished in England before the Conquest were the progenitors of the first Alexander Burnard who settled on Deeside ". The extent to which genealogy should or could be based on *moral certainty* would be strongly argued against by those who contend that, unless it can be authenticated, it cannot be considered to be fact. Curiously, Burnett does not elaborate on the pre-Conquest Saxon Burnards.

There are alternative schools of thought, one of which is presented by Jackson.[(4).] He suggests that evidence, which George Burnett appears to have either not considered or perhaps omitted, indicates that the ancestors of the Burnards/Burnetts were most likely not Saxon but Norman in origin. Jackson points out that, in an article, by J. G. Nicolls on the Arlesey estates of the Abbey of Waltham, published in 1840 in *Collectanea Topographica et Genealogica*, there are several references to Burnards/Bernards including one recorded in the Doomsday Book as the mesne tenant of Alrichsey (Arlesey) held by William de Ow (d'Eu), a known member of the Norman nobility.[(5)]

There is documented proof of the existence of Burnards and/or Bernards in England from 1066 as they are included in the aforementioned Doomsday Book, the Chartulary of St. Neot's and, as we have seen, in the Charters relating to the Abbey of Waltham. The charters of the religious establishments show records of land gifted to them, owned by them and leased or sold by them. It is through these records that the genealogy of the Burnards has been traced from the Norman Conquest through to the 13th century but, irrespective of George Burnett's statement, there is no apparent trace of them prior to the arrival of William the Conqueror.

Burnard not only held the Manor of Arlesey and land at Haneslawe in Bedfordshire but also an unnamed Manor in Hampshire, the Manors of Cholderton (or Celdraton/Chalvertoun) and Codford in Wiltshire. In the reign of Henry I, his son *Rogerus filius Burnardi* (Roger son of Burnard) is shown in the charters of St. Neot's to have made gifts to the monks there of parts of the Bedfordshire and Wiltshire estates. These records also mention that he had two wives, Rohays who predeceased him and Elita who survived him. The charters show that he had a son who founded a branch of the family at Beston in Bedfordshire where in 1230 reference is made to Matilda, widow of a William Burnard, along with sons Richard and Robert. Jackson draws attention to the fact that "the Priory of St. Neot's with which the Burnard family were closely associated was re-founded after the Conquest by Roheise (daughter of Walter Gifford I) and her husband Richard de Bienfaite (uncle of William d'Eu) ". [(6)]

The Charters of the Abbey of Waltham refer to two sons of Roger Burnard called Gilbert and Stephen. Roger is known to have had an eldest son, also named Roger, who gifted churches at Boscumbe, Cheldreton, Cotford and Eddeworth to St Neots for the souls of his father and mother whose bodies lie there. The fact that Roger the younger's wife was called Margaret is also recorded at St Neot's. Roger's son Odo Burnard confirmed the gifts made by his father. He, in his own right, granted several charters to Waltham Abbey. Burnett [(7)] makes the definitive statement that Odo's seals, which were attached to these charters, are the chief evidence " that the Burnards of Wiltshire and Bedfordshire were the progenitors of the Burnetts of the North ". He bases this on the similarity of the leaf device contained in the seals of Roger and Odo Burnard to that of the later Richard Burnard of Farningdoun, in southern Scotland who, in 1252, appended his seal with a single leaf device to a charter to the Abbey of Melrose. [(Fig. 1.1)] A letter preserved at St. Neot's, refers to Roger Burnard, son and successor of Odo who was apparently alive in 1192 and to Odo's wife Matilda.

References:

1. Coutts, J., *The Anglo-Norman Peaceful Invasion of Scotland 1057-1200. Origin of Great Scottish Families*, p.viii, (1922). Edinburgh.
2. Rowley, T., *The Normans* 86. (1999. Tempus Publishing Ltd., England and USA).
3. Burnett, G., (ed. Allardyce J.), *The Family of Burnett of Leys*, 1, (1901), Spalding Club.
4. Jackson, R.N., " The Noble Anglo-Saxons? " in *Aberdeen University Review*, LVII, No. 199, (Spring 1998).
5. *Ibid.* 208.
6. *Ibid.* 213.
7. Burnett, G., (ed. Allardyce J.) *The Family of Burnett of Leys*, 2 –3,(1901), Spalding Club.

Bibliography:

Burnett, G., (ed. Allardyce J.), *The Family of Burnett of Leys*. 1901. Spalding Club.

Jackson, R.N., "The Noble Anglo-Saxons?" in *Aberd. Univ. Review,* LVII, No. 199, (Spring 1998).

Coutts, J., *The Anglo-Norman Peaceful Invasion of Scotland 1057-1200. Origin of Great Scottish Families*. (1922), Edinburgh.

Rowley,T. *The Normans*. (1999), Tempus Publishing Ltd., England & USA.

Reynolds, A., *Later Anglo- Saxon England*. (1999), Tempus Publishing Ltd. England & USA.

Black, G.F., *The Surnames of Scotland,* (1946) New York, reprinted (1993), Birlinn, Edinburgh.

Fig. 1.1 The Seals of Odo and Richard Burnard.

2

THE BURNETS IN SOUTHERN SCOTLAND

Eileen A. Bailey

The historian, essentially, wants more documents than he can really use.
(Henry James, 1909)

King David I of Scotland, who succeeded his elder brother Alexander I, reigned from 1124 until his death at Carlisle on 24 May 1153. Although Alexander initiated a deliberate attempt to enhance loyalty to the Crown in Scotland by encouraging movement from England into land tenancies in Scotland, David encouraged many English nobility who were descendants of Anglo-Norman, French and Flemish settlers to come to Scotland. There they settled with gifts of land and title from the Crown. The Flemish people were particularly welcome because by that time they were regarded as being commercially the most advanced of the European communities. David I had an extensive Norman pedigree, the genealogical tree of which is illustrated in Jackson.[(1)] He was an experienced administrator having gained the Earldom of Huntingdon, along with vast estates in Northumbria and other lands, through his marriage in 1114 to Matilda (often referred to as Maud), daughter of the Earl of Northumbria. He saw the introduction of Saxon and, even more extensively, Norman, families into his kingdom as one of the most effective ways of civilising the country. Bingham [(2)] states that "Some, though by no means all, of the men who received grants of land in Scotland came from the honour of Huntingdon......... Others came from lands granted to David by Henry I and the duchies of Normandy and Brittany".

It was administrative skill that encouraged King David to promote the feudal land system in Scotland thereafter continued by King Malcolm IV and William the Lion. This was a process whereby some of the land which was the property of the King, or had fallen to the Crown by forfeit or absence of an heir, was distributed amongst chosen influential individuals who were given grants of land in exchange for their allegiance to the Crown. Individuals were then able to sub-divide that land to as many tenants as they wished thereby gaining income in money or produce from the annual rents. King David was also responsible for a strong system of law, including, it is said, the system of trial by jury. During his reign the Church was encouraged and supported in taking a strong active role. David I was the first monarch of Scotland to mint his own coinage.

Burnards or Burnets of Farningdoun

Amongst those who came to Scotland at the time of King David I, thus benefiting from the new system of land-holding, were Burnards who were given the large barony of Farningdoun (also known as Fairnington or Farnington) in Roxburghshire in the Border country of southern Scotland. This raises further speculation about the origins of the Burnards/Burnets. As already described, King David I, who was of Norman origin, had a particular wish to introduce Norman and Flemish settlers to his Scottish kingdom. This being the case, it would not be unreasonable to suggest that Burnards/Burnets were likely to be of Norman or even Flemish origin rather than Anglo-Saxon. It is interesting to note, however, that Bingham [(3)] draws attention to the fact that it was common place to stereotype all incomers to Scotland at this time as Normans. In respect of families who settled in Scotland between 1100 and 1250 she quotes Ritchie [(4)] "it is seldom possible to ascertain their continental home, whether in the Duchy (of Normandy) or in Flanders, Picard, Artesian, Cennomanian, Angevin, general-French and Norman Conquest". Similar to the situation of earlier Burnards in England, we find the records of the religious houses providing interesting genealogical information. Melrose Abbey received two grants from the lands of Farningdoun from Roger Burnard circa 1200, one record of which was witnessed by his sons Geoffrey, Ralph, Walter and Richard. The Bishop of Glasgow is shown in the Episcopal Records of Glasgow, circa 1208, as receiving fuel in the form of peat dug from the lands of Ralph Burnard, son and heir of Roger. When Roger Burnard died in 1292, the Bishop, by grant from King Edward, also took custody of the lands of Farningdoun, value assessed at £10, 15s., which he was to hold until the majority and marriage of Roger's son and heir, or the remarriage of his widow.

The Abbey of Melrose bought the Eastmeadow of Farningdoun from Richard Burnard of Farningdoun in 1252. The transaction was confirmed by a charter from King Alexander III, signed during that year and witnessed by Richard Burnard and Hugh Rutherford. The aforementioned Richard Burnard is the same individual who was of such particular interest to George Burnett on account of the above charter of sale having had attached to it a seal with a single leaf. This was the same as that on documents bearing the seal of Odo Burnard on the documents of the Burnards of Wiltshire and Bedfordshire.[(Fig.1.1)] It has been said that the leaf represented was that of the burnet plant thus contributing to the eventual evolution of the surname from Burnarde to Burnet. This is unlikely. The name of John Burnard appeared in the witnessing of various charters in 1338, 1354 and 1358 but by 1381 King Richard II had claimed the Barony of Farningdoun and in 1581 and 1585, King James IV ratified Francis, Earl of Bothwell, in Farningdoun. The present-day dwelling, now spelt Fairnington and located just north of Jedburgh, absorbed a pre-existing Tower-house, probably built in the 1580s by the Earl of

Bothwell. The link between the Burnards and Farningdoun appears to have been lost no later than 1381.

Burnard/Burnet of Burnetland and Barns

Prior to acquiring Barns in Peebleshire, the Burnards or Burnets are known to have owned land in the parish of Manor that was called Burnetland after them. In an early will, dated 30 April 1656, William Burnet of Barns, Treasurer-Clerk of Scotland, refers to Barns having been *to my predecessors and me above these three hundred years*. This being so, it takes the family connection with the lands of Barns back to at least 1356 with their occupation of Burnetland pre-dating that time. John Burnet of Burnetland founded a Chaplaincy at the Church of Manor. The lands of Barns eventually became the Burnets' principal possession. The descendancy of the Burnets of Burnetland and Barns with the Burnards of Farningdoun and of Wiltshire & Bedfordshire is again thought by Burnett [(1)] to be through the bearing of the same arms through to 1585. The use of the name Burnard as well as Burnet appears in association with this branch.

*****

THE GENEALOGY OF THE BURNETS OF BURNETLAND & BARNS

John Burnet of Burnetland married Marion Caverhill, who was the daughter of George Caverhill and was his heiress jointly with her three sisters. It was through this marriage that the Burnets acquired the lands of Barns in the parish of Manor. John Burnet died before 1470.

Their son **John Burnet,** inheritor of Burnetland and also of his mother's portion of Caverhill, married (1) Sibilla Veitch who, from a deed of mortification dated 1497, appears to have died between 1495 and 1497 and (2) Mariota/Marion Inglis daughter of William Inglis of Murdiston. John Burnet died in 1502 by which time he owned only half of Burnetland. His widow Mariot Inglis *relict of John Burnet of that Ilk* was formally served heir to her third of the lands of Barns and Caverhill, in the parish of Manor and Burnetland in the Barony of Broughton, on 15 February 1502 before the Sheriff of Peebles.

Barns Tower was a rectangular Tower-house, part of which still stands, about 3 miles to the south of Peebles and on the south bank of the River Tweed. It was built around 1498 possibly at the time of John Burnet's marriage to Marion

Inglis but it was deserted in 1773 in favour of a new mansion nearby. Details are given in Chapter 14.

John Burnet's successor was a son from his second marriage **William Burnet**, who was a minor at the time of his father's death. William Ingles (sic) of Murditoun, assumed to be William's grandfather, is recorded on 23 September 1505 as tutor in law to William Burnet who came of aged in about 1522. Although he took the designation *William Burnet of Barns*, William also inherited his father's portion of Burnetland. On 20 January 1522 he is infeft in the lands of Nether Crailing and others in Roxburghshire with Sasine recorded on 28 January of the same year. On 30 September 1555, William Burnet of Barns resigned into the hands of William Cranstoun of the Ilk, the lands of Nether Crailing and others in the Sheriffdom of Roxburgh. William Burnet married Elizabeth Veitch, of the family of Dawyck. William Burnet and Elizabeth (who seems to have predeceased her husband) had the following children:

- William Burnet who succeeded his father.
- John Burnet, later styled *of Woodhouse* who died in May 1616 leaving two sons, John and Thomas.
- Agnes Burnet who married John Sandilands of Bold, Peebleshire.
- Marion Burnet
- Thomas Burnet.

On William Burnet's death in 1564, he was succeeded by his eldest son, **William Burnet** who, in a charter dated 15 July 1545, was designated *William Burnet, son and heir apparent of William Burnet of Barns* when he was infeft in the lands of Dollarburn and Dogflat. He was later infeft in lands of Crailing and in others in Roxburghshire on 1 May 1564. The lands of Burnetland do not appear to be mentioned in connection with the family after this time. William Burnet married Isobel Hay, a daughter of Hay of Locharret and Yester, whose family were hereditary Sheriffs of Peebles from 1409 until the 1700s. William who died in 1574 was buried, at his own request, at St Gorgone's Kirk of *Mener* or Manor. William and Isobel Burnet had the following known children:

- William Burnet, who succeeded his father.
- Thomas Burnet.
- Gavin Burnet.
- Isobel Burnet.
- Janet Burnet who married Adam Rutherford of Kidheuch (Kidhaugh) in 1574 and who was infeft in liferent of one third each of Caverhill, Over Glack and Sourlands.

Isobel Hay Burnet married (2) John Govan of Cardrona, Peebleshire after 1574.

William Burnet, who succeeded his father, was served heir on 21 April 1575. He is reputed to have been of immense stature, great bodily strength and to have lived to age 107 years. His nick-name was The Hoolet of Barns, from the Scots word for owl. This he acquired because he was able to see as well in the dark of night as by the light of day which no doubt was a valuable gift in his efforts to suppress the Border freebooters of the time! The property in Teviotdale, which had been held for so long by the family, appears to have been forfeited in his time for non-payment of *waird* and acquired by Cranstoun of that Ilk. Sir John Stewart of Traquair entered into an obligation on 9 August 1576 *to procure & deliver to William Burnet of Barns, the gift of his marriage gratis, from Cranstoun of that Ilk, into whose hands it had fallen by reason of waird.* The same lands must have then been redeemed because, on 5 March 1600, William Burnet resigned the lands of Nether Crailing and others to Sir John Cranstoun and his son William.

In 1576, William Burnet married Margaret Stewart, daughter of James Stewart of Shillinglaw, youngest son of Sir William Stewart, 2nd Baron of Traquair, and Christian Hay, daughter of John Hay, 2nd Lord Yester and Katherine Kerr. William and Margaret Burnet had children of whom nine are known to have survived namely:

- John Burnet was born in approximately 1577. Styled variously *heir apparent*, *Fiar of Barns* and *of Barns*, he predeceased his father having apparently held the family property for only a short time. He married (1) Margaret Scot, eldest daughter of Simon Scot of Bonnington. The marriage contract was dated 15 June 1614, although William Burnet of Barns, with the consent of John, granted a charter of land with houses and rents to Margaret Scot on 30 July 1610. John and Margaret had the following children:
    - William Burnet who was later styled *of Barns*. He succeeded his grandfather.
    - John Burnet who was styled at various times as *in Stanepath*, *in Gledstanes* and *of Wester Kailzie*. He was Chamberlain to the Earl of Southesk. John Burnet married in 1641 (1) Helen Baillie, daughter of James Baillie of Hillis in Lanarkshire and Catherine Inglis. Helen died on 17 January 1654. Their known children were:
        - William Burnet, *of Kailzie*, also in *Glenwrath* and later, on the death of his cousin Captain William Burnet, of Barns. He continued the family line.
        - James Burnet who became a Captain, merchant and shipowner in Leith, Edinburgh. During the absence of Captain William Burnet whilst at war in Flanders, he acted as the Captain's agent in the management of his Barns estate. James married Alison Gibson. Their daughter
            - Alison Burnet married John Dundas, elder son of George Dundas of Blair, and Helen Cooper.

James Burnet died in 1690.

- Margaret Burnet. She married James Lockhart, a Writer to the Signet in Edinburgh.
- Marie Burnet.

John Burnet married, (2) in 1656, Grizzel Menzies, daughter of Menzies of Culterallers in Lanarkshire, and Janet Carruthers. John & Grizzel Burnett had one child, a daughter:

- Helen Burnet who, in 1680, married James Douglas of Muirhousedykes in Lanarkshire, son of James Douglas of Baads and Jean Sandilands.

John Burnet died in November 1659 and was succeeded by his son William. After his death Grizzel Menzies Burnett married (2) William Somerville of Gladstanes who was Commissioner of Supply for Lanark county.

John Burnet, Fiar of Barns, married (2) Marion Ingles, daughter of John Ingles of Mannerhead and one of the Scots of Thirlstane and had a further five children:

- James Burnet, of *Toun of Manner*, born about 1624, who, on 28 March 1650 in Edinburgh, married Marion Brown, daughter of John Brown, Merchant Burgess of Edinburgh.
- Elizabeth Burnet born about 1625.
- Janet Burnet born about 1626
- unknown Burnet born about 1627.
- unknown Burnet born about 1628.

John Burnet is thought to have died about 1642.

- James Burnet was born about 1579. He graduated from Edinburgh University on 27 July 1609 and, having been educated for the church, was admitted minister of Lauder on 17 September 1615. He was presented to Jedburgh by King Charles I on 15 September 1635 and deposed April 1649. James Burnet married Christian Dundas, daughter of George Dundas of that Ilk, and unknown Boswell. James and Christian Burnet had the following children:
  - Robert Burnet who became a Physician in Edinburgh. He married Margaret Murray and died in Edinburgh on 28 September 1663 leaving a son
    - Robert Burnet, also a Doctor of Medicine, who received a legacy of 5000 merks from his uncle, Archbishop Burnet.
  - Alexander Burnet who was born in 1614 and baptised on 6 August 1615 in Edinburgh. He graduated from Edinburgh University on 22 June 1633, became chaplain to the Earl of Traquair and was presented by King Charles I to Coldingham on 10 January 1639. Alexander was in Kent, England until 1650 After that he went abroad where he continued to serve King Charles II with intelligence from England and elsewhere. He was appointed chaplain to General Rutherford who was governor of Dunkirk where Alexander had an English congregation. In 1660 he became Rector of Ivechurch

Alexander Burnet was consecrated Bishop of Aberdeen at St. Andrews on 18 September 1663 and Archbishop of Glasgow on 18 January 1664. He was appointed a member of the Privy Council in April 1664 and an extraordinary Lord of Session in November of that year, an office that he held until June 1668. Also in 1664, he became interim Keeper of the Great Seal on the death of the Earl of Glencairn. He preached the sermon at the state funeral of the Marquis of Montrose.

After the murder of Archbishop Sharp on 3 May 1679 he became Primate of St. Andrews in October of that year. In that office it is interesting to note that he took precedence over all nobility and ranked next after royal princes. Alexander Burnet died on 24 August 1684 and was buried in St. Salvador's College close to the tomb of Bishop Kennedy.

Archbishop Burnet's estate amounted to £41,570 which was a large fortune at that time and included two coaches worth £300, silver plate to the value of over £900 and a large library of books valued at £1050. He left legacies to his nephew Robert Burnet, to Jean Fleming widow of James Smith, minister of Eddleston. The piece of land, which he bequeathed to the poor of St. Andrews for their use, was, for a long time thereafter, known as 'Bishop's Rigg'.

Alexander Burnet married Elizabeth Fleming of Luthrie in Fife, daughter of George Fleming of Kilconquhar and Margaret Philip. Children of the marriage were:

- unknown (son) Burnet who predeceased his father.
- Anna/Anne Burnet who, on 10 September 1667, married (1) Alexander, the 7th Lord Elphinston. On the occasion of her marriage, Anna was presented with a propyric of silverwork from the Corporation of Glasgow for which they paid £887. 2s. After the death of Alexander on 11 May 1669 she married (2) according to contract dated 20 August 1674, Patrick Murray, the 3rd Lord Elibank. Patrick and Anna had the following children:
  - Alexander Murray, of Elibank, who succeeded as 4th Lord Elibank.
  - Anna Murray, born on 23 August 1679, died young.
  - Mary Murray, born on 28 August 1681, married on 28 April 1701 in Aberlady, East Lothian, John, Master of Tarbet, later Earl of Cromarty.
  - Helen Murray, born on 27 February 1687, married on 13 August 1703 in Aberlady, East Lothian, as the second wife of Sir John Mackenzie of Coull.
  - Elizabeth Murray, born 14 November 1686, died unmarried.

- Mary Burnet who married on 28 April 1674 to Roderick Mackenzie of Prestonhall, 2nd son of Sir John Mackenzie of Tarbet. Mary died before 4 January 1700. Their children were:
  - Alexander Mackenzie who, in 1702, married Anne, daughter of Hugh, 10th Lord Lovat and Amelia Murray, daughter of the 1st Marquis of Atholl. Alexander subsequently took the title *Fraser of Fraserdale*.
  - Elizabeth Mackenzie baptised 9 August 1675.
  - John Mackenzie baptised 27 July 1678.
  - George Mackenzie baptised 25 January 1681.

- Alexander Burnet. He was Advocate and Treasurer-Clerk of Scotland until 1639. Alexander is regarded as being the first **Burnet of Carlops** having purchased the lands of Carlops, in the county of Peebles, from Menzies of Weem. The ruins of the Tower-house are close to the village of Carlops which was established in about 1784 for weavers of cotton. He married Margaret Hay before 1636 and died before 1656. Alexander and Margaret had children:
  - Alexander Burnet who was born about 1640. Various land charters, given under The Great Seal of Scotland or in family documents (27 November 1656 onwards), mention *"Alexander Burnet, eldest son of Alexander Burnet of Carlops and Margaret Hay his mother and tutrix"* indicating that Alexander Burnet Snr., advocate, was dead by 1656 whilst his son was still a minor. Alexander Burnet of Carlops, who was also an advocate, married on 18 August 1675 in West Linton parish, Isobel Rutherford, daughter of John Rutherford of Hunthill (also known as Scraisburgh) and Alison, fifth daughter of Andrew Ker, 1st Lord Jedburgh. Their children were :
    - Archibald Burnet.
    - Margaret Burnet born in 1676.
    - Lilias Burnet born in 1678.
  - Archibald Burnet. It would appear that he is a son because, by the time of the calling out of the Militia in 1689 (the Revolutionary Settlement) Archibald Burnet, was a Major in the Edinburgh Regiment and styled *" of Carlops"*. In 1704 he was listed as a Commissioner of Supply for the county of Edinburgh. Archibald Burnet supported the Jacobite cause and was taken prisoner "for being in arms" at the Battle of Preston. In the Court which sat at Liverpool, England, between 20 January and 9 February, seventy-four persons, including about twelve English Jacobites, were tried and sentenced. Archibald Burnet was executed towards the end of January 1715.
  - Anne Burnet married, according to contract dated 7 September 1673, John Melville, son of Lord John Melville of Monimail.

It is relevant to note here that, although members of the family of Alexander Burnet, advocate (who was dead by 1656) continued to be styled *of Carlops*, the

Register of the Great Seal shows a charter, dated 1 February 1656, concerning lands of Stobo as well as the lands of Carlips (sic) in Peeblesshire pertaining to Mr Alexander Burnet of Carlips being granted to Robert Burnett, elder, advocate, his heirs and assignees, for 6175 merks. This Robert Burnett became Lord Crimond and the lands were inherited by his son Thomas Burnett, Physician in Edinburgh, with record in *RGS* dated 1 October 1662. The lands were later disposed of by Thomas to James Naismith on 3 November 1665.

Captain Alexander Burnet, who died in July 1743, was styled of *Carlops* and succeeded by his brother William Burnet, a Lieutenant in General Pultney's Regiment of Foot.

- ❑ Christian Burnet was born about 1584. She married, about 1608, John Scot of Hundleshope, second son of Sir Robert Scot of Eskdale and a daughter of Johnston of that Ilk. John Scot died about 1625 and was succeeded by his son John Scot, a minor, whose curators were Sir Robert Scott of Thirlestane, William Burnett of Barns and Sir John Stewart of Traquair.
- ❑ Robert Burnet was born about 1586. He became an advocate. According to the Register of the Great Seal the lands of Cringeltie were created a barony with manor house in 1633. From this record is taken the information that Robert Burnet's spouse was Margaret Heriot. Robert Burnet married Margaret Heriot on 31 January 1627 in Edinburgh. Their children were:
  - ♦ William Burnet, recorded in 1633. He is referred to as "the late Sir William Burnet of Cringltie" in a charter on Cringltie dated 12 October 1666. A charter dated 3 May 1664 grants lands, including Cringltie, to James Maitland for loyal services rendered. The lands are therein described as *formerly belonging to the deceased Mr William Burnett as heritable tenant and now to the Crown* as William Burnet had apparently sold them without the Crown's permission. A mansion called Cringletie/Cringltie House, now a hotel, was built in the mid-1800s on the site of the original Tower-house, located about 2 miles north of Peebles.
  - ♦ Robert Burnet of Little Ormiston, who was probably a son, is named in documents relating to the Convention of Estates in 1678, the First Parliament of James VII in 1685 and a meeting of Estates in 1689.
- ❑ Agnes Burnet was born about 1590. She married, in 1610 in Peebles, James Nasmyth of Posso who was a Member of the Scottish Parliament in 1627 and also Sheriff of Peeblesshire. Their son
  - ♦ James Naysmith, who succeeded, was an eminent Lawyer in his time. His son
    - ☐ James Naysmith, also a distinguished Lawyer, who succeeeded his father, was created a Baronet of Nova Scotia in 1706. A descendant became Sir James Naysmith of Posso and Dawyck.

- William Burnet. He became a Writer to the Signet. Montgomery Burnet in his genealogy of the Burnets of Burnetland and Barns states that William is thought to have been the later-styled *William Burnet of Cringiltie* but evidence from the RGS indicates that this was not the case. William Burnet was Commissioner of Supply for the county of Peebles and held several Offices of State in the reign of King Charles II (1661).
- Thomas Burnet. On 3 November 1635 he was styled *'Thomas Burnet. Servitour to his Majestie.*
- Gavin Burnet born about 1588, was the youngest son (according to his mother's will) and having been apprenticed to Andrew Hay, became a Writer to the Signet on 12 August 1633. He married Helen Ramsay. One known child, the eldest [according to the Register of Writers to the Signet] was:
  - Robert Burnet, who was born on 13 July 1646, was apprenticed to John Trotter before becoming a Writer to the Signet on 21 December 1671. He was appointed Commissioner of Supply for the county of Peebles in 1699. Robert Burnet married Elizabeth Cockburn, daughter of James Cockburn, Brewer of Yardheads, Leith. Elizabeth died on 29 March 1694 and her husband was killed in a duel with James Wishart of Logie on 16 July 1699. Robert and Elizabeth Burnet had four known children namely:
    - Isobel Burnet.
    - David Burnet.
    - James Burnet.
    - William Burnet.

Gavin Burnet died in October 1660 and his wife Helen died 17 May 1664.

Margaret Stuart Burnet died on 21 December 1625. She requested in her will that she should be buried in the Churchyard of Manor, under the great choir window, where many of her children had already been interred. Margaret appointed her husband and youngest son Gavin as executors and her eldest son John as heir. William Burnet is said to have died in 1645 but if the family tradition that he died aged 107 is correct his death is likely to have occurred around 1668. During his lifetime he made over the estate to his son John Burnet and William's grandson, William was styled *of Barns* from an early date having received a liferent in his favour.

William Burnett, son of John Burnet and Margaret Scot, succeeded to Barns within the lifetime of his grandfather William *Hoolet* Burnet who had earlier made over the lands to William's father John. He was the first of the family line to spell his name with double 't'. William became a Writer to the Signet in about 1638. On 19 October 1639, upon the resignation of his uncle, Alexander Burnet of Carlops, advocate, William Burnett was given several simultaneous appointments by King Charles I. Those were Treasurer-Clerk, Comptroller, Collector and Treasurer of the

Temporalities of Kirk Lands annexed to the Crown, Treasurer of Annuities within the Kingdom of Scotland and the Clerkship of the Principality of the Kingdom. Early in the 1600s William Burnett's family appear to have held a prominent position evidence of which is the extent to which additions were made to the property, but by about 1650 considerable sums were raised by wadsets on the estate. Mary Scot 'Lady Bonnington' died in October 1649. Her will was confirmed by the Commissary of Peebles on 1 March 1656 in favour of *William Burnet of Barns her oye* (grandson) *and Executor Dative.* He married, on 27 April 1648 in Edinburgh, Christian Whiteford, daughter of Dr. Walter Whiteford, Bishop of Brechin and Ann Carmichael, daughter of Sir John Carmichael of that Ilk...William and Christian Burnet had the following children:

- William Burnett, who had an army career and who succeeded his father in Barns.
- Walter Burnett who had an army career and held the rank of Lieutenant. He was killed in the wars in Flanders.
- Henrietta Burnett who married, on 1 January 1680 in Edinburgh, John Stewart, Writer to the Signet.
- Christian Burnett married (1), on 15 June 1682 in Edinburgh, William McGie, minister at Aberlady. They had one known child
    - Daughter unknown McGie

  Christian Burnett married (2) Rev. Robert Cheyne. Their children were:
    - James Cheyne.
    - Jean Cheyne who married, on 1 June 1721 in Edinburgh, Alexander Hay, Writer, Edinburgh.
- Anna Burnett who married unknown Mitchelson of Middleton.
- Marie Burnett married Andrew Naughton, minister at Storie who retired to England in 1688. There was one known child
    - Andrew Naughton.
- Margaret Burnett who died before 1675.
- Agnes Burnett who died before 1675.

Christian Whitford Burnett died in 1674 and William Burnett, WS, in 1675.

William Burnett, WS, Treasurer Clerk, was succeeded by his son **Captain William Burnett** who was apprenticed in law in April 1669 to Archibald Nisbet, Writer to the Signet. Soon afterwards, however, he entered military service. From September 1678 he was an Ensign in the newly raised Regiment of Foot of Charles, Earl of Mar, and made Lieutenant in Captain Thomas Douglas's Company on 15 October 1679. He was promoted to the rank of Captain by 1685. William Burnett served in Flanders, where his brother Lieutenant Walter Burnett was killed, and was wounded at the Battle of Steinkerke on Sunday 24 July 1692. He died, unmarried, in November 1692 in Brussels.

William Burnett, son of John Burnet and Helen Baillie, styled variously as of *of Kailzie*, and *in Glenwrath*, succeeded on the death of his cousin Captain William Burnett, *of Barns* in 1692. Captain William had been seriously worried about the continuing financial difficulties of the family estates but did not live to put his remedial ideas into operation. William Burnett inherited all of these debts! The heirs of Captain James Burnett in Leith, his brother, had wadsets on a large amount of the estate and although eventually redeemed by William Burnett, it was only achieved after long legal intervention. On 14 March 1698, Alison Burnett, daughter of James Burnet and Alison Gibson, finally disponed to 'William Burnett in Glenrath, now of Barns' with the consent of her husband John Dundas.

William Burnett married (1), in December 1663, Jean Chancellor, eldest daughter of Robert Chancellor of Shieldhill, county of Lanark. They had no children. After her death, William Burnett married (2), in 1684, Jean Baillie, daughter of James Baillie, descended from Baillie of Lamington, and Martha Lindsay of Covington. Jean was the widow of John Murray of Glenrath, son of Sir David Murray of Stanhope, with a daughter Violet Murray, who died in 1760 and was heritrix of that property. Violet Murray sold Glenrath in 1698 to the Earl of March. William and Jean Baillie Burnett had children:

- ❑ James Burnett who was born in 1685 and succeeded to Barns.
- ❑ John Burnett *in Glenrat*h. He married, in 1720, Lilias Russell, daughter of William Russell of Ashiesteel and Elisabeth Mitchelson of Middleton. They had children
  - ♦ Jane Burnett.
  - ♦ Elizabeth Burnett who married James Robertson of Currie.
- ❑ Helen Burnett who married, on 14 July 1712 in Manor parish, Peebles, Robert Chisholm, Collector of Cess for the county of Peebles, son of Chisholm of Hairhope. After the death of Helen, Robert Chisholm married (2), in 1732, Mary Findlay, daughter of Rev Thomas Findlay, minister at Preston.

William Burnett, who was ill by 1710, made a will in that year in favour of his son James Burnett. He died in 1712 and his wife Jean Baillie Burnett died in March 1717.

James Burnett who succeeded his father in Barns in 1712 set about with great energy to improve the estate including adjusting the boundaries with Bellanridge which was owned by William Laidlaw. Much of his scheme of improvement was seen as unusual at that time and included the planting of many trees. He re-purchased Glenrath in 1729 from the Earl of March to whom it had been sold in 1698 by Violet Murray, his step-sister. In 1747 he had an interest in purchasing property to the south, in Dumfriesshire. In 1776 he was recorded in a Court of Session document as being over 80 years of age and still improving his property. In fact he would have been over 90 years! This member of the southern Burnets saw, in his lifetime, the Jacobite Risings of 1715 and 1745 and was personally sympathetic to the Stuarts.

James Burnett married, in 1725, Anna Veitch, daughter of John Veitch of Dawyck, Presenter of Signatures to His Majesty's Exchequer, and Margaret Nisbet. Their children, of whom many died early in life, were:

- Margaret Burnett, born on 22 September 1726 who married her cousin James Murray, a Surgeon in Edinburgh, son of George Murray of Polmaise and Christian Veitch.
- Jane Burnett, born on 26 January 1728. She died on 23 September 1728.
- Violet Burnett, born on 25 May 1729 and died a few months later on 2 August 1729.
- Agnes Burnett, born on 29 August 1730 and died in December 1780.
- William Burnett, born on 17 September 1731. He died on 8 July 1740.
- Jean Burnett, born on 23 January 1734 and died in October 1771.
- Anna Burnett, born on 22 April 1735 and lived only until 28 October 1735.
- Violet Burnett, born on 24 May 1736. She died on 20 September 1805.
- James Burnett, born on 28 October 1737. He succeeded to Barns.
- Anna Burnett, born on 20 February 1739.
- William Burnett born on 23 September 1740 and died on 3 March 1783.
- John Burnett, born on 5 June 1742 and lived less than a year, dying on 2 March 1743.
- Janet Burnett, born on 13 February 1744 and died almost exactly a year later on 10 February 1745.
- Charles Burnett, born on 26 June 1745. He died on 31 January 1777 at Fort Marlborough whilst on passage to Bengal. He had been a merchant in Cadiz, Spain.

James Burnett died in his 86th year in January 1771. His wife Anna Veitch Burnett died two years later in October 1773.

James Burnett, born in 1737, was the oldest surviving son when he succeeded his father in 1771. Although he was educated towards a legal career and was apprenticed in 1756 to David Anderson, WS, in Edinburgh where he showed much ability and promise, he gave up law and retired to Bonnington which was a small family inherited property near Peebles. There he followed the life of the country gentry until he came to Barns. James Burnett was what could be described as a classical scholar who enjoyed the handsome library that he had accumulated. His interests did not include his father's enthusiasm for further improvement of Barns apart from the erection of a new mansion house in about 1775. He rented out a large portion of the estate in small farms to tenants, many of whom paid their dues irregularly and, in the old custom, often in kind rather than money. This led him eventually to dispose of part of the estate, in 1807 because of the poor income received from it and the fact that he was unsupported by income from any profession.

James Burnett is said to have been one of the last of the Scottish gentry who held sympathy for the Stuart cause, just as his ancestors had done. He was a staunch member of the Scottish Episcopal Church and attended meetings in Carruber's Close in Edinburgh. James Burnett married, on 27 July 1775, Janet Moir, daughter of John Moir, Merchant in Edinburgh, who was descended from the Moirs of Leckie, and Janet Gellatly. The children of James and Janet Burnet were:

- James Burnett who was born on 16 May 1776 and succeeded in Barns.
- Clementina Burnett who was born on 8 December 1777. She died on 25 April 1866 at Dalkeith, Midlothian.
- Anne Burnett who was born on 7 August 1779 died at Dalkeith on 11 December 1857.
- Janet Burnett who was born on 20 March 1781 died on 3 March 1847 at Dalkeith.
- Joan Burnett who was born on 24 June 1783 married, in 1814, George Gardiner, Comptroller-General of His Majesty's Customs in Scotland. Their known children were:
    - James Burnett Gardiner, merchant of London and of Moulmein who died at Moulmein.
    - Agnes Gardiner.

  Joan Burnett Gardiner died in London on 12 May 1866.
- Violet Burnett, who was born on 17 November 1784, married, in 1808, Dr Thomas Young of Rosetta, Peebles, the Inspector-General of His Majesty's Military Hospitals. Thomas Young joined the Army in 1775 and served in America, the West Indies, Holland, in the Mediterranean and in Egypt. He was present at the battle of Alexandria on 21 March 1801. For service to his country Dr. Young was offered a baronetcy which he declined. They had no family. Thomas Young died on 6 February 1836. Violet died at Rosetta on 1 June 1867.
- William Burnett who was born on 28 May 1788 became a Merchant in Brazil and later in London. He was appointed Colonial Secretary of the Swan River Settlement, which is now Western Australia, under the government of Sir Edward Parry. Soon afterwards he moved his family to New South Wales where he settled. William Burnett married on 30 October 1813 in Edinburgh to Marjory Chalmers Brown, eldest daughter and heiress of Unknown Brown of Newton, county of Lanark. William and Marjory had the following children:
    - James Charles Burnett, FRGS, who served for 20 years in the Surveyor-General's Department. Sir Charles Fitzroy rewarded his esteemed services by naming the Burnet River and District in the north after him. James

Charles Burnett died unmarried at his home near Brisbane, Australia on 18 July 1854 at the age of 39 years.

- John Alexander Burnett became a Merchant in Melbourne, Australia.
  He married Margaret McDonnell and had the following children:
  - Charles John Burnett who became a Major in H. M. 15th Regiment.
  - William Burnett who married, in 1870, Elizabeth Alexander, only child of Alexander Alexander of Hawkes Bay, New Zealand. They had one known child
    - Violet Alexander.
  - James Burnett.
  - Abigail Scott Burnett who died young.
  - Lilias Burnett who married in September 1873 to Frank de Crez McCraken. They had one known child
    - Lilias de Crez McCracken

  John A. Burnett died at his home, St. Kilda, on 25 May 1853 aged 35.
- Marjory Burnett who died young.
- William Burnett of Burnetland, in Hunter District, New South Wales, Australia. He succeeded his father, William Burnett.
- Patrick Graham Burnett.

William Burnett died in Australia in 1858 aged 70.

- Christian Burnett who was born on 19 June 1790. She died in Dalkeith on 16 May 1866.

Janet Moir Burnett died before 1820 and James Burnett died on 19 November 1820, at Barns, aged 83.

James Burnett, born 1776, succeeded his father James in Barns. James became the Deputy Lieutenant and Magistrate in the county of Peebles. He was a Captain in the Dumfriesshire, 4th, Regiment of the North British Militia from 1792 until the Peace of Amiens in 1802. Very active in local and county affairs, he was a staunch Episcopalian who was mainly responsible for the establishment of the Episcopal Church in Peebles. James Burnett married, in 1803, Christian Catherine Lee, daughter of Robert Lee of Greenock and Christian Donald. Christian Lee Burnett was descended from the Earls of Bute. Children of James and Christian Burnett were:

- James Burnett who was born on 2 February 1804 became a Writer to the Signet and was an Attorney at Law in Georgetown, Demerara. He died, unmarried, in Demerara on 6 December 1836 aged 32 years.
- Robert Lee Burnett who was born on 23 March 1805 became a Captain in the 54th Regiment of Bengal Native Infantry. He joined the service of the Honorable East India Company (HEIC) in 1821 and was in India for 22 years. Robert had an extremely active military career and was severely wounded on

several occasions including while in action in Afghanistan on 18 October 1842. He died in January 1843 aged 38 at Ferozepore where his fellow officers erected a monument in his memory. During his military service he was awarded a number of medals.

- Christian Catherine Burnett who was born on 4 July 1806 died unmarried at Mayville, Stevenston, Ayrshire on 15 April 1875.
- Janet Ann Elizabeth Burnett who was born on 6 September 1807 married, on 3 July 1839 in Manor parish, Peebles, the Rev. James Cruickshank. Their children were;
  - Henrietta Hay Cruickshank who died in childhood.
  - Christian Catherine Cruickshank who married, in 1869, the Rev. James Smith, Newhills, Aberdeen.
  - James Burnett Cruickshank who died on 21 January 1877 in Ceylon.
  - John Robert Lee Cruickshank who was in Civil Service in Demerara.

  Janet Burnett Cruickshank died at Stevenston, Ayrshire on 16 June 1877 and her husband on 17 October 1880.
- William Burnett, who was born on 4 January 1810, became a Lieutenant Colonel and was an Assistant Adjutant General in the Militia of British Guiana. He was also a Justice of the Peace in the county of Peebles. William Burnett married, in 1843, Elizabeth Wilday, daughter of Charles Wilday, Colonial Registrar and Secretary of the Supreme Courts of Justice of British Guiana. William and Elizabeth Burnett had the following children:
  - Maitland James Burnett.
  - Kate Egan Fullarton Burnett.
  - Violet Anna D'Urban Burnett who married, on 3 July 1873 in Manor parish, Peebles, John Ogilvie, younger of Inneshewan, in the county of Angus. They had one known child:
    - John Burnett Ogilvie.
  - Edith Carmichael Smythe Burnett who married, in August 1878, Thomas Henderson Orphoot, Advocate and Sheriff-Substitute of county of Peebles. They had one known child:
    - Burnett Napier Orphoot.
  - Annie Elizabeth Boyd Burnett who married, on 15 July 1880, William Anderson of Hallyards in the county of Peebles and of Richmond, Surrey, England.
- John Hamilton Burnett who was born on 10 February 1811 became a Captain in the 16th Bengal Native Infantry, Grenadier Regiment. He entered the service of HEIC in 1827, was made Lieutenant in 1834 and Captain in 1843. After a notable campaign, he fell at the Battle of Ferozeshah on 21 December 1845 aged 34 having won a number of service medals.

- Eleanor Stuart Burnett, who was born on 23 July 1812, died unmarried at Mayville, Stevenston, Ayrshire on 18 April 1870.
- Thomas Young Crichton Burnett who was born on 12 September 1813 became a Merchant and Justice of the Peace in Trinidad, West Indies. He died when the steamship *Amazon* was destroyed by fire in the Bay of Biscay on 3 January 1852. He was then 38 years of age.
- Montgomery Burnett who was born on 16 October 1814 was a merchant in Trinidad, West Indies. He became a Member of the Corresponding Committee of the Society of Arts and a Director of the Botanical Gardens, Trinidad. Montgomery married, in December 1858, Maraval Georgina Fuller, born Devon, England in about 1834, daughter of Hon. Henry Fuller, Judge of Supreme Courts in Trinidad who was deceased by the time of his daughter's marriage. At the UK census recording in 1881, Montgomery Burnett and his wife Maraval were living at Dunreeth, Lower Warberry Road, Tormoham, Devon.

  Montgomery Burnett collected together details of the genealogy of the Burnets of Burnetland and Barns, which he published privately for members of the family. Information extracted from that publication has been included in this genealogy with added amendments and additions.
- Archibald Campbell Burnett who was born on 17 August 1817 was a Merchant in Demerara. He died on 24 January 1868 aged 50 at Mayville, Stevenston, Ayrshire.
- Fullarton Cunningham Burnett, who was born on 5 June 1822, made his home in America. He married Mary Caroline Larkins and had the following children:
  - John Stewart Burnett.
  - Lynn Hall Burnett.
  - Christian Catherine Lee Burnett.

  Fullarton Burnett died at Lillington, Pender Co., North Carolina on 14 February 1876 aged 53 years.

James Burnett died at Mayville, Stevenston, Ayrshire on 20 June 1855 aged 79. He was buried in the family grave in Manor parish, Peebles. His wife Christian Catherine Lee Burnett had died a few months earlier on 21 February 1855. She was buried at Stevenston.

The Bonnington part of the estate was sold in order to raise money in 1824. Thereafter trustees were appointed to oversee the affairs of James Burnett and the Barns estate. In 1838 the sale of Barns was pursued although the time was not a favourable one for the sellers.

The Burnets of Barns then ceased to be landowners in Peebles and the Border counties of Scotland with which they had had family association for several centuries.

Burnard of Ardross and Currie.

John Burnard, who accompanied King David II in the journey south to his defeat and subsequent capture, on 17 October 1346 at the Battle of Neville's Cross, Durham, owned part of the lands of Ardross in Fife and also part of those of Currie in Midlothian. He is thought to have been one of the Burnards of Farningdoun. During the assault to capture the fort of Liddell which lay on the route of the march south, John Burnard was severely wounded and left at Roxburgh Castle where he eventually died. After the battle of Durham, Roxburgh was surrendered to the English. The effigy of a knight in armour, described as being in the parish church of Kilconquhar in Fife, [(6)] supposedly celebrates John Burnard, Laird of Ardross, who received his death-wound whilst fighting with David II in the attack on the fortress of Liddel in 1346.

As a result of being found at Roxburgh Castle when it was surrendered, it was generally believed that John Burnard had been a traitor who had voluntarily joined the enemy. Because of this, his lands were forfeited and bestowed on Alexander Manteland/Maitland. The Treaty of Berwick in 1357 secured the release of King David II and on his return from captivity, the truth was revealed. The grant to the Maitlands was subsequently revoked and the lands formally restored by Royal charter in 1368-69 to William of Dishington, who was the kinsman and nearest heir of John Burnard.

The first record of the Dishington surname, of which the origin is the placename of Dissington in Northumberland, is that of Sir William de Dissingtoun who received a charter of the lands of Balglassy in Angus from King Robert I (1306-1329). Flemington Tower, a seventeenth century L-plan Tower-house, near Forfar, was the property of the Dishingtons from the 1400s and is now ruined. In 1495, John Dissington of Ardrosse had licence from the Crown to export Scottish goods into England. A branch of the family settled in Orkney about 1600 where John Dishington was depute to the Earl of Orkney in 1602 at the Castle of Scalloway, Shetland, and, by 1669, a Thomas Dishington was minister of St. Magnus Cathedral, Kirkwall [(7)]. About the same period some Dishingtons emigrated to Norway where the name evolved to Dessington. In 1517, Thomas Dishington was Captain of the Palace of St. Andrews. Ardross Castle, the site of which is located a short distance to the north-east of Elie on the coast of Fife near St. Andrews, is said to have been built by the Dishington family in the 1300s, possibly after the lands were inherited from the estate of John Burnard. It was later sold and by 1700 was owned by Sir William Anstruther.

References:

1. Jackson, R.N., The Noble Anglo-Saxons?, in *Aberdeen University Review*, LVII, No. 199, (Spring 1998).
2. Bingham, C., *Robert The Bruce*, 21. (1998), Constable, London.
3. *Ibid.* 23.
4. Ritchie. G., *Normans in Scotland*, 157.
5. Burnett, G., *The Family of Burnett of Leys*, 2. (1901), Spalding Club.
6. Rogers, Rev. Charles, *Monuments and Monumental Inscriptions of Scotland*, Vol. II, (1872), 101.
7. Black, G. *The Surnames of Scotland*, (1946).

Bibliography:

Anderson, W., *The Scottish Nation*, 3 vols. , (1868).
Burnett, M., *Genealogical Account of the Family of Burnett of Burnetland and Barns.* (1880). Published privately.
Burnett, G., (ed. Allardyce, J.), *The Family of Burnett of Leys*, (1901), Spalding Club.
Black, G.F., *The Surnames of Scotland,* (1946).
Coventry, M., *The Castles of Scotland*, 2nd ed., (1997), Goblinshead, Edinburgh.
Christie, J.A. et al., *Register of the Society of Writers to Her Majesty's Signet*, (1983), Edinburgh.
Ferguson, J.P.S., *Scottish Family Histories – National Library of Scotland*, (1986), Edinburgh.
Hannay, R.K. et al., *The History of the Society of Writers to his Majesty's Signet*, (1936), Edinburgh.
Registrum Magni Sigilli Regum Scotorum (Register of the Great Seal of Scotland).
Registrum Secreti Sigilli Regum Scotorum (Register of the Privy Seal of Scotland).
Ross, S., *Monarchs of Scotland.* (1990), Lochar Press, Moffat.
Way, G. of Plean, & Squire, R., *Scottish Clan & Family Encyclopaedia*, (1994).

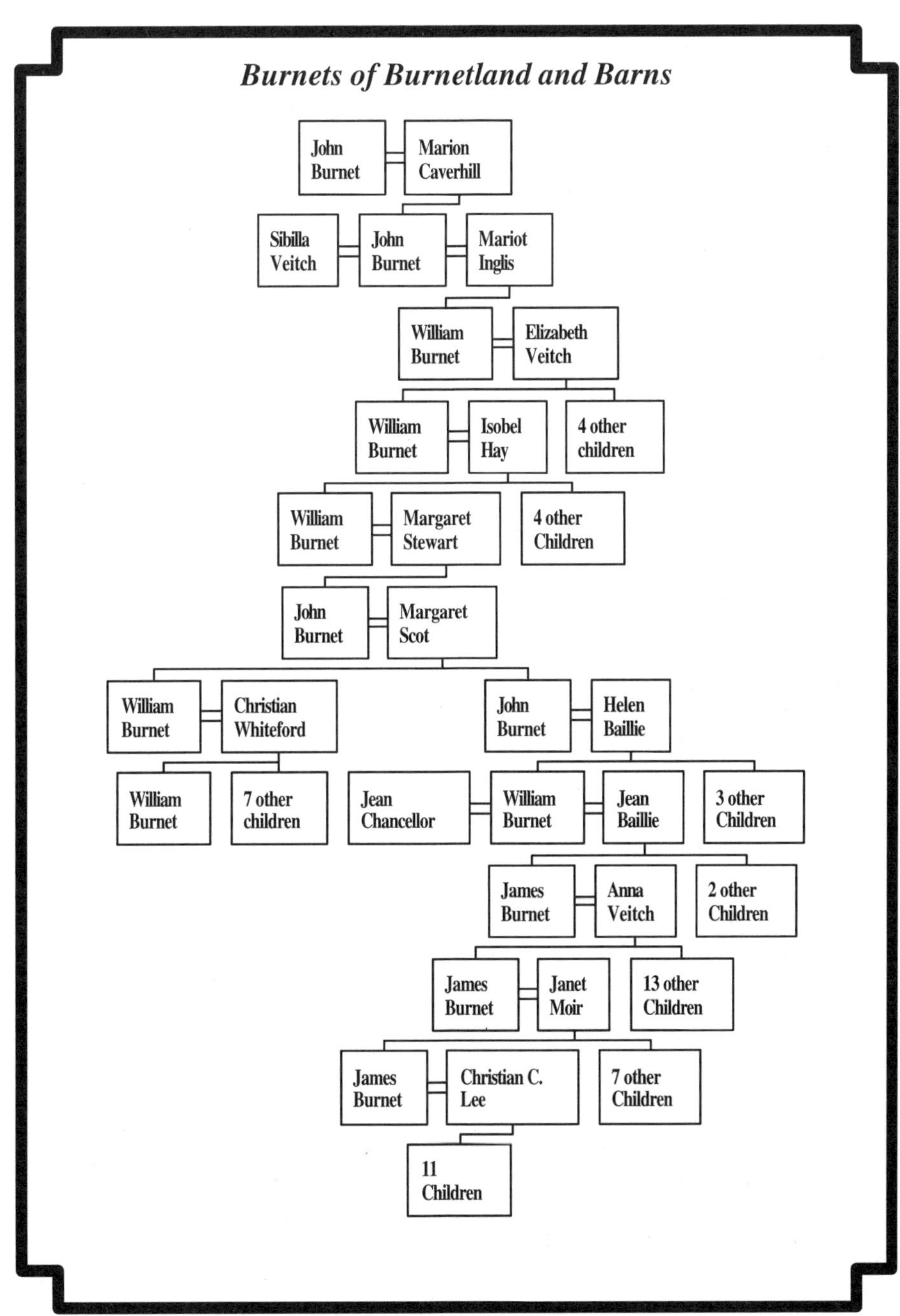
Burnets of Burnetland and Barns
John Burnet
Marion Caverhill
Sibilla Veitch
John Burnet
Mariot Inglis
William Burnet
Elizabeth Veitch
William Burnet
Isobel Hay
4 other children
William Burnet
Margaret Stewart
4 other Children
John Burnet
Margaret Scot
William Burnet
Christian Whiteford
John Burnet
Helen Baillie
William Burnet
7 other children
Jean Chancellor
William Burnet
Jean Baillie
3 other Children
James Burnet
Anna Veitch
2 other Children
James Burnet
Janet Moir
13 other Children
James Burnet
Christian C. Lee
7 other Children
11 Children

3

THE BURNETTS IN NORTH-EAST SCOTLAND

Eileen A. Bailey

To be still searching what we know not, by what we know, still closing up truth to truth as we find it.

(John Milton, 1644)

The Burnetts in the north-east of Scotland, located mainly in Aberdeenshire and Kincardineshire, evolved into several distinct branches of which the detailed genealogy is outlined later. The following branches all stemmed from the ancestors of the present Chief, James C. A. Burnett of Leys.

Burnard/Burnet(t)s of Leys

Alexander Burnard was one of those adherents whose loyalty and many services to King Robert I were repaid substantially by large grants of land on the banks of the River Dee in the vicinity of the parish of Banchory Ternan, Kincardineshire. The charter, outlining the land transaction, dated 28 March 1324 at Berwick-on-Tweed, was confirmed by a later charter by King David II dated 17 November 1358 at Scone.

Fig.3.1. Leys Charter

Alexander Burnard was also Keeper of the Forest of Drum, the badge of office of which is considered to be the Horn of Leys. This still hangs in Crathes Castle and is portrayed in the Coat of Arms of the Burnetts of Leys. Given the feudal system of land tenure introduced from England by King David I, it is likely that the procedure of "Cornage" or use of a symbolic horn in the process of land grants also extended north of the Border. Interestingly, in Chapter 14, Ian Bryce, in describing Castlehill Tower, one of the properties occupied by Burnets in southern Scotland, draws attention to the fact that its contents in 1555 included a "hart horn" hanging in the hall.

Fig. 3.2 The Horn of Leys

The Horn of Leys may, therefore, have had a two-fold significance in not only identifying the role of Keeper of the Royal Forest at Drum but also in sealing the charter. A family tradition that the Horn of Leys must always be in the possession of the family almost certainly arises from the fact that the horn could, if necessary, be produced in support of any claim to land. There is no reference to it, however, in any of the family charters, which is a situation that the Leys horn has in common with a number of other symbolic horns.

Although his exact ancestry is not on surviving record, Alexander Burnard is generally considered to have been a member of the Burnets of Farningdon, perhaps a son of Roger. From the Burnetts of Leys, there derived a number of branches of the family of which the following are the principals:

Burnett of Craigmyle

James Burnett of Craigmyle was the son of Alexander Burnett of Leys and the immediate younger brother of Sir Thomas Burnett, 1st Baronet. By terms of a family contract made in 1598, he married, in 1608, Elizabeth Burnett, daughter and heir of Thomas Burnett of Craigmyle and Tillihaikie and Jane Moncur. This Thomas was the grandson and representative of William Burnett of Craigour,

Campbell and Tillihaikie who fell at the Battle of Pinkie in 1547, ancestor of Burnetts of Campbell/Camphill, Elrick, etc. Thomas Burnett seems to have acquired Craigmyle through his mother, the heiress of a family of Craigmyle of that Ilk who are on record in the fifteenth century as holding Craigmyle directly from the Crown. In November 1608, Thomas Burnett resigned his lands of Craigmyle, Pitmedden and Hill of Craigmyle into the hands of the Earl of Huntly, superior, in favour of his daughter Elizabeth and her husband James Burnett on their marriage. In 1678 the Arms of Sir Alexander Burnett of Craigmyle were recorded in the Lyon Register.

Burnett of Camphill

William Burnett of Wester Camphill, Craigour and Tillihaikie had charters on these lands in 1537, 1546 and 1547 respectively. His successor, Andrew Burnett of Easter Camphill had three sons from whom were descended the Burnetts of Camphill and of Elrick.

Burnett of Crimond

Robert Burnett, born in 1592 and brother of Sir Thomas Burnett of Leys, 1st Baronet, was an eminent lawyer at the Scottish Bar to which he was admitted on 20 February 1617. He married (2) Rachel daughter of James Johnston, merchant in Edinburgh. Robert Burnett acquired Banachtie and Mill of Bourtie in 1628 and, in 1634, the estate of Crimond which became his residence. In 1661 he was made a Judge of the Court of Session and took the title Lord Crimond.

Burnett of Kemnay

Thomas Burnett, second son of the above James Burnett of Craigmyle was a Writer in Edinburgh. He married, in 1655, Margaret Pearson, daughter of John Pearson, Merchant, of Edinburgh. In 1688 he purchased the estate of Kemnay, on Donside, Aberdeenshire, from Sir George Nicholson, a Lord of Session under the title of Lord Kemnay. On 20 July 1688 he had a Crown Charter to Thomas Burnett, Writer in Edinburgh and his heirs, of the barony of Kemnay.

Burnett of Monboddo

The Monboddo branch of the Burnetts also descended from James Burnett of Craigmyle. James Burnett of Lagavin, third son of James of Craigmyle, married (2) Elizabeth, daughter of Robert Irvine of Monboddo in Kincardineshire. Around 1671, Elizabeth's brothers sold the Monboddo mansion and estate to their brother-in-law James Burnett.

Burnett of Elrick

John Burnett, magistrate and Dean of Guild in Aberdeen, descended from William Burnett of Camphill, acquired the property of Elrick, in 1662 as the result of a complicated series of financial and land transactions and debts. This property had earlier been in the hands of Mr. Robert Burnett, Tutor of Leys, but was mortgaged to Gilbert Hervie, burgess of Aberdeen, in 1659. John Burnet died on 9 December 1666. John Burnett married (1) Marjorie Howieson and (2), in 1664, Mary Jameson, daughter of George Jameson, Artist. The estate of Elrick comprised *the land and barony of Elrick with the mill and miln-croft, Smiddieland and Broomiebrae of Elrick, the town and lands of Monacabback, Ord and Scrogley of Monacabback and lands of Snellen.*

Burnett of Countesswells & Kepplestone

Alexander Burnett of Countesswells had a charter, under The Register of the Great Seal [(1)], of Salterhills with Auchries and other lands *apprising from the Earl Marischal.* His daughter and heiress, Marjorie married, in 1640, James Sandilands of Cotton, born 1610, son of James Sandilands of Craibstone and his spouse Catherine Paterson of Granton, Kincardineshire. Her estate of Countesswells descended to his second son John, later Provost of Aberdeen. Salterhill/Satyrhills had been sold earlier.

Burnett-Stuart

Theadosia Stuart, daughter of John Stuart of Dens, married John Burnet, who was born in 1704, the son of John Burnett, merchant in Aberdeen and Katherine Paton of Grandholm. Like his father, John Burnett also became a merchant in Aberdeen. His grandfather was John Burnett of Daladies, descended from the Burnetts of Leys. John Burnett and Theodosia Stuart married in 1729, in St. Nicholas, Aberdeen and had numerous children. Theadosia Burnett inherited the Dens and Crichie estates on the death of her father in 1729 at which time the surname Burnett-Stuart was adopted.

Burnett-Ramsay of Balmain

Through the marriage of Sir Thomas Burnett, 6th Baronet of Leys, with the sister of Sir Alexander Ramsay, 6th Baronet of Balmain, the Burnetts became heirs in line of the Ramsays of Balmain. Sir Alexander Ramsay, 6th Baronet, died without issue in 1806 and in virtue of his settlement, his estates passed to the immediate younger brother of his heir in line i.e. Alexander, born 31st July 1757, second son of Sir Thomas Burnett of Leys. He was admitted to the Scottish Bar and became Sheriff of Kincardineshire in 1779. In 1782 he married Elizabeth, daughter of Sir Alexander Bannerman, 4th Baronet of Elsick. Alexander Burnett died in 1810 and his family, in general, dropped the name Burnett and retained that of Ramsay.

Burnett of Lethenty

Robert Burnett, of Lethenty, became a Quaker and was made to suffer greatly for his adhesion to this faith to which he had become a convert before 1680. His exact descent from the Burnetts of Leys is not stated in *The Family of Burnett of Leys* and has not yet been ascertained from research. In the Meldrum Charter Chest an obligation dated 11 March, registered 7 April 1665 by Adam Urquhart of Meldrum, gives warrant to Robert Burnett of Lethenty *for the lands of Lethenty, tiends, desks in the Chapel of Garioch etc.*, with the consent of James and Patrick Urquhart, brothers of the said Adam.

Burnett of Kirkhill

The first Burnett laird of Kirkhill was Alexander Burnett, merchant, son of Thomas Burnett, merchant of Aberdeen. Alexander married Agnes Moir in 1655. Through marriage Kirkhill passed to the Bannerman family.

Burnett of Daladies

John Burnett of Daladies was, by his Arms, a cadet of Leys. He married Agnes Turnbull, daughter of Turnbull of Stracathro. His son John Burnett, who succeeded, was nicknamed "Bonnie John". He married (1) on 15 June 1703 in Old Machar parish, Katherine/Catherine Paton, second daughter of George Paton of Grandholm.

Burnett of Powis

Alexander Burnett, 4th laird of Kemnay, married Christian Leslie in 1781. Christian inherited Powis through her mother who was the daughter and heiress of Hugh Fraser of Powis.

BURNETTS OF LEYS

The first of the Burnards who is known be associated with the lands of Leys, was **Alexander Burnard**. The surname appears in early north-east records as interchangeable with Burnet and gradually evolved, through a number of variations, to that of Burnett. Alexander is thought to have been a son of Roger Burnard of Farningdoun. Little is known about his ancestry or about his early life but it would appear that he had given loyal service to King Robert I as reward for which land in Kincardineshire was bestowed on him in March 1324. Simultaneously, William of Irvine from the south-west of Scotland, also received lands in the same area. William Irvine is known from Chamberlain Records to have been the Clerk Register or *Clericus rotulorum et register* from 1328-31 and, in addition, is believed to have been the King's Secretary and Armour-bearer.

Such grants of land from the Crown were, in part, an appointment as custodian. King Robert I granted the forests of Kintore and of Drum to two of his followers with whose descendants the lands remain, but the Parks remained in his royal domain until otherwise decreed. For example, although the Forest of Kintore became the property of the Keiths, Marischals of Scotland, the Crown retained the right to reside there as they wished. This right seems to have been exercised only in situations where there was also a place of strength which would provide security and protection to the royal party. A charter by King David II, dated 1361, concerning Kintore mentions *apud Manerium nostrum forestii de Kyntor* indicating that there was such a stronghold or manor within the Forest of Kintore. This keep was known as Hallforest.

Similarly Drum was probably a royal manor, one in the chain which spanned the country. It was important because of its position at one of the two main fords across the River Dee, at the north end of one of the main routes across the high ground between Rivers Tay and Dee. In a later deed, dated 1393, from John de Moigne to Alexander de Irvin, it is stated that certain payments were to be made *apud marerium dicti Alexandri de Droum* or at the manor of the said Alexander of Drum. Many similar types of deeds of the time use the term *manerium* to signify dwelling places at which castles or strongholds existed. Such castles were built for practicality of defence and were far removed from the elegant design and style of the surviving grand residences such as Crathes or Drum.

The lands which Burnard and Irvine received at Drum, on the north bank of the River Dee, were the Forest and Park of Drum which were possessions of the Crown in 1247 and probably for some time prior to that date. The Park was an enclosed area to retain game for hunting. Tyler, in *History of Scotland*, Vol. II, 337, says *It appears to have been the custom of our monarchs to remove their court at different seasons to the various palaces, estates and manors which they possessed in private property.* In 1318, the *Registrum de Aberbrothoc*, 284, records a deed in which King Robert the Bruce grants, to the Abbot and monks of Arbroath, the right of passage through the Park of Drum without fear of challenge by the forester or any other officials, on condition that they erect two gates for their entrance and exit with bolts to allow the gates to be opened or shut as required. [*Antiquities*, Vol. I., 277, Spalding Club.]. The association of Burnetts and Irvines with their adjacent lands in Kincardineshire has continued down through the ages.

The granting of these lands should be considered against the historical background of the times. King Robert the Bruce, was born in 1274. He claimed the throne of Scotland and was crowned at Scone, Perthshire, on 25 March 1306 when he was aged 32. Scots of all walks of life gave enthusiastic support to their new king. In 1307 he defeated the English forces at the Battle of Loudoun Hill. By 1314, King Robert only had to retrieve Berwick and Stirling from English control and on 24 June 1314, a successful Scottish army, who were outnumbered two to one, defeated the English forces of King Edward II at the Battle of Bannockburn, near Stirling. Many of Robert Bruce's campaigns were mounted in southern Scotland and it is reasonably supposed that Alexander Burnard, thought to have been of the Farningdoun family, had contributed to their success.

Whether the link between Alexander Burnard and Robert the Bruce was as a result of his having held an office in the retinue of the royal court, or for his services as a knight fighting for his king in all, or some, of the southern battles, will probably never be known. Certainly the two families and the Irvines were all connected to the same area of southern Scotland. It is quite likely that Alexander Burnard fought at Bannockburn. The very early writer William Bower, Abbot of Inchcolm, in his Latin *Scotichronicon* which he wrote in the 1440s, included detail about the Battle of Bannockburn [*A History Book for Scots*, ed. Watt] In that work, he specifically quotes from the account of the preparations for the battle written in verse by Bernard, Abbot of Arbroath, whose role it was to carry a reliquary of St. Columba to the field of Bannockburn and to spiritually prepare the Scottish troops for the battle to come. Bower notes that Abbot Bernard's verses also refer to King Robert having called upon St. Andrew and St. Thomas a' Becket of Canterbury, to whom Arbroath Abbey was dedicated, to ensure a victory for the Scots.

From various writings it is clear that Bernard was greatly favoured by King Robert and shortly after the coronation he was appointed Chancellor of Scotland, in which office he drafted a treaty between King Robert and the King of Norway which he witnessed at Thurso. An acknowledged outstanding Latin scholar and writer Abbot Bernard is generally regarded as the author of the Declaration of Arbroath. At this time it would be pure speculation to suggest a possible connection between Abbot Bernard and Alexander Burnard but, as has already been mentioned, the Abbey had a grant in 1318 from the King giving them right of passage through the lands of Drum. The relationship between the Burnards of Farningdon and King Robert with Melrose Abbey in the south, and the later long association between the Burnards/Burnetts of Leys and the Abbey of Arbroath over several centuries, is certainly worthy of note.

A further portion of the royal forest of Drum was bestowed on Alexander Burnard before 1 February 1322-23. [Grant of that date in Drum Charters]. On 28 March 1323 a charter was granted to Alexander Burnard proceeding on the narrative that the custody of the Forest of Drum had been transferred to William of Irwyn/Irvine. The grant outlined that Alexander was to receive Killenachclerach and certain other lands in the forest and, in addition, Easter and Wester Cardney as compensation for the loss of the Forestership. The boundaries of the lands in the forest were given as the River Dee from the Ford of Durris to the mouth of the stream that issued from the Loch of Banchory in the south. This stream is now known as Burn of Bennie, and the Loch of Banchory, or Loch of Leys, was later drained. The western boundary was the course of the stream, the Loch and Islands of Banchory/Leys through to marches of Tilliebothville in the north. Easter and Wester Cardney extended eastwards towards the Loch of Skene. The transcript of a charter from Robert the Bruce to Sir Alexander Fraser of Cluny dated 18 June 1325 concerned *our lands of the Cardneys, with the tenandry of the same, belonging to Alexander Burnard, and the fishing on the Loch of Skene belonging to these lands* [Gordon Charters]. The placename Killenachclerach later became Collonach and Canneglerach, both of which are found in subsequent Burnett records. This appears to indicate that Alexander Burnard had originally held the appointment of Royal Forester but that this office had later been passed to William Irvine with resulting compensation in land having been made.

The early habitation of the Burnards was a crannog or lake/loch dwelling, sometimes refer to as the Castle of Leys, constructed on the island in the Loch of Leys where it could be defended. Whether the Burnards were responsible for its construction or simply took possession of an existing dwelling on the site is not known. Suggestions that the lands, and probably the crannog, were previously owned by the Wauchop family and were forfeited before being granted to Alexander Burnard have not been authenticated, although a charter of 1324-5 granted to Alexander Burnard showed that he had been conveyed the lands of Tulliboy and Little Culter which had formerly been the property of *John of Walchop*. A full description of the crannog style of settlement at Loch of Leys is given in Chapter 13.

It is reasonable to assume that the crannog dwelling was eventually abandoned in favour of a "manor" or land-based home with attendant farm and servant accommodation on the shores of the Loch of Leys especially, when one considers that the placename Lochtown/Lochtoun (a farm settlement with associated buildings) of Leys survives to the present day. It seems very unlikely that the Burnett family would have lived on the crannog for some 200 years. This is borne out by details of a ceremony of taking sasine at the house of Robert Burnet in the farm-toun of Leys when Alexander took possession of the lands of "Gannoccleroch and Wester Cardney in the Barony of Leys" dated 2 May 1488. Various archaeological records in Ireland and Scotland show a pattern of crannog dwellings being eventually replaced by land-based structures often in close proximity. There is no doubt that the Burnetts, as they were later styled, had, by the 1500s, constructed a tower-house which came to be called Crathes Castle and is described by Ian Bryce in Chapter 14.

Alexander Burnard had a son, possibly his eldest, **Symon Burnard**, who succeeded him. One Simonis Bayard is to be found in *Early Records of Aberdeen 1317, 1398-1407.* [Scottish History Society 3rd series. Vol. XLIX.] This record concerned *Tenentes Botharum* and *Pistores laganarum.* He is also mentioned in *The Annals of Aberdeen.* It would appear that Simon was one of the earliest of a long line of merchant Burnetts in one of Scotland's most important ports. In 1134, King David I granted a tithe on all ships trading in and out of Aberdeen. The first charter from King William the Lion in about 1179, and second charter granted before 1203, freed the burgesses of the town from paying toll on their goods traded and in so doing indicated how important a role Aberdeen merchants played in the commerce of the land.

By the end of the reign of King Alexander III, Aberdeen not only enjoyed strong domestic trade but, being a sea-port, possessed trading vessels with which its merchants exchanged goods with ports on the Continent. The Bishop of Aberdeen had a grant, from King David I, of one tenth of the "Can" or customs from the ships trading to and from the port of Aberdeen as part of the revenue of his *See*. In the second half of the thirteenth century, the overseas trade was chiefly with the Netherlands to which Aberdeen merchants sent salmon, wool and hides and brought back cloth from the Flemish weavers, salt, wine, iron and other domestic goods. Wool was a strong trading commodity, the fleeces of the Scottish sheep being particularly in demand in Flanders. Indeed, part of the 1357 ransom for the release of King David II was paid in wool produced in the hinterland of Aberdeen. The town was renown for the quality of its salmon, preserved by smoking, and for several types of dried and salted fish. As a result there was considerable trade in fish to England, very large quantities being sent to places such as Yarmouth and London.

The next recorded member of the family was **William Burnard**, son of Simon, who had a charter, dated 26 December 1378 at Arbroath, of the lands of Symon Burnard in Forest of Drum which had been resigned by him. This charter is now in the Crathes Papers. It gave the said lands to be held by William and his heirs in fee and heredity. The Register of Burgesses of Guild and Trade of the Burgh of Aberdeen lists a William Burnet, elected in 1399, who may be the same William or his son. There is a Willelmus Burnet who is mentioned several times in the early records of Aberdeen. It is in examining such records that one is particularly aware of the interchangeable nature of Burnard and Burnet(t).

John Burnard, said to be a grandson of Alexander Burnard, is recorded in the *Register of the Great Seal of Scotland* on 25 December 1370 in a charter from King David II as *Clavigeri nostrum* (Royal Mace-bearer). In the charter there is reference to an annual income to be made payable to him from the lands of Carnousis in Banffshire. Scotland and it is thought that the 10 merks per annum was his token payment for this royal duty. The account of the baillies of the town of Aberdeen, dated 10 February 1372/3, shows that a payment of 28s.8d was made by mandate of the King to John Burnard, *Clavigero*. [*Exchequer Rolls*, (the Royal Accounts) Vol.2, 390]. The word Clavigero translated from the Latin can also mean key-holder. It is impossible to determine whether this was the alternative translation which applied to John Burnard and to ascertain why he might have held keys for the King unless he had local responsibility for the royal mint, located in the Castlegate of Aberdeen.

Robert Burnard, according to George Burnett, was a son of William but is now thought to have been the son of John Burnard, Royal *Clavigero*. Douglas in his *Baronage of Scotland* states that Robert Burnard/Burnet was the son and successor of John Burnard. In 1391-2, Robert Burnard gave account as Deputy Sheriff of Kincardine at which time the principal Sheriff was Sir William Keith. A Robert Burnat, possibly the same person, is recorded as having been one of the Assize on 24 April 1400 on the occasion of the claim to succession of Alexander of Auchterlony to his father William as a Robert Burnarde, who claimed to studied for some time in France, appears in connection with the St. Andrew's Chapter, in a *petition submitted by favour of Walter de Leslie, his kinsman* and dated 21 December 1381. This Robert Burnarde was Clerk to the St. Andrew's Diocese on 29 April 1383 and William de Leslie was said to be his kinsman[Biographical Dictionary of Scottish Graduates to AD1410]. A payment to Robert Burnarde, deputy of the Sheriff of Kincardine was recorded in 1391. [Exchequer Rolls, Vol.3, 264]

John Burnet of Leys. According to George Burnett, he was the first of the family to be styled *of Leys*. It is known that *John Burnet of Leyis* was present, on 22 September 1446, at a deposition regarding the mortgaging of Easter Skene to Sir William Keith Marischal. "Leys" is applied in Burnet records from this date onward although it is known to have occasionally been in use earlier and the spelling of the surname varies considerably. Reference to a Johannes Burnet is to be found in the Burgh Records of Aberdeen 1398-1407. In charters relating to the Burgh of Aberdeen, it is noted that letters of safe conduct for owners of ships and their crews to trade with the city of London were granted to certain Burgesses of the town including one, dated 10 February 1438-9, to a John Burnard. John Burnet died in mid-1454.

Alexander Burnard/Burnet of Leys, was most likely to have been a son of John because he inherited in 1454. He was the first *Baron of Leys* during the reigns of kings James II, III and IV. When King James III made his way through the county of Angus and onwards to Aberdeen at the head of a large following, evidence in the Crathes Charters shows the Laird of Leys to have been one of his supporters, or prudently appearing to be so! On 23 April 1488 at Aberdeen, Alexander Burnard resigned all of his lands into the King's hands. Two days later, on 25 April, he received a charter, under the Great Seal held by Bishop Elphinstone, uniting into one Free Barony the lands of Leys, Killenaglerach, Cullonach, The Hill, Candahill, Crathes with mill, Drumsalloch with the Loch of Banchory and Island, all in the Sheriffdom of Aberdeen, along with Wester Cardney. As land charters centred around a main dwelling which, in the case of Burnetts, had so far been the Crannog on the Loch of Leys, perhaps this may have been the time at which an interim dwelling became the focal point of the Burnett family. A similar ceremony took place in the following century when Crathes became the main dwelling. The same Alexander Burnard was named in papers relating to the Abbey of Arbroath. In 1460, he was an arbiter in an inquest to settle the marches or boundaries of lands belonging to the Abbey. This powerful religious house held a considerable amount of land including some which bounded with Leys, and there are numerous and various charters and grants between Alexander Burnard and Irvine, the Laird of Drum.

Alexander Burnard/Burnet is found, from a reference in a 1485 lease, given by the Abbot of Arbroath, of Glenfarquhar in parish of Fordoun, to have been married to an Elizabeth Forbes. She was the widow of Alexander Riach and daughter of Alexander Forbes, 2nd laird of Echt. Alexander and Elizabeth Burnard had children of whom the following are known:

- Alexander Burnet who was heir to his father.
- Andrew Burnet. He was recorded as having witnessed a sasine in 1507.

- Christian Burnet who married, on a Papal dispensation on the grounds of propinquity dated 11 January 1480, Alexander Cumyn, eldest son of William Cumyn of Culter. Alexander Cumyn's grandmother was an Irvine.

Elizabeth was probably dead by the year 1497 as her name does not appear on a later lease of Glenfarquhar of that date. Alexander Burnet died about July 1505.

Alexander Burnet of Leys, son of Alexander inherited in 1505. Alexander married Janet Gardyne of Gardine, in Angus, in or before 1481. The Gardynes were of that Ilk i.e. of the lands of Gardyne in the parish of Kirkden, Angus, and were noted as being benefactors of the Abbey of Arbroath. On 28 May 1481, according to a charter confirmed at Edinburgh on 2 June, Alexander and his wife received a grant of the possession of Canneglerocht from his father. For some generations thereafter it became a practice to give this possession to the eldest son. Alexander and Janet Burnett had the following children:

- Master Duncan Burnet who became the Vicar of Kirkintilloch, then Rector of Methlick, and finally Canon of Aberdeen. From religious records he appears to have died on 9 March 1552-3.
- Alexander Burnet who married Agnes Lechtoun of the family of Lechtoun/Leighton of Usan in Forfar (later Angus). At least two Lechtouns/Leightons of that family are known to have been Abbots of Arbroath. Alexander and Agnes Burnett had the following known children:
    - Alexander Burnet who died in 1574. He succeeded his grandfather.
    - Robert Burnet.
    - Simon Burnet. He is thought to be the same Simon Burnet who is mentioned in the 1558-9 record of Aberdeen Burgh as objecting to a proposal to pull down the "convents" of the Black and White Friars and the appropriation of their property by the town.

  Alexander Burnet died between 2 September 1525 and 11 February 1526.

Alexander Burnett of Leys died in 1529.

Alexander Burnet of Leys, inherited from his grandfather in 1529, the year after King James V had seized power in Scotland. This representative of the family lived through the period immediately preceding the Scottish Reformation and during the crisis of that movement. In 1542, Mary Queen of Scots succeeded to the Crown and in 1547 the Scots were victorious against the English at the Battle of Pinkie. The circumstance of the Laird of Leys having an uncle who was a prebendary of St Machar's Cathedral brought him into friendly relations with the other members of the Chapter of Aberdeen. Alexander Burnet married, by 1540, (1) Janet Hamilton, the daughter of the rich Canon Robert Hamilton of Aberdeen and of an important family which included the Earls of Arran. Janet died between 1557-67. In his lifetime, Alexander had seen three monarchs on the throne of

Scotland as King James VI was crowned in 1567. Alexander and Janet Burnett had the following children:

- John Burnet who succeeded his father.
- Master Thomas Burnet. Thomas followed a career in the ministry and succeeded his uncle, Master Duncan Burnet, to the Canonry of Aberdeen and Rectory of Methlick. From 1565 until his death he held the office of Commissary of Aberdeen. Thomas Burnett died in Old Aberdeen on 24 February 1582-3.
- Andrew Burnet was given the designation *of Cowcardie.* He married Elizabeth Melville, widow of an Erskine of Drum.
- William Burnet *of Slowy*, married Janet/Jenis Chalmers, daughter of Alexander Chalmers of Cults who was a Provost of Aberdeen, and Jean/Jenis Lumsden, daughter of Robert Lumsden of Clova. [George Burnett suggested that some Burnetts of Warriston and Inverleith appeared to have been descended from one of their sons although the facts to support his thinking were not apparent in his notes. In research for this publication, note has been made of the fact that the brother-in-law of Robert Burnett, Lord Crimond, was Lord Warriston.]
  Children of William and Janet/Jenis Burnet were:
  - John Burnet.
  - Thomas Burnet of Slowie. He became the Minister of Strachan in 1599. He married Christian Strachan, daughter of Andrew Strachan, Minister of Logie Durno. Thomas Burnet died in August 1637.[*Fasti Ecclesiaticae Scotianae*]
    Their children were:
    - Andrew Burnet.
    - Thomas Burnet.
    - James Burnet.
    - Christian Burnet.
- Alexander Burnet *of Kynneskie* who married Elspeth Chalmers of Cults, sister of the aforementioned Janet/Jenis.
- Archibald Burnet who married another daughter of Alexander Chalmers of Cults, possibly Mariore/Marjorie Chalmers.
- James Burnet *in Cardney* .
- Isabel Burnet who married Robert Arbuthnot of Pitcarlies and Little Futhes in 1555. He was grandson of Sir Robert Arbuthnot of that Ilk and the elder brother of Alexander Arbuthnot, Principal of King's College, Aberdeen.
- Janet Burnet who married Master James Skene of Wester Corse and Ramore (Raemoir) whose father transfered the estate to him, on 26 February 1547, before departing to fight at the Battle of Pinkie. James later acquired Ramore on 13 December 1578. Their children were:
  - Alexander Skene born about 1540. He was admitted as a burgess of Aberdeen on 27 April 1582 and died 4 November 1582.

- Gilbert Skene born about 1548. He was also a burgess of Aberdeen and succeeded his father in 1600. Gilbert married Elizabeth Burnet, daughter of Alexander Burnet of Leys and Katherine Arbuthnott.
- Robert Skene born about 1550.
- William Skene born about 1552.
- Janet Skene married (1) Patrick Innes of Tibbertie and (2) on 11 February 1625, John Forbes of Byth.

Janet Burnet predeceased James Skene who married (2) Elizabeth Strathauchin. James Skene died in June 1600. [*Memorials of the Family of Skene*. Spalding Club. Aberdeen.1887]

- Agnes Burnet married, in 1551, Alexander Blackhall of Barra, son of William Blackhall and Katherine Gordon and by whom she was granted the middle third of *Meikle* and *Little Finnarsy*. He succeeded to Barra within the lifetime of his father who died in 1541. They had the following children:
  - Alexander Blackhall who inherited Blackhall from his father, before the death of both his grandfather and father, and became Blackhall of that Ilk in 1574. He remained in possession from that date until 1592 at which time the not inconsiderable estates of Barra were forfeited. From 1613 for a short time, Alexander Burnet, 12th laird of Leys, had a charter of the forfeited lands and offices of Blackhall. Members of the Blackhall family were later tenants on the Leys estate and was termed its constable. [*Blackhalls of that Ilk and Barra*, Spalding Club, Aberdeen.(1905)] Alexander Blackhall acted as Sheriff-depute in 1558/59. He married Grissel Leslie of Crichie. Alexander died about 1635. Their known children were:
  - William Blackhall. He became Blackhall, the 1st laird of Finnersie.
  - James Blackhall born 1591.
  - Adam Blackhall born 1592.
- Isobel Burnet, married (1) Craigmyle of Craigmyle and (2) John Forbes of Sonnahinny/Sunhoney, the 3rd laird of Newe. John Forbes, whose nickname was *Bluebonnet*, built the first House of Newe, in Strathdon. When this magnificent building was pulled down in 1927, a heraldic stone bearing the bears' heads and cinque foils of Forbes of Pitsligo quartered with the holly leaf of Burnett and the initials J.F. and I.B. was unfortunately destroyed, although a stone with the date 1604 was apparently preserved. John and Isobel Forbes had the following children:
  - Alexander Forbes who succeeded.
  - William Forbes who was described as being *of Culquhonny* in 1628. He married Isobel Gordon.
  - John Forbes who was called " Blind John".
  - Marjory Forbes who married William Leith of Newlands.
  - Isobel Forbes who died young.

John Forbes died on 28 January 1616 in Aberdeen and was buried there. Alexander Burnet married (2) before 1567, Marjorie Forbes, widow of Forbes of Brux, daughter of John, 6th Lord Forbes. They had no children and Alexander died before 2 September 1574.

[As there does not appear to be any specific period at which the spelling of the Burnet(t) surname was consistently with or without a double 't' and records have even been found which used both spellings in the same document for the same person, it should be noted that the author has used 'Burnett' in this chapter from this point onwards.]

John Burnett of Leys, inherited from his father in 1574. On 2 September 1574, he signed the Bond of Allegiance of the Barons of the North. John Burnett married Elizabeth Lumsden daughter of John Lumsden of Cushnie. John and Elizabeth Burnett had the following children:

- Alexander Burnett who was heir to his father.
- Margaret Burnett who married, as his second wife, Arthur Forbes, successor of John Forbes of Echt. Arthur Forbes was the first minister of Echt after the Reformation and also had charge of the parishes of Kemnay and Drumoak. He had married (1) Elizabeth/Bessie Lyon, daughter of John, Lord Glamis and Elizabeth Gray, and widow of John, Master of Forbes [Echt-Forbes Family Charters]. Arthur and Margaret Forbes had a child:
  - Robert Forbes *of Finnersie* and later *of Echt*. He married the fifth daughter (name unknown) of Alexander Burnett of Leys and Katherine Gordon and had the following known children
    - Arthur Forbes, born in 1615, who succeeded his father.
    - Thomas Forbes of Knockquharne.

As a result of the research undertaken for this book, John Burnett is considered to have had three other sons and a second daughter namely:

- John Burnett who is thought from research to have been John Burnett of Daladies who married Agnes Turnbull. (details continue in Chapter 9)
- Andrew Burnett of Sheddocksley. (details continue in Chapter 8)
- Thomas Burnett. Merchant. (see this Chapter)
- Katherine Burnett

This is deduced from the following information.

In George Burnett's notes, which he prepared for the manuscript of *The Family of Burnett of Leys* he mentioned further children of John Burnett of Leys as:

- *"John who married and had a daughter Agnes."*
- *" Andrew, of "Shethocksley", married to ------.*
- *"Katherine, married to ----of the Ord".*

Katherine as one of two daughters of John Burnett is also listed in Douglas's *Baronage.*

George Burnett did not leave any evidence to support his thinking on the above or perhaps, as Allardyce thought, some pages of the manuscript may have gone astray. Nor did he indicate if these additional children were from John Burnett's marriage with Elisabeth Lumsden, from a second marriage or outwith marriage. However, amongst the cadets of Leys whose arms were matriculated in the New Register in 1672 (details given in chapter 12), were those of *James Burnett of Shetchocksley whose grandfather was a 3rd son of Leys.* The grandfather of the above James Burnett being Andrew Burnett of Sheddocksley and assuming that the genealogical basis for the grant of arms was correct, it is reasonable to accept that Andrew was the son of John Burnet, laird of Leys, the others being Alexander (who succeeded) and John. That being the case, John Burnett had yet another son Thomas!

On a memorial inscription in St Mary's Aisle of St. Nicholas Church, Aberdeen, the names of Thomas and Andrew Burnett *brothers Burgesses of Aberdeen*, are inscribed on a large stone which has, as a centrepiece, a shield with the Arms of Leys. Andrew and Thomas were killed during Montrose's Battle of Justicemills, or the subsequent rout of Aberdeen, on 13 September 1644 at which time over 150 burgesses and several members of the Council lost their lives. This stone also bears the name of Alexander Burnett of Kirkhill who died in 1685 *son to Thomas*. According to *Chartularium Ecclesiae S. Nicholai Aberdonensis,* compiled by J. Cooper for the Spalding Club, the stone was originally located in a prominent position at the back of the pulpit in the church. If Thomas Burnett, merchant of Aberdeen, was, as the memorial inscription suggests, the brother of Andrew Burnett of Sheddocksley then he too must have been a son, the fourth, of John Burnett of Leys. Looking at a counter hypothesis that the term "brothers" was used simply in the context of both men being burgesses of the town, this is unlikely because of the use of the Arms of Leys and the fact that the name of a descendant of Thomas Burnett is also inscribed on the stone.

At this point in the history of the Burnetts there appear to have been a large number who were merchants and who were prominent people in the burgh of Aberdeen. The records of St. Nicholas church frequently contain Burnett names mainly associated with donations for the support of various aisles of the church. The relationship of these people within the family genealogy has not been confirmed in every case. From the church records, we find that Burnetts were landowners within the developing Aberdeen and were building townhouses in the prime sites of the day such as the Guestrow, Shiprow and Schoolhill. These houses were of similar style to that built by the Jamesons in Schoolhill. (Fig.7.2) In a map which he drew in 1661, James Gordon, parson of Rothiemay, showed how building was focused around the church and harbour. The church of St. Nicholas, which he captioned 'Great Church,' was a focal point of the *New Aberdeen or Aberdee*, the settlement which developed around the harbour at the estuary of the River Dee. The prefix 'Aber' in the context of placenames means 'at the mouth of'. To the north, the original *Aberdon* with its church of Old Machar, was closer to the estuary of the River Don and was the location of the University. In due course the two grew and merged together to form the city of Aberdeen.

❑ Thomas Burnett married, on 8 November 1608 in St. Nicholas parish, Aberdeen, Margaret Johnston(e)/Johnstoun. Thomas Burnett, a merchant of Aberdeen, was killed on 13 September 1644. Thomas and Margaret Burnett had children, the spelling of whose first names is given as recorded in the parish records:

- ♦ Isobell Burnett who was baptised on 31 August 1609 in St. Nicholas parish. Burial records of St. Nicholas show a *young bairne* of Thomas Burnett buried 14 August 1610.
- ♦ Johnne Burnett who was baptised on 25 December 1610 in St. Nicholas parish. He became a merchant in Aberdeen like his father. On 24 October 1635, John Burnett, aged 24, described as *a Merchant of Aberdeen* sailed from London to Virginia, America in the *'Abraham of London'* with ship's master Mr. John Barker. A fellow passenger was a John Johnston aged 35 who may have had some family connection. Three years later, on 2 July 1638, a Royal warrant was issued under the hand of King Charles and signed at Greenwich, London stating: *Warrant from the King to the Governor of Virginia or other officers whom it may concern for John Burnett of Aberdeen, the sole merchant of our Kingdom of Scotland, that hath supplied the plantations of Virginia and become Our tenant there, and his factors to have free commerce and traffic between Scotland and Virginia upon paying the usual customs and entering into bond to unlade anywhere other than the ports of Scotland.*

  The cargo, which John Burnett arranged to ship to Scotland, was primarily tobacco. One of the records of trading between Aberdeen and Virginia notes that a Henry Hay who was master of a vessel arriving in Aberdeen from Virginia paid 1.00 for his anchorage. No doubt the Burnett ships returning home to Virginia carried a variety of Scottish goods as well as those of the European countries with which Aberdeen had strong trading links.

  John Burnett married, in about 1657 in Old Rappahannock County, Virginia, Lucretia who may have been the Lucretia Johnston who was baptised on 22 March 1629 in St. Nicholas, Aberdeen, daughter of Andrew

Johnston and Janet Morison. These were troubled times, as shown by the killing of John Burnett's father, Thomas Burnett, in 1644, which would have encouraged the exodus of new colonists to America. John and Lucretia Burnett had the following known children whose names are those recorded in Lucretia's will, dated 1709:

- John Burnett who was born about 1660.
- Thomas Burnett.
- Sarah Burnett.
- Phoebe Burnett.
- Unknown daughter Burnett.
- Charles Burnett.

[The genealogy of the descendants of John Burnett in Virginia has been extensively researched and described in *The Burnetts and Their Connections* Vol.I, written and published in 1989, by June Baldwin Bork, California, USA]

- Unnamed (son) Burnett who was baptised 25 December 1610 in St. Nicholas parish who died and was buried at St. Nicholas. He may have been a twin of John Burnett. Twins occur again in this family group in 1613.
- Issobell Burnett, who was baptised on 10 March 1612 in St. Nicholas parish. Burial records of St. Nicholas show a *young bairne* of Thomas Burnett was buried on 13 March 1612.
- Cristen Burnett (twin of Davyhd) who was baptised on 28 December 1613 in St. Nicholas parish.
- Davyhd Burnett who was baptised on 28 December 1613 in St. Nicholas parish.
- Robert Burnett who was baptised on 3 September 1615 in St. Nicholas parish.
- Elspet Burnett who was baptised on 17 February 1617. Burial records of St. Nicholas show that a *newborn child* of Thomas Burnett was buried in February 1617.

  Burial records of St. Nicholas also show *1 young child without kist* (without coffin) of Thomas Burnett buried on 7 January 1618.
- Margret Burnett born on 11 May and baptised on 17 May 1618.
- Thomas Burnett born on 13 May and baptised on 15 May 1619.
- Alexander Burnett who was baptised on 4 February 1620. He became the 1st laird of Kirkhill. (details of the Burnetts of Kirkhill are continued in Chapter 7)

Alexander Burnet of Leys, succeeded his father. Alexander married, in about 1560, Katherine Arbuthnot (cousin-german) daughter of Robert Arbuthnot of Pitcarlies, 1st of Fiddes, and Isobel Burnet. Alexander was dead before May 1578. Alexander and Katherine Burnet had children. In the Heralds' Visitation of Norfolk in 1613, and of Essex in 1634, their six sons, in order of seniority, were noted along with the three daughters also in 1613.

- Alexander Burnet, who was heir to his father.
- Robert Burnet who was referred to as a *divine* in a letter written by his brother Duncan.
- Thomas Burnet, born about 1570, who married, in 1611, Jane Foys born in 1581, daughter of John Foys of London. He gained an MA degree from Cambridge University and is known to have been a physician of eminence in Braintree, Essex by 1634. Children:
    - Thomas Burnet was born in 1612 in Braintree. Essex. He died about 1684 in Southampton, Long Island, New York. Thomas married Mary Cooper, born in 1621 in Olney, Buckinghamshire, England. Their children were:
        - Lot Burnet who married on 20 October 1675 in Southhampton, NY, Phebe Mills.
        - Joel Burnet.
        - Lois Burnet who married Robert Collins.
        - Pricilla Burnet who married, in 1679, Samuel Fithian.
        - John Burnet born in 1645 in Southampton, NY, who married a Mary (surname unknown) and died in 1694.
        - Hester Burnet born in 1653 in Southampton, NY, who married there, in 1674, Christopher Leaming. Hester died on 5 November 1714.
        - Aaron Burnet born in 1655 in Southampton, NY, married an Elizabeth Unknown. He died in Madison. NJ.
        - Miriam Burnet born in 1656 in Southampton, NY, married on 25 June 1675 in East Hampton, Long Island, NY, Lt. Enoch Fithian. Miriam died on 1 April 1717.
        - Dan Burnet born in 1664 married (1) Abigail (surname unknown) and (2) Elizabeth (surname unknown). He died on 8 July 1729.
        - Mordecai Burnet born in 1670 in Southhampton, NY. His wife was Hannah (surname unknown). Mordecai died in 1716 in Elizabethtown NJ.
        - Matthias Burnet born in 1674 became a Captain. He married Elizabeth Osborne. Matthias died on 4 October 1765.

[Genealogy of the above New York line of descendancy from Thomas Burnet [1612-1684] was contributed by Jim Fina of Tucson, Arizona from his personal research notes.]

    - Alexander Burnet born in 1613 in Braintree, Essex.
    - Frances Burnet born in 1614 in Braintree, Essex. She married, about 1642, Rev. Thomas Templer, Rector of Weston, Northampton.
- Gilbert Burnett who became Professor of Philosophy at Basle and later at Montauban. In 1634 he was said to have no issue.
- Duncan Burnett who married (1) in 1609, Jane daughter of Robert Marsham of Little Meton, Norfolk. Like his brother Thomas he was a physician, practising in Norwich. Duncan was said to have been a *learned, holy and good man.* He married (2) Sarah Deriche, who had previously been married to Jacque de Hem. Duncan Burnet of Manorcroft died in 1641 in Norfolk, England. Their children were :
    - Mary Burnet who was born on 29 September (Michaelmas Day) 1609. In 1613 she is referred to as his *sole daughter and heir.*
    - Robert Burnet who was baptised on 14 October 1610. He died before 1613.
    - Jane Burnet who was born about 1611 and is assumed to have died before 1613.
    - Thomas Burnet who was born about 1615. He was given the Freedom of Aberdeen on 29 September 1629. His Arms, as Thomas Burnet of Wood Dalling, Norfolk, were shown in the books of the English College of Arms, 3 June 1640. (for details see Chapter 12) Thomas married Judith de Hem who appears to have been his stepsister. For whatever reason, possibly because of the marriage, Thomas Burnett was apparently excluded from his father's will. Thomas and Judith Burnett had children.
- John Burnet who married Helen Wood, widow of Alexander Cumyn of Culter, according to a contract dated 30 April 1603. From a letter written by Duncan Burnet it would appear that the efforts of John's father failed to make him a learned man like his brothers! He had one known child:
    - Master Alexander Burnet, probably later the Master Alexander Burnet in Edinburgh. In 1642 he was described as *minister of God's word at the Kirk of Buckingham Fence in the County of Norfolk, England.*
- Janet Burnett who married Gilbert Keith of Auquhorsk, according to a contract dated 10 February 1578-9.
- Margaret Burnett born about 1566, was unmarried in 1613.
- Elizabeth Burnett, married Master Gilbert Skene (her cousin-german), son and heir apparent of James Skene of Wester Corse and Ramore, according to a Crathes charter dated 15 December 1592.

Alexander Burnett of Leys, succeeded his father in 1578. Aberdeen Burgh records state that he was made an Honorary burgess on 13 October 1598. Alexander Burnett married, about 1578, Katherine Gordon eldest daughter of

Alexander Gordon of Lesmoir. He purchased Muchalls, in the parish of Fetteresso, from Francis, Earl of Erroll on 24 June 1606. In 1609 he had Leys and Muchalls formally incorporated into the barony of Leys. In July 1613 Alexander had a charter of Blackhall in the Garioch along with the offices of coroner and forester of Garioch, the lands and offices having been forfeited by Alexander Blackhall of that Ilk. This possession was short-lived and by 1620 the lands were back in the hands of the Blackhall family. In 1619, which was the year in which Alexander Burnett died, he began work on a new castle at Muchalls which his heir, Sir Thomas Burnett, completed in 1637. A hallmark of this laird is the considerable addition that he made to the family estates during his lifetime. The Coat of Arms of Katherine, impaled with those of her husband, are on a tablet which was formerly at Muchalls Castle but which is now built into an outer wall of Crathes Castle. There are several items of furniture, including a very elaborately carved bed, which were created during the lifetime of Alexander and Katherine and which bear their monogram. These are on display at Crathes Castle. Alexander and Katherine Burnett had the following children:

- Alexander Burnett who, according to the Douglas's *Baronage*, died in France almost certainly before 1604, in which year his brother Thomas is described as *son and heir apparent*, and definitely before his father in 1619.
- Thomas Burnett who succeeded his father and became the 1st Baronet of Leys.
- James Burnett, later styled *of Craigmyle* married, in 1608, Elizabeth Burnett, daughter and heir of Thomas Burnett of Craigmyle and Tillihaikie (details of this line are given in Chapter 4). James Burnett was known to have been a Covenanter and died about 1644. Indeed, he may have been one of the many casualties of the 1644 Rout of Aberdeen. As well as several who died young, James and Elizabeth Burnett had children from whom some of the main branches of Burnetts descend namely:
    - Alexander Burnett *of Craigmyle* who succeeded to the Craigmyle estate.
    - Thomas Burnett *of Kemnay* who purchased Kemnay. He died in 1688 at Kemnay. [details are given in Chapter 5]
    - James Burnett *of Lagavin & Monboddo*. He later became Lord Monboddo. James died on 26 May 1799 in Edinburgh and was buried in Greyfriars Churchyard, Edinburgh. (details are given in Chapter 6)
    - Robert Burnett *of Cowtoun, Muchalls & Criggie*. He was baptised on 18 April 1620 in Fetteresso parish, Kincardine. Robert married (1) on 22 December 1645 in St. Nicholas parish, Aberdeen, Jean Mortimer, daughter of John Mortimer, baillie of Aberdeen with whom he had no family and, in about 1682, (2) Helen Arbuthnot who later married John Sandilands. Robert Burnett is generally referred to as *Tutor of Leys*. Robert and Helen Burnett had the following children who were still young when Robert died in 1687:

- Helen Burnett who married, in 1697, Alexander Burnett (later Sir) the Younger of Leys. She inherited the largest portion of her father's estate including Cowtoun.
- Agnes Burnett followed the marriage arrangements made by her father to marry (1) in 1701, Thomas Burnet of Glenbervie. Agnes married (2) Sir William Nicholson of Glenbervie.
- Jean Burnett who married William Burnett (thereafter *of Criggie*). Child of Jean and Thomas Burnet was:
  - ➢ Thomas Burnett who became Sir Thomas Burnett, 6th Baronet of Leys.

♦ Jean Burnett who married Robert Arbuthnot of Little Fiddes.

♦ Mary/Mariot Burnett who married Alexander Forbes of Corsindae, according to contract dated 1661. Mary died at Kemnay and was buried at Midmar on 1st November 1700.

❑ Robert Burnett who was born in 1592. He was admitted as an advocate in Scotland in 1617 after spending seven years in France where he had been sent to study Law. Having been successful in Edinburgh, he was able to buy Benachtie and the Mill of Bourtie from John Seton of Meldrum in 1628 and later Crimond from John Johnston of Johnston. He also owned the small property of Kendal in Montkegie. Robert Burnett later became a Lord of Session and took the title Lord Crimond. (Details of the Burnetts of Crimond are given in Chapter 4)

❑ George Burnett who died without issue.

❑ John Burnett who became Scots factor at Campvere, Holland. He is thought to have married late in life, although the name of his spouse is unknown. John Burnett is known to have had one child:

♦ Obadiah Burnett who lived in Rotterdam as Scots factor and was later a merchant in London. He died in New Jersey after 1701 without issue. Thomas Burnet of Kemnay made a successful claim on some of his American property in 1786, a long time after Obadiah's death.

❑ Unknown (daughter) Burnett who married George Baillie of Jerviswood.

❑ Katherine Burnett who married Patrick Maitland, elder son of Robert Maitland of Auchincreve, according to a Crathes contract dated 27 September 1607.

❑ Helen Burnett who married (1) John Allardyce of Allardyce, according to a contract dated 3 September 1617, and (2) Sir Robert Graham of Morphie in Kincardine.

❑ Barbara Burnett who married Robert Innes of Balveny.

❑ Isabel Burnett who married, according to a Crathes contract dated 1615, James Cheyne, younger of Arnage.

❑ Unknown (daughter) Burnett, who married to Robert Forbes of Echt. Children were:

♦ Arthur Forbes who succeeded his father.

- ♦ Thomas Forbes of Knockwharn.

❑ Janet Burnett, married (1) Alexander Skene of Skene who died before 1642. Children were:
- ♦ James Skene who succeeded his father.
- ♦ Jean Skene who married Alexander Innes of Pethenick.
- ♦ Margaret Skene who married, about 1646, (1), John Garioch son of William Garioch of Tulliebethie, Auchballoch and, on unknown date, (2) John Skene in Knowheade who died before 1675.
- ♦ Janet Skene who married Rev. Adam Barclay, younger of Towie, minister of Nigg and later of Tarves. Ratification of the contract between them and James Skene of Skene was dated at Edinburgh, 14 August 1656. [*Memorials of Skene of Skene*, p. 34/35, Spalding Club].

Janet Burnett married about 1642 (2), Sir Alexander Cumyn of Culter. Her portrait hangs in Crathes Castle.

❑ Mariot Burnett, married George Symmer/Seymour of Balyordie. She was confirmed as one of her father's executors in 1619.

Alexander Burnett of Leys died at Muchalls on 5 July 1619.

Sir Thomas Burnett of Leys, became **1st Baronet** when he succeeded his father to the estate of Leys in 1619.(Fig.3.3) In the Records of the University and King's College, Aberdeen, he appears as a matriculated student in 1603. During the year 1618-19 Thomas Burnett, at that time the Younger of Leys, was one of the commissioners named by King James VI to visit the Universities of Aberdeen and report on their condition. Thomas was made an Honorary Burgess of Aberdeen in 1619 and knighted in 1620. In 1621 he petitioned for the erection of a church at Fetteresso, the parish in which Muchalls lay. He was one of the first Scots to be created a Baronet of Nova Scotia with his patent having been sealed on 12 June 1626 at Holyroodhouse.

Fig. 3.3 Sir Thomas Burnett, 1st Baronet

The first one hundred and eleven Baronets of Nova Scotia each received grants of 16,000 acres of land as Free Baronies in the "Royal Province of New Scotland" with their titles.

When Montrose marched on Aberdeen in September 1644, he crossed the River Dee between Crathes and Drum and peacefully occupied the Castle of Crathes where his troops camped overnight. John Buchan, in his profile of Montrose, wrote *Sir Thomas Burnet was that rare combination; a friend of*

Huntly's and a staunch Covenanter; he hospitably entertained the royal lieutenant and his staff and offered him a sum of money which was refused. One would like to think that Sir Thomas's attitude towards Montrose was a strategic move to gain maximum protection for the Burnetts and that the sum of money offered may have been an attempt to secure amnesty for his Covenanter kinsmen who were resident in Aberdeen. Whatever the position, the Crathes Burnetts may have been left unscathed by Montrose's visit but the Burnett merchants in nearby Aberdeen, such as Andrew of Sheddocksley and Thomas, Andrew's brother, certainly were not.

In 1627, Sir Thomas completed the work on the castle of Muchalls, which his father had initiated. His portrait hangs in Crathes Castle.

Sir Thomas Burnet married (1) Margaret Douglas, eldest daughter of Sir Robert Douglas of Glenbervie, the second son of the 9th Earl of Angus. Thomas and Margaret Burnett had the following children:

- Alexander Burnet, the Younger of Leys, who was made an Honorary Burgess of Aberdeen in 1633. Alexander married, in that year Jean, eldest daughter of Sir Robert Arbuthnot of that Ilk. From note in the Arbuthnot charter chest it was noted that Jean's *tocher* (dowry) was the sum of 20,000 merks. In May 1639, Alexander was a petitioner against a proposal by Montrose to block up the harbour of Aberdeen to prevent a Royalist force landing there. When he died on 27 June 1648, his three sons and two daughters were left under the guardianship of his father Sir Thomas. In 1651, Jean Arbuthnot married (2) Patrick Gordon of Glenbuchat. Alexander and Jean Burnett had the following children:
  - Alexander Burnett, born 1637, who succeeded his grandfather to become 2nd Baronet of Leys.
  - Thomas Burnett styled *in Pittenkeirie* and *of Clerkseat*. He had Sauchen in wadset(mortgage) from his uncle from 1668-1672. He was made an Honorary Burgess of Aberdeen in 1678. In 1688 *Thomas Burnett of Clerkseat* subscribed £20 to the new buildings of King's College. When he died without issue, his nephew, Sir Thomas Burnett, was served heir general on 24 March 1691.
  - Robert Burnett. He was a student at King's College, Aberdeen in 1664, where he graduated in 1668. Robert was made an Honorary Burgess of Aberdeen in 1674. In 1675 he purchased the lands of Glenbervie from Robert Douglas, eldest son of Sir William Douglas. Robert Burnett married, within a few years of 1675, Katherine Douglas, daughter of Sir William and his heiress to Glenbervie, by whom he had three sons and two daughters:
    - Thomas Burnett of Glenbervie who married, in 1701, Agnes, second daughter and co-heir of Mr Robert Burnet of Cowtoun, the *Tutor of Leys*. Thomas died in January 1712 leaving two children:
      - Thomas Burnett who died shortly after his father.

   - Katherine Burnett who married, in about 1728, George Gordon of Buckie. Whilst still a minor and under the authority of the Court of Session, Katherine sold Glenbervie to William Nicholson who later became Sir William Nicholson of Kemnay. William Nicholson became Katherine Burnett's stepfather when he married (4) Katherine Douglas, widow of Robert Burnett.
- John Burnett who was alive in 1704.
- Robert Burnett who became a merchant in Montrose, Angus, and married, on 17 December 1724, Elizabeth Dunbar. Children of their marriage were:
   - Elizabeth Burnett baptised on 28 September 1725 in Montrose parish.
   - Margaret Burnett baptised on 5 January 1727 in Montrose parish.
   - William Burnett baptised on 16 June 1729 in Montrose parish.
   - Jean Burnett baptised on 26 December 1729 in Montrose parish.
   - Mary Burnett baptised on 31 December 1731 in Montrose parish.
   - Christian Burnett baptised on 29 May 1733 in Montrose parish.
- Margaret Burnett
- Elizabeth Burnett

- Margaret Burnett. The only reference to her is in Sir Thomas Burnett's will.
- Jean Burnett who married, according to contract dated 2 September 1661, John Skene of Skene who died 9 May 1680. After his death she had a new central part built to Skene House and a roof put on the old tower. Jean died at Crathes in the autumn of 1688 having been a widow for more than eight years. Children of John and Jean [many of the births were recorded in a Family Bible kept by John Skene and are included in *Memorials of Skene*] were:
   - Alexander Skene born on 12 September 1664.
   - George Skene born on 2 May 1666.
   - Margret Skene born on 4 June 1667.
   - Andrew Skene born on 16 April 1670.
   - John Skene born on 1 July 1671.
   - Jean Skene born on 1 February 1673. She married Donald Farquharson, son of Charles Farquharson.
   - Barbara Skene born on 4 July 1676. She married, on 19 May 1701 in St Nicholas, John Tytler, merchant in Aberdeen.
   - Catren Skene born on 19 August 1678.
   - Thomas Skene born on 24 July 1679. Thomas was a lieutenant in the Army and was amongst the troops of Queen Anne who were killed in Spain.
   - James Skene born October 1680. He lived for only 3 days.

- Mr Robert Burnett who like his father supported the Covenanters. He became a Member of the Faculty of Advocates on 22 June 1642 and married, on 16 February 1643 in Edinburgh, Katherine Pearson, daughter of Alexander Pearson, Lord Southhall. In 1649 he was a Parliament Commissioner for visiting the University of St. Andrews. Robert Burnett died in 1670. Their children were:
  - Jean Burnett who was born on 6 February 1644 in Edinburgh.
  - Thomas Burnett who was born on 31 December 1646 in Edinburgh. He was served heir but no record thereafter.
  - Alexander Burnett who was born on 30 December 1649 in Edinburgh. He is presumed to have died young as another child was give the same name.
  - Alexander Burnett who was born on 2 June 1653 in Edinburgh.
  - Rachel Burnett who was born on 4 January 1655 in Edinburgh
  - William Burnett who was born on 26 October 1656 in Edinburgh.
  - Elizabeth Burnett who was born on 29 September 1658. She married to William Hamilton, Writer in Edinburgh.
  - Archibald Burnett who was born on 29 April 1660 in Edinburgh.
- Jean Burnet. She married (1) in 1632 Sir William Forbes of Monymusk, 2nd Baronet, son of William Forbes and Elizabeth Wishart of Pitarrow. Jean received sasine of Torrie from Sir William on 21 May 1632. William Forbes died in 1654.

  ["House of Forbes". Published by Spalding Club]. Children were:
  - John Forbes born 1642 who became the 3rd Baronet of Monymusk. He died in 1700.
  - Janet Forbes. She married to George Rickart of Auchnacant.

  Jean Burnet married (2) Robert Cumyn of Altyre. There were no children.
- Katherine Burnett who married in 1638 to Robert Gordon of Pitlurg, eldest son of Robert Gordon of Straloch, who had sasine on Straloch on 11 April 1638.

Sir Thomas Burnett married (2), according to a contract dated 9 August 1621 at Carnbee, Jean Moncrieff, widow of Sir Simon Fraser of Inverallochy, daughter of Sir John Moncrieff of that Ilk. Thomas and Jean Burnett had the following children:

- Thomas Burnett of Sauchen who married, in 1648, as per contract drawn up by his father in February 1642 before he was seventeen, Bessie Burnet daughter of Mr William Burnet of Sauchen and Cairndae and Catherine Reid, daughter of Rev. James Reid minister of Banchory-Ternan. On 6 October of the same year, Thomas Burnett of Sauchen was a witness to the contract pertaining to the foundation of the Leys Bursaries at the University. Thomas, who also owned Tillycairn, seems to have acted as Factor to his father. Thomas Burnett died in 1699. Children were:
  - William Burnett who died young.

- Alexander Burnett who was an MA degree student at Marischal College, Aberdeen in 1677. He became minister of Crossmichael, Kirkcudbright.
- Unknown (daughter) Burnett married Ludovic Gordon, son of Rev. James Gordon, Minister of Rothiemay. Ludovic was a grandson of Sir Robert Gordon of Straloch, the cartographer of the Blaue Atlas. Ludovic Gordon who was minister at Aboyne parish from 1679, ordained as assistant at Rothiemay before 8 October 1680 and transferred to Kirkcaldy after 17 April 1683. Ludovic Gordon died in October 1694 aged about 45. They had one known child:
    - Thomas Gordon who was licensed by the Presbytery of Kirkcaldy, Fife, in 1709. He became minister at Lonmay parish, Aberdeenshire in that year. Thomas married Agnes Coupar who died on 5 November 1778. Thomas died on 12 July 1743. Thomas and Agnes Burnett had the following children:
        - William Gordon baptised on 11 October 1709 at Lonmay. He was a student at Marischal College, Aberdeen in 1747.
        - Alexander Gordon baptised on 28 November 1718 at Lonmay
        - Thomas Gordon baptised 24 January 1722 at Lonmay. He became the minister of Dundurcas parish in 1747 and of Speymouth, Moray, on 6 July 1758.
- Robert Burnett who was born about 1649. He was a student at King's College, Aberdeen in 1664 and gained an MA degree on 9 July 1668. Robert was Minister at Banchory Ternan for 16 years from 7 November 1682, and, on 5 January 1699, was admitted at Fintray parish. On 24 February 1699 Robert was served heir to his father Thomas as laird of Sauchen but died soon afterwards on 18 June 1701 aged 53. He was buried at Banchory Ternan Churchyard. Robert Burnett married Jean Reid, daughter of the Rev. Reid of Banchory, who died on 9 April 1722. The gravestone inscription at Banchory Ternan is now partly worn and shows year of her death as 17-2. They had the following children:
    - Robert Burnett born in 1684. He was the last laird of Sauchen. Robert married Jean Barclay, born about 1715, daughter of John Barclay in Eslie. Robert Burnett died in 1768 aged 84 and was buried at Cluny Churchyard. Jean died in 1786 aged 71 and was also buried at Cluny. Children were:
        - Jean Burnett who was baptised on 2 June 1727 in Banchory Ternan parish. She died, unmarried, on 1 July 1801.
        - Mary Burnett who was born about 1739. She died in 1784 aged 45 and was buried at Cluny.
        - William Burnett who was born in 1742/3. There is a strong possibility that he was also a son of Robert and Jean Barclay Burnett

but, for correctness, as this fact has not yet been proven, his genealogy and descendants have been included in Chapter 11 on "Indeterminate Cadets". This William Burnett became factor to Crathes Estate and the ancestor of Burnetts of Kinchyle and of a Burnett branch in USA.

- ➢ Andrew Burnett who was born about 1746. He died, unmarried, in 1770 at the age of 24 and was buried at Cluny Churchyard.
- ➢ Margaret (Peggy) Burnett who married, on 15 June 1767 in St. Nicholas parish, James Martin, merchant in Aberdeen and Rotterdam. Their children were:
  - ▪ Alexander Martin born on 18 July 1768 in Aberdeen.
  - ▪ Robert Martin born on 19 December 1769 in Aberdeen.
  - ▪ Andrew Martin born on 13 October 1771 in St. Nicholas parish, Aberdeen.
  - ▪ Thomas Martin born on 28 September 1773 in Aberdeen.
- ➢ Katherine Burnett who married, on 1 May 1774 at Cluny, David Scott, Factor of Craigievar Estate. They had one known child:
  - ▪ James Scott born about 1776. He was tenant in Achath, Cluny. He married, on 8 January 1808 in Cluny parish, Elizabeth Cruickshank. James died in 18 January 1815 aged 39 and Elizabeth on 7 August 1856 in Aberdeen aged 72. Their children were:
    - ◊ David Scott, who was baptised on 2 August 1810 in Cluny parish, was also tenant in Achath. He died on 3 May 1864 aged 53 in Aberdeen.
    - ◊ William Scott who was born about 1812. He died on 19 August 1882 aged 70 and was buried at Paterangi, NZ.
    - ◊ Catherine Scott who was born about 1814. She married, on 14 September 1851 at Old Machar, Rev. William Polson, minister of Wemyss, Fife, and died 11 March 1884 aged 70 at the Manse, Wemyss.
- ➢ Janet Burnett who died unmarried in 1791.

- □ Alexander Burnett baptised on 5 December 1685. He was designated *second son* in a bond from his father dated 1691.
- □ John Burnett baptised 21 July 1689. He gained an MA degree from King's College, Aberdeen on 6 May 1712 and was minister of Cluny parish 1719-41. John Burnett married Agnes Skene, daughter of George Skene, minister of Kinkell. John died in November 1741 and Agnes on 24 February 1785. They had 7 sons and five daughters:
  - ➢ Charles Burnett.

- ➢ George Burnett.
- ➢ Robert Burnett.
- ➢ Francis Burnett.
- ➢ Andrew Burnett. Born in 1730, he became a Doctor of Medicine and left Scotland in 1752 for Charleston, South Carolina, where he settle in Black Mine, Craven (later called Williamsburg) County. He married, in 1758, Sabrina Baxter, daughter of Presbyterian minister Rev. John Baxter. Andrew Burnett, physician and land-owner, died about 15 November 1764. Children of Andrew and Sabrina were:
    - ▪ Andrew Burnett who was born in 1763. He also became a Doctor of Medicine. Andrew married, on 25 December 1800, Elizabeth Washington de Saussure, who was born in 1777. Andrew Burnett died on 5 May 1814 and his wife Elizabeth in 1853. Their son Andrew William Burnett was born on 12 June 1811.

    [Source of the information on this line in the USA was Annie Lee (Burnett) Vuillemot]
    - ▪ Sarah Burnett. *
    - ▪ Elizabeth Burnett. *

    [* The last two children are listed by Whyte in *Scottish Emigrants to USA*]
- ➢ Alexander Burnett. At a meeting on 27 July 1753, before Dr James Gordon of Pitlurg, common procurator of Marischal College, Alexander Burnett was presented by his brother Andrew Burnett, Surgeon in Aberdeen, as a bursar under the divinity and philosophy bursaries founded by Gilbert Burnett, Lord Bishop of Salisbury.[Minute of meeting archived in Crathes Papers]. Alexander became Minister of Footdee parish, Aberdeen from 1765-1773. Later he became minister at Careston. He was the last surviving child at 1791. George Burnett in *The Family of Burnetts of Leys* suggested that the male line of Sauchen expired with him but perhaps he was unaware of the male children of Alexander's brother, Andrew Burnett, who were alive in America after 1791.
- ➢ John Burnett.
- ➢ Jean Burnett.
- ➢ Mary Burnett.
- ➢ Margaret Burnett.
- ➢ Catherine Burnett.
- ➢ Agnes Burnett.

- William Burnett, baptised 7 September 1690.
- Katherine Burnett, baptised 7 December 1691.
- Mary Burnett who was baptised on 6 December 1693. She was the twin of Nicholas.
- Nicholas Burnett who was baptised on 6 December 1693, twin of Mary.

- Jean Burnett who was married before 1739 to John Lunan.
- Katherine Burnett who was baptised on 19 September 1696. She married Robert Calder before 1732.
- Anne Burnett who was baptised on 15 November 1697. She married (1) on 25 January 1732, Andrew Burnet, physician in Aberdeen and (2) on 3 September 1770 in St Paul's Episcopal Chapel, Aberdeen, Dr John Gordon, Minister of St. Paul's, who was a member of the Gordon of Straloch family.

- William Burnett. He was a student at King's College, Aberdeen in 1645 and gained MA degree in 1649. He was designated *Master William* in his father's will.
- James Burnett. He was mentioned in a family lawsuit as being alive in 1666. [Burnett v Fraser, 7 February 1673].
- Margaret Burnett was born after 1621. She married John Kennedy of Kermucks [Sasine dated 22 July 1673]
- Elizabeth Burnett married (1) Sir Robert Douglas of Tilliwhilly [Sasine to her dated 31 May 1666] and (2) Fullerton of Kinnaber.
- Anne Burnett. Immediately after her father's death she married, on 20 November 1655 at St. Nicholas, Aberdeen, to the Rev. Andrew Cant, minister of Liberton, Edinburgh, who later became the Principal of Edinburgh University.
- Helen Burnett was unmarried in 1653 but is said to have later married "Col. Barron of Strachan".[Douglas's *Baronages of Scotland*]

Sir Thomas Burnett of Leys died on 27 June 1653. His will, dated 8 December 1652, is reproduced in full in *The Family of Burnett of Leys,* 67-71. His portrait by George Jamesone, thought to have been painted about 1632, hangs in Crathes Castle.

Sir Alexander Burnett, 2nd Baronet, born in 1637, succeeded his grandfather in 1653 whilst a second year student at King's College, his father, Alexander, having died in 1648. He was served heir on 10 March 1654 and, as Thomas Burnett had left many debts and obligations to strangers and to members of the family, it became necessary to wadset (mortgage) parts of the estate. His curators whilst he was still under age were Lord Arbuthnot, Sir Robert Douglas of Tillewhilly, William Coutts of Cluny and Alexander Burnett of Craigmyle. An 8000 marks debt left owed by his grandfather to Alexander Burnett of Countesswells had risen to 20,000 marks by the time Sir Alexander came of age in 1658 resulting in him having to give wadset over Leys to Alexander. He married Elizabeth Coutts, daughter of William Coutts of Cluny and Auchtercoull according to an antenuptial contract dated 21 May 1653 in Crathes Archives (S1/b67.31). Sir Alexander Burnett died in May 1663 aged 26. In his will dated 30 January 1663 he ordained his body to be *honourably buried in the quire of the kirk of Banchory.* Elizabeth married (2) on 25 October 1672 in Banchory Ternan parish, David

Ramsay of Balmain. Mr Robert Burnett, Advocate and Mr Robert Burnett of Muchalls were appointed executors and tutors to Alexander's children.

Petition to the Privy Council *by Dame Elizabeth Coutis, Lady Leyes, for a mortification as a competent provision for maintainance and education of her daughter (left unprovided for by death of Sir Alexander Burnett of Leyes, her father, of a fever) aged 14, neglected by the tutor of Leyes in whose charge she is, both as to apparel and breeding, so that her mother was forced to remove her from a 'landwart schole' and settle her in Aberdeen.*
Crathes Archives. (S2/b43)

Alexander and Elizabeth Burnett had the following children:

- Thomas Burnett who became the 3rd Baronet of Leys.
- Robert Burnett. According to G. Burnett in *The Family of Burnett of Leys*, Robert is thought to have died young as he is only mentioned in his father's will.
- William Burnett. He purchased the lands of Balfour and Woodtoun, in the parishes of Fettercairn and Edzell in 1685 from Stratoun of Lauriston. In the Jacobite uprising late in the 1680s his lands at Balfour were plundered and laid waste three times, by Farquharson of Inverey, then by the Earl of Dunfermline and lastly by the brother of the Laird of Keppach. Eventually, in 1693, William and his tenants received damages modified to the sum of £1000 sterling.

An account due by William Burnett of Balfour to Andrew Burnett, merchant in Aberdeen for various items including a fine French hat, a pair of spurs, and bought at London for the Major, a sword with a fine silver handle and a fine Spanish toledo blade costing £45.10s Scots and a horse whip. 1682-3. Endorsed 1688. Crathes Archives(S2/b53).

An account due by Major Burnett to James Millar, Coppersmith in Canongate [Edinburgh] for a copper stoving pan with a close cover, a fish kettle with a false bottom and a pie pan, 2 snuffing dishes and a dredging box. 30 September 1696. Crathes Archives (S2/b54).

William Burnett married (1) Margaret Douglas, daughter and co-heir to William Douglas, Advocate and his wife Rachel Kirkwood of Pilrig, who were married in North Leith, Edinburgh and whose marriage contract is in the Crathes Archives. Margaret died in 1690 after which William Burnett married (2) in England, Margaret Easton. About 1 June 1700, Major William Burnett was killed in a duel with Captain Maclean near Marylebone, London. The children of his first marriage who were taken under the care of Sir Thomas Burnett of Leys were:

- Thomas Burnett who was served heir portioner general to his maternal grandmother Rachel Kirkwood, Lady Evlick, daughter of Gilbert Kirkwood of Pilrig, on 9 December 1701 and, on 6 June 1706, heir portioner special to his grandfather William Douglas in £2000 Scots, secured over the lands and barony of Chirnside. Numerous papers were generated over the affairs of Thomas and his sisters regarding the sale of Balfour and litigation's arising therefrom, also claims in connection with a mortgage of £1400 over lands in Shropshire.

> A receipt dated at Edinburgh 3 January 1677, by George Porteous, herald painter, boxmaster to the Marie Chapel was to Rachel Kirkwood, relict of Mr William Douglas, advocate, for the sum of £53 Scots as one term's rent of a dwellinghouse which apparently was owned by the Marie Chapel and which she occupied. Crathes Archives(S2/b43).

- Elizabeth Burnett. She married on 4 December 1705 in Banchory-Ternan parish to the Rev. Alexander Shank, baptised 1676, son of Henry Shank of Castlerigg, Kinghorn, Fife. Alexander's older brother Martin Shank was minister at Newhills and succeeded Robert Burnett in Banchory Ternan in 1698. Martin's son, Alexander, who married a Mary Burnett, succeeded to Castlerigg. A gravestone of Martin and his family is in Banchory Ternan Churchyard. Alexander Shank was admitted to the parish of Drumoak in 1709 having gained an MA degree at St. Andrews on 25 June 1700. Elizabeth died on 1 April 1730 and Alexander died on 6 March 1749 after a fall from his horse. Children were:
  - Thomas Shank who was baptised on 11 September 1707 in Drumoak parish.
  - Alexander Shank who was baptised on 4 October 1708 in Drumoak parish. He became the minister of St. Cyrus parish, Kincardine.
  - Margaret Shank who was baptised on 20 November 1710 in Drumoak parish. She married Rev. James Walker, minister of Dunottar parish. Kincardine.
  - Jean Shank who was baptised on 24 December 1712 in Drumoak parish. She married Rev. William Thomson, minister of Marykirk.
  - William Shank who was baptised on 20 June 1714 in Drumoak parish. He became minister of Brechin parish. Angus.
  - Elizabeth Shank who was baptised on 13 August 1715 in Drumoak parish but died young.
  - Elizabeth Shank who was baptised on 4 April 1718 in Drumoak parish but she too died young.

- Henry Shank who was baptised on 30 March 1720 in Drumoak parish.
- Elizabeth Shank who was baptised on 21 November 1721 in Drumoak parish and died young.
- Martin Shank was baptised on 18 January 1723 in Drumoak parish. He gained an MA. Degree in 1740.
- Elisabeth Shank was baptised on 15 March 1725 in Drumoak parish. She died young.
- Elizabeth Shank was baptised on 4 April 1728 in Drumoak parish.

[Note: no gravestone inscriptions have been found for the four children named Elizabeth Shank who died young]

- ♦ Rachel Burnett was born in 1690.

- ❑ Elizabeth Burnett who married Alexander Ogilvie, son of John Ogilvie of Kempcarne, according to contract in Crathes papers dated 22 and 24 April 1679.
- ❑ Jean Burnett.
- ❑ Margaret Burnett who was the youngest daughter married (1) in 1686, her cousin Alexander Burnett of Monboddo. She was the grandmother of Lord Monboddo. Margaret married (2) Dr. Andrew Burnett, one of the clergy of Aberdeen. He gained an MA degree from Marischal College in 1672, also a Degree in Medicine, and was appointed one of the ministers of St.Nicholas in 1686. An Episcopalian, he had a somewhat stormy career, details of which are to be found in Burnett, *The Family of Burnett of Leys,* 77. In 1715 at Fetteresso, he and others presented *a humble address* to King James VIII. Andrew and Margaret Burnett had five known children, all baptised at St Nicholas, Aberdeen:
  - ♦ Robert Burnett who was born in 1692. He died before 1723.
  - ♦ Elizabeth Burnett who was baptised on 20 November 1692. Possibly twin of Robert.
  - ♦ Thomas Burnett who was baptised in October 1693.
  - ♦ William Burnett who was baptised on 9 October 1694.
  - ♦ Andrew Burnett who was baptised on 15 September 1703.

  Dr Andrew Burnett married (2) on 14 October 1705, Elizabeth Reid, the widow of Adam Maltman, a merchant in Aberdeen. Andrew Burnett and his son Robert both died before 1723.

Sir Thomas Burnett, 3rd Baronet, succeeded his father in 1663 whilst still in pupillarity. He was served heir, excluding Invery and Cluny, on 19 May 1664. In 1666 he made up his titles from Mr George Burnett, of Wester Slowie and other lands held by the parson of Kincardine. He also inherited considerable debts, but due to the efforts of his guardian, Robert Burnett of Muchalls, Elrick, Colpy, Cowie, Cowtoun and Criggie, known as the *Tutor of Leys*, the fortunes of the estate had, for the most part, been reversed by the time he reached his majority.

Whilst still under age, Thomas Burnett married, in 1677, his cousin Margaret Arbuthnot, the second daughter of Robert, Viscount Arbuthnot and Lady Elizabeth Keith, daughter of the 7th Earl Marischal. Margaret received the liferent of Muchalls from her husband on 29 June 1677. Sir Thomas was Commissioner to the Scottish Parliament for Kincardineshire from 1689 to 1707, a period which spanned the reigns of William and Anne. As a supporter of King William he was given several appointments of responsibility. Shortly before the death of King William there was an intention of raising him to the peerage. On 13 February 1707 he was elected a Member of the Parliament of Great Britain but appears never to have presented his commission or sat as a Member. He was elected as a member of the Scottish Privy Council, constituted in terms of the Union, on 21 May 1707. Thomas died in January 1714 and Margaret died in Aberdeen in July 1744, having outlived her husband by 30 years. Thomas and Margaret Burnet had, in total, 21 children several of whom died young and whose names are not known. Children who have been identified were:

- Alexander Burnett, born in 1679, who succeeded his father. He was made a Burgess of Aberdeen on 18 January 1689.[Burgess Register]
- Robert Burnet who was made an honorary burgess of Aberdeen on 18 January 1689.[Burgess Register]. He must have died prior to 1697 as another child, born on 6 July of that year, was also named Robert.
- William Burnett *of Criggie* who was baptised on 10 December 1683. He was made a burgess of Aberdeen on 18 January 1689. [Burgess Register]. He married on 19 October 1699 to Jean Burnet, 3rd daughter and co-heiress of Robert Burnet of Cowtoun, *Tutor of Leys*. Children were:
  - Thomas Burnett who was born in 1708 and became the 6th Baronet.
  - James Burnett who was born in 1710. He became Captain James Burnett and married Anne Purves, daughter of Sir William Purves of that Ilk.
  - Margaret Burnett who married, on 27 April 1735, the Rev. John Aitken, minister of Montrose.
  - Unknown (daughter) Burnett who married a merchant in Aberdeen by the name of Smith.
  - Helen Burnett who married (1) in 1733, William Fraser, Advocate in Aberdeen, younger son of Francis Fraser of Findrack. She married (2) on 18 September 1758 at St. Nicholas, Peter Reid, a merchant in Aberdeen.
- Elizabeth Burnett who was baptised on 10 April 1685 but died before 1692.
- Thomas Burnett who was baptised on 27 May 1686. He was made an honorary Burgess of Aberdeen on 18 January 1689 [Burgess Register of Aberdeen]
- Marie/Mary Burnett, baptised on 30 September 1687, referred to as 2nd daughter, who married on 2 October 1712 in Banchory Ternan parish, according to contract in Crathes Papers dated 31 August 1712, Sir John Carnegie 2nd Baronet of Pitarrow. Mary died on 5 June 1754 and was buried at Montrose

(probably in Kinnaber Chapel burial ground). Mary and Sir John had the following children:

- James Carnegie who became the 3rd Baronet of Pitarrow.
- Margaret Carnegie, who was baptised 30 July 1713, died unmarried on 20 April 1747.
- Mary Carnegie, who was baptised 12 August 1714, married (1) in 1748, Colonel John Scott of Comistoun in Kincardineshire. She married (2) a Forbes.
- Helen Carnegie, baptised 17 April 1715, married Alexander Aberdein of Cairnbulg who died in 1758.
- John Carnegie who was baptised at Pitarrow House on 10 October 1716. He died aged 17.
- David Carnegie, who was baptised on 23 December 1717, died before April 1747.
- Jean Carnegie, baptised 13 September 1720 at Pitarrow House, married Robert of Tailor of Kirktonhill. Names of children not known.
- Alexander Carnegie who was baptised on 26 April 1722. He went to Jamaica where he died, unmarried, before 3 February 1747.
- Elizabeth Carnegie who was baptised on 30 November 1724. She lived at Charleton with her brother George. Elizabeth died, unmarried on 23 June 1789 and was buried at Kinnaber Chapel burial ground, Montrose.
- Henry Carnegie who was baptised 31 August 1725. He gained an appointment as midshipman in the ships of the Honorable East India Company but was drowned when *The Prince of Orange* sank in a gale in 1747.
- George Carnegie who was baptised 19 November 1726. When only 18 years of age, he joined Prince Charles at Holyrood after the Battle of Prestonpans. He followed the Prince to England and eventually fought at the Battle of Culloden after which he fled to Europe. In due course, George made his way to, and settled in, Sweden where he became a merchant in Gothenburg. After 20 years he returned to Scotland. With the fortune that he had made he re-purchased some of the Carnegie family properties including Charleton. George Carnegie died there on 12 April 1799, aged 72, and was buried at Kinnaber Chapel burial ground, Montrose. [The Scots Peerage, Vol. III.,72]

- John Burnett was born on 10 October and baptised on 11 October 1688. He too was made an honorary burgess of Aberdeen on 8 January 1689. John is presumed to have died young.
- Charles Burnett was baptised on 1 August 1691. He became an advocate at the Scottish Bar. Charles died, unmarried, after 1717.

- Elizabeth Burnett was baptised 11 August 1692 in Aberdeen. She married, on 15 October 1715, George Beattie, merchant of Montrose, according to contract in the Crathes Papers.
- James Burnett was baptised on 16 October 1693. He is presumed to have died young.
- Jean Burnett was christened on 15 January 1695 in Banchory-Ternan parish. She married, on 11 October 1722, in Banchory-Ternan parish, George Lauder of Pitscandlie, a merchant in Edinburgh, second son of the deceased Sir Robert Lauder of Bellmouth. An antenuptial contract dated 14 September 1722 is in Crathes Archives [S1/b 67.26]
- Margaret Burnett was baptised on 20 July 1696. She married, in 1721, James Ogilvie of Melros, Banff.
- Robert Burnett was baptised on 6 July 1697. He is presumed to have died young.
- Helen Burnett was baptised on 23 July 1698. According to Douglas's *Baronage* the youngest daughter, unnamed, but possibly Helen, married an Allardice of that Ilk.
- Lewis Burnett was born on 6 February, baptised on 6 February 1700. He is presumed to have died young.
- Katherine Burnett married, on 31 August 1712, Sir William Seton of Pitmedden, 2nd Baronet. There were children of this marriage. William died in 1744 and Katherine in 1749.

Sir Alexander Burnett of Leys, 4th Baronet, born 1679, succeeded his father in 1714. He married at the age of 18, in 1697, Helen, aged 14, daughter of Robert Burnett of Cowtoun who had been *Tutor of Leys* to Alexander. On the death of Sir Thomas Burnett in 1714, his financial affairs were found to be in a very serious position with debts exceeding the value of the estate. Sir Alexander Burnett was left with no option but to settle these debts by a variety of methods, and with the help of his competent advisers, which included the sale of Muchalls to Thomas Fullerton and the loss of Cowtoun. Alexander is noted as not being a public character nor perhaps as gifted as some members of the family. Nevertheless he had the reputation of being a kind-hearted and benevolent man. He also apparently had an abnormally strong fear of anything unfamiliar and, in particular, a dread of ghosts.

1715 saw the Jacobite Rebellion in Scotland and in September of that year, Alexander received a letter from the Earl Marischal to the effect that *in his Maj. name and auth...to require you with your best horses and armes, and what men you can raise to meet me at Stonhyve(Stonehaven) on Saturday next, October 1st, at one o'clock, for which this shall be yovr warrand.* Obviously the state of the affairs of Sir Alexander Burnett and his estates would have prevented him from being able to

comply with this request. Helen Burnett died at Crathes on 2 March 1740. Alexander died on 4 February 1758, also at Crathes, in his 80th year.
Alexander and Helen Burnett had the following children:

- Thomas Burnett who was killed by a splinter of rock whilst work was being undertaken to drain the Loch of Leys.
- Robert Burnett who was baptised on 17 May 1720. He succeeded his father as 5th Baronet.
- Alexander Burnett who may have been another son considering the following indenture document.

A indenture between William Cruickshank, Provost of Aberdeen and Alexander Burnet, son of Sir Alexander Burnet of Leys, to learn the trade of merchandise and art belonging thereto, for 3 years. Dated 27 August 1729. Endorsed with discharge, 15 November 1731. In Crathes Archives (S1/b64)

- Helen Burnett married, on 21 June 1733, George Burnett of Kemnay, born on 29 September 1714, son of Thomas Burnet, the second Laird of Kemnay.(see Chapter 5). George was the great-grandson of James Burnett of Craigmyle who was brother of the 1st Baronet of Leys. Helen died at Kemnay on 21 September 1750. Children of George and Helen Burnett were:
  - Alexander Burnett who succeeded his father.
  - Helen Burnett who was born in 1734 and died in 1810.
  - Anne Burnett who was born in 1736 and died in 1782.
  - Jane/Jean Burnett, born in 1739, who married Alexander Dunbar of Boath. They had at least two sons both of whom studied medicine at Edinburgh University. She died in 1764 at Auldearn.
  - Elizabeth Burnett, born in 1738.
  - Mary Burnett, born in 1747, died in 1802.
- Jean Burnett who was baptised on 18 October 1714 in Banchory Ternan. She died young.
- Katherine Burnett who was baptised on 27 February 1716 in Banchory Ternan and died young.
- Mary Burnett who was baptised on 2 April 1719 in Banchory Ternan. According to a contract dated 24 June 1742, she married, on 27 June 1743 in St. Nicholas, Alexander Aberdein of Cairnbulg who was a Provost of Aberdeen. Their children were:
  - Alexander Aberdein who was baptised on 21 January 1745.
  - Robert Aberdein who was baptised on 18 January 1747. He became a member of the Faculty of Advocates and died in London.

Sir Robert Burnett of Leys, 5th Baronet, was baptised on 17 May 1720. As the only surviving son, he succeeded his father, Alexander, on 4 February 1758.

Robert died, unmarried, in August 1759.[Aberdeen Register of Testaments 23 January 1768] There followed a legal dispute as to succession between Alexander, son of George Burnett of Kemnay and Thomas, son of the late William Burnett of Criggie.

Sir Thomas Burnett of Leys, 6th Baronet, was the son of William Burnett of Criggie and Jean Burnett, daughter of Robert Burnett *Tutor of Leys*. He was served heir special to his father in Criggie on 6 May 1748 and heir male special to his cousin Sir Robert Burnett, 5th Baronet, in Leys and Pittenkeirie, on 17 January 1761. His succession ceased to be contested by 1766 and on 7 August 1767 he obtained a Court of Session decree against Alexander Burnett, Younger of Kemnay and Robert Aberdein, heir of line of Sir Robert Burnett. He was made a Burgess of Montrose on 22 September 1757. Thomas Burnett married in 1754 to Katherine Ramsay, daughter of Charles Ramsay, merchant and 3rd son of Sir Charles Ramsay of Balmain, and Katherine Mill. An inventory of the household furniture of Crathes taken in 1759 is to be found in the Appendix of *The Family of Burnett of Leys* published in 1901.

By order of the Commssioner of Supply for the Shire of Kincardine

There are requiring the whole labouring people in the Mill Sucken of Durris to come and work upon the Road leading from Darnford to Water of Cowie upon Monday Tuesday and Wednesday next being the 15,16,17 days of June instant each man to bring with him a spade and shovell and to attend from 8 o'clock in the morning. Also the whole labouring people with the Mill Sucken of Baladrum to come in to repairing of the said roads upon Thursday Friday and Saturday next being the 18,19 and 20 days of June current with Certification that those who refuse to attend on the said Road will be prosecuted in terms of Law given at Banchory the twelfth day of June one thousand seven hundred and seventy two years by

Tho. Burnett J.P.

Crathes Archives. (S2/b10)

Sir Thomas and Katherine Burnett had the following children:

- Robert Burnett, born on 20 December 1755, who was baptised on 28 December 1755 in St Cyrus parish. He succeeded his father.
- Alexander Burnett, born on 31 July, who was baptised on 30 August 1757 in St. Cyrus parish. He was the twin of Thomas. Alexander was admitted to the Scottish Bar and became Sheriff of Kincardineshire in 1779. Alexander Burnett married, on 14 October 1782, Elizabeth Bannerman, eldest daughter of Sir Alexander Bannerman, 4th Baronet of Elsick. Alexander became Sir Alexander Ramsay, Baronet of Balmain. [Details of descendants, many of whom dropped the surname Burnett in favour of Ramsay, are given in Chapter 10.]
- Thomas Burnett, born on 31 July, baptised on 30 August 1757 in St Cyrus parish, who was the twin of Alexander.

- Katherine/Catherine Burnett was baptised on 17 September 1759 in St. Cyrus parish. She married, on 27 October 1783, in Banchory-Ternan parish, Alexander Forbes of Schivas. Catherine died at Banchory Lodge on 14 January 1853, aged 94.
- William Burnett was baptised on 18 February 1762 in Banchory-Ternan parish. He was appointed to the 14th Regiment in 1784, served in Flanders in 1793 under the Duke of York and was created General William Burnett in January 1837. William Burnett acquired Arbeadie, on the north of River Dee, from his brother Robert Burnett and half of the estate of Blackhall on the south of the River, from the trustees of Sir Edward Bannerman. Having retired to Deeside, General Burnett died unmarried on 7 February 1839. A monument to commemorate him was erected by his tenants and neighbours on the summit of Scolty hill, overlooking Blackhall and Banchory, where it is still a prominent landmark.

Sir Thomas Burnett died on 26 July 1783 at Crathes.

Sir Robert Burnett of Leys, 7th Baronet was born on 20 December 1755. He entered the Army on 23 December 1771 and served in the first American War with the 21st Royal North British Fusiliers. Robert was taken prisoner at Saratoga in 1777 at the time of General Burgoyne's surrender to General Gates. He left the Army to succeed his father in 1783. Robert Burnett married, on 16 September 1785 at Logie, to Margaret Dalrymple Elphinstone, 4th daughter of General Robert Horn Dalrymple (son of Lord Drummore and Ann Horn) and Mary Elphinstone, heiress of Logie. On his marriage, Robert Horn Dalrymple had assumed the surname of Elphinstone. In 1807, Robert Burnett purchased Mills of Drum, part of the upper barony of Culter from the trustees of James Duff of Fetteresso. Sir Robert Burnet died on 2 January 1837 in his 82nd year. Margaret died at Crathes, on 18 March 1849. Robert and Margaret Burnett had the following children.

- Mary Burnett who was born on 16 September 1786. She died of cholera on 9 February 1856 at Corsee Bank, Banchory.
- Thomas Burnett who was baptised on 26 May 1788. He became the 8th Baronet. Thomas died on 16 February 1849.
- Alexander Burnett who was born on 17 December 1789 and baptised the following day. He succeeded his brother Thomas to become the 9th Baronet.
- Robert Burnett who was born on 24 January 1793. He was killed in an accident on 5 September 1801.
- William Burnett who was born on 1 August 1798 and entered the Royal Navy in 1811. He served under Sir George Cockburn, Sir Henry Hotham and Sir Thomas Hardy on the *Northumberland* and the *Ramillies* during the French and American Wars. In the attacks on Washington and New Orleans he was employed in the boats of the squadron. He was mentioned in dispatches against

Greek pirates and again during an insurrection on Jamaica. William returned home in 1824 and was promoted post captain. He died, unmarried, on 16 April 1840, in Portsmouth, England where a monument to him was erected at Garrison Church. At the time of his death he had just been appointed to the *Magicienne.* His commissions, which are archived in the Crathes Papers, include that of Lieutenant of HMS *Egeria* dated 20 November 1818, Commander of HM sloop *Ariel* dated 28 April 1827, Captain of HMS *Royal William* dated 11 March 1834 and Captain of HMS *Magicienne* dated 11 February 1840.

- Katherine Burnett who was born on 16 December 1791.
- Margaret Burnett who was born on 9 April 1796. She married, on 28 April 1826, her cousin-german, Thomas Ramsay, the second son of Sir Alexander Ramsay, Baronet of Balmain. Margaret died on 17 January 1828. [Details are give in chapter 10 on the genealogy of Ramsays of Balmain]
- James Horn Burnett who was baptised on 22 June 1801. He became the 10th Baronet of Leys.
- Helen Burnett who was baptised on 30 July 1803.

Sir Thomas Burnett of Leys, 8th Baronet, was born on 22 August 1788. He succeeded his father in January 1837. In 1832 he contested the Parliamentary seat of Kincardineshire against General, the Hon. Hugh Arbuthnott. For his services, he was presented with a silver centre-piece by the Liberal electors of the county. He was a prominent agriculturalist and breeder of Aberdeenshire cattle. Thomas Burnett was appointed Lord Lieutenant of Kincardineshire in 1847. He died, unmarried, at Crathes on 16 February 1849 aged 61.

Sir Alexander Burnett of Leys, 9th Baronet, was born on 17 December 1789. He succeeded his brother in 1849. Alexander, who was in the HEICS, died, unmarried, on 20 March 1856.

Sir James Horn Burnett of Leys, 10th Baronet, was born on 22 June 1801. He succeeded his brother on 20 March 1856. After being apprenticed to John Morison, he was admitted to the Society of Writers to the Signet on 9 July 1824. He was Lord Lieutenant of Kincardineshire from December 1863. James Horn Burnett married (1) on 3 February 1831, Caroline Margaret Spearman, daughter of Charles Spearman of Thornley Hall, County Durham. James and Caroline Burnett had the following children.

- Robert Burnett who was born on 28 August 1833. He became the 11th Baronet.
- Charles Spearman Burnett who was born on 6 July 1835. He died on 21 June 1836.

James Horn Burnett married (2) on 12 July 1837, his cousin-german, Lauderdale Ramsay, born about 1807 at Fasque, Fettercairn parish, Kincardineshire, youngest daughter of Sir Alexander Ramsay of Balmain. Lauderdale was the widow of David Duncan of Rosemount and Parkhill, Angus, whom she had married on 27 June 1832. David Duncan died on 25 January 1833 aged 30 and was buried at Inchbrioch, in the parish of Craig. By the time of the 1881 British census, Lauderdale Burnett was a widow, aged 74, living in her residence at 47 Heriot Row, St. Stephen's parish, Edinburgh with her son, Alexander, and four servants. Lauderdale died on 4 November 1888. James and Lauderdale Burnett had the following children:

- Thomas Burnett who was born on 27 November 1840. He became the 12th Baronet.
- Alexander Edwin Burnett who was born on 17 December 1842. He was a student at the University of Edinburgh from 1862-1867 from which his class cards are archived in the Crathes papers. After being apprenticed to Archibald Watson Goldie, WS, in 1867, he became a member of the Society of Writers to the Signet on 24 March 1873. Alexander was a member of the firm of Baxter & Burnett W.S. in Edinburgh but prior to his death had been involved in commercial interests as a partner in the firm of Weir, Whigham & Vernon, Wine Merchants He was an enthusiastic follower of drama and a talented amateur actor. One of his hobbies was the collecting of playbills of which he had an immense collection. In 1890 he was resident at 37 Drummond Place, Edinburgh and was co-petitioner with Lt. Col. Thomas Burnett in the matter of appointment of a curator bonis for Sir Robert Burnett who at that time was regarded as being unable to manage his affairs. Alexander, who remained unmarried and who was, in 1881, living with his widowed mother at 47 Heriot Row, Edinburgh, died suddenly at Crathes Castle on 8 August 1895 at the age of 53, whilst he was on a visit to his brother. He had been recuperating after a period of indifferent health but his death was unexpected. He was buried at Banchory Ternan Churchyard.
- Elizabeth Bannerman Burnett married, on 2 February 1869 at Crathes Castle, George John Pitt Taylor of the 78th Highlanders. Elizabeth died on 22 February 1877. They had one son and three daughters.

Sir Robert Burnett of Leys, 11th Baronet, was born on 28 August 1833 and educated at Christ Church, Oxford, England. He succeeded his father in 1876. Prior to his succession, Robert Burnett had moved to Los Angeles, USA, where he became the owner of 2,500 acres of Aguaje de la Centinela. This was extended later by the purchase of Rancho San Sal Redondo bring his total land to 25,000 acres, extending from Playa del Rey to Watts and from the Baldwin Hills to Redondo. His initial investment cost $3000 in 1860. Eventually the ranch ran 24,000 head of sheep but, after 1870, Robert Burnett turned to planting extensive orchards. By 1873 he had leased the land, on condition that it continue in orchards, to Daniel Freeman to whom he eventually sold the ranches of San Sal Redondo and

Centinela along with a tract of land called the Stuart Tract on 17 January 1885 for $140,000. A copy of this agreement is in the Crathes Archives. Much of Robert Burnett's land is now the site of the city of Los Angeles development, university, oil fields and the airport of Los Angeles.

Robert Burnett married, in 1864, Matilda Josephine Murphy, born in New York in about 1835, daughter of James and Mary Murphy of New York. Matilda Murphy had been divorced from her first husband Charles B. Polhemus. Robert was appointed a Justice of the Peace for Kincardineshire. At the time of the 1881 census, Robert and Matilda Burnett were living at 3 Charles Street, London, in the parish of St. George, with one servant (a footman). Matilda died on 25 April 1888. Having been ill since 1889, Robert Burnett died, aged 60, on 15 January 1894 at Crossburn House, East Wemyss, Fife where he had been under medical care. At the time of his death, Robert Burnett still had a residence at 3 Charles Street, Berkeley Square, London. He was buried on 18 January 1894 at Banchory Ternan Churchyard. Robert and Matilda Burnett had one son:

- James Lauderdale Burnett who died in infancy in 1874.

Sir Thomas Burnett of Leys, 12th Baronet, was born on 27 November 1840. He succeeded his half-brother in 1894. At the time of his succession, Thomas Burnett was resident at Campfield House, near Banchory. He was a Lt. Colonel and later a Colonel in the Royal Horse Artillery. Thomas Burnett was a member of the Council of the Spalding Club of Aberdeen and contributed much to the Spalding Club's publication of George Burnett's work on the history of *The Family of Burnett of Leys*. Thomas Burnett married, on 2 June 1875 at St Andrew's Church, Aberdeen, Mary Elizabeth Cumine, born 20 November 1842, elder daughter of James Cumine of Rattray and Harriet Hay Cumine. He died on 25 January 1926. Mary died on 8 November 1928. Thomas and Mary Burnett had the following children:

- James Lauderdale Gilbert Burnett who was born on 1 August 1880 at Rattray House, Peterhead. He was a 2nd Lieutenant in the Gordon Highlanders and then a Major General. Later he succeeded as the 13th Baronet.
- Alexander Edwin Burnett who was born on 26 April 1881 at Rattray House. He became the 14th.
- Ethel Burnett who was born about 1876 in India. She was awarded the OBE in 1918. Ethel Burnett died, unmarried, on 10 November 1957 at the Alexandra Hotel, Ballater, Aberdeenshire, aged 81.
- Mary Bertha Burnett who was born on 21 October 1878 at Rattray House. Bertha died on 25 September 1898 aged 19 and was buried on 29 September in an area of Leys Estate set aside as a family burial ground.

Sir James Lauderdale Gilbert Burnett of Leys, 13th Baronet was born on 1 April 1880 at Rattray House, Peterhead. After attending the Royal Military

College, Sandhurst, James Burnett received his commission as a 2nd Lieutenant in the Gordon Highlanders on 6th December 1899 and so began an exceptionally distinguished military career and long association with the Gordons. Such was that career that an extended profile of Sir James has been specially researched for this book by John Mathieson and is included here.

MAJOR GENERAL SIR JAMES BURNETT of LEYS, CB, CMG, DSO.

It was 1899, the end of a century, Queen Victoria's reign, with all it represented drawing to a close and the war in South Africa ... not over by Christmas.

Fig.3.4 James L. G. Burnett

After attending the Royal Military College Sandhurst, James Burnett received his commission as a 2nd Lieutenant on 6 December 1899 and was gazetted to the Gordon Highlanders, the beginning of a distinguished military career and a long association with the Gordons.

The 2nd battalion Gordon Highlanders had completed their first year's foreign service in India when they sailed for South Africa, arriving at the start of hostilities. After the initial action at Elandslaagte, the Gordons, along with the rest of the Natal Field Force retired to Ladysmith and suffered the siege from the beginning of November 1899 till the end of February 1900.

After the garrison was relieved, the Gordons moved to Arcadia, west of Ladysmith, to recuperate, prior to pursuing the Boers. At this point is found the first mention of James Burnett. *Draft of 73 rank and file under 2nd Lt. J. L. G. Burnett joined on 7 April.*

2nd Lt. Burnett saw action at Laing's Nek, Natal, 6 to 9 June. From July to the end of November he took part in operations in the Transvaal, east of Pretoria, including the actions at Belfast, 26-27 August and Lydenberg, 5-8 September. Another notable event at that time was the meeting of the 1st and 2nd battalions. There is a photograph of James Burnett with two fellow officers [Fig. 3.5], taken at Spitz Kop on the 11 September, close to what is now the Kruger National Park.

Fig. 3.5 R. G. Forbes (left), J. R. F. Stansford, James Burnett (right) Spitz Kop, 11 September 1900. (courtesy, Gordon Highlanders' Museum).

James Burnett spent the remainder of the war in the Transvaal, west of Pretoria. From 18 October to 12 November 1900 he is listed as an RTO (Railway Transport Officer); 31 January 1901 promoted to Lieutenant; 4 January to 7 April again listed as an RTO. During the period 21 April to 27 November 1901, he served on the Staff as a Railway Staff Officer.

During the latter half of 1901 James Burnett must still have been on the strength of the 2nd battalion, Gordon Highlanders. There is a series of photographs of a gymkhana at Pietersburg, July 1901 in which most of the officers appear to be dressed as ladies. James Burnett is dressed like a Boer farmer's wife, complete with 'pramhood' type bonnet. (Fig. 3.6)

Fig. 3.6 James Burnett (second right) at Gymkhana, Pietersburg, July 1901. (Courtesy, Gordon Highlanders' Museum)

There also exists a photograph of the Officers Pipe Band, circa August 1901, with J. L. G. Burnett, drummer. (Fig. 3.7)

Fig. 3.7 Officers Pipe Band 1901. James Burnett (fourth from right)
(Courtesy, Gordon Highlanders' Museum)

By all accounts James Burnett achieved quite a reputation as a very skilful drummer. Although there was time for bands, gymkhanas and suchlike, action was never far away. What follows is an account from the regimental history.

On 10 August 1901, 2nd Lt. J. L. G. Burnett and fourteen rank and file left Pietersburg at 1 p.m. and changed at Nylstroom into the down train to return home again. They had an armoured truck. Not half an hour from Nylstroom an explosion took place and the train bumped to a standstill; eight trucks went over the low embankment while the engine and some of the other trucks kept upright although derailed. Almost simultaneously, a second mine was exploded by a man who had placed himself behind an ant-heap close to the line, too close for his own safety, for he was shot. This mine was meant for the armoured-truck but went off too soon and caught the truck in front; the armoured truck stayed on the line. At once from thick bush one hundred yards off, rapid fire was pouring on the train but the escort was equally prompt and their fire was so effective that the enemy was seen to be running. But they only shifted to a safer distance, musketry continued brisk for a quarter-hour or more when shells from an armoured train which happened to be following put the enemy to flight.

Under her cover, Burnett with ten men went out over a mile, finding several dead, while others lay at the scene of the action. The armoured train remained for the night, the Gordons mounted guard over their charge; next morning a breakdown train cleaned up and the party were back at Pietersburg on 12 August. In this affair two passengers were killed and three wounded, a Boer woman among them. The escort had two men hit though their truck bore the marks of over one hundred bullets; two wounded prisoners were taken, sixteen dead Boers were buried and it is stated the enemy removed wounded in the wagons brought for the train supplies. One Lance Corporal McNiven, survivor of the fight on 4th July, had his pipe knocked out of his mouth by a bullet.

A fight on the 4 July refers to a similar attack by a band of train-wreckers on the same stretch of line. In this instance the truck was not armoured, Lt. Best and twenty-two rank and file as escort. The officer and eight Gordons were killed and eight severely wounded, the guard and three soldier passengers were also killed and seven wounded. The engine driver, fireman and two Africans were shot out of hand.

James Burnett was mentioned in Lord Kitchener's despatches of December 1901, for *coolness and resource on occasion of a train being derailed and attacked by Boers near Naboomsprult, August 1901.*

A further reference mentions that James Burnett took part in operations in the Transvaal till May 1902, which explains why he is not included in the list of officers embarking when the 2nd battalion returned to India on 2 January 1902. Also, a note dated 27 November, Pietersburg, *Lt. Burnett severely injured by fall from horse, fracturing left arm.*

James Burnett qualified for the Queen's South Africa Medal, clasps, 'Laing's Nek' and 'Belfast'. Also the King's South Africa Medal, clasps' SA 1901' and 'SA 1902'.

When the Boer War ended, James Burnett sailed for India and rejoined his regiment, at Sialkot, now in Pakistan. There followed a well-tried round of training, sport, the social life of the officers' mess and, of course, parades. Throughout his time in India James Burnett is included in a number of photographs with the band; in addition to his proficiency at drumming he was probably the band president. Also during his service in India, James Burnett acquired the nickname *Maxim* due his rapid-fire style of speech, like a Maxim machine gun.

On 7 December 1905 the battalion has moved to Peshawar. There Lt. Burnett was one of the Colour Party for the Guard of Honour to the Prince and

Princess of Wales (the future King George V). On 22 January 1906, he was promoted Captain.

At 20 February 1908, the battalion transferred to Calcutta, which was not regarded as a good posting because it took them away from the prospect of action on the North-west Frontier, the climate was not appealing and there was an excess of ceremonial parades. The end of 1909 saw the Gordons' final move in India. On 18 December the battalion set off on a four hundred mile march, arriving at Cawnpore on the 24 January 1910.

The Delhi Durbar on 7 December 1911 was a magnificent spectacle of the various units of the British and Indian Armies with their distinct uniforms, plus all the Indian Royalty in their splendid clothes, be-jewelled elephants, etc. The British Raj was at its peak. Capt. J.L.G. Burnett was one of the members of the regiment selected to receive the Delhi Durbar commemorative medal. On 10 December, the King-Emperor, George V, unveiled the all-India Memorial to his predecessor, King Edward VII. Edward VII having been Colonel-in-Chief of the Gordon Highlanders, the Gordons provided the Guard of Honour, James Burnett in command.

The battalion shook the dust of India from its shoes in December 1912 and exchanged it for the sand of Egypt, at Kasr-el-Nil Barracks in Cairo, regarded as a good posting by all; more regimental soldiering. In mid-October 1913, Captain Burnett was appointed 'A' Company Commander.

The fourth day of August 1914 saw the start of the First World War. On 24 September, the 2nd battalion arrived in Southampton and left there on 7 October for Zeebruge. The Gordons did not have to wait long to see action.

On the 29 October, during the First Battle of Ypres, whilst leading his company in counter-attacks near Ghevulet, alongside the 1st battalion Grenadier Guards, Captain Burnett was severely wounded. His servant, Private Christie, carried him to safety. What follows is an account of Private Christie's actions by a fellow Gordon.

> After the successful counter-attack the battalion retired to their own lines, by which time night had fallen. At this point James Christie realized Captain Burnett was missing. Private Christie made his way back across the battlefield to the point he last saw his company commander. James Christie had covered almost three-quarters of a mile and was within a stone-throw of the German trenches when he found the wounded officer. Capt. Burnett spotted a figure on the skyline and hoping it was a friend he sounded a distinctive call on his whistle. Private Christie had promptly responded when they came under fire from the German

trenches. Heaving the wounded officer on to his back, Private Christie returned to the British trenches, still under fire.

Captain Burnett was evacuated from France on the 2 November, eventually to Dublin, where he made a satisfactory recovery. Private James Christie was subsequently awarded the Military Medal. He remained with Capt. Burnett throughout the war and was still his chauffeur in the 1930s.

Capt. Burnett was Mentioned in Despatches, *London Gazette*, (17 February 1915) and also created a Companion of the Distinguished Service Order, *London Gazette*, (18 February 1915), *For services connected with operations in the field.*

After recovering from his wounds, Captain Burnett was appointed an Officer in charge of Gentleman Cadets at the Royal Military College, Sandhurst from 19 May to 6 October 1915. He was promoted Major on 1 September 1915; appointed in command of a Company of Gentleman Cadets, Royal Military College, 7 October 1915 to 31 October 1916; late November 1916 appointed commanding officer 1st battalion Gordon Highlanders. An entry in 1st battalion War Diary for 27 December 1916 at COUIN: *Frost in morning. Work as usual. Major J. L. G. Burnett joined as the new C.O.* He was promoted Acting Lt. Col. 8 January 1917 to 2 December 1917.

On 7 April 1917, the 1st battalion entered Arras where the 1st, 5th, 6th, 7th, 8/10th and 9th battalions Gordon Highlanders met. The Massed Pipes and Drums of the six battalions played Retreat in the Grande Place.

Easter Monday, 9 April 1917, saw The Battle of Arras. An exceptional feature of the battle was the use of vast caves below Arras, created by quarrying for the rebuilding of the seventeenth century city. 25,000 troops could assemble in the caves, which were linked by two tunnels to the front line almost one and three-quarter miles away. This eliminated the hazard of jumping off from a front-line trench and having to confront the danger of crossing no-man's land. The caves still exist and (possibly) in the future may be open to visitors on tours of the battlefields.

The 1st Gordons attacked on a very narrow front, they achieved all their objectives and more, when the general advance ran out of steam. Cyril Falls, the famous historian and author of the Regimental History at this point stated *Lt. Col. J.L.G. Burnett was one of the best officers produced by the regiment during the First World War.* Cyril Falls also described the Battle of Arras as *The most savage infantry battle of the war.*

Lt. Col. Burnett was again Mentioned in Despatches and awarded a bar to his DSO (i.e. a second DSO) *For conspicuous gallantry and devotion to duty in commanding his battalion during the attack and capture of a position. The success of the attack was greatly due to his leadership and the confidence with which he inspired his men.* Supplement of the *London Gazette*, (17 September 1917).

On 1 December 1917, Lt. Col. Burnett was ordered to proceed to take over the 186th Infantry Brigade, 62nd Division, effective from 3rd December. On 1 January 1918, he was promoted Brevet Lt. Col., temporary Brigadier General till 1 March 1919 and Brigade Commander for that period.

James Burnett was created a CMG. (Companion of St. Michael and St. George) in 1919, made an Officer of the Legion of Honour and promoted Brevet Colonel, 3 June 1919.

James Burnett was temporary commanding officer, 5th battalion Gordon Highlanders, as part of the Army of Occupation of Germany from 16 June to 28 July 1919. The War Diary mentions that the battalion spent most of the time doing ceremonial drill to impress the population, also that Lt. Col. Burnett was very keen on mounted paper chases which were held twice a week. The writer comments on the fact that the guards mounted in Cologne were the smartest he had seen during the war.

So ended the Great War. In addition to the decorations already awarded, James Burnett had been mentioned in despatches a total of five times and qualified for the 1914 Star with clasp, indicating he had been under fire between 4 August and 22 November 1914, also the British War Medal and Victory Medal. A bronze oak leaf attached to the ribbon of the Victory Medal signifies one or more mention in Despatches.

James Burnett's first role in the post-war army was as an instructor at the Senior Officers School, Woking, Berkshire, with the temporary rank of Lt. Colonel from 1 September 1919 till 19 December 1922, then the rank of substantive Lt. Colonel. On 31 December 1922, he took command of the 2nd battalion Gordon Highlanders, stationed at Fort George, quite a bleak location, where the barracks were in the process of renovation.

In June 1924 a training march was carried out to Aberdeen, also aimed at attracting recruits. In May 1925 the exercise was repeated, routed through part of the Regimental area not covered in 1924 and including Banchory and Crathes.

In October 1925 the battalion moved to Bordon, Aldershot Command. Despite being the home of the British Army it was more than compensated for by the amenities, also the standard and facilities for sport.

A significant date in his personal life and in the history of his family was 15 January 1926 when J. L. G. Burnett succeeded his father as the 25th laird of Leys and 13th Baronet.

By 20 December 1926, Sir James Burnett had completed four years as commanding officer of the 2nd battalion Gordon Highlanders.

Whilst commanding the 2nd battalion Sir James Burnett's photograph features regularly in the *Tiger and Sphinx*, the regimental journal. There are a number of photographs of him with the tug-of-war teams, the boxing team, the bayonet-fencing team and the pipers. In the latter photograph, Sgt. Piper C. Turnbull is sitting alongside Lt. Col. Burnett. Pipe-Major Turnbull went on to compose a pipe tune dedicated to Sir James, called *Farewell to the 92nd*.

Sir James, promoted Colonel, effective 25 January 1927, received an important assignment overseas leading an expeditionary force to Shanghai to protect British interests threatened by the civil war in China, and became Brigadier, 14th Infantry Brigade, Shanghai Defence Force and North China. He returned to Scotland at the beginning of 1928 and was given command of the 153rd (Black Watch and Gordon) Infantry Brigade, Territorial Army and, in 1930, command of the 8th Infantry Brigade.

In 1932 Sir James was appointed a Companion of the Most Honorable Order of the Bath and in 1939 was appointed Brigadier, Royal Company of Archers (H. M. Bodyguard in Scotland.

Major General Sir James Burnett of Leys became Colonel of the Gordon Highlanders in June 1939. When he succeeded General Sir Ian Hamilton the event was recorded in the last pre-war issue of the regimental magazine, the *Tiger and Sphinx*.

Fig.3.8 Sir James L.G. Burnett of Leys

Sir James's duties during the war included visiting the Gordon battalions in various locations throughout the United Kingdom. He also received a considerable amount of correspondence from the commanding officers of the Gordon battalions serving all over the world, North Africa, Europe and the Far East (Burma). In addition Sir James commanded the 3rd (South) Aberdeenshire and Kincardineshire Battalion Home Guard. For a time Sir James was Chairman of the Kincardine Territorial and Air Force Association and also a member of the county army cadets committee.

Shortly after D-Day Major General Burnett read a message from the Duke of Gloucester, Colonel-in-Chief of the Gordon Highlanders, during a special broadcast in celebration of the regiments one hundred and fiftieth anniversary. Thrilling episodes from the Gordons history were vividly recalled.

In 1945 the war ended but Sir James continued as Colonel of the Regiment till 1948.

On 13 August 1953 Major General Sir James Burnett of Leys died at his home in Deeside. Sir James was buried in the family cemetery in the grounds of his home, Crathes Castle. Over four hundred people from many walks of life came to pay their last tribute. Telegrams expressing sympathy were sent from the Queen and the Duke of Edinburgh, the Queen Mother and the Duke of Gloucester. Throughout the simple but impressive service the mourners stood in torrential rain in the shadow of the centuries old castle. There were distinguished soldiers, fellow lairds from the north-east and civic heads mingling with representatives from the many and varied organisations with which Sir James had been associated.

Sir James's personal standard fluttered at half-mast above the castle, in front of which were eighty-five wreaths laid in a semi-circle. The centrepiece was one in the form of a drum of chrysanthemums and marguerites from the tenants of Crathes estate.

Rain continued to fall heavily as the coffin was borne from the castle by the staff of the estate to a horse-drawn farm cart flanked by officers of Sir James's old regiment, the Gordon Highlanders. It was not a military funeral. Sir James was to be buried as laird of the lands of Leys.

Slowly the funeral procession made its way down the winding, tree-lined slopes to the burial ground in the valley, led by a piper of the Gordon Highlanders, playing *The Flowers o' the Forest.* Once the burial ceremony was completed, the plaintive notes of *The Last Post* faded, the rain stopped and a shaft of sunlight broke through.

While each soldier in turn came forward to stand erect and salute an 'old comrade', the piper struck up the march composed twenty-seven years ago in honour of Sir James when he relinquished command of the 2nd Battalion, *Colonel James Burnett of Leys' Farewell to the 92nd*. As the people turned away, the castle and the wooded estates which he loved so well were framed in sunlight and the ancient Leys standard once again flew proudly at the top of the mast.

The *Tiger and Sphinx* reproduced the following appreciation contributed by Capt. Keith Caldwell:

> Everyone who knew Jim Burnett will deeply mourn his passing. Outstanding personalities are always rare; few in our generation have merited the description so well as Jim. Great Laird of a great estate, he was part and parcel of his land and his life was intertwined with the lives of those who served him. He was the perfect host as all who enjoyed his hospitality well know. Jim was also the perfect guest. Unique as a raconteur, his presence ensured the success of any function, private party or official reception he attended. His capacity for saying

the right thing at the right time coupled with his quick wit and ready tongue ensured that he would be in great demand as a speaker. No one was more popular or had a more attentive audience.

Jim Burnett had an immense number of friends drawn from every walk of life and one of those amazing memories for faces that enabled him to place everyone, even if he had not seen them for years. I had the very real pleasure of working with him daily for most of the war in a Home Guard battalion over 2,000 strong.

I verily believe Jim knew the majority of the men and not only knew them but, when talking to them, could always produce an apposite story about their families, their homesteads or their neighbours. No wonder they adored him and worked with him to make his battalion one of the best in Scotland.

His tastes were catholic. He was a noted horticulturist and one of the greatest living authorities on shrubs. With the help of his talented wife he made the gardens at Crathes, his beautiful Scottish home recently handed over to the National Trust, world famous. How many reading these lines will think back on strolls with him and his bulldog round the gardens, enlivened by his continuous amusing commentaries on the plants, the people and anything else that came into his quick and active mind.

Quite as a sideline he studied railways and could tell one off-hand the timing of trains between two obscure African stations and types of engines used for the journey. A keen fisherman and shot, he never allowed sport to become one of his major preoccupations. His special recipe for shooting rabbits, at which he excelled, will always be remembered by those whom he confided in.

The loss of his only surviving son, killed in action during the last war, dealt him a grievous blow and, though he never showed it, I feel his zest for life was never quite so keen thereafter. Abler pens than mine will write of him as a soldier and others will pay tribute to the public work he did so efficiently for his county, of which he has been Vice-Lieutenant since 1944. I write of him as a friend and a man, to whom, like all who knew him well, I was devoted. With his passing something great has gone from the world and from the lives of all of us.

James Burnett married, on 10 July 1913, Sybil Aird Crozier, born 25 November 1889, daughter of William Crozier-Smith of Whitehill, St Boswells. Sir James L. G. Burnett died on 13 August 1953 at Crathes. Sybil died on 6 April 1960. A memorial inscription is in the private burial ground at Crathes. James and Sybil Burnett had the following children:

- Thomas Gilbert Alexander Burnett who was born on 17 April 1914. He died, unmarried, in 17 March 1934.
- Roger William Odo Burnett who was born on 19 August 1920. He became a Captain in 3rd Tank Battalion of the Scots Guards but was killed in action on 16

February 1945. Roger was buried in Plot XLV, Row D, Grave No. 12, Reichswald Forest War Cemetery in Germany. His name is recorded, along with that of others from the area who fell in WW 2, on the War Memorial at Banchory. A memorial inscription is in the private burial ground at Crathes.

- Elizabeth Rohays Mary Burnett who was born on 30 August 1916. She married (1) on 15 December 1938 at St Margaret's, Westminster London, Hon. Henry Kerr Auchmuthy Cecil of 7th Hussars, son of the late Captain Hon. William Amherst Cecil and Lady Amherst of Hackney. Henry, who on his marriage took up farming in Suffolk, was killed in action in North Africa on an unknown date between 30 November and 2 December 1942. Rohays and Henry Cecil had the following children:
  - John Strongbow Amherst Cecil who was born on 20 October 1939. After education at Sandroyd School and Eton, he served in the Scots Guards. John Cecil married Elizabeth Clare Hughes, daughter of C. Michael Hughes of Penton Manor, Andover, Hants., in 1966. John Cecil was formerly a stockbroker and is currently a business consultant. Their children are:
    - Richard Strongbow Amherst Cecil born in 1973. He is employed in Banking in London.
    - Miranda Elizabeth Rohays Cecil born in 1974 and working in Public Relations in London.
    - Michael John Amherst Cecil born in 1977 is employed in Turf Accountancy in Gibraltar.
  - James Comyn Amherst Cecil (now Burnett) of Leys was born on 24 July 1941. Like his eldest brother, he was educated at Sandroyd College and Eton. He was formally recognised in the surname Burnett of Leys by the Court of the Lord Lyon in 1966 and is now Head of the Burnett Family worldwide. James married in 1971 to Fiona Mercedes Philips, daughter of Lt. Col. Harold Philips. Their children are:
    - Alexander James Amherst Burnett who was born on 30 July 1973. He was educated at Crathes, Caldicott School, Eton College, Newcastle University and London Law School and is currently involved in property development in Azerbaijan.
    - Eliza Amelia Burnett who was born on 13 June 1977. After education at Crathes, Croftinloan, North Foreland Lodge School and Don Quixote College in Granada, she now works in publishing in London.
    - Victor Cecil Tobias Burnett who was born on 1 October 1982. He was educated at Crathes and Caldicott and is now at Eton College.
  - Henry Richard Cecil, twin of David, was born on 11 January 1943 in Aberdeen, just after his father had been killed in North Africa. He was educated at Sunningdale and Canford Schools. His career after attending the Royal Agricultural College at Cirencester followed a series of courses and

jobs in the horse-racing world thus gaining experience in thoroughbred management in France, USA and Great Britain. Henry became an assistant trainer and in 1969, aged 26, he took out his trainer's licence. He was assistant trainer to his step-father, Sir Cecil Boyd-Rochfort, who was trainer of the Queen's racehorses in Newmarket. By 1999, Henry Cecil had set a record in training 21 classic English winners and had been champion trainer 10 times. Henry Cecil can claim to be the English Trainer of the 20th century. Curiously, his family had no connection with the racing world until his mother re-married.

Henry married (1) in 1966, Julia Murless, daughter of Sir Charles Francia Noel Murless of Warren Place, Newmarket, England. Their children are:

- Katrina Henrietta Amherst Cecil or Mackenzie, who married Craig Mackenzie in 1999.
- Arthur Noel Amherst Cecil.

The marriage of Henry and Julia Cecil was dissolved in 1990. He married (2) in 1992 to Natalie Payne and they have a child:

- Jake Henry Richard Amherst Cecil.

♦ David Henry Amherst Cecil, twin of Henry, was born on 11 January 1943 in Aberdeen. He was educated at Sunningdale and Canford Schools and later attended the Royal Agricultural College at Cirencester before gaining thoroughbred management in France, USA and Great Britain. David was initially a racehorse trainer at Lambourn. Thereafter he managed thoroughbred studs in the USA and Yorkshire. He is currently the owner of the successful *Hare & Hounds* Public House and Restaurant near Lambourn. David Cecil married, in 1966, Hon. Fiona Elizabeth Cameron Corbett, daughter of Thomas, 2nd Baron Rowallan but their marriage was dissolved in 1972. Their children are:

- Rupert Lawrence Amherst Cecil who has followed a career in banking in London. He married Nellie Shone in 1966.
- Benjamin David Amherst Cecil who married Jenine (Jennie) Sahardi, daughter of Fred Sahardi of California, in 1998.

David Cecil married (2) in 1973, Vanessa Wladyslaw Gallica. Their marriage was dissolved in 1995. Their children are:

- Anoushka Henrietta Amherst Cecil.
- Sapphire Rose Cecil.

David Cecil married (3) Joanna Christian Howes, daughter of David Cecil Howes. Their child is :

- Jemima Rohays Amherst Cecil.

Rohays Burnett married (2) on 24 July 1944, Captain Cecil Charles Boyd-Rochfort, younger son of Major Rochfort Hamilton Boyd-Rochfort of

Middleton Park, County West Meath, Ireland. Captain Cecil Boyd- Rochfort died in 1952. They had a son:

- Arthur Roger Boyd-Rochfort who was born on 28 July 1945. He was educated at Sunningdale School and at Eton. Arthur was formerly owner and manager of a thoroughbred stud in Ireland and latterly in Suffolk. He married Lina Marigueretta Bernie, daughter of Aldo Bernie of Bristol, in 1974. They are now separated. Their child:
  - James Edward Cecil is involved with the organisation of charity fund-raising events.

A memorial inscription to Elizabeth Rohays Mary Boyd-Rochfort, who died on 17 May 1993, is in the private burial ground at Crathes.

Crathes Castle, Banchory was taken into the care of the National Trust for Scotland in 1952. It was formally opened to the public on Saturday 22 May 1952 at a ceremony attended by Major-General Sir James and Lady Burnett of Leys and the Earl of Wemyss and March, Chairman of Council of the National Trust for Scotland.

Sir Alexander Edwin Burnett, 14th Baronet, was born on 26 April 1881 at Rattray House, Crimond parish, Aberdeenshire. He was educated at Wellington College and Trinity College, Cambridge. He was appointed a Justice of the Peace for Kincardineshire and for a time lived at Usan House, Montrose. Alexander became a Major in the King's Own Scottish Borders and served in World War I from 1914-1918 during which he was wounded. He was awarded the Order of the British Empire (OBE) in 1919. He succeeded his brother James L. G. Burnett in 1953. Alexander Edwin Burnett died, unmarried, on 9 May 1959, and was buried at East Dean Churchyard, Sussex. At this point in time the baronetcy became dormant.

Sources and Notes:

Information included in the above genealogy has been extracted from a wide variety of sources including Parish and Civil registers, St. Paul's Episcopal Chapel records, Crathes archives, Burnett family papers and local newspaper notices. For the convenience of researchers some sources are noted beside the relevant text.

Aberdeen Burgh Records 1558-9

Allardyce, J., (ed), *Historical Papers relating to the Jacobite Period*, Vols I & II, Spalding Club, (1896).

Anderson, John A., *Aberdeenshire Epitaphs and Inscriptions*, (1907).

Anderson, Peter J.,(ed), *Records of Marischal College and University,* Vol II, Spalding Club, (1898)

Biographical Dictionary of Scottish Graduates to AD 1410.

Bork, June Baldwin, *Burnetts and their Connections* Vol. I, (1989) USA.

British War Graves Commission.

Browne, Rev. G.F., *Echt-Forbes Family Charters*. Edinburgh (1923).

Buchan, John, *Montrose*, (1928)

Buchan Watt, V.J., *The Book of Banchory*, Oliver & Boyd, (1947).

Burgess Register of Aberdeen.

Burnett, G., ed. Allardyce, J., *The Family of Burnett of Leys*, Spalding Club (1901).

Christie, J.A. et al., *Register of the Society of Writers to Her Majesty's Signet*, (1983), Edinburgh.

Cooper, J., *Chartularium Ecclesiae S. Nicholai Aberdonensis*, Spalding Club.

Dobson, D., The Original Scots Colonists of Early America 1612-1783, USA (1989)

Douglas, Sir Robert, *Baronage of Scotland* (1798)

Early Records of Aberdeen 1317, 1398-1407, Scottish History Society, 3rd series, Vol. XLIX.

Fasti Eccesiaticae Scotianae

Fyfe, J.G., Scottish Diaries and Memoirs 1550-1746, Stirling, (1927).

Gordon, James, Aberdoniae Vtrivsque Descriptio; A Description of Both Touns of Aberdeen, (1661), reproduced by Spalding Club.

Hannay, R.K. et al., *The History of the Society of Writers to his Majesty's Signet*, Edinburgh, (1936).

Henderson, John A., *History of the Society of Advocates in Aberdeen*, Spalding Club, (1912)

Huntly, Charles, Marquis of, (ed), *The Records of Aboyne*, Spalding Club (1894).

Jamieson D., & Wilson, W. S., *Old Banchory*, [photographs of], Stenlake Publishing, (1999).

Keith, A., *A Thousand Years of Aberdeen*, (1972)

Morison, Alexander, *Blackhall of that Ilk and Barra*, Spalding Club (1905).

Munro, A. M., *Memorials of the Aldermen, Provosts and Lord Provosts of Aberdeen 1272-1805*, (1896)

Registrum Magni Sigilli Regum Scotorum (Register of the Great Seal of Scotland).

Registrum Screti Sigilli Regum Scotorum (Register of the Privy Seal of Scotland)

Rogers, Rev. C., *Monuments and Monumental inscriptions in Scotland*, Vols I & II, London, (1871).

Scottish Biographies 1938, published by Thurston (London) and Jackson (Glasgow).

Skene, William Forbes, *Memorials of the Family of Skene of Skene*, Spalding Club, (1887).

Tayler, A., & H., *The House of Forbes*, Spalding Club, (1937).

Tayler, A., & H., *The Valuation of the County of Aberdeen for the Year 1667*, Spalding Club, (1932).

Tayler, A., & H., *The Jacobite Cess Roll for the County of Aberdeen in 1715*, Spalding Club, (1931).

Temple, Rev. W., *The Thanage of Fermartyn*, Aberdeen, (1894).

The Scots Peerage, Vol III.

Tyler, *History of Scotland.*

Watt, Theodore, *Roll of the Graduates of the University of Aberdeen 1901-1925*, Aberdeen University Press, (1935).

Watt, Theodore, *Aberdeen Grammar School Roll of Pupils 1795-1919*, Aberdeen, (1923).

Whyte, D., *Scottish Emigrants to USA.*

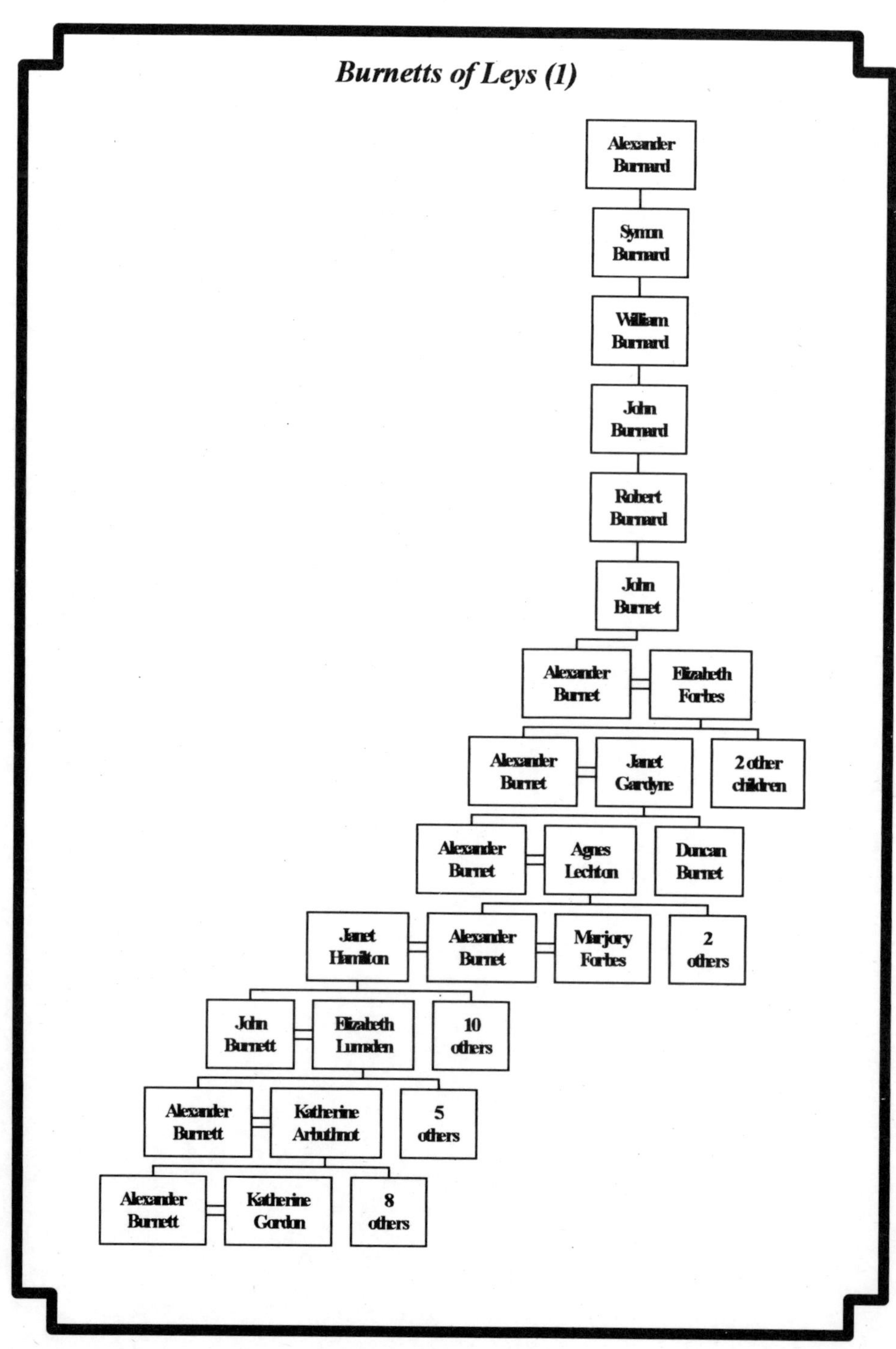
Burnetts of Leys (1)
Alexander Burnard
Symon Burnard
William Burnard
John Burnard
Robert Burnard
John Burnet
Alexander Burnet
Elizabeth Forbes
Alexander Burnet
Janet Gardyne
2 other children
Alexander Burnet
Agnes Lechton
Duncan Burnet
Janet Hamilton
Alexander Burnet
Marjory Forbes
2 others
John Burnett
Elizabeth Lumsden
10 others
Alexander Burnett
Katherine Arbuthnot
5 others
Alexander Burnett
Katherine Gordon
8 others

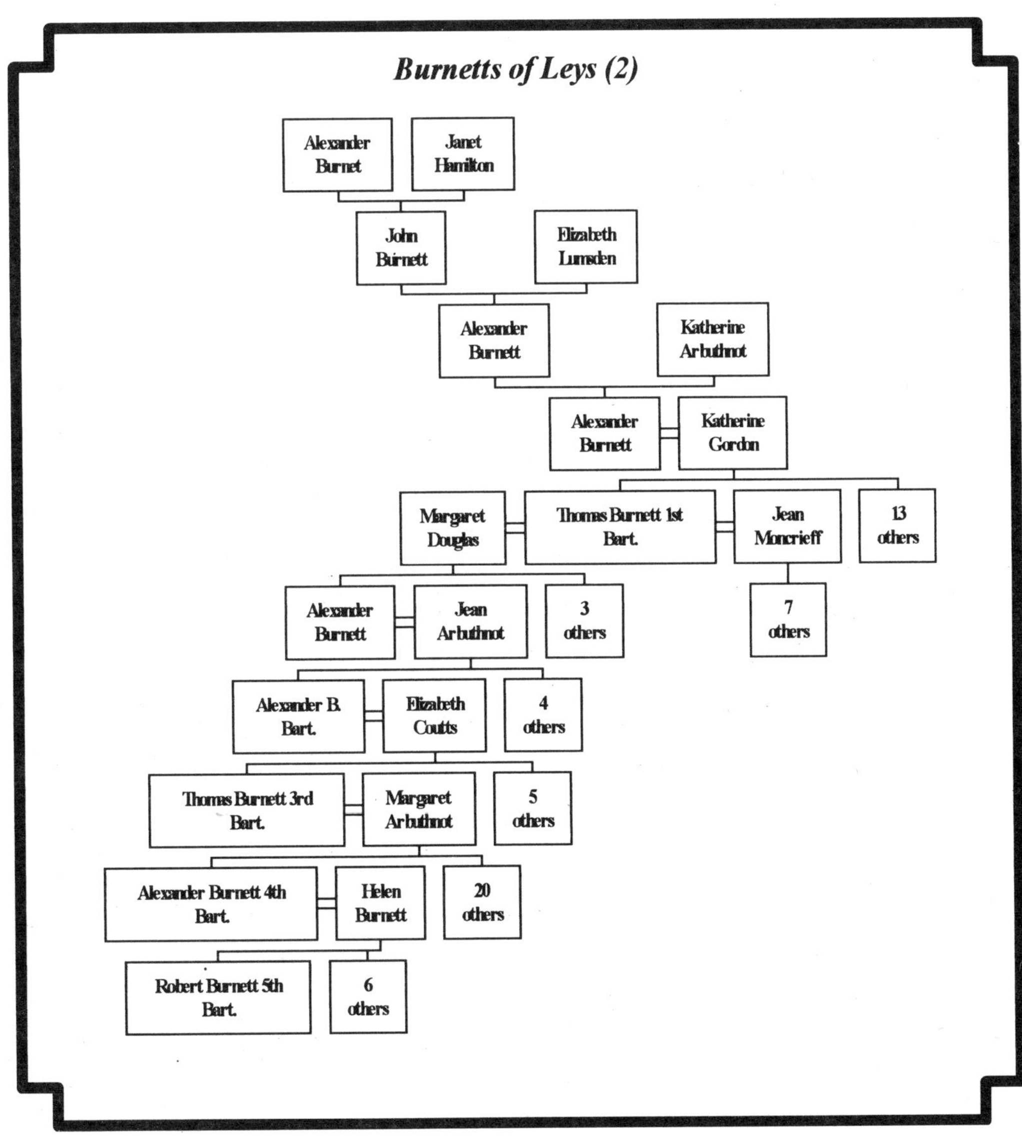
Burnetts of Leys (2)
Alexander Burnet
Janet Hamilton
John Burnett
Elizabeth Lumsden
Alexander Burnett
Katherine Arbuthnot
Alexander Burnett
Katherine Gordon
Margaret Douglas
Thomas Burnett 1st Bart.
Jean Moncrieff
13 others
Alexander Burnett
Jean Arbuthnot
3 others
7 others
Alexander B. Bart.
Elizabeth Coutts
4 others
Thomas Burnett 3rd Bart.
Margaret Arbuthnot
5 others
Alexander Burnett 4th Bart.
Helen Burnett
20 others
Robert Burnett 5th Bart.
6 others

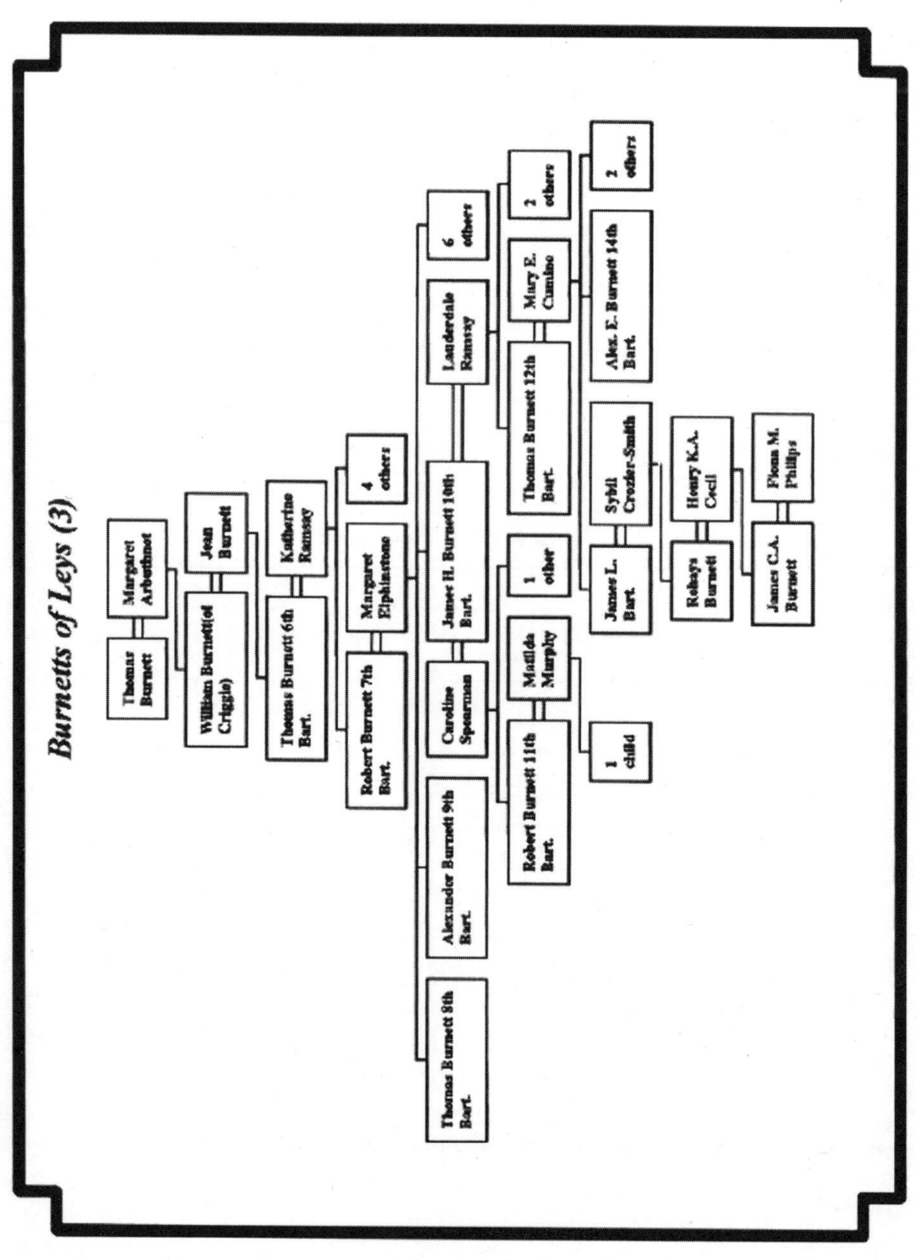
Burnetts of Leys (3)
Thomas Burnett
Margaret Arbuthnot
William Burnett(of Criggie)
Jean Burnett
Thomas Burnett 6th Bart.
Katherine Ramsay
Robert Burnett 7th Bart.
Margaret Elphinstone
4 others
Thomas Burnett 8th Bart.
Alexander Burnett 9th Bart.
Caroline Spearman
James H. Burnett 10th Bart.
Lauderdale Ramsay
6 others
Robert Burnett 11th Bart.
Matilda Murphy
1 other
Thomas Burnett 12th Bart.
Mary E. Cumine
2 others
1 child
James L. Bart.
Sybil Crozier-Smith
Alex. E. Burnett 14th Bart.
2 others
Rohays Burnett
Henry K.A. Cecil
James C.A. Burnett
Fiona M. Phillips

4

THE BURNETTS OF CRAIGMYLE & CRIMOND

Eileen A. Bailey

BURNETTS OF CRAIGMYLE

James Burnett of Craigmyle was the son of Alexander Burnett of Leys and immediate younger brother of Sir Thomas Burnett, 1st Baronet of Leys. A peacemaker, his name occurs often in the role of negotiator and adviser of moderate councils, for example, shortly before his death he tried to make Huntly disband his troops.

In terms of a family compact made in 1598, he married in 1608, when not much more than 18 years of age, **Elizabeth Burnett**, daughter and heir of Thomas Burnett of Craigmyle and Tillihaikie. This Thomas was the grandson and representative of William Burnett of Craigour, Campbell and Tillihaikie who fell at the Battle of Pinkie in 1547, an ancestor of Burnetts of Campbell, Elrick, etc. Thomas Burnett seemed to have acquired Craigmyle through his mother, the heiress of a family of Craigmyle of that Ilk who appear on record in the fifteenth century as holding Craigmyle directly from the Crown. In November 1608, Thomas Burnett resigned his lands of Craigmyle, Pitmedden and Mill of Craigmyle into the hands of the Earl of Huntly, superior, in favour of his daughter Elizabeth and her husband James Burnett on their marriage. They had sasine, on 9 November 1608, reserving the life-rent of half to Thomas Burnett.

By his marriage to Elizabeth, James Burnett was able to add large properties in the parishes of Kincardine o' Neil, Skene and Fetteresso to those that he already held at Craigmyle and Pitmedden. These additions were partly in absolute property and partly in wadset from the Earl Marischal, Sir William Douglas of Glenbervie and others. This made James almost as considerable a laird as his brother, Sir Thomas Burnett, the 1st Baronet. The parish records of Fetteresso (Stonehaven) show him as resident in, and an elder of, that parish with six of his children being baptised between 1620 and 1633. It is not known whether his residence at that time was Muchalls or Auquhorthies which was wadsetted to him for 3000 marks from the Earl Marischal. James and Elizabeth Burnett had the following children:

- Alexander (Mr.) Burnett. He was successor to his father in Craigmyle.

- Thomas Burnett who became the 1st laird of Kemnay (details are given in Chapter 5).
- James Burnett of Lagavin & Monboddo (details are given in Chapter 6).
- Robert (Mr.) Burnett was baptised in Fetteresso parish on 18 April 1620. He became Robert Burnett of Cowtoun, Muchalls & Criggie, Tutor of Leys and guardian of Sir Thomas Burnett, 3rd Baronet. Robert Burnett married (1) on 22 December 1646, Jean Mortimer, daughter of John Mortimer, Baillie of Aberdeen. There were no children of the marriage. Robert married (2) in 1682, Helen Arbuthnot who later became the wife of John Sandilands of Countesswells. Robert and Helen had the following children:
  - Helen Burnett who inherited the largest share of her father's estate, including Cowtoun. She married, in 1697, Alexander Burnett the Younger of Leys who later became the 4th Baronet.
  - Agnes Burnett who married in accordance with her father's wishes (1), in 1701, Thomas Burnet of Glenbervie. Agnes later married (2) Sir William Nicholson of Glenbervie.
  - Jean Burnett who married William Burnett, later of Criggie. They were the parents of Thomas Burnett, 6th Baronet.
- Jean Burnett who married Robert Arbuthnot of Little Fiddes.
- Mary Burnett who married, according to contact made about 1661, Alexander Forbes of Corsinday. She died at Kemnay and was buried at Midmar on 1 November 1700.
- Helen Burnett who was baptised in Fetteresso parish on 21 January 1623 and died young.
- William Burnett who was baptised in Fetteresso parish on 10 February 1624 and died young.
- Margaret Burnett who was baptised in Fetteresso parish on 9 September 1625 and died young.
- George Burnett who was baptised in Fetteresso parish on 10 April 1628 and died young.
- John Burnett who was baptised in Fetteresso parish on 6 June 1633 and died young.

James Burnett of Craigmyle died in late 1644 or early 1645.

(Mr.) Alexander Burnett of Craigmyle was the eldest son of James Burnett of Craigmyle. He was admitted to the Scottish Bar on 12 July 1642. By 1646 he was Commissioner of Supply for Aberdeenshire and a member of the Committee of War for Kincardineshire. In the Indemnity Act of 1662, Alexander Burnett of Craigmyle's fine for indemnity was £2,400. Alexander Burnett married, on 5 June 1649, Christian Fraser, daughter of Thomas Fraser of Strichen and Christian Forbes, daughter of John Forbes of Pitsligo. Alexander and Christian Burnett had the following children:

- ❑ Alexander Burnett who succeeded his father in Craigmyle.
- ❑ Thomas Burnett who died unmarried. His brother Alexander was served Tutor to him on 3 September 1678.
- ❑ Elizabeth Burnett who married, according to contract dated 8 February 1688, James Gordon of Corfarroch.
- ❑ Anne Burnett who married George Gordon of Terpersie. They had a child:
  - ♦ Charles Gordon.
- ❑ Jean Burnett who was born in 1667. She married her cousin-german, Andrew Burnett, son of Thomas Burnett of Kemnay. Her brother Alexander was served Tutor to her on 3 April 1678.

Alexander Burnett died in about 1677.

Sir Alexander Burnett of Craigmyle was the eldest son of Mr Alexander Burnett and succeeded him in about 1677. The lands which made up his titles were Craigmyle and Pitmedden, Easter Skene, Milboy, Hill of Keir, Rogershill, Garlogie, and from 1678, the barony of Easter Skene, Craigour and Mill of Campbell, Fordyce, Cormore and Croft of Wester Campbell (called Alehousecroft), all of which were held by Sir Thomas Burnett of Leys. His arms were recorded in the Lyon Register in 1678. On 7 September 1681 Alexander Burnett was granted authority from Parliament to hold two annual fairs and a weekly market at Kirkton of Skene. At the end of 1682 or early in 1683 he was knighted by King Charles I. It is said that he had built *a very fine loaft (loft) in the Church of Kincardine, fairly coloured and to be seen intire.* [William Robertson, *Description of Parish of Kincardine o' Neil*, (1725)].

Alexander Burnett married Nicholas Young, daughter of Peter Young of Auldbar. Alexander died in 1694 after which Nicholas married (2) in 1696, Sir Charles Maitland, 2nd Baronet of Pittrichie. Alexander and Nicholas had the following children:

- ❑ Isabel Burnett, born before 1684, married in 1695 or 1696, John Farquharson of Invercauld. All of their children died young. She predeceased her husband who married (2) Christian daughter of Robert Menzies of that Ilk, (3) Margaret daughter of Lord James Murray and (4) Jean Forbes of Waterton. John Farquharson died in 1750 at which time his brother, Alexander Farquharson of Monaltries, purchased Craigmyle.
- ❑ Anne/Anna Burnett, born before 1684, died unmarried in 1697. Her inheritance went to her two sisters.
- ❑ Margaret Burnett married (1) Sir Charles Maitland of Pitrichie, the son of her stepfather and (2) on 24 April 1705, Sir Thomas Erskine of Pittodrie. He died in 1750. Margaret and Thomas Erskine had the following children:
  - ♦ William Erskine, baptised on 21 November 1708 in St. Nicholas parish. Being of feeble mind, he did not succeed to Pittodrie and died before November 1746. The succession went to a daughter of Sir Thomas Erskine,

from his second marriage to Anne Forbes, daughter of James 15th of Forbes who later married Col. Henry Knight.
- Nicholas (daughter) Erskine was baptised on 12 June 1712 in St.Nicholas parish.

The Craigmyle branch then became extinct in the male line.

BURNETTS OF CRIMOND

The Burnetts of Crimond descend from **Robert Burnett**, brother of Sir Thomas Burnett of Leys, 1st Baronet. Robert was born in 1592 the third son of Alexander Burnett and Katherine Gordon. He spent seven years in France for his early education studying law. A letter to his elder brother, Thomas, was written from Castres on 24 November 1611. In it he complained about the level of allowance from his father which was not sufficient. Robert Burnett was admitted to the Scottish Bar in 1617. He was regarded as a man of great learning, high moral and religious principles. Robert acquired several estates in Aberdeenshire namely Banachtie and Mill of Boutie, from William Seton of Meldrum, in 1628 and Crimond, from John Johnston of that Ilk, in 1634, plus the smaller property of Kendal near Montkegie. He also acquired Carlops and Stobo, in 1656. These lands, which have been mentioned earlier in this volume in connection with the Burnets of Barns, later passed to his son and heir, Thomas Burnett. On account of his opposition to, and refusal to subscribe to, the Solemn League and Covenant, Robert was compelled to go into exile on three occasions, once for a period of five years. On his return to Scotland, and after Charles II came to the throne in 1649, he was made a Judge of the Court of Session in 1661, with the title Lord Crimond. He lived only a few months thereafter and died on 27th August 1661.

Robert Burnett married (1) in 1620, Beatrix Maule, daughter of William Maule of Glaster, son of Robert Maule of Panmure. Beatrix died in 1622. Robert & Beatrix Burnett had one child:
- Bethia Burnett, born in 1622 who died in 1624.

Robert Burnett married (2) before 1629, Rachel Johnston, daughter of James Johnston, merchant in Edinburgh, and sister of Lord Warriston. Robert and Rachel had the following children:
- Alexander Burnett who was born in 1629 and died young.
- Robert Burnett who was born in 1630. He was admitted to the Scottish Bar in 1656 and died unmarried in 1662.
- James Burnett who was born in 1635 and died young.
- Thomas Burnett who was born in 1638, probably in Edinburgh. He was a student of medicine in Montpellier, later a practising physician in Edinburgh. Dr Burnett became Sir Thomas Burnett, Physician successively to King Charles II, James II, William III and Queen Anne. He was a founder member of the

Royal College of Physicians of Edinburgh along with his great friend, Sir Robert Sibbald. He married, in 1662, Janet, daughter of Robert Bruce of Blairhall, granddaughter of Sir George Bruce of Carnock & Broomhall, Fife, and sister of the Countess of Kincardine. On 1 October 1662, Thomas Burnett was infeft in the lands, which had formerly belonged to the deceased Alexander Burnet of Carlops, Sir Michael Nasmith of Posso and George Browne of Scotstoune. These lands which included Carlops in the Sheriffdom of Peebles and Stobo with its manorplace in the Sheriffdom of Edinburgh, had been acquired by his father, Robert Burnett of Crimond, on 6 March 1656. Thomas Burnett sold them to James Nasmith, eldest son of Sir Michael on 9 September 1665. [*Reg. Great Seal*, XI, 824, Edinburgh, (3 Nov 1665)]. Janet was buried on 30 April 1699 in Greyfriars Churchyard, Edinburgh. Sir Thomas Burnett died in February 1706 in Edinburgh. Their children were:

- ♦ Gilbert Burnett who became an advocate and married a daughter of Sir William Hamilton of Preston. Their daughter was:
  - ☐ Anna Burnett who married James Halyburton of Pitcur.
- ♦ Helen Burnett who married (1) William Crawford, the Younger of Auchinarnes and (2) Ralph Dundas of Manor. Names of their children are not known.
- ♦ Euphemia Burnett who married James Robertson, an advocate. Their daughter was:
  - ☐ Janet Robertson who became Countess of Kincardine from whom the Elgin family are descended.

❑ Gilbert Burnett was born Edinburgh on 18 September 1643. After being instructed in Latin by his father, who by that time had retired to his Aberdeenshire estate, he was sent to Marischal College, Aberdeen, at the age of ten and gained a Master of Arts degree in 1657 before the age of 14. Although originally inclined to the study of law he applied himself to divinity and was licensed to preach in 1661 before he was 18 years of age. In 1663, after the death of his father, he went to England for about six months visiting the universities of Oxford and Cambridge. Gilbert appears to have inherited his father's property of Kendal in Aberdeenshire. He travelled in Holland and France in 1664 and on his arrival back in London he was admitted as a member of the Royal Society. In 1665 he was ordained as a priest by the Bishop of Edinburgh and entered the charge of Saltoun, East Lothian. In 1668 Anne, Duchess of Hamilton, with whom he was acquainted, entrusted him with family papers from which he compiled *Memoirs of the Dukes of Hamilton*, published in London in 1677.

Fig. 4.1 Bishop Gilbert Burnett

Appointed Professor of Divinity at the University of Glasgow in 1669, he married (1) in Glasgow in 1669, Lady Margaret Kennedy, daughter of John, 6th Earl of Cassillis. They had no children. In 1673 Gilbert Burnett became Chaplain to King Charles II but this honorary appointment only lasted one year. In 1675 he resigned his Chair at the University and settled in London for nine years during which time he was appointed Chaplain to the Rolls and Lecturer at St.Clement's.

As a result of his opposition to the Court party in 1683, the year of the Rye House Plot, and his friendship with Lord Russell who was sent to the scaffold, Gilbert returned from a tour of France in 1684 to find himself discharged from the Chaplaincy of the Rolls and also from lecturing at St. Clement's. After the death of King Charles II, Gilbert travelled on the continent before settling at the Hague where he formed a lasting friendship with King William of Orange and his consort Mary. Indeed he accompanied William of Orange to England as his Chaplain. It was at the Hague that Gilbert Burnett married (2) in 1688, Mrs. Maria Scot who died from smallpox in 1698. She was described as "a Dutch lady of large fortune and noble extraction". Maria was descended from the Scots of Buccleuch. For services to King William, Gilbert Burnett was appointed Bishop of Salisbury in 1689 and also Chancellor of the Order of the Garter. Gilbert and Maria had the following children:

- William Burnett who was born at The Hague in 1688. He was educated as a gentleman-commoner at the University of Cambridge, England, and made his profession in Law. William Burnett was one of those who lost financially from the South Seas scheme of 1720. He became Governor of New York and New Jersey in 1720, of Massachusetts in 1728 and then of New Hampshire. William Burnett married (1) Maria Stanhope, daughter of Dr George Stanhope, Dean of Canterbury. Their children were:
  - Gilbert Burnett, born in 1714, whose child
    - Thomas Burnett, born in 1740, became a surgeon at Chigwell, Essex. Thomas Burnett married Margaret (surname unknown) who died at Chigwell on 27 August 1811 aged 83. Thomas Burnett was said to be the last in the male line of descendants of Bishop Burnett. Thomas and Margaret had a daughter:
      - Mary Burnett who died, unmarried, in 1795.

William Burnett married (2) Mary Van Horn, daughter of Abraham Van Horn of New York. William died 17 September 1729 in Boston. Their children were:

- William Burnett who took Holy Orders.
- Thomas Burnett who entered the Army and died unmarried.
- Mary Burnett who married, in 1737, Hon. William Brown of Salem, Massachusetts. Mary Burnett Brown died in 1745 and William in 1763.

- Gilbert Burnett, the second son, was educated at Leyden University and Merton College, Oxford. He took Holy Orders, later becoming Chaplain to King George I in 1718 and Rector of East Barnet. Gilbert was considered to be a distinguished author contributing to a periodical *Hibernicus's Letters* published in Dublin in 1725-26 and *The Free Thinker* which was later collected into 3 volumes. In 1719 he published an abridged version of the third volume of his father's work on the History of the Reformation. Gilbert Burnett died, unmarried, in 1726.
- Thomas Burnett (Sir), the third son, was born in 1694. He studied at Leyden University and Merton Collage, Oxford for a career in Law. In 1712 and 1713 he wrote several political pamphlets in favour of the Whigs and against the administration of the last four years of Queen Anne's reign. As a result of one of these he was arrested in January 1713. Considered to be one of the best lawyers of his time, Thomas was, for several years, employed in the diplomatic service as Secretary to the King at Ratisbon, and then as Consul at Lisbon. In November 1741 he was made a Judge of the Common Pleas. Thomas Burnett edited his father's work *The History of my own Time* and was author of a memoir of the Bishop published within it. He was knighted on 2 November 1745 and was admitted as a member of the Royal Society. Sir Thomas Burnett died, unmarried, at his home in Lincoln's Inn Fields on 7 January 1753 (an inscription found on his coffin apparently read 17 May 1753) in his 59th year. He was buried in the vault of St James's at Clerkenwell beside his father.
- Mary Burnett married in 1712 to David Mitchell, nephew of Admiral Mitchell. They had:
  - James Mitchell
  - Mary Mitchell.

  Mary Burnett Mitchell and the children died before 1788.
- Elizabeth Burnett married to Lord Chancellor Richard West, of Ireland. Their children were:
  - Richard West who had no children.
  - Mary West who married John Williams of Pembroke. They had a child:
    - Unknown son Williams who was the Vicar of Wellisbourne, in Warwickshire, by 1789 and had three children.

Gilbert Burnett, shortly after the death of Maria in 1698, married (3) Elizabeth Blake, widow of Robert Berkley of Spetchley, Worcester, and eldest daughter of Sir

Richard Blake. Gilbert and Elizabeth Burnett had two daughters who died in infancy. Elizabeth died in 1708 and Gilbert Burnett died of pleurisy on 17 March 1715 at St. John's Court, Clerkenwell where he had spent the last five years of his life in retirement. He was buried in the vault of St. James's Church, Clerkenwell. The letter to Sir Alexander Burnett of Leys announcing the death of Bishop Burnett is preserved in the Crathes Papers.

Bishop Burnett made a bequest of twenty thousand merks Scots to the parish of Saltoun and to Marischal College, Aberdeen. He wrote *in remembrance of my education there...and I order the Lairds of Leys, as long as the Estate is in the Family of Burnetts, to have every year a Scholar in the First Class of the College...as I do also desire, that to the said Scholarships, one of the Name of Burnett may be preferred, if he is duely qualified for it.*

Sources (additional to those noted within the text):

Burnett, G., (ed.) Allardyce, J., *The Family of Burnett of Leys, (1901), Spalding Club.*

Parish registers, Fetteresso.

Irving, J., *The Book of Eminent Scotsmen*, (1880), Paisley.

Crathes Archives.

5

THE BURNETTS OF KEMNAY

Eileen A. Bailey

Fragments they leave us of the world's old story. Fragments we muse and gaze upon and sigh. Had we been there – in those bright days of glory! Had we a faithful record 'neath our eye!
(Christina Leslie Burnett, *The Shades of the Past*, 1857) (1)

James Burnett was the immediate younger brother of Sir Thomas Burnett, 1st Baronet of Leys, both being sons of Alexander Burnett of Leys. James Burnett married Elizabeth Burnett, daughter and heiress of Thomas Burnett of Craigmyle and Tillihaikie, in 1608.

The second son of James and Elizabeth Burnett was **Thomas Burnet of Kemnay, 1st laird,** who was a Writer (lawyer) in Edinburgh. Thomas Burnet married, on 5 October 1655 in Edinburgh, Margaret Pearson, daughter of John Pearson, a Merchant in Edinburgh and Margaret Byres. They made their home in Edinburgh at Parson's Close (formerly called Pearson's Close). In 1688, with a charter dated 20 July, Thomas purchased Kemnay estate on Donside from Sir George Nicolson, a Lord of Session under the title Lord Kemnay. The mansion house there was built by Sir Thomas Crosbie in the seventeenth century reputedly in place of, and in a higher location to the south-east of, an older residence which had belonged to the Auchinlecks and the Douglases of Glenbervie. The original house is said to have closely resembled Muchalls. Thomas and Margaret Burnett had the following children:

- Thomas Burnett who was born in 1656 and died on 26 February 1729 He succeeded his father to become the 2nd of Kemnay.
- Andrew Burnett who became a Writer to the Signet in Edinburgh. He married, in 1697, Jean Burnett, daughter of Alexander Burnett of Craigmyle. Andrew died in 1726. Both he and his wife were buried in the Drum Aisle of St. Nicholas Church, Aberdeen.
- Robert Burnett who was born in 1662 in Edinburgh and died young
- Alexander Burnett who was born in 1668 in Edinburgh and died young.
- James Burnett who was born in 1672 in Edinburgh and died young.
- Margaret Burnett who was born in 1676 in Edinburgh and died young.
- Rachel Burnett who was born in 1679 in Edinburgh and died in 1732.

There was little time to enjoy the newly purchased property, however, as Margaret Burnett died that year, in November 1688. Both Thomas Burnet who died in February 1689, and his wife, were buried at Kemnay.

Thomas Burnett of Kemnay, 2nd laird, born in 1656, succeeded his father in 1689. After studying abroad, he was admitted to the Scottish Bar. Thomas was part of the Court Circle of the Electress Sophia in Hanover. Whilst in Paris in 1702 he was arrested on some fictitious charge because of his association with Hanover and spent eighteen months in the Bastille. On his release in 1703 he went to Geneva. When he was 57, Thomas Burnett married in 1713, Elizabeth Brickenden (known by the family as Betty Brickenden), daughter of Richard Brickenden of Inkpen, Berkshire, England. Thomas died on 26 February 1729. His widow Elizabeth later married (2) Dr. George Lamont who had been tutor to the children and this caused some family upset at the time. Dr. Lamont went on to become a distinguished physician in London. Elizabeth died there and was buried in St. Pancras Churchyard as was her daughter Anna. George Lamont died on 8 November 1789 at Tunbridge Wells, Kent where he owned a large amount of property. Thomas and Elizabeth Burnett had the following children:

- George Burnett who was baptised on 29 September 1714 in Aberdeen. He became the 3rd laird of Kemnay.
- Anna Burnett was born in 1717 and died in 1787.
- Elizabeth Burnett was born in 1721 and died in 1723.

George Burnett of Kemnay, 3rd laird, was born on 29 September 1714 and succeeded his father in 1729. He married (1) in 1734, Helen Burnett, daughter of Sir Alexander Burnett of Leys. George Burnett was known as an agricultural improver. He was very interested in horticulture resulting in his undertaking extensive planting of trees and laying out of gardens at Kemnay. George and Helen Burnett had the following children:

- Helen (Nellie) Burnett who was born in 1734 and died in 1810.
- Alexander Burnett who was born on 3 July 1735 and died in 1802. He became the 4th laird of Kemnay.
- Anne Burnett who was born in 1736 and died in 1782,
- Jane/Jean Burnett who was born in 1739. She married, in July 1763, Alexander Dunbar of Boath, Auldearn, in the county of Nairn. They had at least two sons both of whom studied medicine at Edinburgh University. Jean died in 1764 and was buried at Auldearn.
- Elizabeth Burnett who was born in 1738 or 1740 and died in 1807.
- Mary Burnett who was baptised on 15 June 1743 in St. Paul's Episcopal Chapel, Aberdeen. Godparents were Dr James Gordon of Hilton and John Burnet of Elrick. [St. Paul's Baptismal records] Mary died in 1802.

Helen Burnett died on 21 September 1750 and was buried at Kemnay.

Every year, the five daughters were sent to school in Edinburgh, travelling the long distance between Kemnay and Edinburgh on horseback with a male servant to take care of them.
George Burnett married (2), on 25 October 1751, Janet Dyce, daughter of James Dyce of Disblair. There were no children of this marriage. George who died on 31 October 1780 was buried at Kemnay. His second wife, Janet, died on 16 July 1802. Both wives were buried in the same grave in Kemnay Churchyard.

Alexander Burnett of Kemnay, 4th laird, born on 3 July 1735, succeeded his father George in 1780. He was educated at Leyden and, in 1756, was appointed Secretary to Mr. Mitchell of Thainston (who later became Sir Andrew Mitchell), the newly appointed Ambassador to the Prussian Courts. Alexander Burnett attended Frederick the Great during the Seven Years War and after Sir Andrew Mitchell's death remained for a further year at Berlin as Charge' d'Affaires. Alexander Burnett married, in 1781, Christian Leslie, born 1 October 1761, daughter of John Leslie, Professor of Greek at Aberdeen and Christian Fraser (the heiress of Powis). Christian Fraser was the granddaughter of Alexander Fraser, 1st laird of Powis. Alexander and Christian Burnett had the following children:

- George Burnett, who was baptised on 17 May 1783 and died in January 1784 of smallpox.
- Helen Burnett who was born on 19 December 1784. She married, on 26 April 1805 at Kemnay, Dr. James Bannerman, Professor of Medicine at University of Aberdeen, 2nd son of Sir Alexander Bannerman of Elsick. Dr Bannerman's father inherited Kirkhill (see also Burnetts of Kirkhill in Chapter 7). Helen died at Old Aberdeen on 23 April 1864 aged 80, her husband having predeceased her. There were no children of their marriage.
- John Burnett, who was born on 5 June and baptised on 8 June 1786 at Kemnay, became the 5th laird of Kemnay. John died on 22 December 1847.
- Elizabeth Burnett was baptised on 9 December 1787 [memorial inscription at Kemnay gives birth date as 5 January 1788]. She remained unmarried and died on 18 July 1806.
- Christian Burnett who was born on 17 October and baptised 21 October 1789, remained unmarried. She lived latterly at Don Street, Old Aberdeen where she died on 9 May 1874.
- Lamont (daughter) Burnett who was born on 2 June and baptised on 7 June 1791 also remained unmarried. She died on 27 September 1842.

Alexander Burnett died on 30 December 1802. Christian Burnett, died in Old Aberdeen on 14 February 1842 aged 80 [ref. *Aberdeen Journal* Obituaries in 1842 although memorial inscription at Kemnay Churchyard gives date of death as 1841].

John Burnett of Kemnay, 5th laird, who was born on 5 June 1786, succeeded his father in 1802. He proceeded to add to and improve the property and woodlands. John Burnett married, on 10 June 1814 in St. Cuthbert's parish, Edinburgh, Mary Stuart, born 14 July 1786, daughter of Charles Stuart of Dunearn, Fife. The Stuarts of Dunearn trace their family ancestry back to the Regent Moray. John and Mary Burnett had the following children:

- Mary Erskine Burnett who was born on 5 May 1815 in St. Cuthbert's parish, Edinburgh. In 1881, at the time of the British census, she was living at Balbithan House, Keithhall, near Inverurie with her brother Stuart Burnett. Mary died on 25 April 1890 and was buried at Kemnay.
- Alexander George Burnett who was born on 6 November 1816. He became the 6th laird of Kemnay and died in 1908.
- Christian/ Christina Leslie Burnett who was born on 1 September 1818 and died on 20 October 1866. She was buried at Kemnay.
- Charles John Burnett who was born on 18 August 1820 and died in 1907.
- George Burnett who was born on 9 March 1822 at Kemnay. George was admitted to the Scottish Bar in 1845, was appointed Lyon Depute in 1863 and Lord Lyon of Arms in 1866. He married, on 13 August 1870 in Dresden, his cousin, Alison Stuart, daughter of John Alexander Stuart, son of Charles Stuart of Dunearn. In the 1881 British census, George Burnett, his wife and children were resident at 21 Walker Street, Edinburgh where their household included four servants - nurse, cook, tablemaid and housemaid. George Burnett was the original author of *The Family of Burnett of Leys* but died on 23 January 1890 before his research could be completed and published. The final manuscript was prepared from his notes by James Allardyce in 1901. George Burnett was buried at St. Cuthbert's, Edinburgh. George and Alison Burnett had the following children:
  - John George Burnett who was born on 30 March 1876 in Edinburgh. He gained an MA degree and was appointed a Justice of the Peace. John became the **7th laird of Powis** in June 1894 on the death of Isabella Leslie, 6th in the succession of Powis (niece of Christian Leslie Burnett). He married, in 1901, Catherine Sarah Helen Irvine, daughter of Capt. Duncan Malcolm Irvine of Killadeas, Co. Fermanagh, Ireland. John Burnett served as Member of Parliament for North Aberdeen from 1931-35. (details of the Burnetts of Powis are continued in Chapter 8)
  - Alice Christina Burnett, born on 19 September 1874 in Edinburgh, married a Mr. Holloway and had children whose names are not known.
- Stuart Moubray Burnett who was born on 5 July 1824. In the 1881 British census he is recorded as living at Balbithan House, Keithhall parish, where he farmed 15 acres. He died unmarried on 9 January 1893 and was buried at Old Machar, Aberdeen.
- Henry Martyn Burnett, born on 2 April 1826, died on 12 July 1881 at Perth and was buried at Kemnay.

- Erskine William Burnett, who was born on 16 December 1828 died, unmarried, at Dunoon, on 31 October 1848 aged 19. He was buried at Kemnay.

John Burnett died on 22 December 1847 at 5 Church Terrace, Great Malvern and was buried at Kemnay as was his wife Mary who died on 1 March 1872.

Alexander George Burnett of Kemnay, 6th laird, was born 6 November 1816 and succeeded his father in 1847. He married (1) on 2 September 1849 at Kemnay, Letitia Amelia Kendall, born 25 December 1826, daughter of William Kendall of Bourton, Glos. She died on 30 April 1855 and was buried at Kemnay. Amelia Kendall was a direct descendant of Oliver Cromwell (1599-1698), General and Lord Protector, through the line of his son Henry. Alexander and Letitia Burnett had the following children:

- Letitia Wilkins Burnett who was born on 27 November 1850 at Kemnay. In 1881, she was a boarder with Martha Anne Lloyd at 3 Otway Terrace, Lambeth, England. Letitia died in 1936.
- John Alexander Burnett who was born on 12 August 1852 at Kemnay and died in 1935. He became the 7th Laird of Kemnay. John married, in 1877, Charlotte Susan Gordon, daughter of Arthur Forbes Gordon of Rayne. They had 4 sons and 2 daughters whose names are not known.
- William Kendall Burnett who was born at Kemnay House on 6 February 1854. He was educated at Oxford, gaining MA and LLD degrees in 1876. William was apprenticed to the firm of Duncan & Morice and was admitted as an Advocate in Aberdeen in 1880. He was a Notary Public, a Justice of the Peace and a Magistrate of Aberdeen from 1904-8 and 1910-11. An enthusiastic genealogist, William married (1) in Colraine on 14 June 1883, Margaretta Mary Carson, daughter of Dr. James C. L. Carson, JP, of Coleraine. Margaretta died on 17 July 1905. Children of the marriage were:
    - Ian Alistair Kendall Burnett, who was born in Aberdeen on 20 June 1885, was a pupil at Aberdeen Grammar School. He gained an MA degree in 1907 and took up a post as Assistant Librarian, Royal Scottish Museum, Edinburgh in 1909, then at the British Museum Rare Books Division, London in 1910. He gained a second degree of BSc. in Economics, at London in 1913. Ian served in the 8th Battalion, East Lancashire Regiment from December 1914. He saw active service in France from April 1915, was promoted to the rank of Captain in January 1917 and was killed in action on 31 May 1917.[ref. Aberdeen Grammar School]
    - Kathleen Elizabeth Burnett.
    - Amy Verena Carson Burnett who was born on 6 August 1889 at The Grove, Kemnay.
    - Olive Kendall Burnett.

William Kendall Burnett married (2), on 25 April 1907, Florence Emma Hargreaves, younger daughter of T. L. Hargreaves of Hull. He died in 1912.

- Amelia Burnett, who was born on 22 April 1855 at Elie, Fife, married Rev. James Stark in December 1908. Amelia died in December 1941.

Alexander George Burnett married (2) on 1 August 1877 at Pembury, Kent, Anna-Maria Pledge, born 7 March 1849 in Old Machar parish, daughter of Rev. Ebenezer Pledge of Pembury Chapel, Kent, and Frances Sarah Sangford. Anna died in September 1885 and was buried at Kemnay. Alexander and Anna-Maria Burnett had the following children:

- Ebenezer Erskine (known as Erskine) Burnett who was born on 25 June 1878, at Kemnay House. He was a pupil at Aberdeen Grammar School. In 1897 he went to Agricultural College at Guelph, Ontario, Canada and latterly was engaged in farming and fruit growing at Vernon, British Columbia. Erskine died in 1951.
- Alexander Douglas Gilbert Burnett was born on 7 June 1879, at the Cockburn Hotel, 1 Cockburn Street, Edinburgh but his birth was registered in Kemnay parish. He was a pupil of Aberdeen Grammar School and followed a career as manager of tea and rubber estates in Ceylon. Alexander served as a Private in *Service Automobile*, 39th Division, French Army, from April 1916 to March 1918 and was awarded the Croix de Guerre on 17 July 1917. Like Bishop Burnett, he married a Margaret Kennedy. Their children were:
  - Arthur Burnett whose spouse is unknown. He served as a regular officer in the Royal Navy.
  - Ian Burnett.
  - Elizabeth Burnett.

  Alexander D.G. Burnett died in 1962. A memorial inscription is close to the wall of Kemnay Church.
- Henry Martyn Burnett was born on 5 August 1881 at Kemnay House. Henry was a pupil of Aberdeen Grammar School and later a Clerk in the Union Bank of Scotland, Aberdeen in 1899. He then had a post at the National Bank of India in London in 1902 before going to the London & Brazilian Bank in Para, Brazil in 1904. Henry became involved in the rubber business in Para and Northern Brazil from 1909 to 1911 and was latterly with Manaos Harbour Ltd. He died in Manaos, Brazil, on 12 April 1915. [ref. Aberdeen Grammar School] His name is inscribed along with that of his brother A. D. Gilbert Burnett on a memorial at Kemnay churchyard.
- Octavius Winslow Burnett was born and died in 1882.
- Stuart Alexander Burnett was born on 31 May 1883 at Kemnay House and died in the same year.
- Frances Mary Stuart Burnett was born on 20 May 1884 and died on 23 October 1976.

Alexander George Burnett married (3) in 1893, Emily Julia Burch, daughter of Joseph Burch, Woolgrower, and Margaret Wainwright, Tuddenham Hall, Ipswich. There were no children of this marriage. Emily died of pneumonia and chronic diabetes on 15 February 1908, at Kemnay House aged 71. Her husband Alexander died of influenza a few days later, on 19 February 1908, at Kemnay House, aged 91.

John Alexander Burnett of Kemnay, 7th laird, was born on 12 August 1852. He married, in 1877, Charlotte Susan Forbes Gordon, daughter of Arthur Forbes Gordon of Rayne. At the time of his father's death, John was resident at 14 De Lanne Street, Knightsbridge, London S2. John Burnett died in 1935 in London. John and Charlotte Burnett had the following children:

- Arthur Moubray Burnett who was born at Saplinbrae, Old Deer, Aberdeenshire on 24 December 1878 and died on 10 July 1948. In April 1881, he was recorded in the census as a visitor at the home of his grandmother, Charlotte F. Gordon, at 16 Rutland Square, Edinburgh. In the same census, Charlotte Gordon was recorded as aged 66, born in Ireland. Arthur became the 8th laird of Kemnay.
- Lettie Muriel Burnett who was born at Saplinbrae, Old Deer, Aberdeenshire on 1st June 1880. In April 1881 she, too, was recorded as a visitor at the home of her grandmother, Charlotte (Forbes) Gordon at 16 Rutland Square, Edinburgh. After she returned from being a governess at the Russian Imperial Court, she became a Roman Catholic at the age of 23 and was admitted to the Sacred Heart Order of Nuns in 1913. She became Mistress-general at the Sacred Heart Convent at Roehampton. Lettie died at Daviot, Aberdeenshire in 1966.
- Charles Stuart Burnett who was born at Brown's Valley, Minnesota, USA, on 3 April 1882 and died in 1945. His distinguished career deserves specific mention. The following details are from a short biographical article by A.W. Clarke. (2)

  Charles Stuart Burnett was educated at Bedford Grammar School from where he joined the Imperial Yeomanry at 17 and served in the South African War from 1899-1901. Charles received the Queen's Medal with three clasps for his service. He was wounded during a three-year secondment, from 1903, to the West African Frontier Force. He was twice mentioned in dispatches and received the Queen's Medal with four clasps. By 1907, he had been promoted to the rank of Lieutenant in the Highland Light Infantry. In 1909 he was involved in a business venture in Portuguese Guinea and by 1911 he was in Government service in Northern Nigeria.

  Charles Burnett returned to the services at the commencement of World War I and qualified as a pilot on 24 November 1914, becoming a flight commander in No.17 Squadron of the Royal Flying Corps in 1915 and in command of No. 12 Squadron in France in 1916-17. He was again mentioned in dispatches. In 1917 he was in the Middle East and in 1918 commanded No. 5 Wing of the

Palestine Brigade of the RAF. Charles was awarded the DSO in 1918, created a CBE in 1919 and gained an additional three mentions in dispatches. In 1920 he commanded RAF operations in Iraq and returned there as Air Chief Staff Officer with the rank of Air Commodore. He was again in Iraq in 1932 as Air Officer Commanding. He was created a CB in 1927 and a KCB in 1936. In 1939 he became Inspector General of the RAF and was part of the British military mission to the Soviet Union in that year. A few months later, in December, he was chosen to become Chief of Air Staff, Royal Australian Air Force, from February 1940, a post which he held until March 1942. In 1943 he was recalled from retirement to take up the post of Commandant, Central Command, Air Training Corps.

Charles Stuart Burnett married on 30 November 1914 at the Registry Office, St. Martins, London, Sybil Maud Bell, daughter of John Bell of Saltburn, Yorkshire. Sybil, a relation of Gertrude Bell, was the former wife of Henry Pack-Beresford. Charles and Sybil had the following children:

- Sybil (Buntie) Burnett who was born on 23 August 1913. Sybil and her husband, Marcus Swann, whom she married in Australia, had the following children:
  - Charles Swann who was born on 18 December 1943 in Australia and married Jenny Smith.
    - Gilbert Swann.
    - Martha Swann.
  - Ann Swann who was born on 30 May 1946 in Australia married (1) Robert Hudson and (2) James Martin with whom she had the following children:
    - Stewart James Martin born in Inverurie.
    - Christina Martin born in Aberdeen.

  Sybil Burnett Swann died in Aberdeen in September 1983.
- Joan Burnett who was born in 1915 and died in 1997 in Argyllshire.
- Katherine Burnett who married James Crearer and had the following children:
  - Alison Sybil Crearer
  - Helen Crearer who married Shaun Roper. Their children:
    - Clare Roper.
    - Lucy Roper.
- Ann Burnett who married Humphrey Stratton and had the following children:
  - Jane Stratton who married Junior Bellamy. Their children:
    - Eliza Bellamy.
    - Robyn Bellamy who married John Taylor in 1999.
  - John Stratton who married (1) Teresa Sheahan. Their children:

- ➢ Finella Stratton.
- ➢ Rosalind Stratton.

Teresa died in 1990-1996. John married (2) Lucy Cole. Their child:

- ➢ Isabella Stratton.

- □ Diana Stratton who married Richard Paxman. Their children:
  - ➢ Oliver Paxman.
  - ➢ Lucy Paxman.
  - ➢ Rebecca Paxman.
- □ Louise Stratton.

Air Chief Marshall, Charles Stuart Burnett died on 9 April 1945 at the RAF Hospital, Halton.

- ❑ Thomas Leslie Forbes Burnett who was born at Devil's Lake, Dakota, USA on 29 September 1885 and died in Old Aberdeen in 1940. He married (1) Helen Morton Corsar. They had the following children:
  - ♦ Thomas Alexander Forbes Burnett who was born in 1913. He married Olive (surname not known) who died in 1996. Their children:
    - □ Thomas Alexander Forbes Burnett who married Elizabeth Draiw. Their children:
      - ➢ Thomas L.F. Burnett.
      - ➢ Carol Burnett.
      - ➢ Dawn Burnett.
    - □ Sandra M. Burnett .
    - □ David A.F. Burnett who married (1) Morag Laing. They had one child:
      - ➢ Grant Burnett.

      David Burnett married (2) to Kim (surname not known). Their child:
      - ➢ Cameron Burnett.
  - ♦ Florence Burnett who was born in 1911, died in 1914.
  - ♦ Moubray Burnett who was born on 5 February 1916. He married Mary Cartwright. Their children:
    - □ Nigel Moubray Forbes Burnett who married Maureen Gunn. Their children are:
      - ➢ Christopher Forbes Burnett.
      - ➢ Paul Alexander Burnett.
      - ➢ Nicola Mary Burnett.
    - □ Alexander Donald Burnett who married Elaine Scott. Their children are:
      - ➢ Elizabeth Mary Burnett.
      - ➢ Alexander James Burnett.
      - ➢ Robert Charles Burnett.
    - □ Victoria Mary Rohays Burnett married Michael Stewart who resides in Argentina. Their children, all born in Argentina, are:
      - ➢ James Michael Stewart.

- ➢ Edward Stewart.
- ➢ Thomas Stewart.
- ➢ Charles Stewart.

- Dorothy Burnett was born in 1918 and married Walter Low. Dorothy died in childbirth. Their child:
  - ➢ Diana Low who married Allan Grove. Their children:
    - Daughter Grove.
    - Daughter Grove.

Helen died in 1969. Thomas L.F. Burnett married (2) Eve Diana Fitzgerald. Their children:

- ♦ John Burnett who married Billie (surname not known) and has children.
- ♦ Diana (Pat) Burnett who married and had children.
- ♦ Hazel Burnett who married and had children.
- ♦ Nesta Burnett who died young.
- ♦ Bridget Burnett who married and had six sons.

- ❑ Robert Lindsay Burnett who was born at Saplinbrae, Old Deer, Aberdeenshire on 22 July 1887. Robert Burnett was another member of the family whose distinguished career deserves to be outlined in more detail. The following notes precis an article written by Robert O'Neill. (3)

Robert was educated at Bedford Grammar School and Eastman's College. At an early age, he made up his mind to join the Navy, a career which he commenced by joining the *Britannia* in 1903. An athlete, he qualified as a physical training instructor and had gained the rank of Lieutenant by 1910. Robert served on a number of ships, was given his first command in 1915 and, later, command of destroyers within the Grand Fleet up to 1918. After World War I until 1928, his appointments were in the area of physical training. Robert Burnett was promoted Captain in 1930 after being the executive officer of the *Rodney*. A series of appointments led to him becoming Commodore of the Royal Naval Barracks at Chatham in 1939, followed in 1940 by promotion to acting Rear-Admiral, confirmed shortly thereafter. Following appointment to Vice-Admiral in 1942 he became commander-in-chief, South Atlantic in 1944. He was knighted in 1944. He played a significant role in the strategic countering of the *Scharnhorst*, which contributed to its eventual destruction. Robert became an Admiral in 1946 and retired in May 1950.

Robert married, on 12 July 1915, Ethel Constance Shaw, daughter of R.H. Shaw. They had no children. Sir Robert L. Burnett, who, in his lifetime, was made an O.B.E., C.B., D.S.O., K.B.E., K.C.B., C. St. J., G.B.E., received an honorary degree of LL.D. (Aberdeen 1944) and honours from the Soviet Union, Greece and the Netherlands, died at his London club on 2 July 1959.

- ❑ Irene Dorothy May Burnett, who was born at Braehead, Bridge of Don, Aberdeen on 12 January 1893, died at Daviot, Aberdeenshire on 26 March

1982. She married Quentin Hugh Innes Irvine of Barra and Straloch, second son of Francis Irvine of Drum and Mary Agnes Ramsay of Barra and Straloch. Their children are:

- Mary Dorothea Forbes Irvine who was born in Edinburgh on 28 October 1916. She married Dr. Andrew Bogdan(ovitch) whose parents had escaped from Russia at the time of the Revolution. Their children are:
  - Nicholas Quentin Bogdan, born in Aberdeen.
  - Robert Andrew Bogdan, born in London.
- Francis Charles Quentin Irvine of Barra and Straloch who was born in Edinburgh on 26 January 1918 and married Eve Molly Leicester. Their children:
  - Hugh Ramsay Innes Irvine, born in Old Aberdeen in 1942, died in 1984.
  - David Howard Irvine, born in October 1944, died in 1983.
  - Susan Mary Irvine who married Gerhardt Fichner. Their child:
    - Tobias Alexander Fichner Irvine born in Germany.
- Jean Christian Charlotte Irvine who was born in Edinburgh on 27 January 1924 and married Roger Ker Gibson. Their children:
  - Christina Ker Gibson born at Straloch, Newmachar parish, Aberdeenshire.
  - John Ker Gibson married(1) Nicola (surname not known) and (2) Ginny (surname not Known).

ARTHUR MOUBRAY BURNETT of Kemnay, 8th laird, born at Saplinbrae, Old Deer, on 24 December 1878, succeeded his father in 1935. He served as a midshipman with the Royal Naval Reserve, India to China, during the Boxer Rising 1900-1901. He then served in East Africa with the Calcutta Volunteer Battery 1914 and from 1915-1916 was Captain and Company Commander, 1st Battalion, King's Africa Rifles. He was at GOC's Staff Brigade Office, Bombay until 1918. Arthur became a Partner in Perman & Hynd, Calcutta. He was appointed Justice of the Peace for Aberdeenshire in 1938 and Deputy Lieutenant of the County of Aberdeen in 1946.

Arthur Mowbray Burnett married, on 1 October 1921, Muriel Speed, born 1894 in Daquhai, widow of Seymour Langham who died 1919, and daughter of Col. Henry Andrews Speed, Enmore, Somerset. Children from Muriel's first marriage were Geoffrey Langham born in 1914, Philip Langham born in 1916 and Michael Langham born in Somerset in 1919. Arthur and Muriel Burnett had the following children:

- Susan Letitia Burnett who was born October 1922, in Calcutta and became the 9th laird in the succession of Kemnay.

- ❑ Jean Muriel Moubray Burnett who was born in 1926 in Somerset. And married on 2 November 1946 to Ronald Charles Hicks, Captain in the Royal Artillery. She died in April 2000. Their children:
  - ♦ Robert Moubray Hicks.
  - ♦ Simon Hicks.

SUSAN LETITIA BURNETT, 9th of Kemnay, born on 16 October 1922, married Frederick James Milton, Royal Air Force, in Orange Free State, South Africa. Their children:

- ❑ Timothy Jan Frederick Milton who was born on 16 February 1946 and died on 21 October 1948.
- ❑ Letitia Irene Milton who married Calum Smith. Their child:
  - ♦ Alexandra Smith Burnett.
- ❑ Caroline Milton who married Jock (surname not known) and had a child.
- ❑ Alice Milton who married (1) Peter (surname not known) and (2) Peter (surname not known) and had children.

[Additional information about the more recent generations of the Burnetts of Kemnay was provided by Mrs. M. Bogdan and Nicholas Q. Bogdan]

Susan Burnett of Kemnay compiled *Without Fanfare* which she describes as "the story of my family". This detailed 300-year history of the Burnetts of Kemnay, published in 1994, contains, in addition to the genealogy of the family, many extracts from personal letters and papers giving a fascinating 'behind the scenes' insight into the lives and relationships of this branch of the Burnetts.

References and Sources:

(1) (Title Quote) from C. L. Burnett, "The Shades of the Past", in *Without Fanfare*, 242, S. Burnett, (1994)

(2) A.W. Clarke, *Admiral Sir Robert Burnett.*

(3) Robert O'Neill, *Air Chief Marshall Sir Charles Burnett.*

G. Burnett, (ed.) J. Allardyce, *The Family of Burnett of Leys*, (1901), Spalding Club.

T. Watt, Aberdeen Grammar School Roll of Pupils 1795-1919, (1923), Aberdeen.

S. Burnett, *Without Fanfare*, (1994), Kemnay.

Descendants of Burnetts of Kemnay, as indicated in text.

1881 British census.

International Genealogical Index for Aberdeen and Midlothian.

Civil Birth, Marriage and Death Registers for Aberdeen and Kemnay.

Memorial Inscriptions at Kemnay Churchyard.

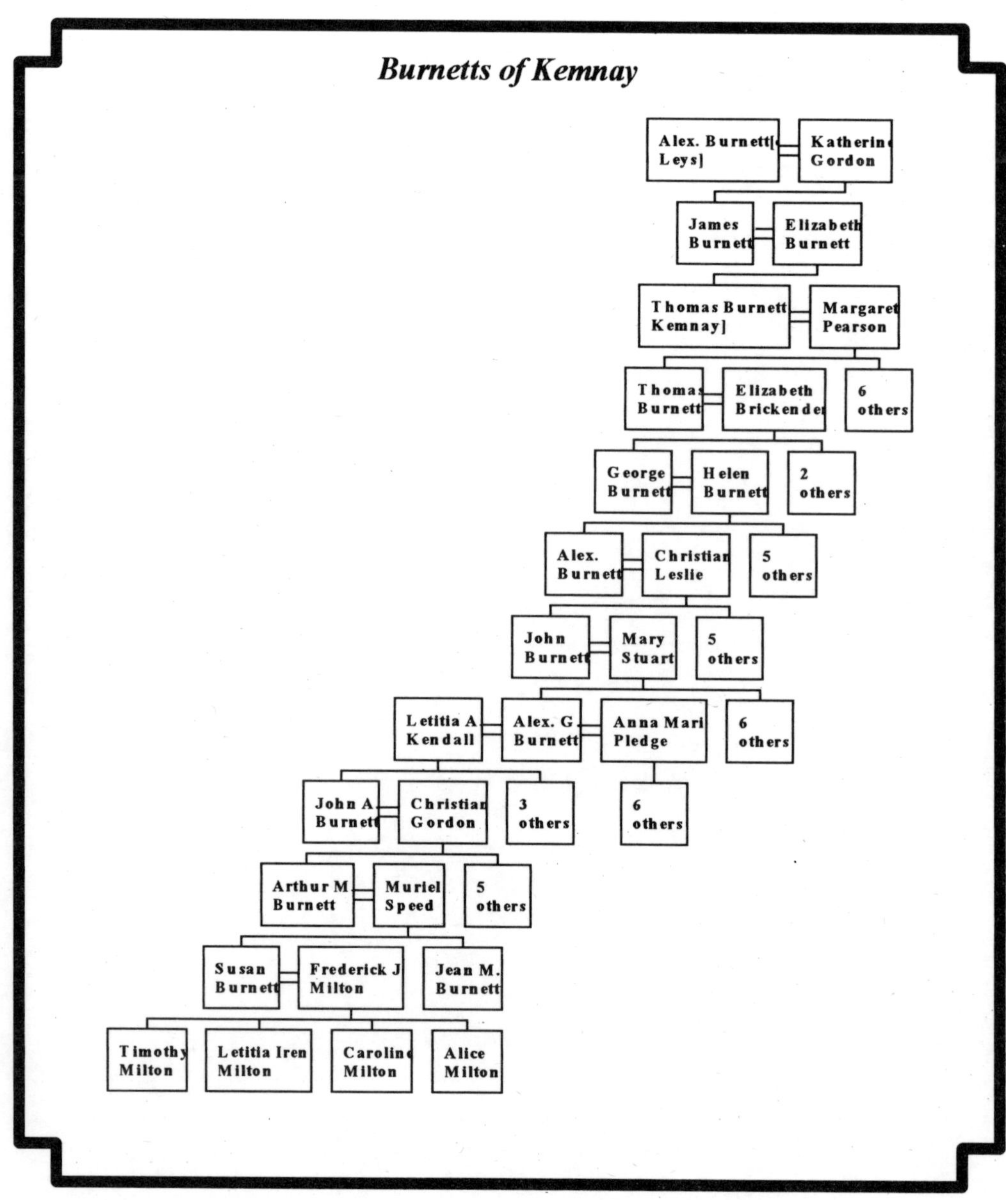
Burnetts of Kemnay
Alex. Burnett[of Leys]
Katherine Gordon
James Burnett
Elizabeth Burnett
Thomas Burnett[of Kemnay]
Margaret Pearson
Thomas Burnett
Elizabeth Brickender
6 others
George Burnett
Helen Burnett
2 others
Alex. Burnett
Christian Leslie
5 others
John Burnett
Mary Stuart
5 others
Letitia A. Kendall
Alex. G. Burnett
Anna Mari Pledge
6 others
John A. Burnett
Christian Gordon
3 others
6 others
Arthur M. Burnett
Muriel Speed
5 others
Susan Burnett
Frederick J Milton
Jean M. Burnett
Timothy Milton
Letitia Iren Milton
Caroline Milton
Alice Milton

6

THE BURNETTS OF MONBODDO

Eileen A. Bailey

In science the credit goes to the man who convinces the world, not to the man to whom the idea first occurs.
(Sir Fancis Darwin , son of Charles Darwin, 1914)

The Burnetts of Monboddo, as a distinct branch, descend from **James Burnett of Lagavin**, Kincardineshire, who was the third son of James Burnett of Craigmyle, younger brother of Sir Thomas Burnett of Leys, 1st Baronet. After his second marriage, James Burnett of Lagavin purchased the old estate of Monboddo in about 1671 from his brothers-in-law, the Irvines, and in addition, he purchased six other Kincardineshire lands namely Kair, Whitefield, Sillyflat, Hallgreen, Johnshaven and Ballandro.

James Burnett, 1st of Monboddo, married (1) Isobel Forbes, possibly on 27 November 1642 at Fetteresso. They had no children. He married (2) Elizabeth Irvine, daughter of Captain Robert Irvine of Monboddo and Elizabeth Douglas. Captain Irvine died on 6 July 1652 aged 80 and was buried at Fordoun. Both James and Elizabeth were buried at Fordoun Churchyard. Children of the marriage were:

- Alexander Burnett, the heir, predeceased his father. He married, on 22 September 1686, his cousin, Margaret Burnett, daughter of Sir Alexander Burnett of Leys, 2nd Baronet. Both Alexander and Margaret were buried at Fordoun Churchyard. Their children were:
    - James Burnett who was born in 1688 succeeded his grandfather.
    - Unknown Burnett, who died as an infant.
    - Unknown Burnett, who died as an infant.

  After Alexander Burnet's death, his widow Margaret married Dr. Andrew Burnett, who was born in 1663, son of Andrew Burnett in Foveran. Andrew and Margaret Burnett had five children details of whom are given in Chapter 3 on the genealogy of the Burnetts of Leys.
- Robert Burnett who became *of Kair & Ballandro.* He died before 1695 leaving no issue.
- Jane/Jean Burnett, who was born about 1652, married Sir David Carnegie, 1st Baronet of Pitarrow, whose ancestors had formerly owned Monboddo. There is no record of a marriage contract but a bond was dated 9 and 30 April 1697. Jean Burnett survived her husband. She died on 15 May 1740 and was buried at Montrose.

- ❑ Elizabeth Burnett, whose birthdate is not known, married, George Garioch of Kinstair in 1683.
- ❑ Margaret Burnett who married (1) Alexander Steele and had the following children (the spelling of whose names is as found in records):
  - ♦ Margarat Steil, baptised on 16 November 1700 in Marykirk parish.
  - ♦ Magdalen Steil, baptised on 17 September 1702 in Marykirk parish.
  - ♦ Alexander Steele, baptised on 23 November 1708 in Marykirk parish.

  Margaret Burnett married (2) on 6 April 1727 in St. Cyrus parish, Kincardineshire, David Wyse of Lunan who was the first son of Alexander Wyse of Mains of Thornton. David Wyse had married (1) in 1681, Margaret Nairne of Pitboddo with whom he lived at Mains of Lauriston in St. Cyrus parish. At the time of his marriage to Margaret Burnett he was resident in Montrose. [A. Jervaise's *Epitaph & Inscriptions*, concerning his observations at Laurencekirk Churchyard also the Mortifications of Montrose Parish Church.]

James Burnett of Monboddo died in 1699.

James Burnett, 2nd of Monboddo, was born in 1688 and succeeded his grandfather. He was a student at Marischal College, Aberdeen, from 1702-1706 where he was recorded in the University records as *Jac Burnet a Monboddow*. James Burnett was listed as a Jacobite in the 1715 Rebellion, the catalist for which was Jacobite outrage at the crowning of King George I, known as "The Wee German Lairdie", in succession to Queen Anne who died in 1714. The Earl of Mar and supporters of James Stuart "The Old Pretender" raised his standard at Braemar, Aberdeenshire, on 26 August 1715. On 14 November 1715, Jacobites under the command of the Earl greatly outnumbered government troops under the Earl of Argyll at Sheriffmuir, near Stirling. Whilst the final outcome has never really been established, the Hanoverian troops were not overcome. James Burnett was taken prisoner and kept at Stirling Castle and Carlisle. After a long period of imprisonment, he eventually returned to Kincardineshire where, in due course of time, he had to sell all of his estates except Monboddo and Lagavin.

James Burnett, married on 3 November 1709, Elizabeth Forbes, daughter of Sir William Forbes of Craigievar and sister of Sir Arthur Forbes. James and Elizabeth Burnett had eleven sons and three daughters all of whom are said to have died young or in infancy, other than two noted below. James and Elizabeth Burnett were both buried at Fordoun Churchyard.

- ❑ James Burnett, who succeeded his father, was born on 14 October and baptised on 25 October 1714 at Monboddo, parish of Fordoun. He became Lord Monboddo. James died on 26 May 1799.
- ❑ William Burnett, the younger son, was baptised on 23 August 1731. He was a student of Marischal College from 1746-50 then apprenticed to Thomas Burnett, son of Thomas Burnett of Kirkhill. At one time he was in partnership with his son, Thomas, in the firm of William & Thomas Burnett. William became

Procurator Fiscal for Aberdeenshire, a post that he held from 17th January 1759 until 13 December 1805. He was admitted as a Burgess of Aberdeen in February 1757 and served as Fiars Juror from 1758-98. William Burnett married, on 11 July 1754, Margaret Taylor, daughter of John Taylor, advocate in Aberdeen, and Elizabeth Fyffe. They had the following children. There were several other children who died young.

- James Burnett was baptised 3 August 1760 in Aberdeen. He died as an infant.
- Elizabeth Burnett was baptised 14 October 1761 in Aberdeen.
- Arthur Burnett was baptised on 5 March 1763. He died of yellow fever in Jamaica on 22 May 1794.
- John Burnett was born about 1764. He became an eminent lawyer and was admitted to the Scottish Bar on 10 December 1785. John became Advocate-depute in 1792 and was created Sheriff of Haddington on the resignation of Lord Elvingston, in October 1803. In April 1810, on the death of R. H. Cay, he was appointed Judge-Admiral of Scotland. John Burnett married Deborah Paterson, daughter of Dr. John Paterson of Baulk, Jamaica. John died on 7 or 8 December 1810, aged 46, whilst preparing his work, the *Criminal Law of Scotland* which was published posthumously. Their known children were:
  - William Burnett who died unmarried in 1852.
  - Anne Rebecca Burnett, who was twin of John, married, on 23 June 1828 in Edinburgh, William Grant, son of Alexander Grant of Redcastle. Anne Burnett died in 1874.
  - John Burnett, twin of Anne. He served in the Indian Army and died unmarried.
  - Elizabeth Deborah Burnett married, on 30 December 1830 in Edinburgh, Col. Edward Twopenny of 78th Highlanders. Elizabeth died in 1856.
  - Roberta Dundas Burnett married, on 25 July 1836 in Edinburgh, Lieutenant Joseph North.
- Marjory Burnett was baptised in February 1766 in Aberdeen.
- James Burnett was baptised on 10 September 1767.
- Margaret Burnett, born in 1768, died unmarried.
- William Burnett, baptised on 14 February 1770 died on 12 November 1788.
- Alexander Burnett was baptised on 11 May 1771 in St. Nicholas parish. He became a Land Measurer.

- Thomas Burnett, of Park and Kepplestone, was baptised on 6 March 1773 in St. Nicholas parish. He was a student of Marischal College from 1787-89 then apprenticed to Alexander Shand. Admitted as Advocate on 7 March 1796, he was appointed Joint Procurator Fiscal for Aberdeenshire from 1805- 1811 and was also County Clerk of Aberdeenshire.

Fig. 6.1 Thomas Burnett of Kepplestone, Advocate

Thomas Burnett married (1) on 30 June 1800, Anne/Annie Rebecca Paterson, born 31 March 1779, daughter of Dr. John Paterson of Baulk, Hanover, Jamaica. Anne Rebecca died on 13 November 1804 aged 25. Their children were:

- Margaret Burnett who was born in 1801 and died unmarried in August 1837.
- John Burnett. Born on 26 June 1802, he entered the HEICS in 1823 and married Harriet Bourchier, daughter of Samuel Bourchier of the East India Civil Service. John died on 3 March 1834. Children of the marriage were:
  - Henry Burnett who died young.
  - Peter Burnett who died young.
  - Marianne Burnett.
- Newell Burnett, of Kepplestone and Kyllachie, was born on 12 June 1803. He was a pupil of the Grammar School and thereafter a student at Marischal College from 1817-1819. Newell was first of all apprenticed to Duncan Davidson and then to his father. He was admitted to the Society of Advocates in Aberdeen on 5 July 1825 and was later also County Clerk of Aberdeenshire.

Fig. 6.2 Newell Burnett of Kyllachie, Advocate

In 1825 he was in practice with his father Thomas Burnett, advocate, in the firm of Thomas & Newell Burnett at 11 Belmont Street, Aberdeen and living at 9 Belmont Street. Newell Burnett held a wide range of appointments. He was a Justice of the Peace, a Notary Public, Keeper of the Register of Sasines for Aberdeen and Kincardine, Clerk of Supply, Clerk to the Prison Board, a Director of the Great North of Scotland Railway and many more. Records show that between 1840 and 1861 he was a Fiars Juror on twelve occasions. At one time he was the proprietor of Kepplestone, Aberdeen. In 1872 he was listed as proprietor of Kyllachie, Moy, near Inverness, an estate of 3,015 acres valued at £471. Newell Burnett, who was unmarried, died on 20 November 1878 aged 75.

- Thomas Burnett was born on 30 October 1804. He was killed in an accident on board the *Buckinghamshire*, East Indiaman, on 20 July 1820.

Thomas Burnett, of Park and Kepplestone, married (2) at Ballater on 26 August 1806, Mary Garden/Gardyne, daughter of Peter Garden of Troup & Dalgety & Katherine Balneaves (who became heiress of Glenlyon). Peter Garden succeeded his brother Lord Gardenstone in the estate of Troup and became Peter Garden Campbell of Troup and Glenlyon. Thomas and Mary had three sons and six daughters:

- Francis Burnett was born on 13 April, baptised 3 May 1810. He became an MD. Francis died unmarried on 6 August 1843.
- William Farquharson Burnett was born on 18 February 1815. With the rank of Captain, he served in the Royal Navy at Sebastopol. William drowned in the shipwreck of the *Orpheus* off the coast of New Zealand on 7 February 1863.
- James Burnett was born on 17 February 1820. He became Superintendent of the Royal Bank of Australia. James accidentally drowned crossing the Lower Murray River, New South Wales, on 29 October 1851.
- Marianne (Mary Ann) Burnett was baptised 29 June 1808 in St. Nicholas parish, and married, on 2 July 1833 at Kepplestone, Rev. Charles Edward Birch, Rector at Wiston, Suffolk. [as recorded in St. Paul's Episcopal Chapel Marriage Records]. Mary Anne died at Colchester on 26 October 1895 aged 87. Records of two children have been found:
  - Mariana Helen Birch who was baptised on 24 January 1837 in Wissington parish, Sussex, England.
  - Margaret Elizabeth Agnes Birch who was baptised on 21 April 1839 in Wissington parish.
- Helen Christian Burnett, born about 1813, married on 29 July 1839 at Old Machar (marriage also recorded 2 August 1839 in Banchory-Ternan parish), Thomas Innes of Learney, advocate, born 31 October 1814, second son of William Innes of Raemoir and Jane Bremner of Learney. Children:

- William Innes was born in 1841. He became a Captain in the Royal Engineers and was killed at Passir Sala in Malacca on 7 November 1875 aged 34. William was buried at Banda Bahru on the Perak River.
- Thomas Innes was born in 1843. He died at sea on 18 June 1888 aged 45 while returning from the Phillipines.
- Francis Newell Innes was born in 1845. He became a Lieutenant Colonel in the Royal Artillery, serving in the Egyptian Expedition as Staff Officer. He received the Medal & Clasp for Tel-el-kebir and the Bronze Star & Order of the Medjidie. Francis Newell Innes married Margaret Anne Irvine, daughter of Archer Irvine-Fortescue of Kingcausie. Their children were:
  - Thomas Innes who became Lord Lyon. He married Lady Lucy Buchan, third daughter of the 18th Earl of Caithness.
  - Helen Christian Innes of Cromney who was born on 6 December 1895. Helen died on 9 March 1982 and was buried at Echt Churchyard.

  Francis Newell Burnett died at Learney on 12 April 1907 aged 62. Margaret Anne, his wife, died on 15 October 1923 and was buried at Echt Churchyard.

Thomas Innes, CVO, LLD, a Colonel in 3rd Battalion, Gordon Highlanders, died on 12 November 1912. Helen died on 30 October 1901 aged 88. Their memorial inscriptions are included on the gravestone of the Innes of Learney family in Kincardine o' Neil Churchyard.

- Catherine/Kate Burnett was baptised on 14 August 1811 in St. Nicholas parish. She died on 20 February 1814.
- Penelope Burnett was baptised on 8 February 1816 in St. Nicholas parish. She married, on 10 April 1834, Captain, afterwards Major, Napier Turner Christie of the 79th Highlanders and latterly of the 11th Regiment, son of James Christie of Durn, Fife. Penelope died at Liverpool on 10 August 1882. Children found were:
  - Mary Harriet Christie, but recorded as Burnett, was baptised on 4 June 1840 in Episcopal Church, Aberdeen. This record names her mother (only) as Penelope Burnett.
  - Napier Thomas Christie was baptised on 13 September 1844 in Kincardine o' Neil parish, Aberdeenshire.
  - Penelope Christie was born on 10 August 1847 in Old Machar parish, Aberdeen.
- Harriet Hay Burnett married, at Leamington on 20 January 1842, James Cumine of Rattray, who was born on 30 March 1810, son of Adam

Cumine and Elizabeth Williamson Burnett. He succeeded his father in 1841. James was, at the time of his marriage time, in the HEIC, Bengal Civil Service. Their children were:

- Elizabeth Cumine who was baptised 14 December 1842 in St. John's Episcopal Church, Aberdeen.
- Mary Elizabeth Cumine who was born on 20 November 1842 in Old Machar parish. She married, on 2 June 1875 in St. Nicholas parish, Aberdeen, Thomas Burnett, of the Royal Horse Artillery, son of Sir James Horn Burnett. Their family is described in the genealogy of the Burnetts of Leys.
- Harriet Cumine, who was baptised on 1 January 1844 at Lonmay Episcopal, died in infancy.
- William Adam Cumine, who was born on 24 November and baptised 27 December 1844, died on 12 June 1849. He was buried at Old Machar Churchyard.
- Thomas Cumine who was born on 11 April and baptised on 15 May 1847 in St. John's Episcopal, Aberdeen. He joined the Royal Artillery and inherited Rattray from his father. Thomas married Emmeline Jones by whom he had two known children:
    - Sylvia Hay Kate Cumine, born in 1885, died in 1975. She inherited Rattray on the death of her brother George in 1941.
    - George James Gordon Gerald Cumine born in 1881, died in 1941. George Cumine was the successor to his father in Rattray.

  Thomas Cumine died on 21 June 1887 and was buried at Rattray.
- James Cumine was baptised on 16 January 1849 in St. John's Episcopal, Aberdeen. He died, unmarried, in 1870 and was buried at Lower Norwood Cemetery.
- Alexander Cumine was baptised 18 August 1851 in Lonmay Episcopal. He served in the Bombay Civil Service.
- Harriet Cumine, known as "Aunt Harriet" died on 15 February 1935 and was buried at Rattray.
- George Lewis Cumine born 25 October in Crimond parish was baptised on 19 November 1857 at Lonmay Episcopal. George became a Civil Engineer and pursued his career in the Americas, notably in Columbia, Mexico and Canada. On 10 August 1894 he married Isabel Victoria Maria Carmen Dudley-Bateman y Ospina, born in 1875, in Bogata, Columbia on her 19th birthday. George and Isabel had seven children:
    - Adam Cumine.
    - George Louis Cumine.
    - Alan Cumine.
    - Robin Cumine born in 1901, died in 1981.

    - Isabel Cumine.
    - Philip Arthur Cumine. He inherited Rattray on the death of his aunt, Sylvia Hay Kate Cumine in 1975. He was succeeded by his son:
        - ◊ Peter Cumine
    - Alice Cumine.

    George Lewis Cumine died in 1934 and his wife, Isabel, in 1962. Both are buried at Rattray.

Harriet died on 21 November 1884. James Cumine of Rattray died on 17 December 1894. Both James and Harriet were buried at Rattray.

[The genealogy of the descendants of Harriet Hay Burnett and James Cumine was enhanced and updated with the assistance of Peter Cumyn]

- Eliza/Elizabeth Deborah Burnett, married on 16 June 1844 in Old Machar parish, John Paton of Grandholm, Persley and Ferrochie, a Major in Royal Aberdeenshire Highlanders (Militia). Their children were:
    - ➢ Mary Louisa Paton who was born on 6 February 1846 at RMC Sandhurst, England. She married the Hon. Charles Home Sinclair. Their children were:
        - Euphemia (Effie) Helen Sinclair who married Col. H. A. Duncan. Children:
            - ◊ Elspeth Mary Duncan who married General Westrop.
            - ◊ Andrew Duncan
            - ◊ YD (daughter) Duncan
        - Mary Esme Sinclair who married Thomas Holman.
    - ➢ Ida Margaret Helen Paton who was born on 19 June 1847 at Strutts Farm. Histon, Suffolk (now Cambridge county) England. She married (1) R. Garde. The had one known child:
        - Olivia Garde who married G. Williamson.
    - ➢ Sarah Matilda Paton who was born on 23 May 1850 at Grandholm, in Old Machar parish. She married Kildare Robinson. Their child was:
        - Ida Robinson who married Captain Cecil Hunt.
    - ➢ William Roger Paton who was born on 9 February 1857 at 10 The Chanonry, Old Aberdeen, in Old Machar parish. He married Irene Olympitis. They had the following children:
        - George Paton born on 13 August 1886 in Mindus, Turkey, who married R. Horrocks.

- John Paton born Grandhome on 30 March 1890 who married Fenella Crombie. They had 6 children.
- Thetis Paton born on 21 November 1887 at Grandhome, who married Cokostaki Svinos.
- Emanuel Paton born in 1895 in Mindus, Turkey. He died in the same year.
- Augusta Paton born on 17 June 1899 in Mindus, Turkey who married Baron Janos Kemney of Vich, Transylvania. They had 5 children whose names are not known.

➢ Elizabeth Bertha Paton who was born 16 February 1860 at Elmbank in Old Machar parish. Her birth was not registered until 7 March 1860 because of the death of her mother on 24 February. Her godparents were Mary Cumine, Harriet Hay Burton and William Innes. Elizabeth Bertha died on 11 June 1861 aged 16 months.

Eliza Burnett Paton died on 24 February 1860 aged 37. John Paton died on 27 August 1879 aged 61.

[The above information on the descendants of Elizabeth Deborah Burnett and John Paton was enhanced and updated with the help of David Paton of Grandholm.]

Mary Garden Burnett died on 28 May 1863, aged 83, at Kepplestone. Thomas Burnett died at Kepplestone on 1 December 1854 aged 81. [Register of St.Andrew's Episcopal Church] and was buried in St. Nicholas, Aberdeen.

Other children of William and Margaret Taylor Burnett were:

- Jean Burnett was baptised on 2 April 1774 in St. Nicholas parish.
- George Burnett was born on 1 August, baptised on 9 August 1777 in St. Nicholas parish.
- Mary Burnett married John Taylor. She died in 1838.

Margaret died on 23 August 1806 in her 73rd year. William Burnett died on 8 March 1811 at Lochhead.

JAMES BURNETT, 3rd of Monboddo, and Lagavin, was born on 14 October 1714, the year in which Queen Anne died and George I was crowned King of England. James was tutored by Robert Milne before being sent, at the age of eight, to the local parish school of Laurencekirk and then on to college in Aberdeen when he reached fourteen. He went on to Holland to the University of Groningen for 3 years to study Civil Law. After returning to Scotland in 1736, James Burnett was called to the Scottish Bar in February 1737 and, during the 1745 Jacobite Rebellion, which culminated in the defeat of the Stuart supporters at the Battle of Culloden in 1746, he went to London.

Fig.6.3 Lord Monboddo

James was appointed Sheriff of Kincardineshire then raised to the Scottish Court of Session where he succeeded Andrew Fletcher of Milton in February 1767. He took his title, Lord Monboddo, from his estate. Although his was one of the smaller Scottish estates in terms of its generated income, which was never more than 300 pounds per annum, James Burnett would not raise his rents or dismiss a poor tenant for the sake of obtaining rent from one who could pay more. Indeed he boasted that his lands were more highly populated than another estate of comparable size.

James Burnett was regarded as a man of great intellect and achievement; an eccentric who was a cultured, original thinker. His pre-Darwin theory on evolution which traced man back to the orang-utan was greeted with a great deal of scorn and he, personally, was subjected to public ridicule and caricature because of it. During the summer recess of the Courts, he was known to travel every year on horseback to London which, in the face of highway robbers and rough tracks of the time, would have been an extreme test of stamina. Tradition has it that he not only rode to and from London but that he also read during the journeys. This seems unlikely as he was very short-sighted in addition to suffering from deafness, both afflictions which necessitated his sitting with the Clerks of Court rather than on the Bench in order to properly hear a case. His literary works of note were the *Origin and Progress of Language* (1773-92), and *Ancient Metaphysics* (1779-97). He also collected together the *Decisions of Court of Session 1738-60.* James Burnett married, about 1760, to Elizabeth Farquharson, said to be related to the Earl Marischal. Elizabeth died in childbirth, probably in 1767.

Lord Monboddo lived latterly in his town house at 13 St. John's Street, off the Canongate, Edinburgh, in the company of his youngest daughter, Elizabeth who predeceased him. James and Elizabeth Farquharson Burnett had the following children:

- Arthur Burnett who was born in 1763 and died in 1774.
- Helen Burnett who was born about 1765, succeeded her father. She married Kirkpatrick Williamson, Keeper of the Outer House Rolls, who assumed the Burnett surname. Helen Burnett died on 17 February 1833 and was buried at Fordoun Churchyard. Their children who were recorded under the surname Williamson were:
  - James Burnett (Burnett) Williamson, born in 1792, was baptised on 22 March 1792 at Fordoun. He succeeded to the Monboddo estate. James died in 1864 and was buried at Fordoun Churchyard.
  - Arthur (Burnett) Williamson was baptised on 12 January 1797 at Fordoun. He died in 1877. Arthur became Sheriff - Substitute for Peebles.
  - John (Burnett) Williamson was baptised on 25 March 1793 at Fordoun. A surgeon by profession, John died, unmarried, in India.
  - Elizabeth (Burnett) Williamson was baptised on 25 October 1780 at Fordoun. She married, in 1808, Adam Cumine of Rattray who was born on 5 May 1767, son of William Cumine of Pithullie in Buchan and Jean Moir, daughter of William Moir of Lonmay. Adam entered the Royal Navy and afterwards joined the H.E.I.C Naval Service. He was in command of the H.C. ship the *Bengal.* It was Adam Cumine who purchased the estate of Rattray. Their children were:
    - William Cumine who was baptised on 19 March 1809 at Old Machar & St. Nicholas. He followed an Army career and died at Corfu in 1834.
    - James Cumine who was baptised on 30 March 1810 at Old Machar. He married, in 1842, Harriet Hay Burnett, daughter of Thomas Burnett, Advocate. James Cumine died in 1894. Their children are previously listed under the genealogy of Harriet Hay Burnett.
    - Elizabeth Cumine who was baptised on 9 May 1811 at Old Machar & St. Nicholas. She died on 5 November 1887 at 5 Albyn Place, Aberdeen aged 75 and was buried beside her parents at Old Machar.
    - Jane Cumine who was baptised on 6 July 1812 at Old Machar. She died, unmarried, on 5 September 1886 at Albyn Place, Aberdeen aged 73 and was buried beside her parents at Old Machar.

- George Cumine who was baptised on 17 July 1813 at St. Nicholas. He became a Captain in the Madras Cavalry. George Cumine married Mary Forbes, daughter of Rev. G. Forbes. They had two known children:
  - Charles Cumine who entered the Army and died in an accident whilst on duty in India.
  - Mary Cumine.
- Alexander Cumine who was baptised on 9 April 1815 at Old Machar. He was admitted to the Scottish Bar and was killed by the accidental explosion of his gun in 1841.

Elizabeth Burnett Cumine died on 4 May 1815 aged 34. Adam Cumine died, aged 74, on 17 January 1841 at his house in Albyn Place, Aberdeen. Both are buried at Old Machar.

- ♦ Helen (Burnett) Williamson who was baptised on 8 July 1783 at Fordoun. She remained unmarried.
- ♦ Henrietta (Burnett) Williamson who was baptised on 23 March 1789 at Fordoun.
- ♦ Grace or Grizzel (Burnett) Williamson who was baptised on 28 March 1794 at Fordoun. She died unmarried, in 1864 and was buried at Fordoun.
- ♦ Margaret (Burnett) Williamson who was baptised on 21 July 1795 at Fordoun, She died unmarried and was buried at Fordoun.

- ❑ James Burnett who was baptised on 10 September 1767 in St. Cyrus parish.
- ❑ Elizabeth Burnett, who was born in 1767, remained unmarried and died from consumption on 17 June 1790 at the age of 22. She was buried beside her father at Greyfriars Churchyard, Edinburgh. The poet Robert Burns was a frequent visitor at 13 St. John's Street during his stay in Edinburgh in 1788 and was obviously one of the admirers of the beauty for which Eliza was famous. In his *Address to Edinburgh* Burns wrote

Fair Burnet strikes th' adoring eye,
Heaven's beauties on my fancy shine,
I see the Sire of love on high,
And own his work indeed divine.

Robert Burns commemorated the early death of Eliza Burnett in his *Elegy on the late Miss Burnet of Monboddo*

Life ne'er exalted in so rich a prize
As Burnet, lovely from her native skies;
Nor envious death so triumph'd in a blow,
As that which laid the accomplish'd Burnet low.

Thy form and mind, sweet maid, can I forget?
In richest ore the brightest jewel set!

In thee, high Heaven above was truest shown,
As by His noblest work the Godhead best is known.

In vain ye flaunt in summer's pride, ye groves;
Thou crystal streamlet with thy flowery shore,
Ye woodland choir that chaunt your idle loves,
Ye cease to charm – Eliza is no more!

Lord Monboddo died on 26 May 1799 aged 85 and was buried beside his daughter in the burial place of the Grants of Elchies located in the South Ground of Greyfriars Churchyard, Edinburgh. There has been some speculation as to why Lord Monboddo was buried with the Grants but this can perhaps be explained by the fact that Lord Patrick Grant, who died in 1754, was also a Lord of Session and James's mentor.

JAMES BURNETT (Williamson) BURNETT, 4th of Monboddo, was baptised on 22 March 1792. He succeeded through his mother. As well as being a landed proprietor, he was a Captain in the service of the H.E.I.C.S. James Burnett married Jane Ashe Carter, daughter of John Carter and Jane Ashe. Their children were:

- ❑ James Cumine Burnett who was born on 21 March 1835 in Devon and baptised on 21 November 1836 at Fordoun.
- ❑ Arthur Coffin Burnett who was baptised on 10 October 1840 at Fordoun. He died, unmarried, in 1871, at Southampton while en route from India to his home, and was buried at Fordoun.
- ❑ Helen Burnett who was born on 18 July 1858 in Fordoun parish.
- ❑ Eliza Jane Burnett who married, on 15 June 1864 at Monboddo, James Badenoch Nicholson, born 1832, an advocate and the Younger of Glenbervie [Aberdeen Journal Marriages in 1864]. Their child was:
  - ♦ Arthur Badenoch Nicholson of Glenbervie who was born on 18 May 1865. He succeeded his father and became a Writer to the Signet on 13 July 1891. Arthur married, on 1 July 1897, Elizabeth Isobel Napier, elder daughter of Alexander John Napier WS, of Dales, Linlithgow (now West Lothian). Arthur died on 25 February 1924. Their child was:
    - ❑ Edward Nicholson who became an advocate in Edinburgh.
- ❑ Helen Amy Burnett who was born on 18 July 1858 in Fordoun parish. Helen Amy was aged 19 and living at Arbeadie Cottage, Banchory, when she married, on 12 December 1877 in St Ternan's Episcopal Church, Banchory, William Disney Innes who was aged 26, of Raemoir House, Banchory. [in *Aberdeen Journal* Marriages and recorded in the Civil Marriage Register for Banchory Ternan, 1877]. William, who was baptised 11 December 1851 at Fetteresso, was the second son of Alexander Innes of Raemoir and Ann Katharine Leith. Their child was:
  - ♦ Alexander Innes.

Helen died in 1891.

James Burnett died in 1864 at 4 Castle Street, Edinburgh, and was buried at Fordoun. Jane Carter Burnett, died on 4 January 1878 at Arbeadie Cottage, Banchory, aged 64, after suffering from progressive muscular atrophy for 4 years.

JAMES CUMINE BURNETT, 5th of Monboddo, was born on 21 March 1835 in Devon, England. James was with the Hon. East India Company Service (HEICS) and became a Captain in Madras Cavalry, Indian Army. He was later appointed as a Justice of the Peace and served as Deputy Lieutenant of Kincardineshire. James Burnett married, on 12 February 1863 in Bombay Cathedral, India, Georgina Keith, born about 1840. The estate of Monboddo in 1872 was estimated at 3,013 acres and valued at £2,542. The 1881 British census lists the household staff at Monboddo House as comprising a cook, nurse, housemaid, laundress, maid, dairy maid, kitchen maid, indoor servant (male), all of whom were said to have been born in Aberdeen or Kincardine counties, plus a governess (aged 20) and lady's maid (aged 38) both of whom were French. James and Georgina had the following children:

- Mary Bertha Violet Burnett who was born in 1865 in India. She married Charles Francis Wright, a barrister of London. Their children were:
    - Charles Wright.
    - James Wright.
    - Stewart Wright.
    - Violet Georgina Lilian Wright who was born on 21 September 1891 and died on 25 October 1891. There is a memorial inscription at Fordoun.

  Mary died in October 1891 just after the birth of her child Violet and has a memorial inscription at Fordoun. Her husband also died in 1891.
- Lillian May Burnett who was born on 18 May 1866 at Inchmarlo Cottage, Banchory. [Her birth was registered in both Banchory-Ternan and Fordoun civil registers]. She died on 17 May 1931 aged 64 and was buried at Fordoun.
- Georgina Burnett who was born on 4 September 1867 at Monboddo House, Fordoun. She died on 19 December 1905 and was buried at Fordoun.
- James Shank Burnett who was born on 23 December 1868 at Monboddo House, Fordoun.
- John Burnett who was born on 30 August 1871 at Monboddo House, Fordoun. He married Catherine Burnett. John Burnett died on 20 March 1942 and was buried at Fordoun.
- Arthur Burnett who was born on 5 November 1878 at Monboddo House, Fordoun. Arthur married Annie Aberdein, daughter of Francis Aberdein of Garvocklea, Laurencekirk in 1908. Arthur and Annie Burnett had a daughter:
    - Marjorie Eliza Burnett who was born on 12 October 1909. She married on 30 November 1940 to Ronald Stamford Lingen Hutton. Their child:

- Malcolm Usheen Lingen Hutton married Jacqueline Patricia Grant of Grant in 1966.

Arthur Burnett died on 22 February 1934 and was buried at Brechin. Georgina Keith Burnett died on 5 March 1897 aged 57. James Burnett died on 9 May 1905 aged 70. Both were buried at Fordoun.

JAMES SHANK BURNETT, 6th of Monboddo, born 23 December 1868, succeeded his father in 1905 and married, in 1897, Cecilia Mary Barnes. Their children:

- Elizabeth Mary Burnett who was born on 13 February 1898. She died in May 1900.
- James Malcolm Burnett who was born on 6 October 1899 and succeeded his father.
- Cecilia Daphne May Burnett who was born on 13 March 1903. She married, on 23 May 1934, Dennis Marescaux Lees CB. DSO, Acting Rear Admiral, Royal Navy. Their children were :
  - David Brian Lees who married Mary Bernard.
  - Jeremy Marescaux Lees.
  - Rodney Burnett Lees.
- William Arthur Burnett who was born 22 May 1906. He died unmarried in New Zealand.

James Shank Burnett was killed by an elephant on 19 December 1910, whilst in India.

JAMES MALCOLM BURNETT, 7th of Monboddo, was born on 6 October 1899. He succeeded his father in 1910. James Burnett married (1) Germaine, daughter of Henri de la Rue of Paris. On 2 June 1942, he married (2) Gladys Ingram, daughter of John Ingram of Newburgh.

[David Lees of Shropshire who is a descendant provided additional details on the younger generations of the above family]

Sources: (for the convenience of researchers, some sources have been inserted beside the relevant text)

Descendants as indicated in text.

Tayler, A., & H., *Aberdeenshire Valuation Roll, 1667,* (1933), Spalding Club.

McDonnell, F., *Jacobites of 1715 in North East Scotland.*

List of members in *The History of the Society of Writers to His Majesty's Signet*, (1936).

Jervaise, A., *Epitaphs and Inscriptions in the North-east of Scotland.* (1875-79)

Aberdeen Journal, Marriage and Death notices.

Henderson, J., A., *History of Society of Advocates in Aberdeen*, (1912), Spalding Club.

P.J. Anderson (ed.), *Records of Marischal College and University*, (1898), Spalding Club

also

International Genealogy Index for Kincardine, Aberdeen and Midlothian counties.

Records of St. Paul's Episcopal Chapel, Aberdeen.

Records of St. Andrew's Episcopal Church, Aberdeen.

Civil Births, Marriages & Deaths Registers for Kincardineshire & Aberdeenshire.

1881 Census of Great Britain.

Memorial Inscriptions in Fordoun Parish Churchyard.

Memorial Inscriptions at Kincardine o' Neil Churchyard.

Mortifications of Montrose parish church.

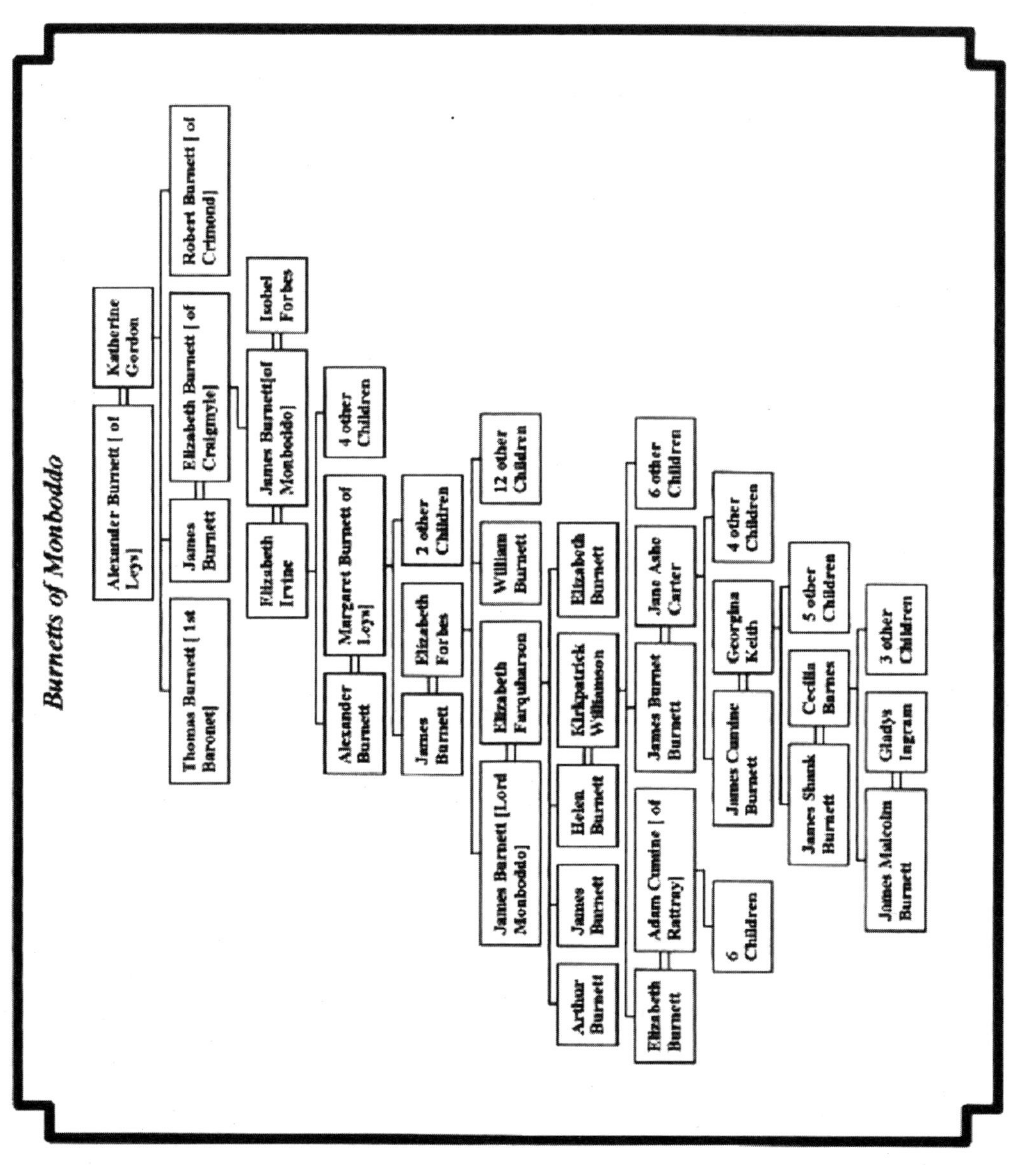
Burnetts of Monboddo
Alexander Burnett [of Leys]
Katherine Gordon
Thomas Burnett [1st Baronet]
James Burnett
Elizabeth Burnett [of Craigmyle]
Robert Burnett [of Crimond]
Elizabeth Irvine
James Burnett[of Monboddo]
Isobel Forbes
Alexander Burnett
Margaret Burnett of Leys]
4 other Children
James Burnett
Elizabeth Forbes
2 other Children
James Burnett [Lord Monboddo]
Elizabeth Farquharson
William Burnett
12 other Children
Arthur Burnett
James Burnett
Helen Burnett
Kirkpatrick Williamson
Elizabeth Burnett
Elizabeth Burnett
Adam Cumine [of Rattray]
James Burnet Burnett
Jane Ashe Carter
6 other Children
6 Children
James Cumine Burnett
Georgina Keith
4 other Children
James Shank Burnett
Cecilia Barnes
5 other Children
James Malcolm Burnett
Gladys Ingram
3 other Children

7

THE BURNETTS OF CAMPHILL, ELRICK and KIRKHILL

Eileen A. Bailey

BURNETTS OF CAMPHILL

The lands of Camphill/Campfield were part of the Leys estate. In 1605 Alexander Burnett of Leys had a Crown charter from Sir Henry Charteris of lands, in the parishes of Lumphanan and Kincardine O' Neil, which included Easter, Wester and Milltown of Camphill in which Alexander Burnet of Craigour and William Burnett of Camphill, grandsons of William Burnett of Tillihaikie, were tenants. Parts of the genealogy of the Burnetts of Camphill are given in a variety of sources some of which are contradictory. The following information is as the author has assembled it to date. The findings so far are shared here on the understanding that further research is required.

William Burnett of Wester Camphill, who fell at the Battle of Pinkie in 1547, had a son Andrew who succeeded in Camphill.

Andrew Burnett, son of William Burnett of Wester Camphill, married Constance Pitcairn and had the following children:

- Andrew Burnett, who was a Burgess and Merchant of Aberdeen. He married Katharine, eldest daughter of John Lichtoun. Andrew was a Burgess in Cracow, Poland before 1592 [ref. Miscellany of Spalding Club.1940]. Their children were:
  - John Burnett who became 1st of Elrick. (of whom further details are given later)
  - Catherine/Katherine Burnett who was baptised on 27 February 1623 in Aberdeen.
  - Andro(Andrew) Burnett who was baptised on 18 September 1824 in Aberdeen.
  - Christiane(Christian) Burnett who was baptised on 13 October 1631 in St. Nicholas parish, Aberdeen.
  - Alexander Burnett who was baptised on 12 November 1632 in St. Nicholas Parish, Aberdeen.
  - Jeane Burnett who was baptised on 17 December 1634 in Aberdeen.

- Thomas Burnett who was baptised on 12 July 1636 in St. Nicholas parish, Aberdeen.
- Robert Burnett who was baptised on 19 September 1637 in St. Nicholas parish, Aberdeen.
- James Burnett who was baptised on 2 July 1640 in St. Nicholas Parish, Aberdeen.

- Alexander Burnett.
- Robert Burnett who was a traveller in Poland in 1597
- William Burnett who succeeded his father in Camphill.

William Burnett of Camphill married Elspeth Leslie on 25 February 1589 in St. Nicholas parish, Aberdeen. Their child:

- Thomas Burnett of Camphill who married Margaret Keith. Thomas received eight hundred merks in the will of Sir Thomas Burnett of Leys, dated 1652, but their exact relationship has not yet been established. Children of Thomas and Margaret Burnett were:
    - William Burnett who succeeded in Camphill. In the 1696 Poll Book he is entered as the heritor and possessor of Camphill. His children were:
        - William Burnett, Younger of Camphill, who had sasine on 25 November 1709. He married, in October 1711 to Anne Guthrie, daughter of Sir John Guthrie of Breda, Alford. William and Anne had children:
            - Mary Burnett who was baptised on July 1712. She married Donald Farquharson of Auchriachan on 2 July 1734 in Alford parish. Mary died in January 1795.
            - Margaret Burnett who was baptised on 4 September 1713, Kincardine O' Neil parish.
            - Anne Burnett who was baptised on 11 October 1714 in Kincardine O' Neil parish.
            - John Burnett, Younger of Camphill, who was baptised on 5 April 1716 in Kincardine O' Neil. John took part in the 1745 rebellion in which he was said to have been a trained gunner officer. Taken prisoner at Carlisle he was held in the Newgate prison. John Burnett later became a merchant trading in Holland. He married, in 1743, Jean Lumsden, daughter of Harry Lumsden, 15th of Cushney and Catharine Gordon. They had the following known children:
                - Katharin Burnett baptised 10 May 1740 in Kincardine O' Neil parish.
                - Anne Burnett baptised 18 April 1744 in Kincardine O' Neil parish.
                - William Burnett baptised 14 May 1745 in Kincardine O' Neil parish.

        - Mary Burnett baptised 25 February 1751 in Aberdeen.
        - Unknown (daughter) Burnett.
    - William Burnett who was baptised on 9 January 1718 in Kincardine O' Neil.
    - Thomas Burnett who was baptised on 30 October 1719 in Kincardine O' Neil
    - Elizabeth Burnett who was baptised in May 1723.

    William Burnett of Camphill died in January 1764.
  - Alexander Burnett
  - Agnes Burnett
  - Jean Burnett
  - Nicholas Burnett, baptised on 27 January 1690, who married Thomas Keith on 3 August 1710 in Kincardine O' Neil parish.
  - Margaret Burnett
  - Isobel Burnett.
- James Burnett, who was later styled *of Dantzig*. His Birth Brieve of 17 June 1652 outlines his ancestry as given above. It states that his parents were Thomas Burnett of Camphill and Margaret Keith and describes him as *merchant in Danseik* (Poland).

According to the Poll Book of 1696, a Thomas Burnett of Camphill was living in Aberdeen at that time

BURNETTS OF ELRICK

William Burnett, of Wester Camphill, Craigour, Tillihaikie evidenced by land charters dated 1537, 1546 and 1547, married and had three sons:

- Alexander Burnett *of Craigour.*
- Andrew Burnett of *Easter Camphill.*
- William Burnett of *Wester Camphill* who married Jane Arbuthnot.

Andrew Burnett, son of William Burnett of Wester Camphill, married Constance Pitcairn. Their children included:

- Andrew Burnett, Burgess and Merchant of Aberdeen. He married Katharine, eldest daughter of John Lichtoun. Andrew was a Burgess in Cracow, Poland before 1592. [ref. Miscellany of Spalding Club.1940] Their children were:
  - John Burnett, born about 1629, who became 1st of Elrick.
  - Alexander Burnett.
  - Robert Burnett who was a traveller Poland in 1597.
  - William Burnett who succeeded his father in Camphill.

John Burnett, *of Colpnay*, became a Merchant, Magistrate and Dean of Guild (1662) in Aberdeen and, having acquired the property of Elrick by assignation from William Innes of Kinnermonie, had a charter of these lands in 1663. Gilbert Hervie, Burgess of Aberdeen, had resigned his wadset on Elrick in 1650. This property had been in the hands of Mr Robert Burnett of Cowtoun, Tutor of Leys but was mortgaged to Gilbert Hervie. The estate of Elrick comprised *the land and barony of Elrick with the mill and miln-croft, Smiddieland and Broomiebrae of Elrick, the town and lands of Monacabback, Ord and Scrogley of Monacabback and lands of Snellen.*

Fig. 7.1 Gravestone inscription of John Burnett of Elrick (from drawing c1890)

John Burnett married (1) Marjorie Howieson, who died in 1663. They had the following children, (the spelling of surnames is as recorded):

- Androw Burnett who was baptised on 29 May 1649.
- Rachell Burnett who was baptised on 12 April 1653.
- Catherine Burnett who was baptised on 4 May 1654.
- Alexander Burnett who was baptised on 8 July 1655.
- Johne Burnett who was baptised on 12 March 1657. Died young.
- Elspet Burnett who was baptised on 9 January 1658.
- Isobell Burnett who was baptised on 26 June 1659.
- Johne Burnett who was baptised on 23 October 1660 and succeeded his father at age of six. He died aged fifteen.
- Christen Burnett who was baptised on 9 January 1662.

John Burnett of Elrick married (2) in 1664, Mary Jameson(e), daughter of George Jameson, the celebrated Portrait Painter, and his spouse Isabel Toasch/Tosh. She was often referred to as "Bonnie Mary". Some of the excellent work of George Jameson, who was a student of Van Dyke, is to be found at Crathes castle.

The house where Mary Jameson would have been born stood on the north side of Schoolhill and very close to the Church of St. Nicholas. Andrew Jameson, her grandfather, was a master mason. In 1586 he acquired land in Schoolhill from the church and built a house, which was considered to be an outstanding piece of work. (Fig.7.2) By 1625, the house was recorded in the name of George Jameson and it was here that he lived and worked until his death in 1644. The house stood until

Schoolhill was 'improved' in 1886 during which process, and amidst much public outcry, *Jameson's Castle* was demolished.

Mary Jameson had obviously inherited some of her father's artistic talents because she took great pleasure in designing and embroidering a series of tapestries which were hung in St. Nicholas Church.

John & Mary (Jameson) Burnett had the following children:

- George Burnett, born on 10 June, baptised on 20 June 1665 in St. Nicholas parish. He succeeded his brother John and was served heir on 14 May 1675 but died in or before 1684.
- Robert Burnett, baptised on 11 December 1666, succeeded his brother George to whom he was served heir on 6 March 1684.

Fig.7.2 The Jameson House (from a 19th century sketch by G. Gordon Burr)

Their marriage was short-lived for John Burnet died on 9 December 1666. The gravestone of John Burnett and his two wives was originally within the church of St. Nicholas.[(Fig.7.1)] Mary Jameson married (2) in 1669, her cousin, Professor James Gregorie, Astronomer and appointed Professor of Mathematics at St. Andrews University. James Gregorie was the inventor of the reflecting telescope. James and Mary Gregorie had a son James Gregorie, a daughter Helen Gregorie who married Alexander Thomson of Portlethen and a second daughter Janet Gregorie who married the Rev. William Forbes, Minister of Tarves, a son of Forbes of Waterton. Professor Gregorie died in 1675 at the age of 37, having suddenly gone blind just after showing his students the Statellites of Jupiter. Mary married (3) George Aedie, Baillie of Aberdeen and the father of David Aedie of Newark & Easter Echt. She died in July 1684.

John Burnett of Elrick who was born in 1660, succeeded his father in 1666 but was laird of Elrick for only nine years. He died in 1675 when 15 years of age.

George Burnett of Elrick, brother of John Burnett, was served heir on 14 May 1675 in the lands and barony of Elrick, the lands of Monicaboc, Chappeltack etc. He, too, was laird for about nine years and died young.

Robert Burnett of Elrick, brother of John & George Burnett, was served heir to George in the lands and barony of Elrick on 6 March 1684. Robert Burnett married (1) on 21 June 1683, Bessie Burnett, daughter of Andrew Burnett of Durris. Their children were:

- John Burnett baptised on 3 April 1684 in Aberdeen
- Andrew Burnett, baptised on 14 April 1685 in Aberdeen, who succeeded his father. He was listed as a Jacobite in the 1715 Rebellion and died in 1720.
- Alexander Burnett baptised on 22 July 1686 in Aberdeen.
- Robert Burnett baptised on 31 August 1687 in Newmachar parish .
- Thomas Burnett baptised on 6 August 1688 in Newmachar parish.
- Patrick Burnett baptised on 6 August 1690 in Newmachar parish.

Robert Burnett of Elrick married (2) Isobel Irvine. Their children were:

- James Burnett baptised on 27 December 1694 in Newmachar parish.
- Mary Burnett born in 1697.

Robert Burnett of Elrick died on 28 March 1697.

Andrew Burnett of Elrick was served heir special to his father Robert, in the lands and barony of Elrick, Monycabok etc. on 16th August 1706. He married, in Aberdeen on 1 May 1707, Marjorie Johnston, elder daughter of Sir John Johnston, 4th Baronet of Caskieben from whom Andrew bought New Place (Caskieben) in the same year. The property of Caskieben was all sold to the Burnett family about 1730 as Sir John Johnston died in Edinburgh in 1724 without having male heirs, his only son having been killed at his side at the battle of Sheriffmuir. Marjorie's sister Janet Johnstone married Charles Forbes of Sheils. Marjorie Johnstone Burnett had sasine on the lands of Monycabock on 1 June 1708. Andrew Burnet was 'out', that is to say an active Jacobite, in the 1715 uprising. He died in November 1720 aged 35 and was buried in St. Nicholas. Marjorie died in October 1723 and was also buried in St Nicholas, Aberdeen.

Records of the wills of Andrew Burnet of Elrick and of Mrs Marjory Johnston, his widow, were dated 11 January 1722 and 2 February and 15 Nov 1726, 18 January 1727 respectively.

Andrew and Marjorie Burnett had children:

- Janet Burnett who was baptised on 22 January 1709. She died on 28 May 1782 in Aberdeen
- Beatrice Burnett who was baptised on 3 October 1710 in Aberdeen. She married James McRobert on 12 February 1740 in Pitsligo parish, Aberdeenshire.Children:
    - Elizabeth McRobert baptised 5 June 1745. Pitsligo.

- Robert Burnett who was baptised on 12 February 1712. He was served heir to his father on 11 February 1721 but died in 1737.
- John Burnett who was baptised on 14 February 1714 was served heir to his brother on 3 September 1737. John Burnett sold Newplace in 1739 to the Synod of Aberdeen. John married Margaret Strachan of Balgall. He died in his 35th year, in November 1748 and was buried at St. Nicholas. Margaret married (2) in about 1750 to Sir Arthur Forbes, 4th Baronet of Craigievar and had five sons and four daughters.
- Marjory Burnett was baptised on 29 August 1716. She married George Mowatt in Aberdeen. Marjory died in October 1761 and was buried at St. Nicholas. They had the following children:
  - Andrew Mowatt was baptised on 2 April 1745.
  - George Mowatt was baptised on 6 November 1741. He became a merchant in Jamaica, and died unmarried in New York in 1796.[*Scots Magazine*, June 1796]
  - Andrew Mowatt was baptised on 13 April 1755.
  - Margaret Mowatt was baptised on 2 February 1758. She married, on 26 April 1787, in St. Nicholas parish, John Stuart of Inchbreck, Professor of Greek at Marischal College and University of Aberdeen, and had several children including
    - John Stuart born on 26 February 1788 in Aberdeen.
    - Marjory Stuart baptised 11 December 1789, St. Nicholas, Aberdeen.
    - Mary Stuart baptised on 17 January1792 in Aberdeen.
  - Marjory Mowatt was baptised on 26 April 1759. She married in about 1758 to Rev. Alexander Peter (later Doctor of Divinity) who was a minister in Dundee for many years. They left no children.
  - Helen Mowatt was baptised on 22 August 1753.
  - Isobel Mowatt was baptised on 13 October 1749.
  - James Mowatt was baptised on 2 January 1751.
  - Janet Mowatt was baptised on 6 May 1752.
  - John Mowatt was baptised on 11 April 1748.
- Helen Burnett was baptised on 14 June 1719 in Aberdeen.
- Andrew Burnett was baptised on 28 August 1720. He was admitted to the Aberdeen Burgess Register in January 1740 which records that Andrew Burnett, a merchant in Campvere (Holland) was admitted as a Guild brother. He returned to Aberdeen about 1750 and married Elizabeth Keith, daughter of George Keith of Bruxie, Old Deer. Elizabeth died in May 1786 and was buried at St. Nicholas. From correspondence it would appear that Andrew & Elizabeth Burnett had lived for a time at Bruxie.They had no children. Andrew Burnett became a member of Aberdeen Town Council and a Magistrate He died at his house in the

Shiprow, Aberdeen in February 1806 aged 86 and was buried at St. Nicholas. [Obituary in *Scots Magazine*,1806].

Robert Burnett of Elrick was served heir to his father Andrew on 11 February 1721. He died in 1737.

John Burnett of Elrick was served heir general on 17 September 1737. He married Margaret, daughter of Strachan of Balgall. In 1742 John Burnett was made Dean of Guild and, in 1744, a Baillie of Aberdeen. After his death on 26 October 1748 at the age of 34, Margaret married (2) about 1750, Sir Arthur Forbes, 4th Baronet of Craigievar. John and Margaret Burnett had the following children:

- ❑ Andrew Burnett who was baptised on 15 March 1742 and succeeded his father.
- ❑ William Burnett who was baptised on 13 February 1742 (he was probably twin of Alexander) and died in 1776.
- ❑ George Burnett was baptised on 17 May 1744 in Aberdeen. He became a Captain in the 33rd Regiment of Foot and married Mary Rigail but died without issue. His will was registered in Aberdeen 10 February 1777.
- ❑ John Burnett was baptised on 20 July 1745 in St. Nicholas parish. He succeeded his brother Andrew.
- ❑ Alexander Burnett was baptised on 9 June 1748 in Aberdeen. He became a Quarterly Deputy Commissioner General in the H.E.I.C.S. and Commissary of Ordnance in the Bengal establishment. He married on 25 December 1788 in St. Nicholas parish to Barbara Maxwell. A memorial inscription at Newmachar churchyard indicates that Alexander died on 2 January 1811 and Barbara died on 20 April 1819 aged 53. They had one known child:
    - ♦ Agnes Burnett, born about 1790, died on 15 April 1805 aged 15. She was buried at Newmachar.
- ❑ Mary Burnett was baptised on 29 April 1740 in Aberdeen.
- ❑ Marjorie Burnett was baptised on 8 April 1841 in Aberdeen.
- ❑ Hope Burnett was baptised on 10 October 1746 in Aberdeen. She married (1) James Davidson of Midmar on 22 March 1772 in Midmar parish and (2) Dr Alexander Donaldson, Professor of Medicine at Marischal College, on 3 August 1779. Alexander Donaldson died on 19 May 1793. Several other members of the Donaldson family were also Professors of Medicine.

Andrew Burnett of Elrick, born in 1742, succeeded his father John but died in 1767.

John Burnett of Elrick, born in 1745, succeeded his brother Andrew. In 1781 he was designated as *of Bencoolan, East Indies.* John married, in 1785 Helen, daughter of Patrick Garden of Troup and Glenlyon. John Burnett died on 9 June 1822 in his 77th year. His widow died on 30 December 1839.

John and Helen had the following children:

- Margaret Burnett was baptised 28 June 1788, Newmachar. Margaret married, on 26 February 1811 in her father's house, Archibald Norman McLeod of Montreal. Witnesses were Francis Garden of Troup and Sir William Forbes of Craigievar. [as recorded in St Paul's Episcopal Chapel Marriage Records]
- John Burnett was baptised on 17 June 1790 in Newmachar parish. He predeceased his father.
- Peter Burnett was baptised on 25 March 1792 in Newmachar parish. He succeeded his father.
- Andrew Burnett was baptised on 30 August 1794 in Newmachar parish.
- Francis Burnett was baptised on 5 May 1796 in Newmachar parish and became a Merchant in Aberdeen. He married, on 23 April 1826 in Old Machar parish (also recorded on 28 April 1826 in Newmachar parish), Elizabeth Tower. They had the following children:
    - Francis Burnett, baptised on 3 June 1831 in Newmachar parish, died young.
    - John Burnett baptised 11 November 1828 in Newmachar parish.
    - Peter Burnett baptised on 1 June 1837 in Newmachar Parish
- William Burnett was baptised on 4 March 1801 in Newmachar parish. He married, on 19 December 1826 in Newmachar parish, Isabella Morison Pitcairn and had a daughter.
- David Burnett was baptised on 6 January 1804 in Newmachar parish. He married Unknown Forsyth.
- Catherine Burnett was born in 1787 and died unmarried, in 1810.
- Hay Burnett was baptised on 10 June 1799. She married, on 8 February 1821 in her father's house, Thomas Lumsden (later Colonel, C.B.), of Belhelvie, of the Bengal Horse Artillery. He was the son and heir of Harry Lumsden, advocate in Aberdeen, and Catherine McVeagh. Harry Lumsden purchased Belhelvie in 1782. Witnesses to the marriage of Hay and Thomas were John Menzies of Pitfodels and Col. Arthur Forbes [as recorded in St Paul's Episcopal Chapel Marriage Records]. Hay died at Belhelvie Lodge on 11 October 1873 aged 74 and Thomas Lumsden also died there on 8 December 1874 aged 85. A memorial to them was erected within an enclosure in the Churchyard of Belhelvie. Their children included:
    - Harry Burnett Lumsden born on 12 November 1821. He became Lt. General H.B. Lumsden, KCSI, CB and served in the Indian Mutiny. Harry died at Belhelvie Lodge on 12 August 1896 and was buried at Belhelvie churchyard. His wife, Fanny, died on 21 January 1919 and is also buried there.
    - Thomas Lumsden born in 1825.
    - William Lumsden born in 1831

- Hugh David Lumsden born on 7 September 1844 in Old Machar parish, Aberdeen.
- Peter Stark Lumsden (later Sir Peter Lumsden GCB., CSI), born on 9 November 1829, distinguished himself in the Indian Mutiny and in political missions to Kandahar and Alfghanistan. He latterly resided at Buchromb, Dufftown, Banffshire.
- Helen Garden Lumsden married Rev. James Johnstone, minister of the United Free Church, Belhelvie. She died in 1903.
- Clementina Jane Lumsden who died on 8 November 1895 and is buried in the family enclosure at Belhelvie churchyard.

Peter Burnett of Elrick was served heir to his father John on 22 March 1824. He held the rank of Captain and married (1) in 1849 to an unknown spouse and had a child:

- Peter Burnett who succeeded his father.

Peter Burnett married (2) Unknown (possibly Mary Ann) Demidoff. An obituary in the *Aberdeen Journal* states " 6 July 1864, at Elrick House, Mary Ann, wife of Peter Burnett of Elrick". He died in 1870 in Nice, France.

Peter Burnett of Elrick (Captain) succeeded his father. He married on 27 November 1849 at Elrick in Newmachar parish to Guillemina, daughter of Sir William Curtis.

- Rodber William Stapylton Burnett married in the British Embassy on 9 April 1874, Aida Maria Willhelmia, third daughter of Sir Roderick Hartwell.

George H.M. Burnett of Elrick, Newmachar (Captain), son or grandson of Peter Burnett, married, in 1897, Kate Wallis, daughter of Edward Wallis.

- Donald Rodber Burnett born 1 July 1900. He became a Private in the Argyll & Sutherland Highlanders on 21 January 1918, transferred to RAF on 9 November 1918. He was demobbed on 19 March 1919 but re-enlisted in the Scots Guards on 16 September 1919. He was made a 2nd Lieutenant (Hon) in RAF in June 1920. Donald became a Cadet in Auxiliary Force, Royal Ulster Constabulary.
- Alexander F. Burnett born 2 September 1904.
- Malcolm Valentine Burnet born 14 February 1906.

BURNETTS OF KIRKHILL

Alexander Burnett, 1st laird of Kirkhill, near Dyce, was baptised on 4 February 1620, son of Thomas Burnett, merchant, and Margaret Johnston(e). Records of

Marischal College show Alexander Burnett was an entrant to the MA degree class in 1636. He became a Baillie of Aberdeen and was designated *Polls or Poles* which was a term used to identify those merchants who had strong trading links with Poland. Alexander married, on 26 June 1655 at St. Nicholas, Agnes Moir and their children (as recorded in St. Nicholas registers) were:

- Margaret Burnett baptised 20 August 1657. Godfathers were Alexander Burnett, late Baillie and Patrick Moir.
- Thomas Burnett baptised 16 January 1659. He succeeded his father in 1685 as the 2nd laird of Kirkhill.
- Geils (Grace) Burnett baptised 19 February 1661. Godfather was Mr Robert Burnet of Colpnay.
- Agnes Burnett baptised 15 March 1663. Godfather was John Jaffray of Dilspro (later known as Grandholm), late Provost of Aberdeen.
- Alexander Burnett baptised 2 February 1665.
- Marjorie Burnett baptised 14 August 1669. She married James Moir, Regent of Marischal College.
- Robert Burnett baptised 7 March 1672.
- John Burnett baptised 24 April 1673.
- John Burnett baptised 15 August 1674.
- David Burnett baptised 14 March 1676.
- George Burnett baptised 21 August 1677. Godfathers were George Skene of Fintray and Mr. George Peacock.
- Andrew Burnett baptised 8 January 1679. Godfather was William Cuming of Auchry.
- Patrick Burnett baptised 7 November 1680. Godfathers were Patrick Moir and Patrick Gellie.

Alexander Burnett who died on 2 April 1685 and his wife Agnes, who died on 18 June 1686, were buried at St. Nicholas and recorded on the previously mentioned stone of Andrew and Thomas Burnett (Alexander's father) in St. Mary's Aisle.

Thomas 'Poles' Burnett, 2nd laird of Kirkhill, was baptised 16 January 1659. He was a student at Marischal College where he gained an MA degree on 23 June 1687 and was admitted to the Society of Advocates in Aberdeen in 1691. He succeeded his father in Kirkhill in 1685 and was noted as being a Jacobite in the 1715 Rising. [A Thomas Burnett, of Kirkhill, son of Alexander Burnett of Kirkhill, was transported on 2 April 1716 from Liverpool to South Carolina in the *Wakefield*. This may have been the 2nd laird but could have been his nephew, son of Alexander Burnett (1665)]. Thomas Burnett married Anna Leslie and they had the following family:

- Agnes Burnett who was baptised 23 October 1687 in Aberdeen.
- Thomas Burnett who was baptised 28 April 1694 in Aberdeen. He succeeded his father.

- David Burnett who was baptised 28 April 1694 in Aberdeen.
- Alexander Burnett who was baptised September 1695 in Aberdeen
- Anna Burnett who was baptised 16 January 1697 in Aberdeen.

Thomas Burnett of Kirkhill died in 1722.

Shortly after the collection of poll tax in 1696, the estate of Tilliecorthie, in the parish of Udny, was sold by the Lumsdens to the Burnetts of Kirkhill. It remained in the family until sold, about, the mid 1700s, by an Alexander Burnett of Kirkhill to James Clark a merchant in Old Aberdeen.

Thomas Burnett, 3rd laird of Kirkhill, baptised 28 April 1694 in Aberdeen, succeeded his father who died in 1722. He was educated at Aberdeen Grammar School and was a student at Marischal College from 1704-6. After leaving the University he was apprenticed to George Keith and admitted to the Society of Advocates in Aberdeen on 15 August 1722. He was made an honorary burgess of Old Aberdeen on 5 April 1735. Thomas Burnett was styled *of Kirkhill* when he married, on 25 December 1716, in Aberdeen, Margaret Turner, born about 1695, daughter of Robert Turner of Turnerhall. Thomas and Margaret Burnett had the following children:

- Thomas Burnett baptised on 22 October 1717 in Aberdeen and died young.
- Margaret Burnett baptised 21 April 1719. She was co-heir to her father.(see details below)
- Anna Burnett baptised 10 December 1719 in Aberdeen.
- Clementina Burnett baptised 14 February 1721 in Aberdeen. She married, on 4 August 1752, Robert Sandilands, advocate, baptised 23 December 1719 in Newhills parish, son of John Sandilands of Craibstone and Isabella Baillie. (Marriage proclaimed on 25 July in Cruden parish and on 27 July 1752 in St. Nicholas parish). Robert Sandilands was apprenticed to Thomas Burnett and admitted to the Society of Advocates in Aberdeen on 26 July 1743. He became the Collector of Cess for Aberdeen county. Clementina and Robert had a daughter:
    - Margaret Sandilands baptised on 9 August 1753 in Cruden parish.

  Clementina died in January 1756 and was buried in Aberdeen. Robert Sandilands married (2) on 17 August 1765 in Cruden parish, Anna Kinnaird, heiress of Wester Draikies, Inverness-shire. She died in 1768 and was buried in Gordon's Aisle, Old Machar. Robert died on 26 December 1774 in Aberdeen, in his 54th year.
- Thomas Burnett baptised 1 July 1722 in Aberdeen and died young.
- Alexander Burnett baptised 2 November 1723.
- Robert Burnett baptised 18 April 1725 in Aberdeen.
- Helen Burnett baptised 21 July 1726 in Aberdeen.

- ❑ Mary Burnett, baptised 22 September 1729 in St. Paul's Chapel, Aberdeen. Godfathers were John Burnet 'Poles', Merchant, John and George Turner. [St. Paul's baptismal records]. Mary died in May 1734 aged 5.
- ❑ Thomas Burnett, baptised 14 August 1733 in St. Paul's Chapel, Aberdeen. Godfathers were James Moir of Stoneywood and John Burnett of Poles. [St. Paul's baptismal records]. Thomas died in 1734.

Thomas Burnett of Kirkhill died on 3 November 1763. Margaret Turner Burnett died on 8 December 1775 aged 80.

Margaret Burnett, born 1719, daughter of Thomas Burnett of Kirkhill, succeeded in due course of time. The estate of Kirkhill passed to the Bannerman family through her marriage to Alexander Bannerman of Frendraught, a merchant in Aberdeen. Margaret and Alexander Bannerman had the following children:

- ❑ Margaret Bannerman baptised 18 February 1738 in St. Nicholas, Aberdeen and died young.
- ❑ Patrick Bannerman baptised 9 April 1739 in St. Nicholas, Aberdeen
- ❑ Alexander Bannerman baptised 22 December 1741 in St. Nicholas, Aberdeen. He became Dr. Bannerman of Kirkhill, Professor of Medicine at the University of Aberdeen, and in October 1796, inherited from Sir Edward Bannerman to become Sir Alexander Bannerman, 6th Baronet of Elsick, in Kincardineshire. Sir Alexander died in December 1813.
  - ♦ Thomas Bannerman baptised 19 May 1743 in St. Nicholas, Aberdeen. He was a wine merchant in Aberdeen in 1787. Thomas died in January 1820 aged 77.
  - ♦ Margaret Bannerman baptised 3 November 1744 in St. Nicholas, Aberdeen.
  - ♦ Anna Bannerman baptised 3 November 1744 in St. Nicholas, Aberdeen.
  - ♦ Mordaunt Bannerman baptised 2 May 1746 in St. Nicholas, Aberdeen.
  - ♦ Charles Bannerman baptised 7 May 1750. He became Charles Bannerman of Crimondgate and was a manufacturer in Aberdeen. Charles died in September 1813.

Research is continuing into the above Burnett families and their complex inter-relationships.

Sources (for the convenience of researchers, some sources are indicated beside the relevant text) **:**

Baptismal records of St. Paul's Episcopal Chapel, Aberdeen.

Parish registers of St. Nicholas.

Civil Registers of Births, Marriages and Deaths of Newmachar and Old Machar.

Henderson, J.,A., *History of the Society of Advocates in Aberdeen.*(1912), Spalding Club.

8

THE BURNETTS OF SHEDDOCKSLEY , COUNTESSWELLS, and POWIS

Eileen A. Bailey

Burnetts of Sheddocksley

Sheddocksley was part of the Freedom Lands of Aberdeen. In 1398 it was leased for £3 Scots. In 1551 it was divided into two feus which combined were the highest set at that time. In 1629 they were held by Andrew Burnett who leased the Town's Mills which lay on either side of his property for £66 13s 4d each. These mills had been built around 1617. As a merchant, Andrew Burnett was obviously a man of enterprise.

Andrew Burnett of Sheddocksley is considered to be the son of John Burnett of Leys. He was the brother of Thomas Burnett, merchant in Aberdeen. An Andreas Burnett was recorded in 1619 in the Register of burgesses of Aberdeen. He married an unknown spouse and had the following children:

- Johnne Burnett baptised 10 June 1607 in Aberdeen.
- Alexander Burnett baptised on 13 September 1610 in St. Nicholas parish. He succeeded his father.
- Andrew Burnett who married on 8 June 1647, Isobel Drum, daughter of James Drum. In 1658 the name of Andrew Burnett, son of Andrew Burnett of Sheddocksley appears in the Register of Burgesses.
- Margaret Burnett who married on 20 May 1628 in Old Machar parish, William Moir, son of Patrick Moir of Chapeltown.

Andrew Burnett of Sheddocksley was killed in Aberdeen on 13 September 1644.

Alexander Burnett of Sheddocksley, who succeeded his father in 1644, became a merchant. He married, on 23 October 1638, Margaret Skene, widow of William Black and daughter of Patrick Skene. Alexander Burnett was an active Covenanter and was involved in the battle against Montrose at Aberdeen on 13 September 1644. He survived that day and, on 16 October, was one of the burgesses appointed a Captain, of the Futtie (Fittie) division, of the town forces and designated to meet Montrose on his return march from Speyside to try to dissuade him from bringing his army into the town. Alexander and Margaret Burnett had the following children:

- Andro (Andrew) Burnett baptised on 20 August 1639 in Aberdeen.
- Alexander Burnett born on 11 July 1640, and baptised on 11 August, in St. Nicholas parish. He died unmarried in Turkey.
- Bessie Burnett baptised on 12 September 1641 in Aberdeen. She married on 17 September 1668 in St. Nicholas parish, Alexander Ker, minister of Grange parish. They had one known child
    - Isobel Ker.
- Isobel Burnett baptised on 22 April 1642 in Aberdeen.
- Cristian Burnett baptised on 20 September 1646 in St. Nicholas Parish. She married, on 29 January 1678, in St. Nicholas parish, John Findlater. Their children were:
    - Margaret Findlater baptised 1 December 1678 in St. Nicholas parish. Died young.
    - Bessie Findlater baptised 26 September 1680 in St. Nicholas parish.
    - Alexander Findlater baptised 20 December 1681 in St. Nicholas parish.
    - Unknown (daughter) baptised 27 April 1684 in St. Nicholas parish.
    - Margaret Findlater baptised 24 May 1685 in St. Nicholas parish.
- James Burnett of Sheddocksley baptised on 14 April 1648 in Aberdeen. He succeeded in Sheddocksley.

James Burnett of Sheddocksley, born in 1648, succeeded his father, Alexander in Sheddocksley. James, as a burgess of Aberdeen, conveyed the estate of Sheddocksley to the Dean of Guild of Aberdeen in 1677. As described in detail in Chapter 12, James Burnett had his Arms recorded in the New Register in 1672 when he is described as *James of Sheddocksley whose grandfather was a 3rd son of Leys.*

Burnetts of Countesswells

Countesswells now lies on the western perimeter of the city of Aberdeen, to the north of Cults. The point at which the lands of Countesswells came into the hands of Burnetts is uncertain but an Alexander Burnett of Countesswells is recorded in the mid-seventeenth century. An 8000 marks debt left owed by Sir Thomas Burnett, 1st Baronet to Alexander Burnett of Countesswells had risen to 20,000 marks by the time Sir Alexander Burnett, 2nd Baronet, came of age in 1658 resulting in him having to give wadset over Leys to Alexander.

Alexander Burnett of Countesswells had a charter, under The Register of the Great Seal [(1)], of Salterhills with Auchries and other lands *apprising from the Earl Marischal.* His daughter and heiress, Marjorie married, in 1640, James Sandilands of Cotton, born 1610, son of James Sandilands of Craibstone and his spouse Catherine Paterson of Granton, Kincardineshire. Her estate of Countesswells descended to his second son John Sandilands, later Provost of Aberdeen. Salterhill/Satyrhills had been sold earlier.

Countesswells, at a later date came into the possession of another branch of the family through James Burnett, who was born 1742, an ancestor of the Burnett-Stuarts. He became James Burnett of Countesswells having purchased that estate with a fortune that he made in India and built the mansion house of Countesswells. James married Elizabeth Grant, born at Orton on 2 February 1746, second daughter of Sir Ludwick Grant of Dalvey,

Burnetts of Powis

The earliest mention of Powis *trans pontem et rivulum de Powis* (the bridge and stream of Powis) occurs in a Sasine dated 4 May 1526 from Bishop Gavin Dunbar to King's College. The Powis burn which took its source from Forresterhill, crossed Kittybrewster and through the lands of Powis until it met the main street of Old Aberdeen where there was a bridge forming one of five entrances to Old Aberdeen. The burn also provided the water supply for the southern part of Old Aberdeen. Alexander Fraser, Regent of King's College, was the 1st laird of Powis, in the parish of Old Machar, Old Aberdeen. His possession initially comprised a house on the west side of the street opposite the college gate, a small yard and some short riggs (strips of land) which he bought from William Anderson. He proceeded to build two large houses and three smaller ones near the street and twelve houses along the Powis burn from which he gained income in the region of 500 merks per year.

His successor on his death in 1742 was Captain Hugh Fraser whose daughter Christian married John Leslie, Professor of Greek. Their daughter Christian married Alexander Burnett of Kemnay. Her niece, Isabella Leslie, the last surviving daughter of Hugh Leslie, 4th laird of Powis, became the 6th in succession as John Leslie of Powis died unmarried. Isabella Leslie and her unmarried sister, Helen, moved from Calsayseat to Powis where they devoted much of their income to public and charitable causes. In 1885 they entailed what was left of the Leslie estate on George Burnett, Lord Lyon, and his heirs but George predeceased them on 24 January 1890. Helen Leslie died on 11 April 1893 and Isabella on 12 March 1894 at which time John Burnett succeeded as 7th laird.

John George Burnett of Powis, who was born on 30 March 1876 in Edinburgh, was a son of George Burnett, Lord Lyon, and Alison Stuart. He achieved an MA degree and was appointed a Justice of the Peace. John became the **7th Laird of Powis** in June 1894 following the death of Isabella Leslie, 6th of Powis (niece of Christian Leslie Burnett, his grandmother). He married, on 13 November 1901 at St. Stephens, Dublin, Catherine Sarah Helen Irvine, daughter of Capt. Duncan Malcolm Irvine of Killadeas, Co. Femanagh. John Burnett served as Member of Parliament for North Aberdeen from 1931-35. He was the author of the *Powis Papers* [(1)] John and Catherine Burnett had the following children:

- George Irvine Leslie Burnett who was born on 10 April 1903 at Powis House, Old Aberdeen. He married Alice (surname not known).
- Malcolm Stuart Leslie Burnett who was born on 22 September 1904 at Powis House, Old Aberdeen. Malcolm married Mary Rydall, born 7 August 1921. They had the following children:
  - Anthea Burnett who married Richard Skilbeck. Their known children were:
    - Virgina Skilbeck.
    - Edward Skilbeck.
    - Henry Skilbeck.
  - Anthony Burnett married Kathie (surname not known). They had three children of whom only one name is known i.e.
    - Adam Burnett.
  - Charles Burnett married Donna (surname not known). Their children:
    - Pamela Burnett.
    - Haylie Burnett
  - Callum Burnett married Roberta Mair. Their children:
    - Andrew Burnett.
    - Catriona Burnett.
    - Emma Burnett.
    - James Burnett.
    - Robert Burnett.

  - Denys Burnett married and had a son
    - Sam Burnett.
- Helen Mary (Maysie) Burnett who was born on 15 December 1905 at Powis House, Old Aberdeen, married in 1930, Denys Foster. They had the following child:
  - Rosemary Foster who married Robert Tasker Paice.

References:

(1) Burnett, John G., *Powis Papers 1507-1894*, Third Spalding Club, Aberdeen.

Sources:

Burnett, G.,(ed) Allardyce, J., *The Family of Burnett of Leys*, (1901), Spalding Club.

Burnett, John G., *Powis Papers 1507-1894*, Third Spalding Club, Aberdeen.

Civil Registers of Births, Marriages and Deaths, Old Machar district.

Parish Registers, St. Nicholas and Old Machar.

Tayler, A., & H., *The Valuation of the County of Aberdeen for the Year 1667*, (1932), Spalding Club.

Taylor, A., & H., *The Jacobite Cess Roll of the County of Aberdeenshire in 1715*, (1931) Third Spalding Club.

9

THE BURNETT-STUARTS and BURNETTS OF DALADIES

Eileen A. Bailey

Burnett-Stuart

James Stuart/Stewart (Colonel) was a Jacobite in 1689. His children included:

- Anna Stuart who married, on 4 September 1697 in Foveran parish, to James Ferguson of Pitfour, Sheriff-Substitute of Aberdeenshire.
- John Stuart who was born in 1659. Captain John Stuart, 1st of Crichie, had an active military career during which he served in Brigadier Maitland's Regiment in several campaigns. He lost his left hand at the Siege of Namur in 1689. The wooden prosthetic replacement is still in the possession of his descendants. In spite of close connections with the Jacobites, Captain Stuart was a Williamite and served on the staff of King William of Orange. He bought the lands of Dens and Little Crichie in the parish of Deer, Aberdeenshire from the Earl Marishal in 1695 completing the purchase in 1702. He built the first house of Crichie in 1709. John Stuart married Agnes Gray of Shivas House, Ellon. He died in 1729 and his will was recorded in the Commissariat dated 11 December 1729.

  John and Agnes Stuart had the following children:
  - James Stuart. He died unmarried in 1749.
  - Theodosia Stuart, born in about 1702, married, on 25 September 1729 in St. Nicholas parish, Aberdeen, John Burnet, born 1704, son of John Burnett of Daladies, Merchant in Aberdeen and Katherine Paton of Grandholm. John Burnett followed in his father's footsteps to become a Merchant in Aberdeen. His grandfather was John Burnett of Daladies, descended from the Burnetts of Leys. John Burnett and Theodosia Stuart had numerous children some of whom died young. Theodosia inherited Dens & Crichie from her father and the family thereafter assumed the surname Burnett-Stuart. Theodosia died a widow on 3 March 1769 aged 67 and was buried in St. Nicholas churchyard along with children as indicated below:
    - John Burnet who was baptised on 6 August 1730 at St. Paul's Episcopal Chapel, Aberdeen. He built a significant fortune in Aberdeen trading and manufacturing linen. John Burnett laid out and established the village of Stuartfield, Aberdeenshire, in 1773 naming it after his grandfather

Captain John Stuart. He died on 9 November 1784 aged 57 and was buried at St. Nicholas. John Burnet bequeathed the majority of his fortune to St. Nicholas Kirk for the poor, indigent and improvident, to Robert Gordon's college for bursaries, to the University of Aberdeen for a prize for an essay on the nature and existence of God and to Aberdeen Free Hospital (Cornhill). His mortification was finally ratified in 1804.

- James Burnett who was baptised on 4 March 1732 at St Paul's Episcopal Chapel. He died in infancy and was buried at St. Nicholas.
- George Burnet who was baptised on 4 December 1733 at St Paul's Episcopal Chapel, Aberdeen. Witnesses were recorded as James Cattanach, late Baillie, James Stuart of Dens, Alexander Bannerman, Merchant and James Burnet, Merchant.
- Agnus(Agnes) Burnet who was baptised on 21 January 1735 at St Paul's Episcopal Chapel. Witnesses were recorded as James Catanach, late Baillie and James Stewart of Dens. Agnes died on 2 January 1768 aged 33 and was buried at St. Nicholas.
- Katharine Burnet who was baptised on 16 July 1737 at St Paul's Episcopal Chapel. Witnesses were recorded as Pa. (Patrick) Trumbel (Turnbull), Merchant and James Nicholson of Glenbervie.
- Robert Burnet who was baptised on 5 March 1736 at St Paul's Episcopal Chapel. Witnesses were recorded as James Stuart of Dens and James Stuart, Merchant.
- James Burnet who was baptised on 14 February 1739 at St Paul's Episcopal Chapel. James died in infancy and was buried at St. Nicholas.
- Theodosius Burnet who was baptised 20 May 1740 in St Paul's Episcopal Chapel. Witnesses were recorded as James Stuart of Dens and James Burnet. He married Frances Crosmier, Marquise de Mont Giron. They lived in Dominica, West Indies, where children, including John (1775) were born. Theodosius Burnet died on 13 February 1778 aged 38 and was buried at St. Nicholas. Their son was
  - ➢ John Burnett-Stuart was born in 1775 in Dominica, West Indies. He married in 1801 to Elizabeth Horsfall who died in 1855. John died in 1847. Their children:
    - John Burnett -Stuart (Rev.) died in 1873.
    - Theodosius Burnett-Stuart (Rev.) became Prebendary of Wells, Vicar and Lord of Manor of Wooken. He married in 1839 to Maria Love Robertson of Keavil, Fife. Their children were:
      - ◊ Eustace Robertson Burnett-Stuart born April 1846.
      - ◊ Augustina Burnett-Stuart born September 1848. She died unmarried in 1896.
      - ◊ Theodosius Burnett-Stuart

- ◊ Lilias Mary Burnett-Stuart married in 1869.
- ◊ Amy Frances Magdalene Burnett-Stuart died unmarried in 1908.

- James Burnet who was baptised 8 January 1742 at St. Paul's Episcopal Chapel. Witnesses were James Stuart of Dens and James Burnet. He became James Burnett of Countesswells having purchased that estate with a fortune that he made in India and built the mansion house of Countesswells. James married Elizabeth Grant, born at Orton on 2 February 1746, second daughter of Sir Ludwick Grant of Dalvey, Morayshire. James Burnett died on 5 July 1782. Elizabeth died at Dunkeld on 1 January 1831. Their children were:
  - ➢ John Burnett christened 8 September 1781. He married, in 1804 at Troup House, Penelope Isabella Hayes, eldest daughter of Sir Henry Hayes. For some time she had lived, as their daughter, with Mr Garden Campbell of Troup and his wife Penelope Smythe. John and Penelope Burnett lived at Countesswells until the estate was sold and then built Woodend Cottage on the Leys Estate.
    - Charles James Francis Burnett was born in 1805 at Countesswells. He served in the Army and died in India.
    - Elizabeth Boscawen Burnett was born in 1806 at Countesswells. She died on 29 May 1820 aged 12 years and 7 months and was buried at St. Nicholas.
    - Penelope Smyth Burnett was born on 16 November 1808. She died in 1820 aged 12 years and 10 months and was buried at St. Nicholas.
    - Unknown daughter Burnett was born in 1809 at Countesswells.
    - Mary Jane Burnett was born in 1810.
    - Henrietta Patricia Burnett was born in 1811.
    - Francis Burdett Burnett was born in 1813 at Woodend Cottage. He died on 14 February 1818 aged 4 years, 11 months and 14 days and was buried at St. Nicholas.
    - Charlotte Burnett was born in 1814 at Woodend Cottage, Crathes.
    - James Ludwick Burnett was born in 1815 at Woodend Cottage.
    - John Burnett was born in 1817 at Woodend Cottage.
    - Mary Gascoigne Burnett was born in 1819 at Woodend Cottage. She married the Rev. John Lillie. They lived for a time in Tasmania and then in Christchurch, New Zealand.
    - Athole Burnett was born in 1821 on Isle of Man. He was named after the Duke of Athole who owned the island at that time.
    - Marianne Jane Burnett was born in 1824 on Isle of Man.

[the above information on the descendants of John Burnett of Countesswell was submitted by Jennifer Mackenzie of Gisborne, New Zealand]

- Robert Burnet who was baptised on 10 December 1747. St. Paul's Episcopal Chapel.
- Peter Burnet who was baptised on 14 January 1749. St. Paul's Episcopal Chapel.
- Elizabeth Burnet who was baptised on 16 April 1750. St Paul's Episcopal Chapel.
- Jean Burnet who was baptised on 22 August 1751. St. Paul's Episcopal Chapel.

The baptism on 11 September 1774 in Peterculter parish of an Untong Burnett has puzzled some researchers. Untong was a native servant employed by James Burnett of Countesswells who presumably arranged for his baptism. After James Burnett died in 1782, Untong (also spelt Ontong) went to work in Morayshire, perhaps arranged through Mrs Elizabeth Grant Burnett's family connection with that area. He is known to have married (1) on 12 April 1788 in Elgin to Margaret Ritchie with whom he had a son William Burnett who was baptised on 12 November 1788 in Drainie parish. Ontong Burnett married (2) Elspeth Hay on 19 December 1790 in Drainie parish.[information provided by Jean Calder of Aberdeen, a researcher of Burnetts in north-east Scotland]

Eustace Robert Burnett-Stuart. JP of Dens & Crichie (representative of Burnett of Daladies) was born in 1846. He married, in 1874, Carlotta Jane Lambert, daughter of Joseph Lambert of Cottingham, Yorkshire. Carlotta died in 1920. Eustace Robert Burnett-Stuart died in 1925 [ref. Fox-Davies, *Armorial Families*, Vol.1, (1929)]. Both were buried at Old Deer. Their son:

- John Theodosius Burnett-Stuart was born on 14 March 1875. He became General, Sir, GCB. KBE.ADC.CMG.DSO.DL. Sir John was a Knight of the Thistle. He served in Rifle Brigade and was at the North-west Frontier of India from 1897-98. From 1931-1934 he was General Officer Commanding in Egypt, Palestine and the Sudan. Sir John was ADC to the King and a leading soldier of his generation. During his distinguished career he trained others who also went on to excel in military command such as Montgomerie and Wavell. He married in 1904 to Nina Nelson, daughter of Major A.A.C.Nelson. Sir John died in 1958 and was buried at Old Deer.
  - Elizabeth Burnett-Stuart, born in 1905, married in 1926 to Evelyn Stuart Arthur, son of James Arthur of Montgomerie, Ayrshire. Their son

- ➢ Adrian James Arthur Burnett-Stuart of Crichie was born in 1932. He held the rank of Captain. Adrian died in 1958 and buried at Old Deer.
- ♦ Kathron Lilias Burnett-Stuart born in 1917 married, in 1939, Brigadier Henry Cotesworth Slessor of the Royal Horse Artillery. Kathron died in 1997. Their son was:
  - ➢ John George Slessor who was born in 1948. He assumed the surname and Arms of Burnett-Stuart in 1969. In 1975 Geordie married Patricia Beatrice de Laverne de la Montoise. Their children are:
    - Cerise Marie Burnett-Stuart.
    - Julia India Marie Burnett-Stuart.
- ❑ George Eustace Burnett-Stuart. CBE of Ardmeallie, Bridge of Marnoch. Born in August 1876, he joined the Egyptian Civil Service in 1900 and returned in 1923. He married in 1924 to Ethelreda Cecily Edge, daughter of T.L.K. Edge DL. JP. of Stretley Heath, Nottinghamshire, England. They had the following children:
  - ♦ Joseph Burnett-Stuart born 1930
  - ♦ Thomas Burnett-Stuart born 1934
- ❑ Francis Burnett-Stuart, born on 7 December 1877, became a Writer to the Signet on 24 March 1902 having been apprenticed to John Cowan and J.A. Dalmahoy. He married on 13 July 1912 to Mary Campbell Martin, daughter of Edward Martin and step-daughter of Mrs Hugh Lang of Brackley Lodge, Northampton. Francis died on 26 April 1949.
- ❑ Gilbert Robertson Burnett-Stuart born 2 March 1885 at Crichie House.

[additional details on the Burnett-Stuart family were provided by Geordie Burnett-Stuart of Crichie]

Burnetts of Daladies

The lands of Daladies lie on the north bank of the River North Esk, on the current border of Kincardineshire with the county of Angus. From Arms recorded, it has been deduced that this family were of Burnett of Leys. Charles Burnett, Ross Herald, demonstrates, in Chapter 12, how John Burnett of Daladies recorded Arms containing the three holly leaves and hunting horn in 1676.

A record of John Burnett's exact relationship to Leys has not been found other than the reference in George Burnett's notes to one of the other sons of John Burnett, of Leys, *John who married and had a daughter Agnes.* John Burnett of Daladies married Agnes Turnbull, daughter of Turnbull of Stracathro, and it is reasonable to assume that Daladies was acquired through this marriage as the two locations are in close proximity. John Burnett appears to have been one of the prominent Aberdeen merchants of the day, as was George Burnett's other suggested son of Leys, that is Andrew of Sheddocksley. The Arms of Burnett of Daladies are contained in the heraldry decorating the ceiling of the south aisle of St. Andrew's Episcopal Cathedral in Aberdeen. John and Agnes Burnett had at least one known son:

- John Burnett of Daladies, nicknamed *Bonnie John*, who married, on 15 June 1703 in Old Machar parish, Katharine/Catherine Paton, second daughter of George Paton of Grandholm. He succeeded his father. John Burnett was listed as a Jacobite of 1715. John and Katharine Burnett had the following children whose names are as spelt in records:
  - John Burnett who was baptised on 12 August 1704. John married Theodosia Stuart of Dens from whom are descended the Burnett-Stuarts.(details are given in this Chapter)
  - Issobell Burnett who was baptised on 13 August 1705 in Aberdeen.
  - Agnas Burnett who was baptised on 5 January 1707 in Aberdeen.
  - George Burnett who was born on 17 August and baptised on 21 December 1708 in Aberdeen
  - Catherine Burnett who was baptised on 28 January 1711 in Aberdeen.

John Burnett married (2) on 23 December 1714, Katherine Gordon, third daughter of John Gordon of Fechil. John and Katherine (Gordon) Burnett had the following children:

- Marjorie Burnett who was baptised on 11 October 1715. She married Patrick Turnbull of Stracathro, brother of the laird of Stracathro, a merchant in Aberdeen.
- Rachell Burnett who was baptised on 11 October 1717.
- James Burnett, baptised 10 June 1701, who married Isobel Black, baptised 21 April 1694, daughter of John Black, merchant of Bordeaux and Isobel Gordon of Hallhead. Isobel's brother was Professor Joseph Black, born in 1728 in Bordeaux, who was a celebrated chemist at the Universities of Edinburgh and Glasgow. Children in the large family of James and Isobel Burnett were:
  - John Burnett baptised on 8 July 1742 in Aberdeen.
  - James Burnett baptised on 18 May 1743 in Aberdeen.
  - Margaret Burnett, baptised on 23 May 1744 in Aberdeen, married, according to contract dated 12 November 1770, Robert Byres of Kincraigie, baptised 12 December 1740, son of Patrick Byres and Janet Moir. Robert was a merchant in Memel, Prussia and also in London. He bought the estate of Kincraigie, adjacent to Tonley, from the Leslies on 8 December 1786. Robert Byres also owned considerable property in St. Pierre, Martineque where he died on 17 November 1799 whilst on a visit there. Robert and Margaret had children.
  - George Burnett baptised on 12 December 1745 in Aberdeen.
  - Katherine Burnett baptised on 9 October 1746 in Aberdeen.

- Robert Burnett baptised on 10 December 1747 in Aberdeen.
- Peter Burnett baptised on 14 January 1749 in Aberdeen.
- Elizabeth Burnett baptised on 16 April 1750 in Aberdeen.
- Jean Burnett baptised on 24 August 1751 in Aberdeen.
- Joseph Burnett baptised on 20 March 1753 in Aberdeen, later Lieutenant Colonel, who married Margaret Steele and became Burnett of Gadgirth, Ayrshire.
- Isobel Burnett baptised on 11 August 1754 in Aberdeen.
- Adam Burnett baptised on 7 September 1755 in Aberdeen.
- Alexander Burnett baptised on 5 November 1756 in Aberdeen.
- Isaac Burnett, twin of Alexander, baptised on 5 November 1756 in Aberdeen
- Samuel Burnett baptised on 6 October 1763 in St. Nicholas, Aberdeen.

James Burnett died on 29 September 1787 and was buried at St. Nicholas. Isobel Burnett died on 24 November 17--, aged 6-, and was also buried at St. Nicholas.

Sources: (for convenience of researchers, some sources have been indicated beside the relevant text)

Burnett,G., (ed), Allardyce,J., *The Family of Burnett of Leys*, (1901), Spalding Club.

Baptismal Records, St. Paul's Episcopal Church, Aberdeen.

Fox Davies, *Armorial Families*, Vol.I, (1929).

History of The Society of Writers to His Majesty's Signet with List of Members, (1936), Edinburgh.

Keay, J. & Keay, J., *Collins Encyclopaedia of Scotland*, (1994), Harper Collins.

Parish Registers for St. Nicholas and Old Deer.

10

THE RAMSAYS OF BALMAIN

Eileen A. Bailey

In doing is this knowledge won. To see what yet remains undone.
(Trench)

Sir Thomas Burnett, 6th Baronet of Leys married, in 1754, Katherine Ramsay, daughter of Charles Ramsay and grand-daughter of Sir Charles Ramsay of Balmain.

The Ramsays of Balmain were descended from John Ramsay, a favourite of King James III, who fought with his king at Lauder Bridge in July 1482 but managed to escape the fate of execution which befell the rest of the king's attendants at the hands of the Earl of Angus. He was later created Lord Bothwell and had his estates restored. The lands of Balmain, Fasque, which had reverted to the Crown in 1475, and others in Kincardineshire were created into a barony in his favour in 1510 and inherited by his descendants.

William Ramsay succeeded his father in 1535.

David Ramsay, who succeeded on 12 August 1588, married Catherine Carnegie, daughter of Sir Robert Carnegie. A Charter from the king gave David Ramsay *the lands and barony of Balmane with the pedicles called Blaries and Boginnothie, town and lands of Eslie, pedicle of Burnsyde, town and lands of West Strath, with the grain mill and pedicles called Lonocheid, Burnet Island and Drumhenrie, grain mill of Fettercarne, annual rent of 20s from the lands of Fettercarne, towns and lands of Feskye, Petnamone and Dronmyre, grain mill of Kincardin, walkmill of Petnamone, town and lands of Reidheuch, with pedicles of Petnamone, Gallohillock, Cokhills and Starryhauch, with commonty on the muirs and mosses of Luther, Kincardin, Gallowmyre and Cammock and common hill above Fesky with manor, fortalices. Mills, fishing etc all resigned by the said David and of new incorporated into the barony of Balmane.* In the context of the charter, *town* refers to a farmtown and *Petnamone* was/is Pitnamoon which has the prefix *Pit*, of Pictish origin, which signifies 'a portion of'.

Sir Gilbert Ramsay, son of David and Catherine Ramsay succeeded in 1625 and was made a baronet of Nova Scotia on 3 September of the same year.

Sir David Ramsay, who became a Member of Parliament, succeeded. He married Margaret Irvine of Monboddo. The Irvine family were owners of Monboddo before it was acquired by Burnetts.

In 1674, **Sir Charles Ramsay,** MP, succeeded. His wife was Elizabeth Falconer of Glenfarquhar.

Sir David Ramsay, MP, who succeeded his brother Sir Charles in 1697, married, on 25 October 1672 in Banchory-Ternan parish, Elizabeth Coutts, widow of Sir Alexander Burnett of Leys, 2nd Baronet.

Sir David Ramsay was succeeded, in 1710, by another brother, Alexander.

In 1754, **Sir Alexander Ramsay** was succeeded by his nephew, **Sir Alexander Ramsay Irvine.** Sir Alexander Ramsay, 6th Baronet of Balmain, died without issue or heir in 1806 at which time he was succeeded by the immediate younger brother of his heir in line.

Alexander Burnett, born on 31 July 1757, was the second son of Sir Thomas Burnett of Leys and Katherine Ramsay. He was admitted to the Scottish Bar and in 1779 became Sheriff of Kincardineshire. Alexander Burnett married, on 14 October 1782, Elizabeth Bannerman, daughter of Sir Alexander Bannerman, 4th Baronet of Elsick. With her sister, Mrs Russell, Elizabeth co-inherited extensive lands in the valley of the River Feugh, including the whole of the parish of Strachan, when Sir Edward Bannerman, 5th Baronet, died without issue. The southern portion of these lands went to Elizabeth Bannerman Burnett. Both Elizabeth and her sister were said to have been extremely handsome, causing heads to turn as they made their way around Edinburgh during visits there.

Sheriff Alexander Burnett did not enjoy good health and travelled much in southern Europe. At the outbreak of the French Revolution he returned to the north-east of Scotland. Alexander Burnett assumed the surname Ramsay by royal licence and corresponding Arms by warrant of the Lord Lyon. He was created a Baronet of the United Kingdom on 13 May 1806 with the title Sir Alexander Ramsay of Balmain. Irrespective of this, the original Baronetcy of Balmain continued until 1859 held by Sir Thomas Ramsay, the last descendant in the male line from Lord Bothwell. On inheriting Balmain, Alexander gave up his Sheriffdom and decided to settle at Fasque, Kincardineshire where, in 1809, he demolished a existing smaller eighteenth century house and, some yards to the south of it, built Fasque House, a palatial mansion at a cost of £30,000. He ruined himself financially by so doing. The architect of Fasque is generally considered to have been John Paterson of Edinburgh who had been appointed as the Scottish representative of the famous designers Robert and John Adam after they went to London. Sir Alexander (Burnett) Ramsay, sold the estate of Fasque and Balfour in 1829 to Sir John Gladstone, the eldest son of Thomas Gladstone, Corn Merchant in Leith, Edinburgh. Sir John, who forty-three years earlier had left home to make his fortune in Liverpool, returned to Scotland where Fasque became his home, and that of his heirs who included William Ewart Gladstone, a Prime Minister of Britain. Gladstones are still resident at Fasque to the present day.

Fig.10.1 Fasque House, Fettercairn. 1998 (Bailey)

Sir Alexander (Burnett) Ramsay, 1st Baronet, and Elizabeth Bannerman had the following family most of which dropped the surname Burnett and retained that of Ramsay:

- Alexander (Burnett) Ramsay, born on 14 February 1785, who succeeded as 2nd Baronet of Balmain.
- David (Burnett) Ramsay who died after 1807 and before 1816.
- Thomas (Burnett) Ramsay who was born on 24 February 1786. He became a Captain in the 47th Regiment and served in the Peninsular war and at the Battle of Waterloo. Thomas married (1) on 9 November 1816, Jane Cruickshank, second daughter of Patrick Cruickshank of Stracathro. By the late 1820s, the family resided at 25, Royal Circus, Edinburgh. Their children were:
    - William Burnett Ramsay who was born on 11 April 1821 in Fettercairn parish.

      From 1829-32, William was a pupil of Edinburgh Academy. By settlement of his great-uncle, General William Burnett who died on 7 February 1839, he succeeded to Arbeadie in Banchory Ternan on the north of the River Dee and to the southern half of Blackhall estate extending towards Strachan. William was a 2nd Lieutenant in 1828, Lieutenant in 1829 and Captain in the Rifle Brigade by 1846 and a Lieutenant Colonel of the Forfar and Kincardine Militia. He retired from military service in 1848. William married, on 24 July 1854, Anne Davidson, born on 12 December 1824, daughter of Duncan Davidson of Inchmarlo. They had the following children:

- Thomas Burnett-Ramsay, later of Banchory Lodge, who was born on 29 March 1862 in Banchory Ternan parish. He, too, became a Captain in the Rifle Brigade. Thomas died in South Africa.
- Frances Mary Burnett-Ramsay, born on 29 May 1855 in Banchory Ternan parish, who married on 20 August 1879 W.D. Robinson-Douglas of Orchardtoun, Kirkcudbrightshire.
- Katherine/Catherine Jane Burnett-Ramsay who was born on 21 June 1856 in Banchory Ternan parish. In the 1881 census she was recorded, aged 24, at Banchory Lodge with her aunt, Williamina Davidson.
- Annie/Anne Elizabeth Burnett-Ramsay who was born on 2 July 1858 in Banchory Ternan parish. In the 1881 census, she was recorded, aged 22, at Banchory Lodge with her aunt, Williamina Davidson. She married Thomas Bentick and became Baroness Bentick. Anne died on 19 January 1934 and was buried at Banchory Ternan Churchyard.
- Wilhelmina (Ina) Margaret Burnett-Ramsay who was born on 9 December 1859 in Banchory Ternan parish. In the 1881 census she was recorded, aged 21, at Banchory Lodge with her aunt, Williamina Davidson. She died on 15 April 1889 and was buried in the Burnett-Ramsay enclosure at Banchory Ternan Churchyard.

William Burnett Ramsay of Banchory Lodge died on 6 November 1865 aged 44 and was buried in the Crathes enclosure in Banchory-Ternan Churchyard. His wife Anne Davidson Burnett-Ramsay died on 13 October 1880 aged 56.

- Elizabeth Marjory Ramsay who was born on 1 January and baptised on 17 January 1820 in Fettercairn parish. She married the Rev. Alexander J. Murray of Jersey in 1858 and had children whose names are not known.
- Catherine Forbes Ramsay, who was born on 16 April 1822 in Fettercairn parish, was killed in an accident on 21 August 1843 aged 21. She was buried in the Crathes enclosure at Banchory Ternan Churchyard.
- Jane Ramsay who was born on 1 November 1823 at Balbegno Castle in Fettercairn parish. She married, on 7 October 1852 at Glenbervie House, (marriage also recorded in Banchory Ternan parish) Dr. Alexander Thom, medical practitioner, born 7 November 1818 at Crathes, Banchory Ternan

parish, son of William Thom and Margaret Burnett. Alexander and Jane Thom had two known children:

- Alexander Thom baptised on 2 October 1853 in Banchory Ternan parish.
- William Ramsay Thom born on 9 February 1855 at Woodside Cottage, Banchory, and baptised the same day.

Captain Thomas Ramsay married (2) on 28 April 1826, his cousin-german, Margaret Burnett, second daughter of Sir Robert Burnett, 7th Baronet of Leys. Their child was:

- Thomas Ramsay who was born on 13 January 1828 in Fettercairn parish. He served in the Royal Navy and died on 17 January 1856 aged 28. Buried in the Crathes enclosure at Banchory Ternan Churchyard.

Margaret Ramsay died in February 1828. The following poem written by her mother, Lady Margaret Burnett of Leys, was found amongst the family papers at Crathes.

A MOTHER'S LAMENT

And art thou, Margaret, then no more?
In death's dark bed dost thou repose?
'Nor hear'st this stormy whirlwind's roar;
Nor heed'st thy loved child's lonely woes.

To me, it seems a little while,
Since in my lap I with thee played,
And heard thy prattle, mark'd my smile,
Or in thy soft couch saw thee laid.

When woman grown – in hall or bower,
I felt a mother's pride to see,
My lovely blushing op'ning flower
Please others, as it has pleased me.

'But late thou wort a married wife-
Content, tho' full of anxious care;
Ah! Who can tell what ills of life
May meet us, ere we are aware?

I little thought thy last 'farewell'
Was thy last accents I should hear:
Thy voice remember'd is a knell;
Thy look a thought I cannot bear.

God's will be done! I am old and gray;
And thou were ripe for Heaven, I know.
'Tis better thus. Lord guide my way;
And to my daughter let me go!

Thomas Ramsay, Snr., died on 18 December 1857 aged 71.

- Robert (Burnett) Ramsay, born on 27 February 1787, became a Captain in the 14th Regiment of Foot. He married on 23 June 1817 (recorded in the parishes of Dun and of Montrose, Angus county), Margaret Cruickshank, third daughter of Patrick Cruickshank of Stracathro. Robert and Margaret had the following children:
  - Robert Ramsay, born in 1818 who married, in 1855, Susan Fullerton-Lindsay-Carnegie, daughter of William Fullerton-Lindsay-Carnegie of Spynie. Their children were:
    - Marmaduke Francis Ramsay born in 1860.
    - Robert Christian Ramsay born in 1861.
    - Edward Lauderdale Ramsay born in 1865.
    - Arthur Douglas Ramsay born in 1868.
    - Norman Ramsay born in 1869.
    - Agnes Mabel Alice Ramsay
    - Nina Mary Ramsay.
    - Edith Patricia Ramsay.
    - Wilfred Ramsay.
    - Helen Ramsay.
  - Alexander Ramsay, born in 1823, died in 1857.
  - Marmaduke Ramsay, born in 1834, died in 1865.
  - Ellen Ramsay.
  - Elizabeth Patricia Ramsay who married, in 1877, Major Francis Fenwick Laye of the 90th Regiment. He died in 1881.
- Edward Bannerman Ramsay was born on 31 January 1793 and spent his early years in Yorkshire with his grandfather Sir Alexander Ramsay. Edward was educated at Durham School and Cambridge University where he gained the degree of LL.D. He was ordained in 1816 and was a curate in Rodden and Buckland, Somerset, England before moving to Edinburgh in 1729 and settling there. His first appointment in Edinburgh was as curate to the Rev. Shannon at St. George's, York Place. He then became the incumbent of the old Church of St. Paul for one year. Edward's last church was St. John's in Princes Street where he was firstly a curate to Bishop Sandford and later the incumbent. He became Dean of Edinburgh in the Scottish Episcopal Church in 1846. He was an accomplished musician of the flute and organ, an author and lecturer. Edward Ramsay married, in 1829, Isabella Cochrane, daughter of Rupert Cochrane of Nova Scotia. They had no children. Isabella died on 23 July 1858 and the Very Reverend Dean Edward Ramsay on 27 December 1872.
- Marmaduke Ramsay became a Fellow and Tutor of Jesus College, Cambridge. He died, unmarried, in 1831.

- William Ramsay was born on 27 May 1798(?) and entered the Royal Navy at aged 13. Sir William Ramsay received a knighthood in 1869 and achieved the rank of Admiral in 1870. He had a career of distinction which is detailed in Burnett, *The Family of Burnett of Leys*, 106-7 and in The Burnett Family, 56. Latterly he lived in Edinburgh, with Dean Ramsay. An obituary was printed in *The Scotsman* of 4 December 1871, following the death of Admiral Sir William Ramsay in Edinburgh on the previous day.
- Edwin Hewgill Ramsay was born in 1804 and died unmarried.
- Elizabeth Ramsay was born on 17 September 1783. She married, on 7 April 1808, Henry Taylor of Brookfield, Kincardineshire. In a letter, dated 26 January 1807 at Montrose, and preserved in the Crathes Papers, Alexander Ramsay intimated the forthcoming marriage. He asked Sir Robert Burnett to provide him with a drawing of Robert's Arms, suggesting that the coachmaker's painter could do a sketch, as he wished to have them done in stone and placed in a vacant shut up window on one of the side towers of the house.
  Elizabeth and Henry Tailyour had children whose names are not known.
- Catherine Ramsay died in infancy.
- Helen Ramsay died in infancy.
- Mary Ramsay died in infancy.
- Isabella Ramsay died in infancy.
- Frances Ramsay died in infancy.
- Lauderdale Ramsay, born in 1806, married (1) on 10 July 1832, David Duncan of Rosemount, Angus. She married (2) on 12 July 1837, Sir James Horn Burnett, 10th Baronet of Leys. Lauderdale died on 4 November 1888.

Sir Alexander Ramsay, 1st Baronet, died at Fasque on 17 May 1810. The Executry papers of Elizabeth Ramsay, Lady Ramsay of Balmain, dated 1841-45 are archived in the Crathes Papers and include the list of household furniture sold on 31 January and 1 February 1845 at 7 Darnaway Street, Edinburgh.

Sir Alexander Ramsay, 2nd Baronet, was born on 14 February 1785 and succeeded his father who died in 1810. He married (1) on 1 August 1811, Jane Russell, eldest daughter and co-heiress of Francis James Russell (deceased), of Blackhall, Kincardineshire. Their children were:

- Alexander Ramsay, born on 26 May 1813, who succeeded as 3rd Baronet.
- William Ramsay who was born in 1814 and died in 1840.
- Francis Ramsay who was born in 1815. He served in the Royal Artillery attaining the rank of Captain. In 1848, he married Georgina Hay Home, daughter of William Foreman Home of Wedderburn and had the following children:
  - William Alexander Ramsay who was born on 5 December 1848 and became Major, then Colonel in the 4th Hussars. William married, on 2 September

1873, Susan Newcombe Minchiner, daughter of William Minchiner of Clontarf, Co. Dublin, Ireland.
- Francis Farquharson Ramsay who was born on 28 July 1855. He was a Captain in the 92nd Gordon Highlanders and died on 7 April 1898.
- Fanny Jane Ramsay.

- Mary Ramsay who married (1) in 1837, the Rev. Bruges Lambert of Misterton, Somerset, England. He died in 1843. Mary then married (2) on 25 February 1845, John Sparks of Crewkerne, Somerset. She died in 1890.
- Elizabeth Ramsay who married (1) John Carr, son of John Carr of Dunstanhill, Co. Durham, England. John died in 1856. Elizabeth married (2) in 1860, Charles Murray Barstow who died in 1885. She died on 14 February 1887.

Following the death of Jane Russell Ramsay in 1819, Sir Alexander Ramsay married (2) on 26 December 1822, Elizabeth Maule, second daughter of William, Lord Panmure. Their children were:

- Fox Maule Ramsay who was born on 18 March 1824 in Fettercairn parish. He became a Captain in the 56th Regiment. Fox Ramsay died, unmarried, on 15 March 1860.
- Edward Bannerman Ramsay who was born on 12 October 1826 in Fettercairn parish. He became a Major-General in the Madras Staff Corps and died, unmarried, on 25 December 1883.
- George Dalhousie Ramsay, who was born on 23 May 1828 in Montrose parish, was Secretary to his uncle, Lord Panmure who was at the time Secretary of State for War, Director of Army Clothing Department and a KCB. George Ramsay, CB, married, on 23 April 1864, Julia Charteris Crawford, daughter of John Crawford FRS. They had the following children:
  - Alexander Panmure Oswald Ramsay who was born on 15 April 1867. He died on 16 February 1897.
  - Elizabeth Edith Ramsay who was born on 27 July 1865. She married, on 11 January 1894, the Rev. Barton R. V. Mills. They had children whose names are not known.
- Marmaduke Ramsay who was born in 1837. He was a colonel in the Bengal Staff Corps and married, in 1858, Anne Innes, daughter of Lieutenant-General Innes. They had the following children:
  - Marmaduke Ramsay who was born in 1859
  - Alexander Ramsay who was born in 1866.
  - Elizabeth Maule Ramsay.

  Marmaduke Ramsay, Snr., died in 1893.
- Patricia Ramsay, who was born on 5 August 1825 in Fettercairn parish, married, on 14 May 1872, W. John de Coucey Agness, Commander RN.

- Christina Ramsay who married, on 14 February 1859, Major Charles Elliot, CB, of the Madras Staff Corps, youngest son of James Elliot of Wolflee. Christina died on 13 March 1873.
- Georgina Ramsay who was baptised on 22 August 1833 in the parish of Dun, Angus, married, on 20 April 1861, Lieutenant-General Sir R.J. Hay, KCB, RA, second son of Admiral Hay of Belton, Haddington.
- Caroline Ella Ramsay who was baptised on 16 June 1835 in Dun parish, Angus. She died in 1845.

Sir Alexander Ramsay died on 26 April 1852 and Elizabeth Maule died on 12 September of the same year.

Sir Alexander Ramsay, 3rd Baronet, who was born on 26 May 1813, succeeded his father. For a time he was Member of Parliament for Rochdale, England. Alexander married, on 29 December 1835, Ellen Matilda Entwisle, daughter of John Entwisle of Foxholes, Lancashire, England. Alexander and Ellen had the following children:

- Alexander Entwisle Ramsay, born 14 January 1837, who succeeded as 4th Baronet.
- Hugh Francis Ramsay who was born on 23 September 1838. He married, on 24 February 1868, Jane Maria Sandys, daughter of General F. H. Sandys of the Bengal Army. They had the following children:
    - Hugh Entwisle Ramsay who was born in 1871.
    - Noel/Nowell Bannerman Ramsay who was born in 1875.
    - Rhoda Beatrice Ramsay.
    - Sybil Ramsay.
    - Olive Ramsay.
- John Ramsay, who was born on 30 June 1843, became a Captain in the Royal Engineers. He married, on 5 September 1876, Florence Mary Hilton, daughter of Richard J. Hilton of Preston House, Faversham, England. Their three sons and three daughters were:
    - Hector Alexander Ramsay who was born in 1878.
    - Norman Ramsay who was born in 1880.
    - Ethel Ramsay who was born in 1882.
    - John Richard Ramsay who was born in 1883.
    - Hilda Ramsay who was born in 1885.
    - Evelyn Ramsay who was born in 1887.
- Bertin Ramsay who was born on 13 October 1850 married, in 1881, Kate King, daughter of Dr. David King of Jamaica and USA. Their children were:
    - Hallie Ramsay.
    - Ellen Ramsay.
    - Ethel Ramsay.

- Ellen Augusta Ramsay who married, on 2 December 1885, Ernest de S. Hamilton Brown, son of Major George Brown, DL of Comber House, Co. Londonderry, Ireland.

Sir Alexander Ramsay died on 3 March 1875.

Sir Alexander Entwisle Ramsay, **4th Baronet**, born on 14 January 1837, succeeded his father. Alexander married (1) on 22 January 1863, Octavia Haigh, youngest daughter of Thomas Haigh of Elm Hall, Liverpool, England. Their children were:

- Ellen Georgina Ramsay who was born in 1864.
- Alexander Haigh Ramsay who was born in 1866 and died in 1870.
- Herbert Ramsay who was born on 6 February 1868 and succeeded.
- Nora Mabel Ramsay who was also born in 1868.
- Arthur Ramsay who was born in 1871.
- Florence Augusta Ramsay who was born in 1874.

Alexander Ramsay married (2) in 1880, Caroline Ireland, daughter of T. J. Ireland MP. They had one known child:

- Gilbert Ireland Ramsay who was born in 1881.

Sir Herbert Ramsay, 5th Baronet, born in 1868, succeeded his father. He married, on 3 January 1902, Mabel Hutchison, daughter of William Joseph Hutchison of Aldingham, Winton, Australia. Their children were:

- Alexander Burnett Ramsay who was born on 26 March 1903 and became the 6th Baronet.
- Herbert William Alexander Ramsay who was born on 20 May 1907. Herbert married on 28 March 1936, Bessie Billingsby Dight, daughter of Dr. Alfred Billingsby Dight, of Sydney, Australia.
- Nora Marjorie Ramsay who was born in February 1905. She married on 5 September 1928, Captain Adrian B. Baltrop, MC, of the 3rd Queen Alexandra Gurkha Rifles, son of Rev. Arthur Baltrop. They had children.
- Constance Agnes Ramsay who was born on 1 October 1912.

Sir Alexander Burnett Ramsay, 6th Baronet, born in 1903, succeeded his father in 1924. Alexander married on 5 September 1935, Isabel Ellice Whitney, daughter of Arthur William Whitney of Wangoola, Australia. Their children were:

- Enid Ellice Ramsay who was born on 30 March 1937.
- Alexander William Ramsay who was born on 4 August 1938.
- Patricia Thirza Ramsay who was born on 15 February 1940.

Sources:

Burnett, G., (ed) Allardyce, J., *The Family of Burnett of Leys,* (1901), Spalding Club.

Burnett, C., H., *The Burnett Family and Collateral Branches*, (1950), Los Angeles.

The Edinburgh Academy Register 1824-1914, (1914), Edinburgh.

Rogers, C., *Monuments and Monumental Inscriptions in Scotland*, Vol II, (1872).

International Genealogical Index for Kincardine, Aberdeen, Angus and Midlothian counties.

Parish Registers for Banchory Ternan and Fettercairn.

1881 British Census.

Civil Birth, Marriage and Death Registers for various Kincardineshire and Aberdeenshire districts.

Crathes Archives.

Memorial Inscriptions Banchory Ternan Churchyard and Fettercairn.

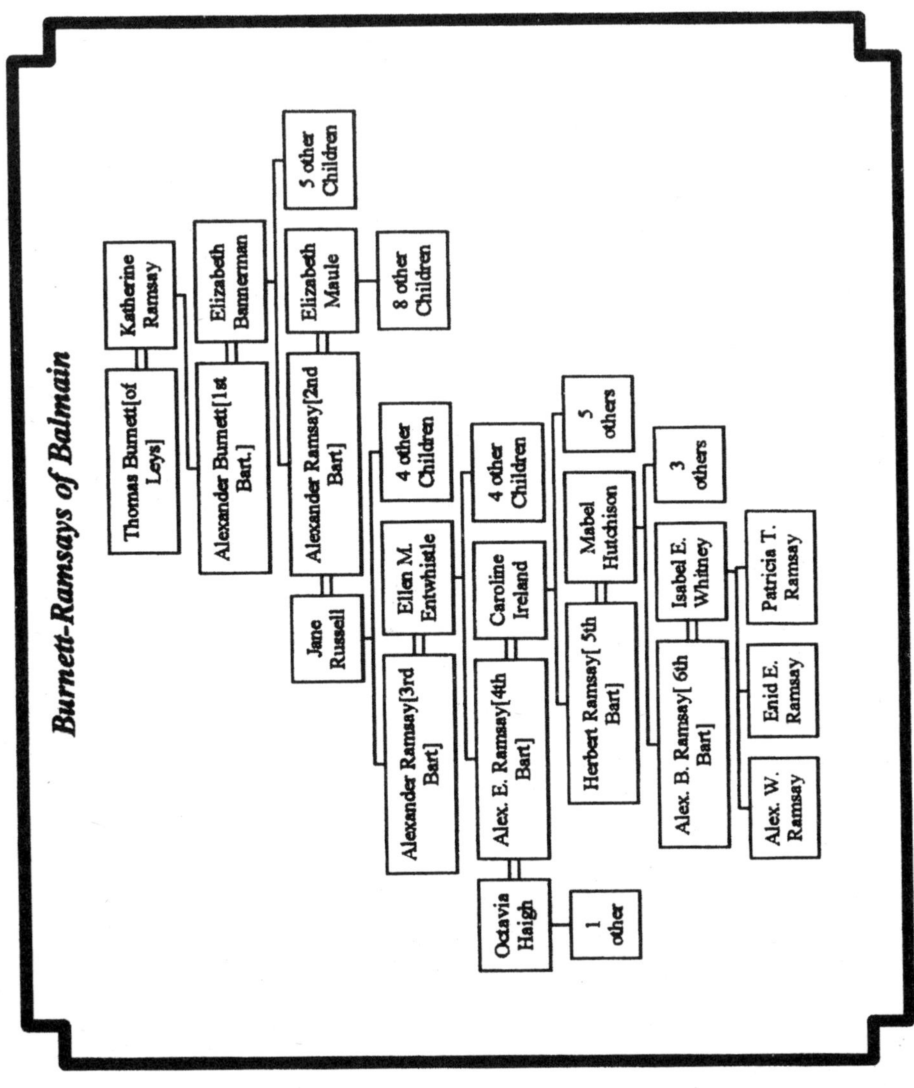
Burnett-Ramsays of Balmain
Thomas Burnett[of Leys]
Katherine Ramsay
Alexander Burnett[1st Bart.]
Elizabeth Bannerman
Alexander Ramsay[2nd Bart]
Elizabeth Maule
5 other Children
8 other Children
Jane Russell
Alexander Ramsay[3rd Bart]
Ellen M. Entwhistle
4 other Children
Alex. E. Ramsay[4th Bart]
Caroline Ireland
4 other Children
Octavia Haigh
1 other
Herbert Ramsay[5th Bart]
Mabel Hutchison
5 others
Alex. B. Ramsay[6th Bart]
Isabel E. Whitney
3 others
Alex. W. Ramsay
Enid E. Ramsay
Patricia T. Ramsay

11

INDETERMINATE BURNETT CADETS

Eileen A. Bailey

Some Burnett families are, by tradition, said to be descended from lines such as that of Burnett of Leys. In research for this work there have been instances where that descent has not been fully validated and so it is appropriate at this time to include them here in the hope that further research will reveal new information.

BURNETTS OF KINCHYLE

William Burnett who was born in 1742-43, is thought, from recent research to have been a son of Robert Burnett, the last laird of Sauchen, and his wife, Jean Barclay. William became a farmer and the tenant in Hirn on the Leys Estate, Banchory. He was factor at Crathes from 1764 to Sir Thomas Burnett, 6th Baronet and to his successor Sir Robert Burnett, 7th Baronet of Leys. William Burnett married, on 19 March 1778 in Banchory-Ternan parish, Helen Lighton (Leighton). On his retirement from Leys, a portrait of him was hung in the Estate Office which, at that time, was within the Castle. William and Helen Burnett's children were:

- William Burnett who was baptised on 25 April 1784 in Banchory Ternan parish. He became the Rev. William Burnett, a Methodist Minister & Publisher and settled in Brooklyn, New York, where he married Mary Ogden, who was born in 1800, of the Ogden family of Elizabeth, New Jersey. William died on 1 June 1861 at Brooklyn and was buried Evergreens Cemetery (Greenwood Shade) along with his wife who died at Brooklyn in 1881. Children of William and Mary Burnett were:
  - William Burnett who died unmarried.
  - Mary Isabella Burnett who was born on 10 August 1827 and married to Captain Edward Hart of the US Navy.
  - Helen Burnett who died unmarried.
  - Anna Amelia Burnet who married to Edward Storer.
  - Joseph Mosher Eaton Burnett who was born on 17 January 1837. He married Mary Louisa Knapp.
- Alexander Burnett who was baptised on 11 June 1786 in Banchory Ternan parish, and married, on 1 July 1811 in Cluny parish, Anne Gillanders. Alexander Burnett, later styled *of Kinchyle*, was a farmer and the Factor for the Estates of Lady Saltoun and later for those of her son, Lord Saltoun, at Ness

Castle, Inverness-shire. He was also Factor for the Dochfour Estates of the Baillie family in the same county. Their children were:

- ♦ Anne Burnett who was baptised on 29 October 1811 in Cluny parish, Aberdeenshire. She married George Marquis, an Aberdeen accountant, on 27 June 1839 in the parish of Dores, Inverness-shire. Their children were:
  - Ann Burnett Marquis who was baptised on 1 May 1842 in Old Machar parish, Aberdeen. She married John Robert Hall on 4 November 1863 in Old Machar parish. Anne and Robert had the following children:
    - ➢ Anne Margaret Hall born 1864.
    - ➢ Isabella Moir Clark Hall born 1866.
    - ➢ Other child who died in infancy.

    Anne died in 1868 and John Robert Hall in 1885
  - Isabella Marquis who was born on 6 June 1843 in Old Machar parish. She married, in 1861, John Moir Clark, born in 1836. Child:
    - ➢ John Moir Clark born 10 October 1862. He died unmarried in 1928.

    John Clark died in 1896 and Isabella in 1902.
  - George Marquis who was born on 22 October 1844 in Old Machar parish.
  - Alexander Burnett Marquis who was born on 28 December 1845 in Old Machar parish. Alexander died in 1873.

  Anne Burnett Marquis died on 28 February 1849 at 16 Albyn Place, Aberdeen.
- ♦ Helen Burnett who was baptised on 30 October 1812 in Cluny parish, married, on 7 November 1833 in Dores Parish, Duncan McTavish, son of Archibald McTavish, tackman at Garthbeg (who died on 23 January 1831 aged 76 years) and Ann McGillivray (who died on 5 February 1834 aged 61 years). Duncan McTavish followed his father in the duties of tackman of Garthbeg. Helen's marriage was also recorded on 7 November 1833 in Boleskine parish, Inverness-shire. Helen & Duncan McTavish had the following children:
  - Anne McTavish born on 13 August 1834 in Boleskine parish.
  - Archibald McTavish born on 8 August 1835 in Boleskine parish. Archibald was Commander of the Steamship *'Armenian'* in the Indian Seas and died at Singapore on 21 June 1862 aged 26 years.
  - Helen Mary McTavish born on 24 November 1836 in Boleskine parish.
  - Alexander Burnet McTavish born on 2 October 1838 in Boleskine parish.
  - Robert McTavish born on 5 April 1840 in Boleskine parish. Robert McTavish died at Berbice, West Indies on 16 (the month is unclear on the family gravestone) 1857.
  - Duncan McTavish born on 14 February 1842 in Boleskine parish.
  - William Burnett McTavish born on 10 October 1843 in Boleskine parish.

- George McTavish baptised on 26 December 1845 in Boleskine parish.
- Catherine McTavish born on 8 December 1846 in Boleskine parish. Her name appears on a gravestone in Boleskine Churchyard but the dates are no longer legible.
- Elizabeth McTavish baptised on 4 September 1849 in Inverness.
- Margaret McTavish born on 15 July, was baptised on August 1852 in Inverness.
- Josephine McTavish born on 27 March 1856 in Inverness.

Duncan McTavish died at Heathmont, Inverness on 30 July 1884 aged 80 years. Helen Burnett McTavish died at Planefield, Inverness on 28 December 1859 aged 46 years.

♦ Agnes Burnett who was baptised on 26 February 1814 in Cluny parish. She married, on 23 November 1838 in Inverness, Archibald Hill Rennie. Their marriage was also recorded on 29 November 1838 in Dores parish, Inverness- shire. Agnes and Archibald Rennie had children:

- Agnes Emily Rennie baptised on 15 November 1839 in Inverness. She died, unmarried, on 5 March 1933.
- Anne Rennie baptised on 27 November 1840 in Inverness.
- Catherine Amelia Rennie baptised 8 July 1842 in Inverness. She is believed to have died unmarried.
- Mary Mortimer Rennie baptised 10 October 1843 in Inverness. She is believed to have died unmarried.
- Alexander Rennie baptised on 21 January 1848 in Inverness. It is understood that he never married.
- Charles George Rennie baptised on 1 May 1849 in Inverness. He is believed to have died unmarried.
- William Rennie baptised on 18 June 1850 in Inverness. He is believed to have died unmarried.
- Jane Allan Rennie baptised on 24 October 1851 in Inverness. She died, unmarried, on 22 May 1940 and was buried in Winbourne Cemetery, Bournemouth. England.

♦ Robert Burnett baptised 7 September 1816 in Cluny parish. He died in America. Robert married Elizabeth Smith and had one child:

- Robert Burnett

♦ Elizabeth Burnett, whose birth/baptismal record has not been found, married Duncan McLennan on 7 July 1841 in Dores parish, Inverness-shire. Their children were:

- Alexander Evan McLennan who was born on 12 February 1860 in Inverness.
- Duncan McLennan who was baptised on 9 March 1847 in Inverness.

    - Annie McLennan.
- William Burnett baptised 15 September 1821 in Cluny parish. He is said to have left Scotland.
- Katherine Burnett baptised 24 February 1820 in Cluny parish. She died unmarried.
- Amelia Burnett baptised 8 June 1823 in Cluny parish. She died unmarried.
- Jane Burnett, whose birth/baptismal record has not been found, married, on 5 October 1848 in Dores Parish, Inverness-shire, Andrew Stewart Oliver, born on 1 January 1809, Boleskine parish, Inverness-shire, son of Robert Oliver and Isabel Stewart. Children:
    - Robert Stuart Oliver born on 8 June 1849 in Dores parish. Thought to have died unmarried.
    - Andrew Oliver born on 20 June 1863 in Inverness. Thought to have died in childhood.
    - Duncan Stewart Oliver who died unmarried in Italy.
    - Alexander Burnett Oliver who became a Planter in Ceylon. He died unmarried.
- Barbara Burnett baptised on 6 July 1826 in Dores Parish. She died unmarried.
- Mary Burnett baptised on 8 May 1828 in Dores Parish and died young.
- Alexander Burnett baptised on 27 November 1829 in Dores parish. Twin of George. He is thought to have left Scotland.
- George Burnett baptised on 7 December 1829 in Dores parish. Twin of Alexander. Thought to have left Scotland.

- Catherine Burnett who was baptised on 3 April 1780 in Banchory Ternan parish. She married, on 27 September 1804 in that parish, William Taylor. Their children were:
    - Ellen/Helen Taylor who was baptised on 20 March 1810 in Banchory Ternan parish.
    - Elizabeth Taylor who was baptised on 2 December 1813 in Banchory Ternan parish.
    - Robert Taylor who was baptised on 3 January 1818 in Banchory Ternan parish. He married Mary Gibbon on 10 June 1852. They had the following children:
        - William Taylor who was baptised on 15 December 1852 in Banchory Ternan parish.
        - Catherine Taylor who was baptised on 12 July 1854 in Banchory Ternan parish.

- Mary Taylor who was born on 11 November 1856 in Banchory Ternan parish.
- James Taylor born 23 September 1858 in Banchory Ternan parish.
- Alexander Taylor born 8 July 1860. Banchory Ternan.

♦ Alexander Taylor baptised 24 July 1823 in Banchory Ternan parish.

❑ William Burnett who was baptised on 21 April 1805 in Banchory Ternan parish.

❑ Jean/Jane Burnett who was baptised on 13 May 1782 in Banchory Ternan parish. She married, on 2 September 1805, Joseph Taylor. Jane/Jean died on 22 November 1844 aged 61 and is buried close to her parents in Banchory Ternan Churchyard. Joseph Taylor was a farmer in Hirn, Banchory Ternan, and is recorded in the Rental Lists of Leys Estates as paying £13 13s in rent for Hirn in 1815 and £32 for the same in 1835. He died on 14 January 1842 aged 58 and was buried at Banchory Ternan. Their children were:

♦ Helen Taylor who died on 20 April 1824 aged 19 and was buried at Banchory Ternan churchyard.

♦ William Taylor who died on 25 April 1824 aged 16 and was buried at Banchory Ternan.

♦ Alexander Taylor who was baptised on 14 August 1810 in Banchory Ternan parish.

♦ Jane Taylor who was baptised on 23 March 1813 in Banchory Ternan parish.

♦ Robert Taylor who was baptised on 28 March 1816 in Banchory Ternan parish.

♦ Joseph Taylor who was baptised on 1 December 1818 in Banchory Ternan parish.

♦ Catherine Taylor who was baptised on 2 August 1823 in Banchory Ternan parish.

❑ Robert Burnett born on 1 August, was baptised on 3 August 1788 in Banchory Ternan parish. Robert married, in August 1816, Amelia Shirrefs, born 14 August 1797, daughter of Reverend James Shirrefs minister of West Church, Aberdeen and Amelia Morison. The Shirrefs family home was Friendville, which is now within the district of Mannofield, Aberdeen. Robert and Amelia lived at 11 Nelson Street, Edinburgh, and later, by 1827, at 16 Dublin Street, Edinburgh. Robert Burnett became an Advocate and, on 7 June 1821, a Writer to the Signet in Edinburgh. He died on 9 August 1828 at age 41. Amelia died on 23 June 1886 at the home of her daughter, Catherine La Forge, in Port Ewen, NY, USA, aged 88. Children of Robert and Amelia were:

♦ Amelia Burnett who was born on 28 June 1817 in Edinburgh. She married, on 22 August 1839 at St.Nicholas and Old Machar, Aberdeen, Rev. Henry Hine, a Wesleyan Minister, born on 8 August 1812 at Bellbroughton, Staffordshire, son of John Hine. Henry died on 27 January 1899 and Amelia on 13 April 1899 at Liverpool, buried in Southdown Road Cemetery, Liverpool, England. Their children were:

- John Burnett Hine born on 20 May 1840 who died in infancy.
- Robert Burnett Hine born on 6 December 1841.
- Henry Hine born on 5 June 1843.
- James Hine born on 9 April 1845 who died in infancy.
- William Hine born on 8 March 1846
- Amelia Burnett Hine born on 5 April 1848. She died unmarried on 17August 1927.
- Margaret Hine born on 28 June 1851.
- Frederick Hine born on 2 February 1853.
- Elizabeth Jane Hine born on 8 December 1854.
- James Balmain Hine born on 27 November 1858.

♦ Ellen Leighton Burnett born on 24 October 1818 in Edinburgh. She lived for a time with her sister, Amelia Hine, after their mother left Scotland for America in 1842. Ellen married, on 20 July 1856, William Willis Joyce, born on 5 March 1856 in Glasgow, son of William Willis Joyce. William was a Rancher in Monterey, CA. Ellen died on 21 February 1877 at Salinas, CA and William Joyce at Monterey on 13 January 1902. Their children were:

- Wilhelmina May Joyce born on 1 May 1857.
- Louisa Jane Joyce born on 10 November 1858.
- Mary Augusta Joyce born on 5 August 1860.
- Willis Burnett Joyce born on 15 November 1862.

♦ James Gilbert Burnett born 6 November 1819 in Edinburgh. James married (1) Sarah (surname unknown) and (2) on 7 June 1865, Julia Maria Chipp, niece and adopted daughter of Warren Chipp. She was descended from a John Chipp who went from England to America in 1764. During his early 20s, James Burnett went to America where he became an actor, manager and producer. They had a child:

- James Gilbert Burnett who was born on 5 August 1868 and died on 20 April 1894.

♦ Jane Farquhar Burnett born in 1822, was the twin of Margaret. Jane married, on 20 August 1840 in Old Machar parish, Lieutenant (later General) James George Balmain, born on 1 May 1814. James died on 3 August 1893, aged 79, at Wimbledon, England. Their children were:

- Marion Margaret Balmain born on 14 July 1841.
- Mary Jane Balmain.
- Charlotte Amelia Balmain.
- Helen Isabella Balmain.

- Alice Hope Balmain.
- Louis Farquhar Balmain who settled in Canada and was the twin of Millicent.
- Millicent Balmain, twin of Louis, died in infancy.
- James Hilaro Farquhar Balmain.

♦ Margaret Morison Burnett, born 1822, was the twin of Jane. She married, on 11 August 1841 in Old Machar parish, Major William Smith Thom, a merchant in Aberdeen who married (2) on 23 April 1854, Elspet Rose. Margaret died March 1844 and was buried, as was her husband at St. Nicholas, Aberdeen. Margaret and William had a child:

- Alexander Thom, baptised 25 February 1843 in St. Nicholas, Aberdeen, who became Cotton Planter in Ceylon

♦ Elizabeth Graham Burnett born on 20 March 1823. Elizabeth went to stay with her Uncle, Alexander Burnett, in Inverness-shire for a time after her mother left for Milford, NJ. Elizabeth went to America in about 1841. She married, on 15 April 1845, Warren Chipp, a Merchant & seedsman, born on 8 December 1814, son of John Chipp & Hannah Van Steenbergh. Elizabeth died on 21 December 1874 and Warren on 23 April 1887. Their children were:

- Amelia Margaret Chipp born on 10 October 1846.
- Charles Winans Chipp. Birth date unknown.
- Anna Graham Chipp born on 14 December 1852. She died unmarried on 23 April 1886.
- Elizabeth Burnett Chipp, born on 7 September 1855, who died in infancy.
- Alice Warren Chipp born on 12 January 1858.
- Katherine Burnett Chipp born on 19 May 1861.
- Agnes Marion Chipp born on 6 May 1864. She died on 25 November 1947.
- Warren Sidney Chipp born on 30 April 1867 in Kingston. NY.

♦ William Burnett born about 1825. He married Abby Pike. William was a US Inspector of Steamboats who died on 9 January 1893 aged 68.

♦ Robert Burnett born on 19 May 1826. He left home at age 15 in 1841 to go to sea. Three years later Robert was in America and married, on 12 March 1860, Elizabeth Orr Hopkins, born 22 December 1834, daughter of William Orr Hopkins and Martha Donaldson. Robert Burnett owned and operated towing boats on the Hudson River. He died on 22 October 1882 in Port Ewen. NY and Elizabeth died on 12 April 1904.

- Catherine Hunter Burnett. She married to John B. La Forge and together they lived in Port Ewen. NY. Catherine died on 15 March 1893. They had a child:
    - Amelia (Amy) Juanita la Forge who died unmarried on 25 September 1882.

Helen Leighton Burnett died at Woodhead, Banchory on 29 November 1817, aged 63, and was buried at Banchory Ternan Churchyard. William Burnett died on 5 May 1829 at Woodhead, Banchory, aged 86, and was also buried at Banchory Ternan.

BURNETTS OF LETHENTY

The Burgess Register of Aberdeen records that **Robert Burnett of Lethenty** was entered as a Burgess on 22 September 1671 and describes him as being son of Alexander Burnett of Countesswell, at one time baillie of Aberdeen. His exact ancestry has not yet been confirmed.

Robert Burnett of Lethenty became a Quaker who was made to suffer greatly for his adhesion to this faith to which he had become a convert before 1680. In 1663, municipal laws against Quakers began to be made and enforced in Aberdeen. On 16 December of that year, three known Quakers were ordered to be conveyed out from the town with orders that, should they return, they would be handed over to the hangman. Robert's relationship to the Burnetts of Leys was not stated by George Burnett and Temple in *The Thanage of Fermartyne* concluded that the Burnetts of Lethenty were descended from Alexander Burnett, brother of the first John Burnett of Elrick. This would seem to indicate that he was descended from Leys through the Burnetts of Camphill.

In the Meldrum Charter Chest an obligation, dated 11 March and registered 7 April 1665 by Adam Urquhart of Meldrum, gives warrant to Robert Burnett of Lethenty *for the lands of Lethenty, tiends, desks in the Chapel of Garioch etc* with the consent of James and Patrick Urquhart, brothers of the said Adam. This is thought to refer to the transfer of the estates of Patrick Urquhart (Adam Urquhart's father) to the family of Burnett. In 1696 (*List of Pollable Persons*), Robert Burnett was "still at Lethenty with his Lady, Robert Burnett his son, Margaret and Jean two grandchildren".

Robert Burnett became deeply involved in America with the New Jersey Quaker Settlement, of which he was a proprietor, no doubt because of the climate of intolerance of his faith. On 13 May 1702,he and his family settled at Milston Brook, Freehold, Monmouth County, NJ. It has been concluded that Robert Burnett's spouse was Anna Forbes. Children were:

- Mesdie/Maisie/Marjorie Burnett baptised on 7 June 1673, in Aberdeen.
- Jeane Burnett baptised on 16 June 1661 in Aberdeen.
- Patrick Burnett.
- John Burnett baptised on 2 December 1669 in Aberdeen.
- Robert Burnett baptised on 11 October 1666 in Aberdeen.
- Allen Burnett baptised on 25 March 1665 in Aberdeen.
- Isabel Burnett baptised on 5 September 1663 in Aberdeen. Isabel Burnett married, on 8 January 1684 in Edinburgh, William Montgomerie, born about 1654, the eldest son of Hugh Montgomerie and Catherine Scott. Isabel, who had gone to America with her family to settle in East New Jersey, was sent back to Scotland to complete her education. It was there that she met and married William. After the birth of several children, William and Isabel Montgomerie and family settled in Doctor's Creek, Monmouth County, East New Jersey where on 20 May 1706 William purchased, from his father-in-law Robert Burnett, 500 acres of land, which he later called Eglinton after his family's Ayrshire estates. William Montgomerie was alive in 1721 but the exact date of his death is not known. Known children of William and Isabel were:
  - Robert Montgomerie who was born in 1687 at Bridgend, Cumnock, Ayrshire. He married, on 8 February 1704 at Burlington, Sarah Stacey, daughter of Henry Stacey, originally from Spitalfields, Stepney, Middlesex, England. Sarah died 9 March 1743 and was buried at Crosswicks. Robert & Sarah Stacey Montgomerie, lived at Eglinton Estate and had the following children:
    - Robert Montgomerie born in 1705 at Eglinton Estate, NJ. He married Sarah (surname unknown). Sarah died in 1775 and Robert in 1776, both in Dauphin County. Pennsylvania.
    - Mary Montgomerie.
    - Elizabeth Montgomerie.
    - William Montgomerie who died young.
    - Sarah Montgomerie.
    - William Montgomerie.
    - Anna Montgomerie.
    - James Montgomerie who is presumed to have died young.
    - John Montgomerie.
    - James Montgomerie.
  - Alexander Montgomerie.

- Anna Montgomerie born on 1 February 1690 at Bridgend, Maybole, Ayrshire.
- William Montgomerie born on 7 February 1693 at Bridgend, Ayrshire.
- Elizabeth Montgomerie born on 12 July 1691 at Bridgend, Ayrshire.
- Jane Montgomerie.

[The genealogy of Isobel Burnett and William Montgomery has been compiled from parish records in Ayrshire and from the contributed research of Charles B. Roe, Jnr. of Washington who is a descendant.]

Sources (some sources have, for convenience of researchers, been inserted beside the relevant text)**:**

Burnett, C., H., *The Burnett Family with Collateral Branches*, (1950), Los Angeles.

Memorial Inscriptions at Banchory Ternan Churchyard, Cluny Churchyard, Boleskine Old Churchyard, Dores Churchyard.

Parish Registers of Banchory Ternan, Cluny, Dores, Boleskine, Inverness, Maybole.

Temple, Rev., W., *The Thanage of Fermartyne*, (1894), Aberdeen.

12

THE HERALDRY OF THE BURNETT FAMILY

Charles J. Burnett, Ross Herald

Heraldry, the floral border in the garden of history, is of its very nature colourful and gay. But it is not just a border of the tallest tulips with a background of ancient laurels: a picturesque record of the achievements and courage of past leaders of the people. It is also part of the flowered pageantry that brightens the living present for the ordinary man.
(Sir Iain Moncreiffe of Easter Moncreiffe, Kintyre Pursuivant, in *Simple Heraldry Cheerfully Illustrated*, 1953)

Although the Spalding Club volume on the Burnetts of Leys described several cadet branches, along with their various armorial ensigns, there was no succinct review devoted specifically to Burnett heraldry or its use as architectural decoration.

Since 1672 several grants of Arms have been made to Burnetts living in Scotland and England, either by the Lord Lyon King of Arms or by the English College of Arms in London. This chapter will list them all, but it will be helpful to begin with a few introductory comments.

In Scotland the assumption is made that all bearing the same surname are related, however distantly. Individuals who can prove descent from the chiefly House of Leys are known as determinate cadets, other Burnetts who cannot do so for lack of proof are regarded as indeterminate cadets. The kinship is expressed in armorial terms by granting specific charges on a shield of Arms which have a long association in the Arms of the principal family of the name. In the case of the Burnetts of Leys these are a silver shield with three green holly leaves and a black hunting horn with red strings.

Lord Lyon George Burnett featured early seals used by English Burnards, but in the 1891 volume he did not mention any heraldic sequence of events from when the English seals were in use until the late sixteenth century when armorial decoration was extensively employed at Crathes Castle. His researches were incomplete at the time of his death in 1890. Another reason why he gave no heraldic history is the almost complete lack of documentary evidence showing use of armorial ensigns by the Burnetts of Leys up to the end of the sixteenth century.

For the student of Scottish heraldry seal impressions are a primary source of information. Apart from a seal used by a Richard Burnard 'dominus de Farningdoun' (in Roxburghshire) which bears a single leaf, there are no Burnett of Leys seals until 1621. Another source of information is the collections of hand-painted coats of arms, bound in book form, known as *Armorials*. There are several of these dating from c1350 to c1630, either containing some Scottish Arms, or devoted solely to Scottish examples. Four of the Armorials are foreign, the remainder are Scottish, and it may be of interest to the reader for all to be listed:

1. c1350 Armorial de Gelré, Flemish, Brussels (contains 42 Scottish examples)
2. c1425 Armorial de l'Europe, French, Paris (contains 33 identified Scottish coats)
3. c1445 Armorial de Berry, French, Paris (contains 93 identified Scottish coats)
4. 1542 Sir David Lindsay of the Mount Armorial, Edinburgh
5. c1562 Queen Mary's Roll , Edinburgh
6. c1565 Sir Robert Forman of Luthrie Armorial, Edinburgh
7. c1565 Hamilton Armorial, London
8. c1566 Forman Lyon Office Armorial, Edinburgh
9. c1580 Armorial belonging to a Mrs C M Kerr in 1891, present location unknown.
10. c1583 Hector Le Breton Armorial, London
11. 1591 Seton Armorial, Edinburgh
12. c1592 The Hague Roll, The Hague, Holland
13. c1598 Lindsay Secundus Armorial, Balcarres House, Fife
14. c1620 Dunvegan Armorial, Isle of Skye
15. c1620 Workman Armorial, Edinburgh
16. c1625 Sawer's Armorial, Edinburgh
17 c1630 Sir James Balfour of Denmiln Armorial, Edinburgh
18. c1630 Gentlemen's Arms, Edinburgh

These prime sources of Scottish armorial ensigns, borne by Scots at the time each was painted, contain no early references to Burnett of Leys until the first reference, c1592 in *The Hague Roll.*

With no evidence of early heraldic use from seals or Armorials, can other clues be found?

There are two pieces of evidence to be considered. The first is second-hand from the pen of Sir George Mackenzie of Rosehaugh who wrote in his book, *Science of Heraldry* (published 1680), that in 1550 Burnet of Burnetland, "pursued Burnet of Leys before Lindsay of the Mount, then Lyon, to change his motto." Both Burnets apparently used the motto, *Virescit vulnere virtus* (Strength draws vigour from an injury) and Burnet of Burnetland obviously considered himself the senior Burnet Representer who wished to verify his claim. Apparently after the action Burnet of Leys began to use the motto *Alterius non sit qui potest esse suus* (He would not be another's who could be his). Apart from the reference by Mackenzie of Rosehaugh we have no physical evidence of armorial use by Burnet of Leys. One would imagine that if Burnet of Leys and Burnet of Burnetland (later Barnes) were armigerous, their Arms would have appeared in the Armorial created by Lyon Sir David Lindsay of the Mount – the Lyon King who had heard their case.

Lindsay's Armorial is dated 1542. Eleven years later a very fine carved stone panel, dated 1553, (Fig.12.1) was carved to commemorate the marriage of Alexander Burnet of Leys (1529-1574) and Janet Hamilton, the daughter of a rich cleric. The panel is now located on the east face of the tower of Crathes Castle. Above the multi-curved shield, bearing the impaled Arms of Burnett and Hamilton, is a gothic arch, decorated with crockets, and around the shield is a beautifully-carved folded ribbon carrying the words ALE(X)AND(ER) BURNET AND JANE(T) H(AMIL)TOUN. This panel is the earliest hard piece of evidence for the Arms of Burnett of Leys.

It would appear that although the Burnetts of Leys were landholders in Kincardineshire by right of a royal grant from Robert I, King of Scots, the family were 'small' lairds who kept a low profile in the political life of the realm of Scotland. Through marriage and good management the Burnetts slowly added to the original royal grant of land by purchase and lease until great good fortune occurred as a result of the marriage, about 1540, of Alexander Burnet of Leys and Janet Hamilton. This marriage was the foundation for the wealth which led to an architectural and heraldic climax during the lairdship of Alexander Burnet of Leys (1578-1619).

His completion/transformation of Crathes Castle provided an ideal opportunity for heraldic decoration – the public symbol of status which reached its apogee in Scotland at the end of the sixteenth century. It is interesting to note that this included a set of three heraldic panels on the south front of the tower which were carved around 1596. (Fig.12.2) Included in the set are the impaled Arms of Alexander Burnett and Janet Hamilton, the heiress, dated 1553. This reinforces the importance of that marriage. The other two panels show the Royal Arms of Scotland surrounded by the English Order of the Garter (James VI, King of Scots was created a Knight of that Order in 1590, and this is the earliest carved stone to commemorate that fact. As the shield and Garter are now badly weathered urgent treatment is required to save the stone); the third panel bears the impaled Arms of Alexander Burnet and his wife Katherine Gordon of Lesmoir, originally dated 1596. The date numeral 6 and the third boar head in the Gordon Arms have weathered away since 1891.

Inside Crathes Castle the significance of the Burnet/Hamilton marriage is further highlighted in the Great Hall. The plastered roof vault was originally highly decorated overall with tempera paint, and surviving fragments provide an indication of its one-time colourful splendour. Painted versions of the Burnet/Hamilton, Burnet/Gordon armorials are prominent, (Figs.12.3, 12.4) as are the Hamilton Arms carved on the central pendant boss. (Fig.12.5)

With this sudden blossoming of heraldic display at Crathes it is not surprising that Burnet of Leys at last appears in a Scottish armorial, albeit one now held in a foreign country at The Hague in Holland. Before looking at other decorative usage of Leys heraldry, the development of the family coat of arms should be considered.

By 1553 Burnet of Leys was using a shield, charged with three holly leaves and a hunting horn, presumably blazoned:
Argent, three holly leaves in chief Vert and a hunting horn in base sable stringed Gules
The crest *may* have been a right hand holding a knife pruning a vine, with the motto, after 1550, *Alterius non sit qui potest esse suus* (He would not be another's who could be his) or this variant, *Alterius non sit qui suis esse potest* (Who can be his would not be another's). About 1592 confirmation of the shield and its tinctures is given in *The Hague Roll,* without indicating crest and motto. Further confirmation of heraldic colours is given in the tempera decoration within Crathes Castle executed in the late 1590s, by order of Alexander Burnet of Leys. It is with Alexander's heir, Thomas, who inherited Leys in 1619, that the next stage of armorial progression occurs.

Thomas Burnet of Leys was knighted in 1620. Thereafter he used a seal which described him as SIR THOMAS BURNET KNIGHT. An impression of the seal survives, 1¾" dia., bearing a shield with holly leaves and hunting horn, set within foliage decoration, and encircled with the name and rank. There is no crest or motto. On 9 August 1621 Sir Thomas married, as his second wife, Jean Moncreiffe, daughter of John Moncreiffe of that Ilk. Five days after the marriage he used his seal to sign a legal document which is now in the Moncreiffe Charters.

Along with Crathes Castle, Sir Thomas Burnet of Leys also inherited the unfinished Muchalls Castle, near Stonehaven, which his father had started to re-model in 1619. Sir Thomas completed construction in 1627 and this delightful, compact building provides good visual heraldic information in the form of plasterwork and two carved stone panels.

The first panel (Fig. 6) bears the impaled Burnet of Leys/Gordon of Lesmoir Arms, but for the first time they are flanked by supporters, that on the dexter is weathered away completely, enough remains of the sinister supporter to show it was an animal. The supporters stand on a debased strapwork panel which once carried a motto. There are sufficient letters left to indicate it read ALTERIUS NON SIT QUI SUUS ESSE POTEST. Above the shield is a helmet with mantling, and the remains of a crest, a hand pruning a vine. Surmounting the crest are the remains of a double scroll which undoubtedly carried the motto VIRESCIT VULNERE VIRTUS. This panel must date from after 1620 when Sir Thomas Burnet of Leys was knighted. Sir Thomas chose a huntsman and a hunting dog, namely the greyhound. These particular supporters reflect the original grant of the Barony of Leys which was a royal game forest. He purchased his Baronetcy of Nova Scotia six years later, the Letters Patent being dated 21 April 1626, though he did not come into full possession of this hereditary knighthood until 13 June of the same year. Sir Thomas Burnett of Leys, 1st Baronet, was the twenty-second individual to acquire this honour (out of a final total of 205) which had been founded by King James VI and I on 18 October 1624.

Sir Thomas caused a second very fine stone carving to be executed for Muchalls Castle which was later moved to Crathes Castle where it is now located on the south wall of the tower. (Fig.12.7) It shows the impaled coat of arms of Sir Thomas and his second wife, Dame Janet Moncreiffe. On the dexter side of the shield the Burnett Arms have the addition of a canton bearing a saltire – a simplified version of the Arms of Nova Scotia to indicate the owner's Baronetcy. The huntsman supporter, in contemporary dress, has a hunting horn suspended from his left shoulder and resting on his right hip. The sinister supporter, a greyhound, has a collar. The supporters stand on a debased strapwork panel bearing the motto ALTERIUS NON SIT QUI SUUS ESSE POTEST, and above the hand, knife and vine crest is the usual Burnett motto VIRESCIT VULNERE VIRTUS. Obviously the ruling by Lyon Sir David Lindsay of the Mount in 1550 was completely ignored! This key Burnett heraldic panel is contained within a handsome frame enlivened with grapes and vine leaves.

A short period after this panel was completed a curious mistake in recording the Burnett Arms was made, not only once but twice! In both *Balfour of Denmiln Armorial* and *Gentlemens' Arms* the Burnett of Leys shield is shown as a silver with a black hunting horn *between* three *red* holly leaves. Someone made a mistake which was copied by another.

A significant event for Scottish heraldry was the decision of the Scottish Parliament to have every coat of arms recorded. The decision was implemented in 1672 when Volume one of The Public Register of All Arms and Bearings in Scotland was begun. It took twenty years to fill up the first volume because armigers were slow to record their Arms and some never did so initially. However Sir Thomas Burnett of Leys, 3rd Baronet (1663-1714) was one to do his duty and his Arms appear on folio 122 of the first Register Volume. Curiously the entry mentions no supporters, and only one motto VIRESCIT VULNERE VIRTUS.

We have to wait until the 8th Baronet, another Sir Thomas (1837-1849), before a significant change occurs to the Burnett Arms. Sir Thomas was never married but the year he inherited he informed the Lord Lyon that he was the new Baronet (it is normal custom to do so though few are so thoughtful in this day and age). He also requested supporters for his armorial achievement. Baronets of Nova Scotia are not entitled to supporters. Sir Thomas argued that he was the male representative of one of the minor Barons of Scotland prior to the year 1587, and as such could be granted supporters. He also requested the dexter supporter be a Highland huntsman. The reasons for doing so should be explained.

In 1822 the first Royal visit to Scotland since 1651 took place. The visitor was the newly-crowned King George IV, the former Prince Regent. The arrangements for his visit were masterminded by Sir Walter Scott who encouraged the Highland Chiefs to appear before their sovereign in tartan. Indeed the same sovereign also donned the kilt. Very few Chiefs knew what their tartan was, and an enterprising weaver, Mr. Wilson by name, who resided in Bannockburn near Stirling, obliged by producing suitable tartan patterns. Thus the great tartan industry began, further fuelled when Queen Victoria fell in love with Scotland. Her interest had yet to happen when Sir Thomas Burnett of Leys, Head of an established Lowland House, decided the Burnetts too should be considered Highlanders. He petitioned the Lord Lyon to turn his huntsman supporter into a Highlandman, complete with green doublet, wearing a kilt of red/brown tartan with a hunting horn worn on the left hip, and holding a bow in his right hand. The greyhound supporter remained unchanged, as did the single motto. The new armorial achievement of Burnett of Leys (second matriculation) was recorded on folio 33, Volume Four of The Public Register of All Arms and Bearings in Scotland, (Fig.12. 8) dated 24 October 1838.

An interesting use of this 'new' version of the Burnett Arms is an undated embroidered pipe banner, now set in a frame and adapted as a fire screen. (Fig.12.9)

The screen is located in the Victorian bedroom at Crathes Castle. The shield carries the three-point label of difference used by the heir to a coat of arms while the father is still alive. The banner was probably made for James Lauderdale Burnett, later Major-General Sir James Burnett of Leys, 13th Baronet, CB, CMG, DSO, (1926-1953) when he was a young 2nd Lieutenant in The Gordon Highlanders Regiment.

To bring the Burnett of Leys heraldic story up to date, one hundred and twenty-nine years have to pass before a Burnett of Leys once again petitioned a Lord Lyon King of Arms. The current Head of the House of Burnett, James Comyn Amherst Burnett of Leys, Baron of Kilduthie, did so in 1966 when he asked the Lord Lyon to recognise him as the heir to the undifferenced Arms of Burnett of Leys. The Lord Lyon duly granted Arms on 22 May 1967 by authorising the third matriculation of the Burnett of Leys armorial ensign. Again there are significant changes.

The silver shield has the three green holly leaves, black hunting horn decorated with gold with its red strap, and the crest is the hand with a knife pruning a vine. The crest now sits on a red baronial chapean, the heraldic symbol for the Barony of Leys and for the Barony of Kilduthie. This is a new element in the Arms. Above the crest is the motto VIRESCIT VULNERE VIRTUS. The tartan kilt worn by the Highlander supporter is officially recognised by the Lord Lyon as the Burnett of Leys tartan and the exact pattern is given.

The Highlander and Greyhound supporters stand on a *compartment* which is in the form of a grassy mound. On the mound is a ribbon bearing the motto ALTERIUS NON SIT QUI SUUS ESSE POTEST – the first time this motto has been officially recognised since 1550, a time lapse of four hundred and seventeen years. Thus in the armorial achievement of our current Head of the House over four hundred years of heraldry has been brought together! (Fig.12.10)

As this volume shows, world-wide Burnetts wished to establish kinship in a formal way. The movement started in the United States of America where the Clan Burnett Incorporated was formed in 1986. Following a meeting of the Burnett kin during 1993 the title was changed to the more appropriate House of Burnett. As a result of this desire to formalise the wider Burnett family, a fourth petition was submitted to the Lord Lyon King of Arms in 1988 for a Standard and Pinsel so that the place of the Head of the House could be recognised at a gathering of the family. The Lord Lyon King of Arms granted both flags on 26 February 1989. (Figs.12.11, 12.12)

This armorial sequence of events is not unique in Scotland. Most of the long-established families have gone through a similar process over the centuries in order for armorial ensigns to reflect changes of status, kinship or circumstance. The strength of Scottish heraldry lies in its ability to cater for these changes, and is the main reason for its ongoing practicality in this the new twenty-first century.

HERALDIC DECORATION, CRATHES CASTLE

The Spalding Club volume detailed various pieces of decoration, old and new at Crathes. Exterior panels, bosses in the Great Hall and the new (1890) armorial scheme in The Gallery which shows the shields of families who have married Burnetts of Leys. One exterior carved panel was not featured. (Fig.12.13) This is located on the wall of the tower and commemorates Sir Robert Burnett of Leys, 7th Baronet (1738-1837), and his wife Margaret Dalrymple of Westhall whom he married on 16 September 1785. The stone dates from soon after the marriage. The stone bears a simple full-bottomed shield with the impaled Arms of Burnett and Dalrymple. Above the shield is an uninscribed folding ribbon. However the main point of interest is a well-detailed rendering of the Badge worn by the Baronets of Nova Scotia. This is shown suspended from a ribbon, tied in a bow above the shield, and hangs below the shield.

The panel contrasts with that of Sir Thomas Burnett of Leys, 1st Baronet (Fig.12.7) who symbolised his Baronetcy with a canton on his shield. That was all he could show at the time because it was not until 1629 that King Charles I granted baronets the right to wear a special badge. By the middle of the eighteenth century baronets seldom wore their badges and many did not have a badge at all! As a result of persuasion by James Boswell, Lyon Depute in 1775, Baronets ordered new Badges from a Birmingham jeweller and began wearing them from the orange-tawny ribbon. Sir Robert Burnett of Leys must have purchased a badge and caused a likeness to be carved under the impaled Arms soon after his marriage in 1785. This must be one of the earliest representations of the 'new' Baronet of Nova Scotia badges.

In 1989, the current Head of the House, James Burnett of Leys, came to an arrangement with the National Trust of Scotland, owners of Crathes Castle, to allocate a room on the top floor of the castle as The Family Room. This is furnished with items of Burnett of Leys family interest plus material representing the world-wide kinship of Burnetts. Within a small turret off the Burnett Room are the armorial devices of Burnetts who are in right of Arms. These are painted on metal with a ribbon below carrying the name and date of matriculation. There are fifteen at present and others will be added as new arms are granted. Individuals featured are:

THOMAS BURNETT, Woodalling, Norfolk, 1640 (Fig.12.14)
Argent, three holly leaves in chief Vert, the middle leaf charged with an annulet of the First, Or in base hunting horn Sable, stringed Gules.

ALEXANDER BURNETT of Craigmyle, c1672 (Fig.12.15)
Quartered shield, 1st and 4th, Argent three holly leaves in chief Vert, in base a hunting horn Sable stringed Gules, 2nd and 3rd Azure, two garbs in chief and a crescent in base Or.

THOMAS BURNETT of Inverleith, c1672 (Fig.12.16)
Argent, three holly leaves in chief Vert, the middle leaf surmounted by a crescent Sable for difference, a hunting horn Sable, stringed Gules in base within a bordure invected Vert.

ANDREW BURNETT of Wariston, c1676 (Fig.12.17)
Argent, three holly leaves in chief Vert, a hunting horn Sable, stringed Gules in base within a bordure invected Vert.

ALEXANDER BURNETT, Aberdeen, c1676 (Fig.12.18)
Argent, a battle axe Proper in pale between two holly leaves Vert in chief, a hunting horn of the Last, stringed Gules in base.

JAMES BURNETT of Sheddocksley, c1676 (Fig.12.19)
Argent, a falcon Proper volant recursant descending in bend sinister, wings overture between three holly leaves in chief Vert and a hunting horn Sable, stringed Gules in base.

WILLIAM BURNETT of Barns, c1676 (Fig.12.20)
Argent, three holly leaves, Vert, a chief Azure.

ROBERT BURNETT, W.S., c1676 (Fig.12.21)
Argent, three holly leaves Vert, a chief embattled Azure.

JOHN BURNETT of Dalladies, c1676 (Fig..12.22)
Argent, three holly leaves Vert in chief, a hunting horn Sable, stringed Gules in base within a bordure counter-compony Argent and Vert.

ROBERT BURNETT, Aberdeen, c1676 (Fig.12.23)
Argent a billet Azure between three holly leaves Vert in chief, and a hunting horn Sable, stringed Gules in base.

DR. THOMAS BURNETT, c1676 (Fig.12.24)
Argent, three holly leaves Vert in chief, the middle leaf surmounted by a mullet Gules (should be Or) for difference, a hunting horn, Sable, stringed Gules in base.

LORD LYON GEORGE BURNETT, 1870 (Fig.12.25)
Impaled shield, dexter, Argent, a lion sejant Gules holding a thistle Proper in its dexter paw and an escutcheon Gules in sinister, on a chief Azure a saltire Argent (Arms of the Office of Lord Lyon), sinister quarterly 1st and 4th Argent, three holly leaves Vert in chief, a hunting horn Sable stringed Gules, 2nd and 3rd Azure, two garbs in chief and a crescent in base Or, in the fess point a mullet Sable for difference. Behind the shield two batons saltirewise.

WILLIAM TATHER BRIDGEFORD BURNETT, 1975 (Fig.12.26)
Argent, on a fess Gules a basket-hilted sword fesswise, point towards the sinister Or, between in chief three holly leaves Vert, and in base a hunting horn Sable stringed Gules.

CHARLES JOHN BURNETT, Ross Herald, 1981 (Fig.12.27)
Per chevron Azure and Argent, in chief a holly leaf between two quill pens and a hunting horn in base contournée stringed, all counterchanged. Behind the shield two batons saltirewise.

JOHN CAMERON BURNETT, Oklahoma, 1989 (Fig.12. 28)
Argent, a hunting horn Sable, stringed Gules, on a chief Gules three plates each charged with a holly leaf paleways Vert.

JOHN THEODOSIUS BURNETT-STUART OF CRICHIE (Fig.None)
This achievement is not displayed at Crathes but an illustration has been included for completeness, following (Fig.12.28) . A full description of his Arms, which were recorded in 1938, are given later in this chapter.

Apart from Crathes Castle, heraldic display can also be seen at Muchalls Castle and at The House of Crathes, the present home of James Burnett of Leys.

Two exterior armorial panels associated with Muchalls have already been mentioned, but before considering internal heraldry, one final panel on the exterior should be mentioned. This is a representation of the Scottish Royal Arms of King Charles I, and is dated 1629.(Fig.12.29) Some damage has occurred as a result of weathering. The Royal Arms are on an oval quartered shield with Scotland in the 1st and 4th quarters. France and England are in the 2nd quarter, which is a grand quarter, with Ireland in the 3rd quarter. Around the oval shield is a Thistle Collar and the English Garter with its motto, HONI SOIT QUI MAL Y PENSE. The shield is flanked on the dexter with the Scottish Unicorn (foreleg missing) which has a metal horn issuing from its forehead, and on the sinister is the crowned English lion also minus its foreleg. The two supporters stand on a very weathered strapwork panel which originally carried the English royal motto, DIEU ET MON DROIT. Above the shield is a helmet with mantling, surmounted with an imperial crown, on which sits the Scottish royal crest lion. It has lost both paws and the sword and sceptre held in each. The crest lion in turn is flanked by a ribbon with upward-sweeping ends on which is inscribed the Scottish royal motto IN DE/FENCE. Just visible peeping above the swirling mantling is the St. Andrew banner of Scotland on the dexter and the St. George banner of England on the sinister. In the two uppermost corners of the panel is the date 16/29. This is a very handsome, well-executed carving of the Royal Arms which should be repaired and tinctured to aid its preservation.

The main glory of Muchalls is the internal plasterwork with its heraldic elements. An itinerant team of English plasterers undertook the work during 1624. They had spent the previous ten years plastering houses along the East coast of Scotland using the same set of wooden moulds in each house. Their progress can be followed from Thirlestane Castle in the Borders to Pinkie House and Lennoxlove Castle near Edinburgh, Edinburgh Castle, Kellie Castle and Balcarres House in Fife, Glamis Castle in Angus, to Muchalls Castle and finally Craigievar Castle in Upper Donside. Plaster was the latest fashionable material so Sir Thomas Burnett of Leys was being very modern when he decided to employ workmen skilled in decorating with this new material at Muchalls. He used them to work in the two principal rooms; his own Private Sitting Room and in the Great Hall.

The Sitting Room contains only Burnett heraldry. Above the fireplace is the complete armorial achievement of Sir Thomas Burnett of Leys, before he became a Baronet of Nova Scotia. (Fig.12.30) It consists of shield, helmet, mantling (should be Argent and Vert) crest, and supporters. The huntsman supporter carries a pole-hook, used for restraining wild animals. Above is the usual Burnett motto and below an abbreviated version of the second motto A(LT)ERI(US) NON SIT QUI SU(US) E(SSE) PO(T)EST. On the ceiling are two shields contained within cast strapwork cartouches. The first is the Burnett of Leys shield with STB for Sir Thomas Burnett. (Fig.12.31) The second is the impaled shield of Burnett and Moncreiffe with the letters STB and DIM for Sir Thomas Burnett and Dame Jean Moncreiffe. (Fig.12.32)

The Great Hall contains an elaborate scheme of royal, Burnett, ancestral and friendship heraldry. Above the fireplace is a version of the Stewart Royal Arms flanked by male and female caryatids with linked arms. (Fig.12.33) They had been modelled in situ. Similar paired caryatids can be seen at Glamis Castle, but at Craigievar there is only a single man and woman on either side of the Royal Arms. The Arms have been incorrectly tinctured in places: the lion sejant crest should be Gules; the 1st and 4th quarters in the grand quarter represent France and should have fleurs-de-lis Or on Azure; the royal helmet should be all gold. Although these Arms are dated 1624, unlike the exterior stone carving of the same Arms, dated 1629, the unicorn is crowned.

There are five complete achievements of Arms on the ceiling of the Great Hall. The first three are for Sir Thomas Burnett of Leys alone (Fig.12.34), with two achievements showing wives, Alexander Burnett and Katherine Gordon (Fig.12.35) who began the work at Muchalls, and Sir Thomas Burnett with Dame Jean Moncreiffe who completed the Castle. (Fig.12.36) In each case mantling should be Argent and Vert, not Argent and Gules. Although no measurements have been taken, it would appear that the four plaster versions of the Burnett Arms have all been made from the same mould with differences then modelled directly on the resulting casts. The remaining two full achievements and shield of Arms are those of family and friends.

Alexander Seton, 1st Earl of Dunfermline, Lord Fyvie, Constable of Dunfermline Palace, Keeper of the Palace of Holyroodhouse and Chancellor of Scotland (fl. 1555-1622) was one of the great magnates of Scotland. He was a favourite of Queen Anne, wife of James VI King of Scots, a trained lawyer, scholar and patron of the arts. He remodelled both Fyvie Castle in Aberdeenshire and Pinkie House in East Lothian. His friendship with the Burnetts of Leys may have been cemented during overnight stops at Crathes Castle on his way to and from Fyvie Castle which lies to the north. His interest in heraldry and his use of the English plasterers at Pinkie House may have influenced Sir Thomas Burnett of Leys to create the scheme at Muchalls. The Arms of the Earl at Muchalls (Fig.12.37)were cast from the same mould which the Earl had used several years earlier at Pinkie. These can now be seen in the Seton Room, Pinkie House in their original white plaster finish.

The Arms consist of a quartered shield, 1st and 4th, Or, three crescents within a royal tressure Gules, for Seton, 2nd and 3rd, Argent, on a fess Gules three cinquefoils of the First, for Hamilton of Sanquhar. Above the shield is an Earl's coronet surmounted by a helmet (should be Argent) with mantling and a crescent crest Gules. Overall is the motto SEMPER (Aways). The shield is flanked by supporters, two horses at liberty, Argent, which stand on a strapwork panel bearing a second motto NEC CEDE ADVERSIS REBVS/NEC CREDE SECVNDIS. (Neither give in to adverse circumstances, nor trust in successful ones).

The second achievement of friendship Arms is that of John Maitland, 1st Earl of Lauderdale, President of the Scottish Privy Council, and son-in-law of the Earl of Dunfermline through his marriage to Isabel Seton. (Fig. 12.38) The Earl died in 1645. Sir Thomas may have become a friend as a result of knowing the Earl of Dunfermline. Lauderdale's achievement had been cast for use at his residence, Thirlestane Castle, in 1618, so the same mould was used for Muchalls except the coronet which was remodelled to that of an earl. Lauderdale had been elevated to earl in 1624. Another cast of the same Arms, dated 1632 (with a different version of the Earl's coronet), was used at another Lauderdale home, Lennoxlove Castle, near Edinburgh.

The Arms consist of an impaled shield, dexter Or, a lion rampant dismembered in all its joints, Gules within a royal tressure (should be Azure) for Maitland, sinister, quarterly 1st and 4th Seton, 2nd and 3rd, Hamilton of Sanquhar. Above the shield is an earl's coronet surmounted by a helmet (should be Argent) with mantling and for crest a lion sejant Gules holding in the dexter paw a sword Proper, and in the sinister a fleur-de-lis Azure. Overall is the motto CONSILIO ET ANIMIS (By wisdom and courage). The shield is flanked by supporters, two eagles, wings expanded, Proper, which stand on a strapwork panel. Below the shield is a garland bearing fruit.

The single shield of arms (Fig.12.39) represents John Hamilton, 2nd Marquess of Hamilton and 4th Earl of Arran, Knight of the Garter, died 1625. These Arms are of kinship, rather than friendship, because of the earlier Burnett/Janet Hamilton wedding. The shield is quartered, 1st and 4th Gules, three cinquefoils Argent, for Hamilton, 2nd and 3rd, Argent a lymphad Sable, for Arran. It is set within the same strapwork cartouche as those on the Sitting Room ceiling, but remodelled with a Garter with the usual motto HONI SOIT QUI MAY Y PENSE surmounting this is an earl's coronet.

There are four ingoes on the ceiling of the Great Hall, two on each of the long side walls. They contain the Arms of four progenitor Burnett wives. In chronological order these are: Elizabeth Forbes of Echt, wife of Alexander Burnard/Burnett of Leys, 3rd Laird; Azure a cinquefoil Argent between three bear's heads of the second, muzzled Gules, above a helmet with mantling (should be Argent and Azure), and for crest a horse's head couped Proper, bridled Azure (Fig.12.40): Janet Hamilton, wife of Alexander Burnett of Leys, 5th Laird; Gules, three cinquefoils Argent, above a helmet with mantling and for crest an oak tree penetrated transversely in the main stem by a Saw Proper (Fig.12.41): Katherine Arbuthnot, wife of Alexander Burnet of Leys, 7th Laird; Azure, a crescent between three mullets Argent, above a helmet with mantling (should be Argent and Azure), and for crest a peacock's head couped Proper (Fig.12.42): Katherine Gordon of

Lesmoir, wife of Alexander Burnett of Leys, 8th Laird; Azure, a fess chequy Argent and Azure between three boar's heads Or, above a helmet with mantling (should be Argent and Azure), and for crest a stag's head cabossed Proper. (Fig.12.43)

The armorial display is one of the finest to be found in a domestic setting as small and perfect as Muchalls. The writer has not found another scheme dating from the first quarter of the seventeenth century which combines royal, personal, probative, and friendship heraldry. Sir Thomas Burnett of Leys must have drawn up a comprehensive brief for the plasterers which expressed his desire to show that the Burnetts of Leys had married well and numbered among their friends the greatest in the realm.

The House of Crathes is featured in Chapter 15 so only heraldic items associated with the house will be mentioned here.

The building has been designed in the Scottish vernacular tradition, finished with harling which sets off well-proportioned fenestration and an exterior carved panel set into the entrance wall. The panel bears a simple shield of the Burnett of Leys armorial ensigns. The inner front door is partially glazed and the glass has been engraved by Philip Lawson Johnston with the full achievement of the present Chief of the Name. The engraving is based on the painted version of the Arms executed on the 1975 Letters Patent granted to James A. C. Burnett of Leys.

Immediately behind the inner front door is a square marble-floored hall which contains four nineteenth century hall chairs in the gothick style. The back of the chairs are carved and painted with a Victorian style version of the Arms of Burnett of Leys. The chairs were originally located in the hall of the Victorian wing of Crathes Castle. Other reminders of the nineteenth century are two stained glass windows bearing the horn and holly leaves, presently in store at the House of Crathes, which were above the Victorian porch of Crathes Castle. These were removed after the fire in 1966. Some pieces of Goss ware porcelain emblazoned with the coat of arms, dating from the same century, are also located in the House.

Our chief possesses contemporary articles incorporating design elements from his Arms. There are two examples of wrought ironwork made by Drumoak blacksmiths. The first is a weather vane on the roof of the House of Crathes in the shape of the Horn of Leys made by Mr. Craig. His successor at the Drumoak Smithy, Mr. Anderson, produced an iron firescreen for the Drawing Room which is adorned with the horn.

Another local artist, Jill Adron, who lives on the south side of the river Dee at Maryfield, undertook a commission from American members of the House of

Burnett in 1992 to carve a pair of mirror frames the intricate design of which incorporates holly leaves, burnet rose and hunting horn. The two mirrors now hang on the main staircase of the House. The same craftswoman also made a heraldic triptych frame for family photographs which is displayed in the Drawing Room. Located in the same room are a pair of bookcases inlaid with the Burnett arms. These pieces of furniture were designed and made by Tom Ironside in his workshop at Finzean, near Banchory.

Two other examples of heraldic carving can be found in an unusual place! Jill Adron enhanced two wooden lavatory seat covers with the Burnett crest and motto which are of course the property of the armiger for use as required...

Jamie Burnett of Leys has also commissioned a cast iron fireback for eventual employment at Thistleycrook. An imaginative design was created by the Edinburgh architect, Ben Tindall, which features the Horn of Leys surrounded by curving holly leaves which sinuously flow upwards like tongues of flame.

The final heraldic feature is on a grand scale and can only be seen from the air. In 1990 a plantation of trees was established at New Mill and laid out in the shape of the Horn of Leys. By these various means our present chief has continued the Burnett decorative heraldry tradition which began at Crathes Castle so long ago and provides an artistic continuous link with that formidable pair of imaginative ancestors, Alexander Burnett of Leys and his wife Katherine Gordon of Lesmoir.

The Newsletter of Clan Burnett, Inc.

RECORDED AND OTHER HERALDRY OF THE BURNETT FAMILY

The boast of heraldry, the pomp of power,
And all that beauty, all that wealth e'er gave,
Awaits alike the inevitable hour.
The paths of glory lead but to the grave.
(From Gray's *Elegy*)

Mention has already been made of The Public Register of All Arms and Bearings in Scotland, commenced in 1672. Not only did not all Scots who used a coat of arms at that time bother to Register their Arms, but descendants of armigers were equally lax in proving their right to Arms. In the case of the Burnetts of Leys few of the determinate cadets such as Crimond, Monboddo and Elrick ever recorded Arms. Not many second, third or fourth sons of Burnett of Leys ever matriculated the paternal Arms with appropriate differences. If only they had, it would have made the task of the Burnett genealogist so much easier! The undifferenced Arms of Burnett of Leys passes automatically between father and designated heir, on the death of the former. Where succession to the undifferenced Arms is dubious then a case has to be made out for consideration by the Lord Lyon King of Arms, Her Majesty's Judge of Armorial Matters in Scotland. Our present Chief had to go through this process in 1967, but his eldest son and heir, Alexander, will automatically inherit the Arms in due course. Our Chief's younger son, Victor, will set up his own determinate cadet branch of the Burnetts and when he reaches the age of eighteen should matriculate Arms in his own right. These will be the Burnett of Leys coat of arms with the appropriate difference for a second son.

Some of these differences do feature in Burnett heraldry and here follows a comprehensive list of *registered* armorial ensigns of Burnetts in Scotland and England. It is possible, as this book goes to press, that Burnetts in Ireland, Canada and South Africa are in the process of recording Arms with the heraldic Authorities in these countries.

SCOTLAND

The First Volume of the Public Register contains records of Burnett Arms but unfortunately between 1672 and 1676 not all have an entry date. After 1676 all Burnett entries are dated. Spellings are as used in the Register.

WILLIAM BURNET OF BARNES

Representer of the southern Scottish Burnets who at one time claimed Headship of the House of Burnett. He was a Writer to the Signet and died as Head of the House in 1675.

Argent, three holly leaves Vert, a chief Azure.

Crest: A hand with a pruning knife pruning a vine tree Proper.

Motto: *Virescit Vulnere Virtus*: Strength draws vigour from an injury.

Recorded: Volume 1, Folio 256, 1672-1676

ALEXANDER BURNET, ARCHBISHOP OF GLASGOW 1614-1685

Archbishop of Glasgow 1674-1679, his Arms show he was of the Line of Barnes.

Impaled coat: Dexter, the Arms of the see of Glasgow, sinister, Argent, a cross pattée Gules between three holly leaves Vert, a chief Azure.

No Crest:

Motto: *Non Est Mortale Quod Opto*: It s not a transitory thing that I hope for.

Recorded: Volume 1, Folio 28, 1672-1676

ROBERT BURNET, WRITER TO THE SIGNET 1646-1699, he was killed in a duel.

Again his arms indicate he is of the Line of Barnes.

Argent, three holly leaves Vert, a chief embattled Azure.

Crest: A vine branch split.

Motto: *Tandem Fit Surculus Arbor*: The young shoot shall at last be the tree.

Recorded: Volume 1, Folio 256, 1672-1676

SIR THOMAS BURNETT OF LEES, 1st BARONET OF NOVA SCOTIA

The first Burnett of Leys to record his Arms, but not his Supporters.

Argent, three holly leaves in chief Vert and a hunting horn in base Sable, garnished Gules with the badge of Nova Scotia (a canton Argent, a saltire Azure surmounted of an inescutcheon bearing the Royal Arms of Scotland)

Crest: A hand pruning a vine tree with a pruning knife Proper.

Motto: *Virescit Vulnere Virtus*: Strength draws vigour from an injury.

Recorded: Volume 1, Folios 22, 122, April 1626

THOMAS BURNET OF INNELEITH

Argent, three holly leaves in chief Vert and a hunting horn in base Sable, garnished Gules within a bordure indented of the Second a crescent for difference.

Crest: A holly branch Proper.

Motto: *Virtute Cresto*: I grow with strength.
Recorded: Volume 1, Folio 122, 1672-1676

ANDREW BURNET OF WARRISTOUNE
Argent, three holly leaves in chief Vert and a hunting horn in base Sable, garnished Gules, within a bordure indented of the Second.
Crest: A holly branch Proper.
Motto: *Virtute Cresto*: I grow with strength.
Recorded: Volume 1, Folio 256, 1672-1676

ALEXANDER BURNET OF CRAIGMYLL
Eldest son of James Burnett of Craigmyle and his wife Elizabeth Burnett, heiress of Craigmyle.
Quarterly, 1st and 4th Argent, three holly leaves in chief Vert, with a hunting horn in base Sable garnished...by the name of Burnet; 2nd and 3rd Azure two garbs in chief and a crescent in base Or, for Craigmyle.
Crest: A dexter hand holding a branch of palm Proper.
Motto: *Quae Vernant Crescent*: Those which are green, grow.
Recorded: Volume 1, Folio 122, 1672-1676

ROBERT BURNET, PROCURATOR FISCAL OF ABERDEEN
Presumably of the Line of Burnett of Leys, a determinate cadet.
Argent, a billet Azure between three holly leaves in chief Vert and a hunting horn in base Sable, garnished Gules.
Crest: A hand with a cutlass cutting through a vine branch (Proper).
Motto: *Verescit Vulnere Virtus*: strength draws vigour from an injury:
Recorded: Volume 1, Folio 156, 1672-1676

DR. THOMAS BURNET
Of the cadet line of Crimond and fourth son of Lord Crimond. He was born in 1638, later knighted as a Royal Physician, and died in 1706.
Argent, three holly leaves in chief Vert, and a hunting horn in base Sable, garnished Gules. A mullet for difference.
Crest: A dexter hand with a sword cutting through a vine branch, leaved and fructed Proper.
Motto: *Virescit Vulnere Virtus*: Strength draws vigour from an injury.
Recorded: Volume 1, Folio 256, 1672-1676

ALEXANDER BURNET, MERCHANT IN ABERDEEN
One of several Aberdeen Burnetts, the Arms suggest he was an indeterminate cadet.
Argent, a battle-axe in pale between two holly leaves in chief and a bugle in base Vert, garnished Gules.
No Crest:
Motto: *Quid Ni Pro Sodali*: Why not, for the sake of a comrade?
Recorded: Volume 1, Folio 255, 1672-1676

JAMES BURNET OF SKETCHOCKSLEY (SHEDDOCKSLEY, now within City of Aberdeen)
Argent, a falcon volant Proper between three holly leaves in chief Vert and a hunting horn in base Sable, garnished Gules.
Crest: A hand pruning a vine tree with a pruning knife Proper.
Motto: *Virescit Vulnere Virtus*: Strength draws vigour from an injury.
Recorded: Volume 1, Folio 256, 1672-1676

JOHN BURNET OF DALELADIES
Argent, three holly leaves in chief Vert, and a hunting horn in base Sable, garnished Gules within a bordure counter-compony of the Second and First.
Crest: A branch of holly, slipped Proper.
Motto: *Nec fluctu Nec Flatu*: Neither by flowing nor by blowing.
Recorded: Volume 1, Folio 256, 20 June 1676

SIR THOMAS BURNETT OF LEYS, 8th BARONET OF NOVA SCOTIA
The first Burnett of Leys to have his Supporters recorded at the Court of the Lord Lyon.
Argent, three holly leaves in chief Vert, a hunting horn in base Sable, garnished or, stringed Gules.
Crest: A hand pruning a vine tree with a pruning knife Proper.
Motto: *Virescit Vulnere Virtus*: Strength draws vigour from an injury.
Supporters: Dexter, a highlander in hunting garb, holding in his exterior hand a bow, sinister, a greyhound all Proper.
Recorded: Volume 4, Folio 33, 24 October 1838

GEORGE BURNETT, LYON DEPUTE
Third son of John Burnett, 5th of Kemnay, born 1822, appointed Lyon Depute in 1863.
Quarterly, 1st and 4th Argent, three holly leaves in chief Vert and a hunting horn in base Sable, garnished and stringed Gules, 2nd and 3rd, Azure two garbs in chief and

a crescent in base Or (for Craigmyle) all within a bordure parted per pale Vert and Argent for difference.
Crest: A dexter hand holding a branch of palm Proper.
Motto: *Quae Vernant Crescent*: Those which are green, grow.
Recorded: Volume 6, Folio 82, 16 October 1863.

GEORGE BURNETT, LORD LYON KING OF ARMS (Second Matriculation)
Created Lord Lyon in 1866, married 1870, died 1890, buried in St Cuthbert's Graveyard, Edinburgh
Impaled Coat: dexter, the Arms of Lord Lyon King of Arms, sinister the personal Arms as recorded above.
Recorded: Volume 8, Folio 1, 26 May 1870.

GENERAL SIR JOHN THEODOSIUS BURNETT-STUART OF CRICHIE, GCB, KBE, CMG, DSO
Eldest son of Eustace Robert Burnett-Stuart of Dens and Crichie, the first of his line to record Arms at the Court of the Lord Lyon.
Quarterly, 1st and 4th, Or, a fess chequy Azure and Argent, surmounting a cross-crosslet fitchée Gules, 2nd Argent, three holly leaves in chief Vert, and a hunting horn in base Sable garnished Gules within a bordure counter-compony of the Second and First, 3rd paly of six Or and Sable an ancient galley Gules.
Crest: Dexter, a pelican in her nest feeding her young Proper (for Stuart) sinister, a branch of holly slipped Proper. (for Burnett)
Motto: *Virescit Vulnere Virtus*: Strength draws vigour from an injury.
Nex Fluctu Nec Flatu: Neither by flowing or by blowing.
Recorded: Volume 32, Folio 28, 30 September 1938

JOSEPH BURNETT-STUART OF ARDMEALLIE
Nephew of General Sir John Theodosius Burnett-Stuart of Crichie and eldest son of George Eustace Burnett-Stuart of Ardmeallie.
Quarterly, 1st and 4th, Or, a fesse chequy Azure and Argent surmounting a cross-crosslet fitchee Gules (for Stuart) 2nd, Argent, three holly leaves in chief Vert and a hunting-horn in base Sable, garnished Gules within a bordure counter-compony of the Second and First (for Burnett of Daladies) 3rd, paly of six Or and Sable, an ancient galley Gules (also for Stuart) all within a bordure Or for difference.
Crest: A pelican in her nest feeding her young Proper (for Stuart).
A branch of holly slipped Proper (for Burnett).
Motto: *Virescit Vulnere Virtus* (for Stuart): Strength draws

vigour from an injury.
Nec Fluctu Nec Flatu (for Burnett): Neither by flowing or by blowing.

Recorded: Volume 38, Folio 46, 22 January 1951.

THOMAS BURNETT-STUART

Second son of George Eustace Burnett-Stuart of Ardmeallie.

Quarterly 1st and 4th, Or a fess chequy Azure and Argent surmounting a cross-crosslet fitchee Gules (for Stuart), 2nd, argent three holly leaves in chief Vert, and a hunting horn in base Sable, garnished Gules, within a bordure counter-company of the Second and First (for Burnett of Daladies) 3rd, paly of six Or and Sable, an ancient galley Gules (also for Stuart) all within a bordure engrailed Or.

Crest: A pelican in her nest feeding her young Proper (for Stuart).
A branch of holly slipped Proper (for Burnett).

Motto: *Virescit Vulnere Virtus* (for Stuart): Strength draws vigour from an injury.
Nec Fluctu Nec Flatu (for Burnett): Neither by flowing or by blowing.

Recorded: Volume 40, Folio 146, 30 May 1956.

JAMES COMYN AMHERST BURNETT OF LEYS, BARON OF KILDUTHIE

Maternal grandson of General Sir James Lauderdale Gilbert Burnett of Leys, 13th Baronet, and now the 18th Laird of Leys.

Argent, three holly leaves in chief Vert, a hunting horn in base Sable, garnished Or, stringed Gules.

Crest: Set on a chapeau Gules trimmed ermine: A cubit arm, the hand naked vested Vert doubled Argent, pruning a vine tree with a pruning knife Proper.

Motto: *Virescit Vulnere Virtus*: Strength draws vigour from an injury.

And: *Alterius Non Sit Qui Suus esse Potest*: Who can be his would not be another's.

Supporters: Dexter, a highlandman in hunting garb – a kilt of the proper tartan of Burnett of Leys, a peplummed jacket Vert, broad collar Argent, and across his sinister shoulder a cord Gules, and there from pendant on his right hip a hunting horn Sable, garnished Or, holding in his exterior hand a bow Sable, stringed Or.
Sinister, a greyhound Proper, collared Vert.

Recorded: Volume 49, Folios 101, 102, 103, 22 May 1967.

WILLIAM TATHER BRIDGFORD BURNETT
Indeterminate cadet whose grandfather, William Tather Bridgford Burnett, was born in Edinburgh.
Argent, on a fess Gules a basket-hilted sword fessways, point towards the sinister Or, between in chief three holly leaves Vert and in base a hunting horn Sable, garnished and stringed of the Second.
Crest: A dexter hand issuant in pale holding a dagger and cutting through a vine branch leaved and fructed Proper.
Motto: *Viresco Vulnere*: I draw strength from an injury.
Recorded: Volume 57, Folio 102, 1 September 1975.

SUSAN LETITIA BURNETT OF KEMNAY, BARONESS OF KEMNAY
Daughter and heir portioner of Arthur Moubray Burnett, 8th of Kemnay.
Quarterly, 1st and 4th, Argent three holly leaves in chief Vert and a hunting horn in base Sable, stringed and garnished Gules (for Burnett), 2nd and 3rd, Azure, two garbs in chief and a crescent in base Or (for Craigmyle) all within a bordure Vert.
Crest: On a chapeau Gules furred ermine: A dexter hand holding a branch of palm Proper.
Motto: *Quae Vernant*: Those which are green.
Recorded: Volume 60, Folio 107, 19 September 1978.

CHARLES JOHN BURNETT
Indeterminate cadet from a group of Burnetts associated with Fraserburgh, Aberdeenshire.
Per chevron Azure and Argent, in chief between two quills a holly leaf and in base a hunting horn stringed, all counterchanged.
Crest: A demi angel, wings displayed, vested Argent, having a collar with a fringed pendant Sable, holding in each hand a quill Azure.
Motto: Forward with the Past.
Recorded: Volume 63, Folio 75, 10 March 1981.

JAMES COMYN AMHERST BURNETT OF LEYS, BARON OF KILDUTHIE
Grant of a Standard and Pinsel as Chief of the Name of Burnett.
STANDARD, four yards in length with rounded end: Argent, three holly leaves in chief Vert, a hunting horn in base Sable, garnished Or, stringed Gules, in the hoist, the fly of two tracts Argent and Vert, thereon is depicted three times the crest of Burnett of Leys, a cubit arm, the hand naked, vested Vert doubled Argent, pruning a

vine tree with a pruning knife Proper along with the motto VIRESCIT VULNERE VIRTUS in letters Argent upon two transverse bands Sable.
PINSEL, four feet in length and two and a half feet in height, Argent bearing upon a wreath of the liveries a cubit arm, the hand naked, vested Vert doubled Argent, pruning a vine tree with a pruning knife Proper within a strap Vert buckled and embellished Or, inscribed of this motto VIRESCIT VULNERE VIRTUS in letters Or, all within a circlet also Or, fimbriated Vert, bearing his name and style BURNETT OF LEYS in letters Sable, the same ensigned of a chapeau Gules furred Ermine, and in the fly a sprig of holly leaves Proper as the proper plant badge of the name Burnett.
Recorded: Volume 49, Folio 101, 16 February 1989

JOHN CAMERON BURNETT
Indeterminate cadet descended from a pioneer settler in the United States of America who married in 1796. Tosheadoer of the Chief of the Name of Burnett, in the United States of America.
Argent, a hunting horn Sable stringed Gules, garnished Or, on a chief Gules three plates each charged with a holly leaf paleways Vert.
Crest: A dexter hand Proper, sleeved Sable, cuffed Argent holding scales of Justice Or.
Motto: *Juris Secundum*: According to the law.
Recorded: Volume 71, Folio 81, 11 March 1989.

JOHN McINTYRE BURNETT
Second son and determinate cadet of Charles John Burnett, Ross Herald.
Per chevron Azure and Argent in chief between two quills a holly leaf and in base a hunting horn stringed contournée, all counterchanged, all within a bordure Or.
Crest: A demi angel, wings displayed, vested Argent, having a collar with a fringed pendant Azure, holding in each hand a quill Azure.
Motto: *Forward with the Past.*
Recorded: Volume 72, Folio 88, 24 February 1998.

CHARLES JOHN BURNETT, ROSS HERALD OF ARMS
Second matriculation to show attributes of a Herald.
Per chevron Azure and Argent in chief between two quills a holly leaf and in base a hunting horn stringed countournée, all counterchanged.
Behind the shield a white cross of eight points for a Knight of Justice of the Order of St. John, two batons sable saltirewise and around the shield the Collar of Esses worn by a Herald of Arms of Scotland.

Crest: A demi angel, wings displayed, vested Argent, having a collar with a fringed pendant Azure, holding in each hand a quill Azure.
Motto: *Forward with the Past.*
Recorded: Volume 72, Folio 87, 24 February 1998.

PATRICK BRITTON BURNETT
Second son and determinate cadet of John Cameron Burnett, Tosheadoer of the Chief of the Name of Burnett, in the United States of America.
Argent, a hunting horn Sable, stringed Gules, garnished Or, on a chief Gules three plates each charged with a holly leaf paleways Vert, all within a bordure Or.
Crest: A dexter hand Proper, sleeved Sable, cuffed Argent, holding Scales of Justice Or.
Motto: *Juris Secundum*: According to the law.
Recorded: Volume 80, Folio 37, 30 September 1998.

CAMERON BELEAU BURNETT
Third son and determinate cadet of John Cameron Burnett, Tosheadoer of the Chief of Name of Burnett, in the United States of America.
Argent, a hunting horn Sable, stringed Gules, garnished Or, on a chief Gules three plates each charged with a holly leaf paleways Vert, all within a bordure counter-compony Argent and Gules.
Crest: A dexter hand Proper, sleeved Sable, cuffed Argent, holding Scales of Justice Or.
Motto: *Juris Secundum*: According to the law.
Recorded: Volume 80, Folio 37, 30 September 1998.

ENGLAND

THOMAS BURNETT, Wood-dalling, Norfolk
Third son and determinate cadet of Alexander Burnett of Leys and his wife Katherine Arbuthnot of Pitcarlies.
Argent, in chief three holly leaves palewise in fess Proper, the centre leaf charged with an annulet Or and in base a bugle horn, bell to the sinister, stringed, Sable.
Crest: A dexter hand Proper charged with an annulet Gules cuffed with a frilled cuff Argent holding a knife cutting into a vine branch leaved and fructed Proper.
Recorded: College of Arms, Volume 2, Folio 612, 30 June 1640.

SIR ROBERT BURNETT, Morden Hall, Surrey
The charges suggest this gentleman had military connections.

Per saltire Vert and Gules, a sword erect the point upwards proper, pommel and hilt, and from the blade pendent a bugle horn stringed Or, on a chief embattled erminois three leaves of the Burnet Rose also Proper.

Crest: Within a mural crown Or, a mount Vert thereon a vine tree Proper fructed Gold an arm issuant from a cloud on the sinister in the hand a knife pruning the vine, also Proper.

Recorded: College of Arms, Volume 26, Folio 369, 22 February 1812.

DAVID BURNETT, Dalston, Middlesex

Later Sir David Burnett, 1st Baronet, Lord Mayor of London 1912-1913.

Per chevron Or and Sable, two holly leaves in chief Vert, and in base a hunting horn of the First, stringed Argent.

Crest: Issuing from flames a branch of holly erect Proper.

Motto: *In Arduis Fortitudo*: Fortitude in Adversity

Recorded: College of Arms, Surrey Volume 5, Folio 118, 1906

AIR CHIEF MARSHAL SIR BRIAN KENYON BURNETT, GCB, DFC, AFC, RAF

Determinate cadet of Sir Robert Burnett, Morden Hall, Surrey.

Per saltire Vert and Gules, a sword erect the point upwards Proper, pommel and hilt, and from the blade pendent a bugle horn stringed Or, on a chief embattled erminois three leaves of the Burnett Rose also Proper.

Crest: Within a mural crown Or, on a mount Vert thereon a vine tree Proper fructed Gold an arm issuant from a cloud on the sinister in the hand a knife pruning the vine, also Proper.

Supporters: Two eagles, wings elevated and addorsed Or, the dexter crowned with an astral crown Gold and holding in the sinister claw a Vickers-Wellesley bomber aircraft proper, and the sinister crowned with an ancient crown Gold and holding in the dexter claw a tennis racquet Proper.

Recorded: College of Arms, Volume 26, Folio 369, 21 June 1985.

IRELAND

There are no grants of arms to Burnetts amongst the records in the office of the Chief Herald of Ireland in Dublin. There are however, scattered references to Burnett arms amongst the various documents. One example only can be given here.

JOHN BURNETT of Balelack, County Monaghan
Apparently died on 11 December 1632, and was married to Katherine Kinge by whom he had a son Thomas and two daughters, Joan and Mary. The records show the impaled coat of Burnet and Kinge viz. dexter, three holly leaves in chief and in base a hunting horn stringed sinister, a chevron charged with three crescents and in the middle chief point a mullet.
Record: Office of the Chief Herald, LS 68/191.
The Arms, and choice of the name Thomas, suggests John Burnett was a cadet of Leys.

Twenty-nine Burnetts have recorded or matriculated Arms, not a large number considering the world-wide spread of the Burnett name. Consistent use of the holly leaves and hunting horn ensures that all can be readily identified by the ensigns armorial.

Public and private displays of Burnett heraldry are located in a wide selection of places in and around the City and Royal Burgh of Aberdeen.

ST NICHOLAS KIRK, Aberdeen
There are Burnett grave slabs in the East Kirk and in the Chapel of St Mary under the West Kirk. The chapel also contains a remarkable collection of carved wooden panelling; several panels commemorate Burnetts.

GREYFRIARS KIRK, Aberdeen
This building also contains a find collection of wooden panelling. One panel commemorates a Burnett, and another series of Burnett panels have been incorporated in a cupboard.

MARISCHAL COLLEGE, Aberdeen
In the Mitchell Hall, a superb neo-Gothic building, there is the Great Window filled with stained glass. Bishop Gilbert Burnet, Bishop of Salisbury is featured, and in a south side window the Arms of Sir Thomas Burnett of Leys 1st Baronet, a benefactor to the College, are shown.

ST ANDREW'S EPISCOPAL CATHEDRAL, Aberdeen
The ceiling of the south Aisle of the cathedral is decorated with the Arms of north-east families who were sympathetic to the Jacobite cause. Amongst the Arms are those of two Burnetts, James Burnet of Campfield and Burnett of Daladies, who married the heiress of the Stewarts of Crichie.

ARBUTHNOT MUSEUM, Peterhead
In the Museum collection there is an oak chair, dated 1661, on the back of which a carved shield of the Burnett of Leys Arms is shown with the initials MB.

SEAVIEW HOUSE, Portsoy, Banffshire
There is a small display of the owner's family heraldry on the ceiling of the Library.

CHANCERY OF THE ORDER OF ST JOHN IN SCOTLAND, Edinburgh
The Chapter Hall contains heraldic stall plates including that of a former Librarian of the Scottish Priory who is a Burnett.

CRATHES CASTLE
Amongst the decorative features included on the re-built wing of the Castle is an exterior metal railing which carries three holly leaves and a stylised horn

The Police Burgh of Banchory, Kincardineshire, was granted Arms on 4 May 1939. The fees to Lyon Office were paid as a gift to the Burgh by Mr James Mortimer Burnett, Provost of Banchory from 1928 until 1945.

The Arms contain heraldic references to the Burnetts of Leys and the Ramsays of Balmain, two Kincardineshire families related by marriage.

Fig. 12.44

Argent, the figure of Saint Ternan, Vested and mitred Proper, with his crosier in his dexter hand and a book and bell in his sinister hand, standing between two holly leaves in chief Vert, and in base a hunting horn and an eagle displayed Salbe, the former garnished Or and stringed Gules, the latter beaked and membered of the Last. (Fig 12.44)

Following the passing of The Local Government (Scotland) Act of 1973 the Burgh Council of Banchory ceased to exist and the Arms reverted to the crown. The current Banchory Community Council could petition the Lord Lyon for a re-grant of the Arms.

BURNETT TARTAN

There are three tartan designs associated with the House of Burnett. The 1838 Grant of Arms to Sir Thomas Burnett of Leys, 8th Baronet, shows a reddish/brown tartan worn by the dexter supporter. The Grant to the present Head of the House, dated 1967, gives the exact pattern. This is the Burnett of Leys tartan (Fig.12.45).

There is also a Hunting version of the Burnett of Leys tartan (Fig.12.46). Another version of the Burnett tartan is that which is normally sold in regular Highland-wear shops (Fig.12.47)

ESTATE TWEED

Most estates have their own tweed for employees who may require country clothes. Gamekeepers and ghillies are usually given a new suit each year.

Some estate tweeds are designed according to the topography and include a blue line if there is a significant river on the estate, or a green line to represent forestry. The Leys Estate has never had its own tweed but around 1965 the Head of the House decided to 'adopt' a standard design (Fig.12.48.).

Since the number of estate employees who might wear the tweed has been reduced to one, it is unlikely the design will be re-ordered once the existing stock has been used.

Fig.12.1

Fig.12.2

Fig.12.3

Fig.12.4

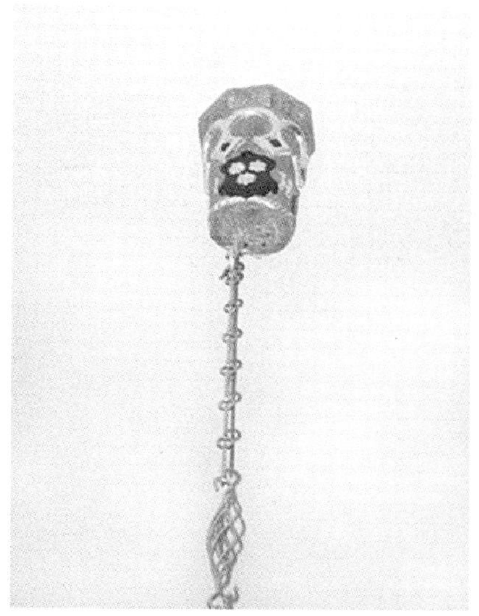

Fig.12.5

Fig.12.6

Fig.12.7

Fig.12.8

Fig.12.9

Fig.12.10

Fig.12.11

Fig.12.12

Fig.12.13

Fig.12.14

Fig.12.15

Fig.12.16

Fig.12.17

Fig.12.18

Fig.12.19

Fig.12.20

Fig.12.21

Fig.12.22

Fig.12.23

Fig.12.24

Fig.12.25

Fig.12.26

Fig.12.27

Fig.12.28

Burnett Stuart

Fig.12.29

Fig.12.30

Fig.12.31 **Fig.12.32**

Fig.12.33

Fig.12.34

Fig.12.35

Fig.12.36

Fig.12.37

Fig.12.38

Fig.12.39

Fig.12.40

Fig.12.41

Fig.12.42

Fig.12.43

Fig.12.45

Fig.12.46

fig.12.47

Fig.12.48

Fig.13.4 Crannog of Leys (green mound in centre of photograph) 2000 (Bailey)

Fig.13.5 Crannog of Leys 2000 (Bailey)

13

THE CRANNOG OF LEYS

Eileen A. Bailey

That tower of strength which stood four square to all the winds that blew
(Tennyson, 1852)

Many references have been made to the fact that the Burnetts, who settled early in the fourteenth century in the north-east of Scotland, did so because Alexander Burnard was rewarded for his service to King Robert the Bruce by being given lands at the Forest of Drum. The Castle of Crathes was not constructed until some 200 years later so where was the early dwelling of the Burnards/Burnetts?

The designation 'of Leys' as applied to the heritor of the Burnard/Burnett lands emerged about 1446 and referred to the property and, in particular, to the area of the Loch of Leys, which was noted in the charter by King Robert the Bruce dated 28 March 1323. This included *lacum de Banchory cum insula ejusdem* or the 'lake (loch) of Banchory with the island within it'. The Loch of Leys, to the north of the present town of Banchory and to the west of Crathes Castle, was located in a marshy area close to Raemoir and formed when meltwater, from glaciers moving towards the coast, was left trapped in a depression below the Hill of Fare. The area still carries the vegetative features of marshland with low scrub and reedbeds. (Fig.13.3) The Loch, when drained in 1850, covered 140 acres.

We are given to understand that the early home of the Burnards was located on a crannog on the Loch of Leys and sometimes refered to as the 'Castle' of Leys. As has been stated earlier, in Chapter 3 on the genealogy of the Burnetts of Leys, there has been no authentication of the tradition that Alexander Burnard not only received land but also took possession of the crannog, a fortallis, which had been built by the Wachopes and of which they were dispossessed by King Robert. Certainly the Wachopes/Wauchopes are known to have been holders of land on Deeside in the reigns of Alexander I (1107-1124) and Alexander II (1214-1449). A charter from the latter to Robert of Walchope, son of Allan Walchope, describes in detail the boundaries of the land said to extend as far as the Loch of Banchory.

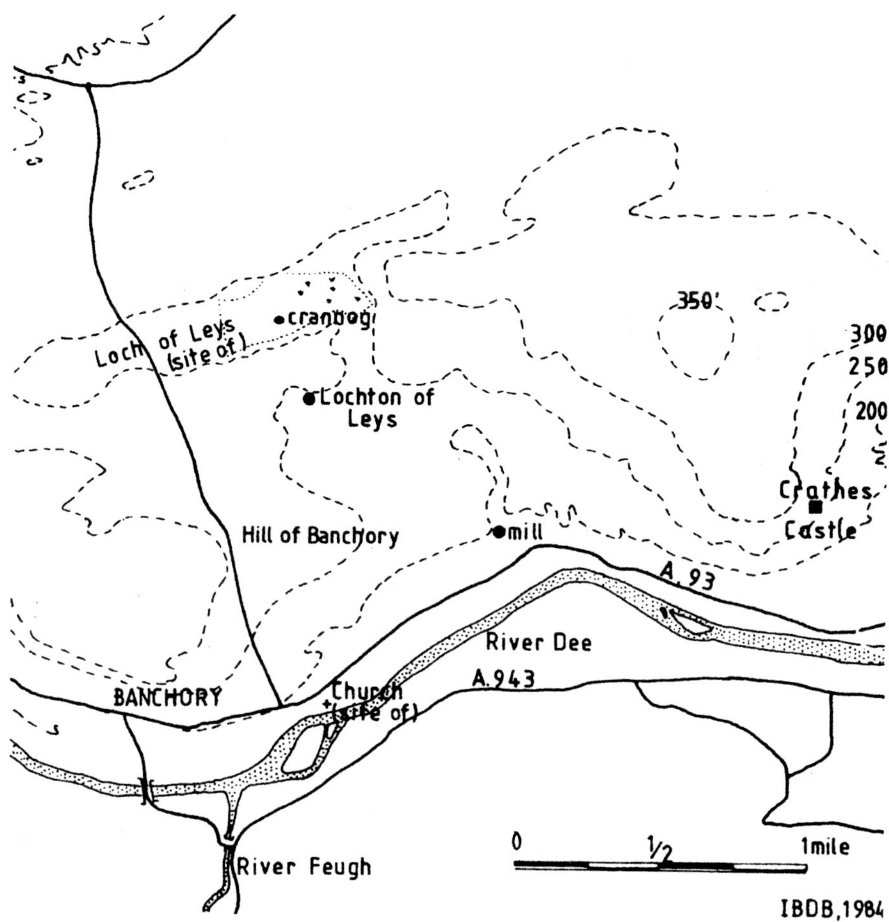

Fig.13.1 Map of Leys and Crathes (Bryce 1984)

In that era, the first priority in selecting a location for a home would have been security and ease of defence. The crannog style of dwelling was used because it provided a homestead with fortification. Chris Tabraham writes that *The landscape of mediaeval Scotland for the most part was altogether more boggy than it appears today and there was thus a greater opportunity to exploit the terrain to this end. Islands had an innate defensive quality requiring little more than an encircling wall of wood or stone to make them reasonably secure.* [(1)] Such a location offered much more security than a building contructed on dry land since any attack required, in the first instance, some means of spanning the area of water between land and the island.

Another factor in the use of crannog dwellings was not only the aspect of defence but also the availability of land suitable for cultivation. In circumstances where tillable land was limited, and what there was had been achieved through much labour, it made sense not to then lose it by building a home on it. The laird's home was certainly his castle whether it was constructed of stone or timber on land or perched on an island surrounded by a natural moat. The crannog, the translation of which from the Gaelic simply means 'made of wood', was not confined to Scotland and Ireland nor was it only associated with very early periods of land occupation. Lake dwellings of similar construction existed throughout many parts of the world and in Scotland archaeological and recorded evidence shows a span from prehistoric times well into the 16th century. Morrison (2) highlights how, in a world perspective, Scotland has one of the largest concentrations of known built-up islands.

A crannog was normally constructed by creating an artificial island, or by enhancing an existing natural one, by driving timber piles, usually of alder or oak, into the bed of the loch often in the shape of a circle. Between the piles, and to well above the high-water line, stones were heaped and levelled so that a platform of timber poles could be laid to form a floor. Excavation of the Leys crannog found it to be composed of earth and stones resting on a foundation of oak and birch trees and surrounded by oak piles. The timber used, along with hazel and alder, was readily available in the vicinity as these were naturally occuring species. Because this was such a valuable resource for the construction of homes, animal shelters, weapons and utensils, the properties of each species were well understood, the timber managed during growth, certain species encouraged by coppicing and any wood used carefully selected. The walls of a crannog building were often constructed from wooden hurdles woven from pliable hazel and the roof trusses made from branches thatched with mature reeds which grew profusely as an annual renewable resource. The floor would have been strewn with straw and bracken. The heat and cooking source came from a central hearth from which smoke seeped through at roof level.

The above description is that of the structure most commonly associated with built-up islands and especially those in early use. This was not exclusively the case, however, and successive research has revealed that some crannog dwellings were more rectangular in shape, the Leys crannog being one. As the 'Castle of Leys' has been described as having been *a strong substantial building* and rectangular in shape (Fig.13.2), the walls, it is reasonable to assume would have been constructed predominantly in stone. Morrison (3) draws a comparison between the footprint of these rectangular island structures and that of the traditional Scottish 'black-house' of similar design.

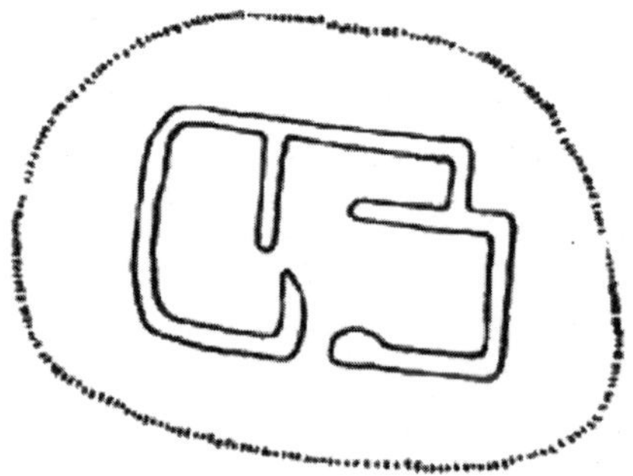

Fig.13.2 The surface of Crannog of Leys (Bryce from *PSAS* Vol.VI)

Of course, depending on the size of the island, a crannog home could have comprised not only the substantial building for the laird and his family but also a collection of other small dwellings for his immediate servants and for crop storage. Supplementary building would most likely have been of timber construction. Henderson quotes Dixon who noted that in relation to the crannogs of Loch Tay, the position *clearly corresponded to areas of lesser slope...and suitable land for cultivation.* [(4)] The position of Leys at the foot of the Hill of Fare very much fits this description. In a paper on *The Isle of Banchory and Other Crannogs* read to the Society of Antiquaries of Scotland in December 1857, Mr. Joseph Robertson expressed the opinion that the loch had, at one time, been four or five times larger than its eventual 140 acres. He wrote, *It had one small island, known to be artificial, oval in shape, measuring nearly 200 feet in length by about 100 feet in breadth*(61m by 30m), *elevated about 10 feet* (3m) *above the bottom of the loch and distant about 100 yards* (91m) *from the nearest point on the mainland.* [(6)]

Robertson [(6)] describes the island as being *a place of very ancient note* on account of it being the burial place of St. Ternan, known as the Archbishop of the Picts, who was one of the first Christian missionaries in the north-east predating the arrival in Scotland of St. Columba by about 100 years. Apart from the fact that an island in the Loch of Leys would seem a logical choice of last resting place for such a person, there does not appear to be any positive proof that his grave was there. St. Ternan, traditionally, is said to have been born at Fordoun in Kincardineshire and baptised into Christianity by St. Palladius to whom Fordoun Church was dedicated. In addition to his monastic teaching centre around which early Banchory grew, St. Ternan, who had been blessed by the Pope in Rome, established other missionary bases in the north-east and his travels are said to have taken him as far as Benbecula. He died before 500AD.

Recorded information about the Leys crannog comes primarily from the efforts of Sir James Horn Burnett to drain the Loch in 1850 as part of the land improvement movement of that period. He noted in his diary on 23 July of that year *Digging at the Loch of Leys renewed. Took out two oak trees laid along the bottom of the lake, one five feet in circumference and nine feet long; the other shorter. It is plain that the foundation of the island has been of oak and birch trees laid alternately and filled up with earth and stones. The bark was quite fresh on the trees. The island is surrounded by oak piles, which now project two or three feet above the ground. They have evidently been driven in to protect the island from the action of the water.* [(5)]

This description matched that of earlier findings at Irish crannogs and was further enhanced by the artifacts found below the surface. Sir James described these as being *bones and antlers of a red deer of great size, kitchen vessels of bronze, a millstone, a small canoe and a rude flat bottomed boat about nine feet long made from one piece of oak.*[(5)]

Fig. 13.3. The present day drained Loch of Leys. 2000 (Bailey)

In spite of the drainage work undertaken, the position of the crannog is still quite clearly visible as a mound.[(Fig.13.3)] The location, photographed recently from the air, is shown in colour in [(Fig 13.4)] and [(Fig 13.5)] facing the beginning of this chapter.

The kitchen vessels found comprised five kettles or cooking utensils (Fig.13.6), located on the bottom of the loch after drainage at between 2-3 feet below the surface. They were described as Roman Tripods or Camp Kettles. One of those presented to the Society was a bronze ewer measuring about nine inches in height which was described as resembling a modern coffee pot in design and was observed to closely resemble *vessels in illustrations of medieval manuscripts such as the 14th century Louterell Psalter.* [6]

Fig. 13.6 Various vessels recovered from the Loch of Leys (after *PSAS* Vol. VI)

The canoe, which was raised from the loch bottom, was said to have disintegrated on exposure to the air. There were also some coins found which were then lost because, as Sir James Burnett wrote, *one of the workmen ran off with them.* In communications to the Society of Antiquaries of Scotland in 1852 [4], Sir James Burnett described the items recovered from the Loch of Leys. Some of the vessels found are on display in Crathes Castle, others were lodged with the Scottish Museum of Antiquities (now the Royal Museums of Scotland).

References:

(1) Tabraham C., *Scotland's Castles*, 22, (1997), Historic Scotland/Batsford, London.

(2) Morrison I., *Landscape with Lake Dwellings. The Crannogs of Scotland,* 2, (1985), Edinburgh University Press.

(3) Ibid. 55.

(4) Dixon T.N. "Unpublished thesis on Scottish Crannogs", p. 173, 1984a, in Henderson J.C., *A Survey of Crannogs in the Lake of Menteith, Stirlingshire* published in *" Proceedings of the Society of Antiquaries of Scotland"* , 286, Vol. 128, (1998).

(5) Burnett J.H., in *Proceedings of the Society of Antiquaries of Scotland,* 26-27, Vol. I, (1851-54).

(6) Robertson J., "Notices of the Isle of Banchory etc. (1857)" in Stuart J., *Notices of Scottish Crannogs,* reprinted from PSAS, Vol. VI, Part I, 13-15.

14

CASTLES AND OTHER RESIDENCES

Ian B. D. Bryce

A house has to my mind a history as enthralling as that of an individual. If it is an old house it has much longer existence and it may be both beautiful and romantic, which an individual seldom is.

(Marquis Curzon in the *Earldom of Mar*)

CRATHES CASTLE

Fig. 14.1 Crathes Castle 2000 (Bailey)

The castle of Crathes is one of the splendours of Deeside, for long the seat of the Burnett family since they settled on the estate of Leys in the early fourteenth century and where they were to remain until 1952, when it was given to the National Trust for Scotland. As the great tower-house now appears it ranks with Fyvie Castle, Castle Fraser and Craigievar Castle as one of that late-sixteenth and early-seventeenth century group which enrich the north-east of Scotland and are of national importance. But, like its sister castles, the Crathes which we know today has undergone many changes, more than appear at first sight.

Scottish castellated architecture started to become a fashionable study in the middle of the nineteenth century and, when the 'Aberdeenshire group' of decorated Jacobean tower-houses was considered (which includes Crathes, although technically in the former county of Kincardine), two divergent lines of thought emerged. The exponent of the composite school, one building being the product of several periods, was R.W.Billings, an English architect and artist who traversed Scotland, drawing its castles and ecclesiastical buildings from which the four volumes of *The Baronial and Ecclesiastical Antiquities of Scotland* were compiled. [(1)] His notes on the north-east castle were based on observation of the elevations from which he deduced, because of its rounded angles similar to those of the Tower of Drum, that the lower portion of Crathes was an old tower upon which the decorative baronial coronet had been raised at a later date. It was, he said, "the gradual accumulation of additions made at various times to the original old square tower".

The second, or homogenous, school arose from the work of David MacGibbon and Thomas Ross who published the first two volumes of *The Castellated and Domestic Architecture of Scotland* in 1887, thirty years after Billings's books and thirteen after his death. [(2)] They argued that castles such as Crathes and Fraser were of one period of construction, that the contrast between plain lower and decorated upper compartments was due to the prevailing fashion, and that Billings "...does not appear to have recognised the importance of the plan". From their reading of the date stones on the outer walls they concluded that Crathes was "probably" begun in 1553 and completed in 1596. As the authoritative Scottish architectural historians, their version was preferred to that of the romantic English artist.

Research has now shown that although Billings' reasoning was wrong his conclusions were right. Reading between the lines of the half-page demolition by MacGibbon and Ross of Billings' ideas on Crathes one suspects that their scholarly caution had been improperly influenced by the rival earlier work.

It has been shown that Castle Fraser is a composite work: a fifteenth century rectangular tower-house with both horizontal and vertical additions of at least three later periods resulting in the present splendid pile. [(3)] It is to be argued here that Crathes is also the product of more than one period, a composite rather than homogenous structure.

After years of uncritical comment Stewart Cruden, then H. M. Inspector of Ancient Monuments for Scotland, sounded a warning note in *The Scottish Castle.* [(4)] He questioned the forty-year span of the supposed building dates and raised several criticisms regarding both the overall design and the applied detail. The improbable time-scale has been accounted for by postulating a succession of short-lived lairds resulting in a period of instability, of which more below, but this does not explain the fundamental flaw which is that the southward mass of the main tower is too great, reducing the eastward *jamb* or wing to a meagre thing by comparison.

Fig. 14.2 Crathes Castle (Bryce 1984)

This is uncharacteristic of any period of castle building where an instinctive sense of felicity and balance was combined with functional requirements to produce buildings with an uncontrived and natural grace. Moreover the wayward structural details of the south front show mishandling. A half-round turret emerges to rise up the centre until corbelled out to the square and oversailed still further on continuous corbelling, enriched with label moulding and stone cannon spouts. It ends in a shallowly crenellated parapet drawn between the copes of the two flanking lums which are thus diminished in significance instead of rising as dominant features of a great house in a cold climate. Most unsatisfying of all is that this seemingly solid finale is only a thin screen between the gables, where its only function is to disguise the gables of the two parallel roofs required to span the abnormal width.

The minor detailing is also weak: a string course applied to the surface descends from the south-west turret, is forced into a framework for armorial panels and the feudal symbol of the Horn of Leys, then continues eastwards until absorbed into the west edge of the central stair turret. In marked contrast to this uncertainty and lack of purpose is the eventful display to the east. The turret emerges on label-decorated demi-corbelling and is then defined by a vertical multi-faceted band which levels off to traverse as a window lintel and base of the south-east angle turret. It continues along the east and south faces of the re-entrant angle to end as the base course of the southern angle turret of the jamb. The change between east and west is other than the conventional division of upper and lower, plain and ornate compartments. A horizontal divide is to be expected but this vertical split requires an explanation applicable to this building alone. Cruden thought that the addition of a stair tower or the enlargement of an existing one of the usual dimensions "are not impossible explanations", a pointer to further research.

In his account *Crathes Castle*, Schomberg Scott, then architect to the National Trust for Scotland, ranges far from the immediate locality and provides a useful chapter under "Scots Baronial" which opens with the provocative sentence "The year 1553 has always been accepted, on somewhat slender evidence, as the date when the building of the castle was begun by Alexander Burnett, 9th laird of Leys." (5) Slender indeed, with the entire literature on the edifice being poised on a nineteenth century reading of a single date-stone, since when some radical revisions of dating have been required due to the realisation that a stone with a date need not signify a new building but a phase in the history of the owners of an existing structure.

In stressing the importance of the plan Cruden follows MacGibbon and Ross when he says it is "too often ignored or merely described where the elevations receive the greater critical attention" but the only readily available plan is that by MacGibbon and Ross. Neither Scott's guidebook nor W Douglas Simpson's *Earldom of Mar* provide this basic key. (6) Following the fire which gutted the Queen Anne wing east of the tower and the Victorian additions to the north, new plans were drawn up for the Trust which were primarily concerned with the re-arrangement of the Queen Anne wing, but which also provide an accurate record of the tower-house walls. By re-drawing these, a new chronology can be shown with an original orthodox L-plan tower, 50 by 43 feet (15.2m by 13.1m) along its north and west flanks, to which a later unit of 20 by 10 feet (6m by 3m) was inserted in the re-entrant angle to contain a new entry, vestibule, and main stair. (Fig. 14.3) It was this addition which gave rise to the need for twin gables, stair turret at the join, and the misapplied decoration, all combining to give the riverward aspect its unique schizoid effect.

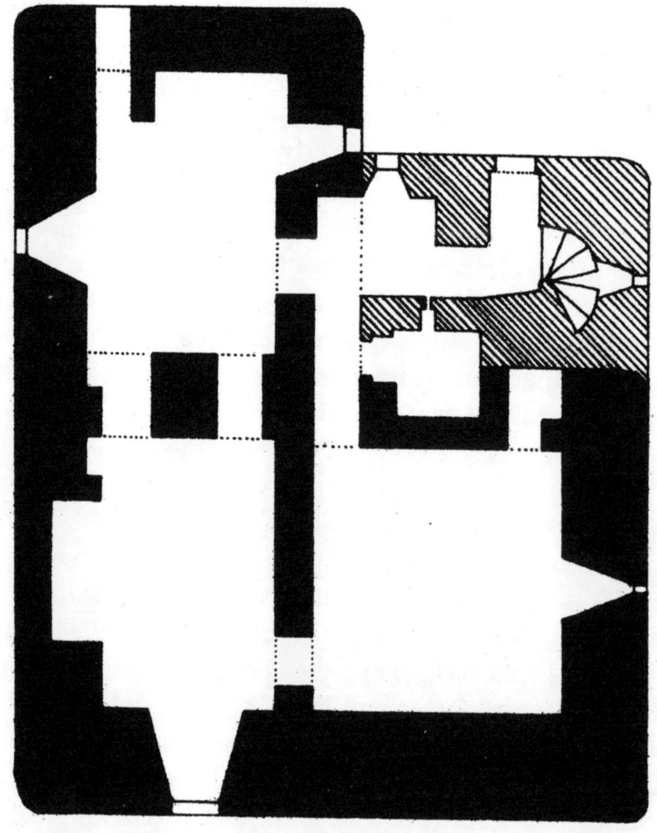

Fig. 14.3 Crathes Castle (Bryce after S.S. & R. McK., 1984)

Although too little used, the technique of comparative analysis is of value. By listing castles of comparable plan, placing them in chronological order, and considering the features common to the group, a pattern may be discerned into which the problematic castle can be assigned a logical place. As shown in the Table of Comparative Analysis (Fig.14.7), there are eight castles which may be considered: the first Huntly (or Strathbogie) of which only the foundations remain; the tower-house of the Dunnottar complex; the first Esslemont, which like Huntly was 'sacked' and demolished to create its successor on the site; Ravenscraig, licensed in 1491;

the shattered ruin of Fedderate and the preserved ruin of Auchindoun. Between Esslemont and Auchindoun was Druminnor of which all trace has vanished in a sequence of ruin, re-development and demolition. Basically similar in plan but with the obviously increased sophistication of the later sixteenth century is Gight. By omitting the intrusive stair unit in the re-entrant the simple L-plan of Crathes can take its place in the fifteenth century pattern by virtue of simplicity of plan and its overlooking of a river crossing.

Criticism of the elevations and re-interpretation of the plan does not constitute proof. As Cruden asserts "in the long run the written record is the last word; all else is supposition." (7) Due to the dearth of early Scottish records such proof may never be found; even where documents do exist the evidence may be negative, as is the case of Castle Fraser where the absence of any reference to a castle led Simpson to reject the existence of a fifteenth century work which has now been shown to have existed whether remarked upon or not. (8) A similar situation would appear to obtain at Crathes. Even if its early history remains as supposition it will be on a sounder basis than past assumptions.

The territorial designation "of Leys" first appears in 1446 and was used of the property generally and the vicinity of the Loch of Banchory in particular. The loch was noted in King Robert Bruce's charter to the Burnetts, dated 28 March 1323, as *lacum de Banchory cum insula ejusdem* - the lake of Banchory with its island. (see also Chapter 13).

On 25th April 1488, King James III issued a charter to *Alexandro Burnard* uniting his lands of *Kellienachclerach* in Kincardineshire and *Westercardney* in Aberdeenshire into the free *Baroniam de Leyis,* given under the great seal in Aberdeen and witnessed by the Bishops of Aberdeen, Moray and Orkney; the earls of Crawfurd, Huntly, Erroll, Buchan and the Marischal, and the lords Glamis, Forbes, Invermeith and Ruthven. It was accompanied by a Precept to William Elphinstone, Bishop of Aberdeen and Chancellor of Scotland with more detailed information on the baronial lands which included *Crathas et molendinum eiusdem...lacum de banchory cum insula eiusdem* - Crathes with its mill...lake of Banchory with its island.

Five days later, 2 May 1488, the ceremony of taking sasine was held and an Attestation drawn up which is of considerable importance in the history of the castle. Freely translated from the Latin it reads:

...at the dwelling house of Robert Burnet in the farm-toun of Leys, by the handing over of earth and stone Alexander took possession of the lands of Gannoccleroch and Wester Cardney in the Barony of Leys...Dated at the farm-toun of Leys,

witnessed by Hugh Robertson (and others), *sealed at Crathes on the same year, month and day given above.*

All three documents: Charter, Precept and Attestation can be read in the original in George Burnett, *The Family of Burnett of Leys* [(9)] .

A number of points emerge from a study of these documents. A baronial revolt in the south of Scotland had forced James III to leave Edinburgh in haste after 23 March 1488. He sailed from Leith in one of Andrew Wood's ships and landed in Fife. Ordering his sheriffs to "call out the host" (raise an army) he rode north to Aberdeen. There he was joined by his chancellor and adviser, Elphinstone, and the other bishops, earls and lords of the north who had gathered in support of the crown. Hence the illustrious roll of witnesses on the Burnett charter, itself a reward for support (although the neighbouring Irvines had been barons since 1324 and with a castle already built). The king and his nobles returned south in early May, to Blackness, Edinburgh and, on 11 June, to the battlefield of Sauchieburn from which James III fled to his death. On Deeside, it would be natural for Burnett to erect a baronial residence as symbol of his new status and insurance against trouble coming north. One final point from the Charter is that the Reddendo was one silver penny payable *apud capitale messuagium* - at the principal house - of the barony, which is not named.

As the Attestation makes clear, Robert Burnet lived beside the loch but his dwelling was not upon the island mentioned in earlier charters. The crannog seemingly unsuitable, the *villa de Leis* - settlement, locally farm-toun - was chosen instead, as the nearest place to the traditional *capitale messuagium.* Here the ceremony of taking sasine by earth and stone was conducted, the Attestation dated and witnessed by a group of more lowly status than those on the charter then, and this is significant, the attaching of the seal was done at Crathes later the same day. So the island on the loch of Banchory, which has invariably been regarded as the residence of the Burnetts until 1533, merits only a fleeting reference in the Precept and there only as one of a number of parts of the baronial lands. After the ceremonial at Leys the technicalities were conducted at Crathes where, doubtless, the celebrations were also held.

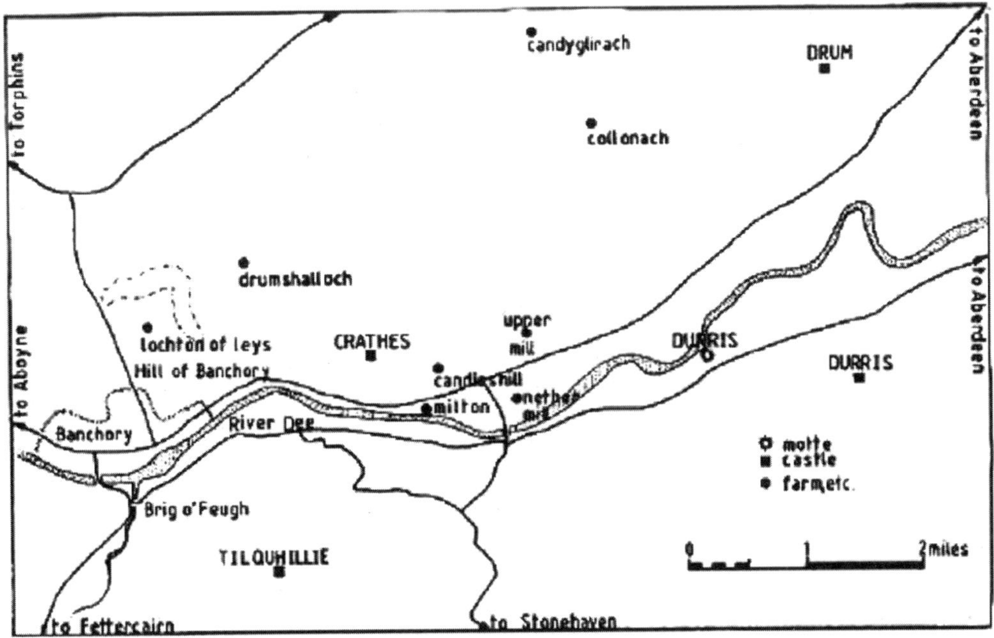

Fig.14.4. Crathes, Drum and other significant locations. (Bryce)

In his paper on "The Early Castles of Mar", W. Douglas Simpson omits Crathes because he assumed it was of the sixteenth century. (10) This results in the eastern branch of the north-south route known as the Cairn-na-Mounth Pass ending in a cul-de-sac at Banchory. (Fig. 14.5)

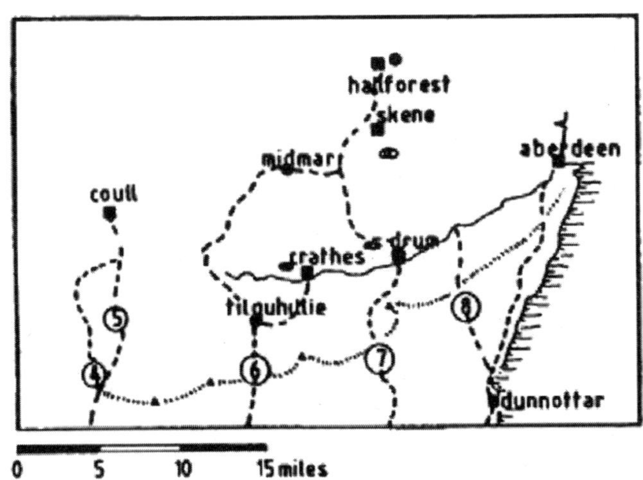

Fig. 14.5 Routes into Deeside showing (6) Cairnamounth Pass (Bryce)

Although not a major route like the western branch to Kincardine O' Neil and Kildrummy, the eastern branch also served a centre of population on the north bank, and a property as old as Drum. The crannog of Leys can never have been a military strength as were the mottes of Strachan and Durris. Postulating a castle at Crathes closes the gap and fulfils the purpose claimed for Drum and Durris: control of the river crossing at Mills of Drum (now confusingly known as Mills of Crathes). The architecture, the cartulary, the geography and the history are all in accord with a date of about 1488 as the commencement of the first castle and therefore the work of the 6th rather than the 9th laird of Leys.

The 7th and 8th lairds married well and acquired lands in the pre-Reformation transfer from church to secular ownership. With the accession of Alexander Burnett as 9th laird and 4th baron in 1529, a tenure of ownership was begun which was to last forty-five years. His coat of arms, with those of his first wife, Janet Hamilton, and the date 1533, appear on the east wall of the re-entrant. It is this stone which has been read as the dating of the castle but, as it is not in its original position, it does not relate to the present building. Bearing the arms of the same couple, dated 1554, is a pendant boss in the hall. It must be accepted that such a place argues new work, but it is also the 25th anniversary of Burnett's lairdship, thus the evidence pulls one way then another. [(11)]

The popular myth that the castle took forty years to build is not acceptable, Cruden considered ten years sufficient.[(12)] Tolquhoun took five and Muchalls eight years respectively. Nor is the idea that a rapid succession of lairds provides a valid reason. The 9th, 10th, 11th and 12th lairds span the period from 1529 to 1619 with periods of lairdship of 45, 1, 3, and 41 years respectively, that is continuity for eighty-six out of a total of ninety years. To this it may be added that it was the 12th laird who commenced his castle at Muchalls in the year of his death. This record of stability and vigour continued, except between 1574 and 1578, with the 12th laird who, even as a minor, showed himself from his known character, to be an energetic laird.

The earlier family chronicler, George Burnett, states that the 12th laird finished the castle which his great-grandfather had begun. However he then adds another detail: *That Crathes was inhabited a few years before 1596 appears by the mention in the Record (sic) Register of the Privy Council of a bond executed at Aberdeen and Crathes on the 3rd and 4th September 1588.* Here we have a repetition of the circumstances attending the issue of the Attestation of a century before. That document crossed the estate from Leys to Crathes on the same day whilst the bond required a lapse of a day to come up Deeside from Aberdeen. If the evidence is good for 1588 it must be good for 1488 also and is persuasive of there being a castle at Crathes on both dates.

In 1595 Alexander Burnett resigned the barony of Leys to the crown and had a new charter issued in which "the tower, manor and fortalice of Crathes" was recognised as the *caput* of the barony, marking the demise of even the symbolic function of either the crannog or the *villa* of Leys. The 12th laird and his wife, Katherine Gordon of Lesmoir, firmly stamped Crathes with their personalities, their arms, their monogram and even perhaps their 'portraits' carved on the doors of a cupboard. It is hardly surprising that he has been so readily accepted as the laird who finished an incomplete building but the facts may be otherwise.

That the present castle is the result of at least two phases of construction is accepted. The point at issue is the time lapse between the first and second and the reason for it. We have considered and rejected the idea that it was begun by the 9th laird about 1533, left unfinished until completed by the 12th laird in 1596. Instead we postulate a fifteenth century nucleus to which others added in due course.

The alterations consist of a stair unit in the re-entrant and the upper floors with their decorative stonework. [(14)] It is possible that the 9th laird began, or even completed, a stair block in addition to the early tower which lacked a large main stair in the manner of the fifteenth century. [(fig. 14.6). (14)]

However the character of the detailing differs from west to east with the central turret in the south wall marking a vertical division. From this it can be argued that the square insert with its new stair, the turret which is the continuation of that stair, the string course and armorial display to the west and all the upper floors are the work of one period - that is by the 12th laird in the late sixteenth century. He would have had to remove his great-grandfather's coat of arms from its place on the old wall to its present situation on the new entry front and included his own and the 9th laird's arms below those of King James VI on the south front, dated 1596 and proclaiming the Burnetts of Leys to be tenants in chief of the king.

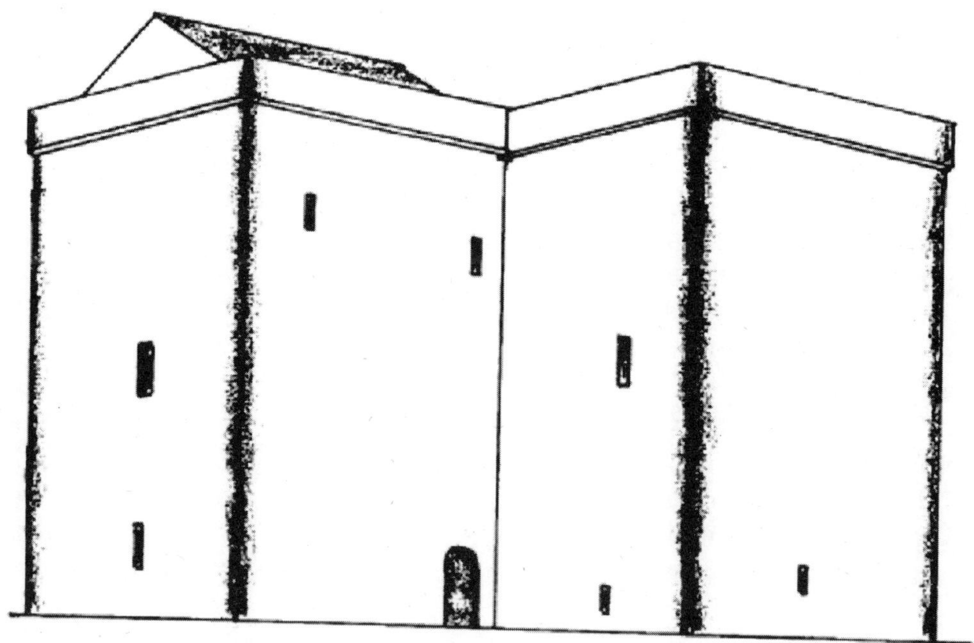

Fig. 14.6 Early Tower of Crathes Castle (Bryce)

On stylistic grounds the upper works have all the appearance of being by the Bell family of master-masons. Traditionally their work has been first identified at Midmar as early as 1575 but this date has now been advanced to either shortly after 1594 or even after 1602. [15] If the latter, then Crathes (1596) may have some claim to be the first of the sequence which continues through Fyvie (1598), Craigston (1604), Fraser (1617) and Craigievar (1627), at all of which, with the exception of Craigston, they were engaged to enlarge or adorn existing buildings. This sequence shows their developing skill in composition, a surer handling of the various elements coming from experience. Thus are the discrepancies at Crathes explained, not only the decision to insert a stair block which disturbed the scale, but also because the elaboration of the new wall-head was an early exercise in the new mode.

Name	Date	AxB	CxD	E	F	G	Family
Huntly	**L14c**	**60x50**	**26x22**	2	**Foundation Preserved**	**Inland**	**Gordon**
Dunnottar	**L14c**	**42x37**	**20x18**	2	**Ruin Preserved**	**Coast**	**Keith**
Esslemont	**E15c**	**55x42**	**20x15**	3	**Foundations**	**Inland (River)**	**Cheyne**
Drumminor	**1445/6**	-	-	-	**Site only**	**Inland**	**Forbes**
Auchindoun	**L15c 1480s**	**48x45**	**22x15**	2	**Ruin Preserved**	**Inland**	**Drummond**
Ravenscraig	**L15c 1491**	**83x73**	**26x22**	3	**Ruin**	**Coast (River)**	**Keith**
Fedderate	**L15c 1490s**	**59x44**	**27x15**	2	**Ruin**	**Inland**	**Crauford**
Crathes	**L15c**	**50x43**	**20x20?**	3	**Occupied Preserved**	**Inland (River)**	**Burnett**

Key: L14c; Late 14th century. E15c; Early 15th century. AxB; Lengths of longest sides. CxD; Lengths of re-entrant angle. E; Number of chambers at ground level. F; Present condition. G; Geographical location.

Fig. 14.7 Table of Comparative Analysis

In December 1990, I visited Crathes Castle at the invitation of Mr. Ian M. Davidson who was accompanied by Mr. Jeffrey Boughey.(16) The main purpose was to consider the origin and function of an aperture between the north-west angle of the White Room and the south-west angle of the Muses Room on the third floor. Hitherto concealed by a tapestry, it had been suggested that it might be re-opened as an additional public access, but on examination it was found that the differing floor levels of the adjoining chambers made this impossible. Whilst the blocking in the White Room is to roof height, the lintel in the Muses Room is considerably lower. No immediately obvious answer emerged but it seemed that the castle being erected in two phases might have some bearing on the matter. The one explanation which seemed to cover the situation was that the spaces in the internal wall at second and third floor levels were originally window voids in the wing of the fifteenth century tower house and that, at the time of the addition of the stair block, the levels in the wing were altered to their present heights, new beams and floors inserted and subsequently decorated. This will have rendered the former windows redundant or, as on the first floor, reused as an access point. This explains the presence of the lintel and jamb in the Muses' Room which will have been the interior face of the former window. It would have been sensible to have blocked the unused voids but, as the insertion of the large window into the south wall of the Great Hall in the last century shows, builders paid scant heed to the future stability of the structure.

The south window is now causing movement of the entire south wall, doubtless already weakened by the sixteenth century alterations. It was also noted that the thickness and alignment of the fourth and fifth floor chambers was clearly different from that of the lower levels, adding further support to the hypothesis that the lower L-plan is earlier, that the stair block is a later insertion, and that the two upper storeys are additions by the Bell school of masons. As the original idea of creating a public access had to be abandoned, the breeze block wall remains *in situ* with two ventilation holes inserted as the 1990s contribution to the 1960s blocking of the 1480s aperture.

The true history of Castle Fraser began to emerge in the 1950s, of Fyvie in the 1960s and of Craigievar in the 1970s and the latter is still on-going. [17] In each case the evidence lay within the walls themselves, revealed in the interval between the removal of old harl and the application of the new cladding. Much highly romantic but quite inaccurate history has had to be revised in each case. For a more accurate history of Crathes we must await the time when it too is obliged to reveal its true age.

Crathes - Notes & References

(1) Billings, R.W., *The Baronial and Ecclesiastical Architecture of Scotland*, (1852) in four volumes, Edmonston & Douglas, Edinburgh. Facsimile Edition,
Heritage Press (Scotland), 1981.

(2) MacGibbon, D. & Ross, T., *The Castellated and Domestic Architecture of Scotland*, (1887-92) in five volumes, David Douglas, Edinburgh. Facsimile edition, James Thin, Edinburgh, 1971.

(3) Slade, H.G., "Castle Fraser: a seat of the ancient family of Fraser", *Proceedings of the Society of Antiquaries of Scotland*, Vol.109 (1977-8), 233-300.

(4) Cruden, S., *The Scottish Castle*, (1960), Thomas Nelson, Edinburgh.

(5) Scott, W.S., *Crathes Castle*, (1971), Aberdeen University Press for the National Trust for Scotland.

(6) Simpson, W.D., *The Earldom of Mar*, (1949), Aberdeen University Press.

(7) Cruden, *Scottish Castle*, 12.

(8) Slade, H.G., "Castle Fraser". *PSAS.*

(9) Burnett, G., *The Family of Burnett of Leys*, (1901), The New Spalding Club, Aberdeen.

(10) Simpson, W.D., "The Early Castles of Mar", *Proceedings of the Society of Antiquaries of Scotland*, Vol63 (1928), 102-138.

(11) In the upper chamber of the Wine Tower, Fraserburgh, there are a series of coats of arms of members of the Fraser family, including the 8th laird and his ancestors. One architectural detail, combined with the known history of the 8th laird, places this structure in the 1580s.
See Bryce, Ian B.D., "The Wine Tower, Fraserburgh", *Double Tressure*, 11 (1989), 3-14.

(12) Cruden, *Scottish Castle*, 170.

(13) This plan is closely paralleled at Balbegno Castle, Fettercairn. The Woods of Balbegno were closely associated with the Irvines of Drum.

(14) There may have been a mural stair in the recess shown in the south wall of the jamb.

(15) Slade, H.G., "Midmar Castle, Aberdeenshire", *Proceedings of the Society of Antiquaries of Scotland*, 113 (1983), 594-619.

(16) Mr Ian M Davidson, Building Surveyor (Grampian) and Mr Jeffrey Boughey, Custodian, Crathes Castle, both National Trust for Scotland.

(17) Bryce, I.B.D., "Cragievar Castle: A Fresh look at Scotland's Premier Tower House" in *Architectural Heritage* (forthcoming), A. Roberts.

MUCHALLS CASTLE

Fig. 14.8 Muchalls Castle (From a drawing by Irene Pratt)

There is no doubt that Muchalls Castle is one of the most benignly charming of all Scotland's baronial residences. Its two long and low-set wings reach out like welcoming arms to gather the visitor into the shelter of its courtyard walls.[Fig.14.8] Once inside, the homely dimensions reinforce the initial impression that this building was designed as a peaceful residence rather than a martial fortification; it is not an overt expression of landed power; there is nothing here of the haughty height of Crathes. [1] This atmosphere has been sustained by the two most recent generations of owners, both of whom have maintained the sensation of friendship and warmth, only too happy to share their love of Muchalls with others. [2]

The received history was admirably expressed by a local journalist who wrote in 1961: There is no mystery about the origins of Muchalls Castle. A commemorative tablet announces:

> **THIS WORK BEGUN ON THE EAST AND NORTH BE Ar. BURNET OF LEYIS, 1619, ENDED BE SIR THOMAS BURNET OF LEYIS HIS SONNE, 1627.** [3]

So is this to be a simple paean of praise for a familiar and former Burnett house? Not so, because whilst the visible structure is undoubtedly by the family of Burnett of Leys, it has a longer and even more complex history than its stately mother house on Deeside. Those who have hailed Muchalls as a modest chateau are correct but have missed the vital point that the present house is only the second, or perhaps even third, phase on the site.

Location

The castle is situated eight miles south of Aberdeen's Bridge of Dee and four miles north of Stonehaven, once the county town of Kincardineshire, and at 72 metres (236 feet) above sea level at Nat. Grid Ref.: NO 892 908. From there it overlooks the least inviting of the seven Mounth passes, the ancient north-south routes across the east-west barrier of hills which stretch along the south side of the river Dee from Aberdeen before merging into the Cairngorm mountains beyond Braemar. The Cowie Mounth Pass was shunned by invading armies, be they Roman, English or belligerent Scots, all of whom chose more westerly routes to avoid the bogs and fogs of the east coast.

To this day the two main northward roads, inland from Perth and coastal from Dundee, converge just south of Stonehaven to leave a single road which only became dual carriageway throughout its length within recent years. (4) Access to the castle is from the Bridge of Muchalls turn-off from which the road ascends the north bank of the Burn of Muchalls for 1 mile north-west to the turn-off to Blackbutts (doubtless once the barony's archery practise ground) where it doubles back eastwards for ¾ of a mile to arrive at the stable/garage yard. There it turns to briefly climb north, arriving at the only practicable entrance on the level ground at the rear, an approach which clearly demonstrates the dramatic defensive potential of the castle's platform site. (Fig. 14.9) To the west especially, although decreasingly so to the south and east, are natural sloping ramparts. Although the modern road at its furthest remove is 850 yards (777m) to the south-east, the ancient Cowie or Causey Mounth track was only half that distance away. Indeed part of the present immediate approach runs on the line of the ancient *Causey*, an alternative name derived from the causeways laid across stretches of marshy ground at its upper levels before its descent to Aberdeen, an unusually early instance of road-works which indicates the importance of this inhospitable but vital route.

Muchalls' Earliest Owners

Fraser

Cowie was an ancient thanage-cum-barony with a promontory castle on the cliffs just north of Stonehaven, now reduced to grass-covered ramparts. What form of residence then stood at Muchalls is not known. Cowy, Collie or Cowie probably became a barony when the property was granted to Alexander Fraser of Corntoun, near Stirling, Chamberlain to Robert the Bruce, in 1368 although the first reference to
Fraser as lord of the barony of Cowie is in 1376. [(5)] After the battle of Harlaw in 1411, Sir William Fraser was disposing of parcels of land when, in October 1413, the baronies of Cowie and Durris were acquired by William de Hay, Lord of Errol and Constable of Scotland.

Hay, Earls of Erroll

In 1314 King Robert the Bruce had granted Sir Gilbert Hay the office of Constable of Scotland and the Aberdeenshire barony of Slains, some 15 miles north-east of Aberdeen. In 1452 William Hay was created Earl of Erroll by James II and about six years later William, Lord Keith, the Great Marischal, was created Earl Marischal. Thus the two men who held the most senior crown posts were now also elevated to the higher nobility [(6)] and both were based in the north-east of Scotland.

Muchalls as an Artillery Castle

Virtually every depiction of Muchalls Castle is from the vicinity of the doocote at the south-west angle which allows a view of the courtyard wall, the stair jamb and the east and north wings. It should be noted here that the orientation of the castle has been misunderstood since MacGibbon and Ross published an inaccurate and misleading plan and text. [(7)] They had *buildings... north, east and part of the west sides of the square* where 'west' should be 'south' and *View from the south-east* which should be 'south-west' although they correctly place the kitchen *At the north-east angle*. Both Cuthbert Graham and Nigel Tranter followed these errors. [(8)]

Also misleading although superficially correct is the impression of a gracious mansion in wooded grounds. Only Sheila Forman, for long a percipient writer on castles, makes the point that "There is no long-distance view of Muchalls. The visitor comes on it suddenly as the last corner is turned on the steep road up from the sea, so that the first shock of delight takes one by surprise". [(9)]

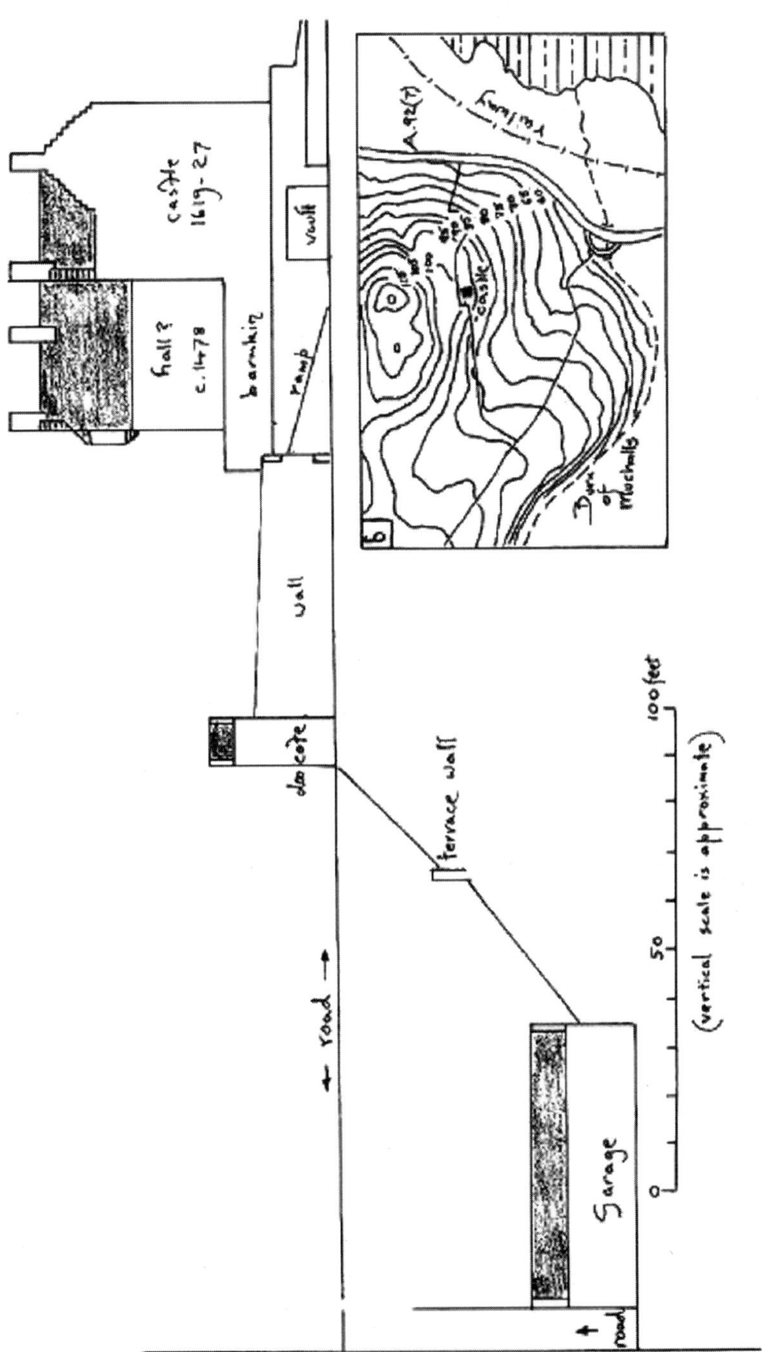

Fig. 14.9 Profile of Muchalls Castle location (Bryce 1997)

A very different delight began in April 1992, when I accompanied my friend and colleague Mr Nicholas Q. Bogdan on a visit to Muchalls at the request of the owner, Mrs Nicol Glenda Cormack. Assisted by her business partner, Mr. Mike Acklon, she had been uncovering features worthy of further consideration. A preliminary survey was undertaken which was supplemented shortly after when the dimensions of the terraces and the doocote were noted with another friend, Mr. Peter Voy, assisting, whilst offering characteristic criticisms of my embryonic hypothesis. My idea was that the previous castle had been a late fifteenth century "castle of enciente" or courtyard erected for William Hay, 3rd Earl of Erroll, the residential hall of which had been incorporated into a new castellated mansion following its acquisition by Alexander Burnett of Leys in 1614. As this volume is principally concerned with the Burnett family, the role of the Hays, Earls of Errol, in the development of the castle must be condensed but cannot be ignored.

In 1478 Errol was engaged in a private war in the county of Angus with James Stewart, Earl of Buchan, laird of Auchterhouse and an uncle of King James III. This was but one of a series of such baronial feuds *in diverss partis of the realm* as noted in the parliament of 1479. [(10)] Another example was when Stewart was "at feud with other nobles, which led to other gatherings of their followers under arms, and necessitated the interference of the Government to preserve the peace". [(11)]

The *caput* of the earldom of Buchan was the Earlshill in Ellon, the bridgehead over the River Ythan north of Aberdeen which controlled the route to the Hays' regality of Slains. However the route from Perthshire through Angus and the Mearns to Aberdeenshire lay along the coast via the Cowie Mounth, so Erroll may well have decided to assert his authority and control by commissioning a castle on his Kincardineshire lands with gun-loops, guns and *a cunning man to shoot them* as Parliament thought desirable in 1456. [(12)] The coastal site of the mediaeval Cowie Castle having long been redundant the plateau on the north bank of the deep declivity of the Burn of Muchalls overlooking the main coast road and the sea was chosen instead. [(13)]

Set into the terrace immediately south of the south flank of Muchalls is a barrel-vaulted chamber which is pointed out as the crypt of the Episcopalian chapel which was destroyed by the Hanoverians in 1746, an identification which appears to be wholly based on tradition. In 1997 two doorways were discovered opening off the main stair at ground and first floor levels, which indicate some form of tall structure had formerly existed above the "crypt".

That there was a building here in the 1619-27 period is shown by the sharp cut-off of the label corbelling of the stair wing and its wall height may be indicated by the projecting spur above. Then there is the ground floor of the two-storey doocote which is barrel-vaulted with an internal wall forming an arc in the south-east angle whilst at first floor level there is a door jamb incorporated into the masonry, neither feature serving any purpose in the present arrangement.

When laying underground cables in the grounds next the north wing some very large stones were found. Where possible they were excavated and stored in the garden but others proved to be set so deep that they had to be circumvented leaving just their tops showing through the gravel drive and paths. The base of the north, west and south walls of the north wing is composed of massive earth-fast boulders but no such stones are visible at the base of either the east range or the main-stair wing.

Since the renovations of 1992, other finds in the ground floor of the north wing have also led to revised ideas regarding its true nature. This wing has been almost wholly disregarded since the account by MacGibbon and Ross with most commentators regarding it as a mere adjunct to the more important main (east) block and confining their observations to the first floor chambers alone.

Although no visible remains indicate the original lay-out, my interpretation of several features is that the eastern section of the north wing was originally a free-standing unvaulted hall-type residential block, entered directly off the courtyard and serving a larger complex. Research by Dr. Joachim Zeune has led to his recognition of at least twelve Scottish castles which were erected between 1480 and 1560, all specifically designed with round towers to be defended by artillery.(14) Thus Muchalls makes a hitherto unrecognised thirteenth example. (15)

The nearest other local instance of this type is Esslemont, near Ellon in Aberdeenshire, which was excavated by Dr. W. D. Simpson in 1938 when he revealed the foundations of an L-plan tower-house. (16) This was surrounded by a curtain wall forming a 110 by 110 feet (33.5m by 33.5m) quadrangle with a triangular western adjunct. The angles appear to have been provided with five 25-foot (7.6m) diameter round towers, one of which appears to have been reused as the base for the 20-foot (6.1m) diameter round tower of the present L-plan tower-house which was built about 1580-90. Following the destruction of the old tower in 1493, Cheyne of Esslemont was granted a royal licence in 1500 to build a new castle and Zeune asserts that this applies to the artillery castle, erected as the successor to the destroyed tower and later superseded by the (now ruined) present tower-house. (17)

Disregarding the triangular adjunct which was a local modification, the dimensions of the Esslemont castle of 1500, on being applied to the Muchalls site with the south terrace as a base-line, encapsulate the south terrace and northern hall-house to give a plan which is closely akin to the other examples except for the absence of a large central tower-house. Thus, based on the scant surviving evidence, the hypothetical castle would have consisted of a southern range of barrel-vaulted cellars built into the terrace with chambers at ground and first floor levels, one of the latter possibly set aside for use as a chapel. On either side there would have been enclosing walls terminated by a south-west round tower, whence the curved wall within the doocote and possibly a south-east round tower, all pierced with gun-loops. At the rear, within the enclosing east, west and north walls, there was a hall-house for the resident castellan.

Prior to the late fifteenth century, the eldest son of Hay of Errol had been granted the barony of Ury, or Urie, a property to the north-west of Stonehaven, three miles south of Muchalls, indicative of the importance of this area to a family who possessed widespread lands. The first earl's uncle, William Hay, was 'of Urie' and the property passed to his younger nephew Gilbert who married Beatrice Dunbar, daughter and heiress of Sir John Dunbar of Crimond. Dunbar had been a gunnery expert from Duchrae in Kirkcudbrightshire, was knighted for repairing a gun at Roxburgh Castle and his last royal payment, for drying gunpowder, was in 1459. He then retired to live with his daughter Beatrice Dunbar and son-in-law Gilbert Hay of Urie at Crimond, seven miles south-east of Fraserburgh, which he had bestowed upon his daughter. Sir John died there in 1478 so Erroll may well have sought advice from his sister-in-law's father living a mere 16 miles north of Slains. He will certainly have been aware of the new fashion in fortifications and of the desirability of having control of the coastal route. The second son of George, 7th Earl of Erroll, was designated 'John of Muchalls' showing Muchalls now being granted to a younger son, as Urie had been before. This then was the disregarded but recognisable earlier phase of Muchalls.

Muchalls as a Burnett House

By 1977, my monthly articles on north-east castles in *Leopard* magazine (founded in Aberdeen in 1974) had led me to realise there could be conflicting reports by different commentators. I found myself especially puzzled and dissatisfied by the varying accounts of Muchalls. Mrs. Diane Morgan, founder and editor of the *Leopard*, gave a characteristic reply, "You write what you think, your opinion is as good as anyone else's". So the Muchalls article was the first intimation of what has subsequently developed into my "leiper theory". (18)

This proposes that between about 1570 and 1624 a group of some sixty-seven castles and other buildings were erected in Scotland, all sharing idiosyncrasies of plan, details or both. They are to be found as far apart as Shetland, Argyll and Galloway but the highest concentration is in Aberdeenshire where there are 24 examples, and 4 in Kincardineshire, which is a relatively high number considering that county was only 629 sq. miles compared with the 1,956 of Aberdeenshire.

It is at Tolquhoun Castle, near Tarves, Aberdeenshire, that all the features of the "classic" leiper plan are to be found: which is securely dated between 1584 and 1589; where something of the builder laird Sir William Forbes, 7th of Tolquhoun is known; and that rarest of persons, the master-mason has been identified as Thomas Leiper from which my generic term "leiper" is derived. A further boon is that it is a ruin, devoid of the camouflage of harl or plaster and has been in state care for many years and therefore readily accessible. Nowhere else is so much information visible and available. A comparison of the main block of Tolquhoun with the east wing of Muchalls shows both consist of a kitchen occupying the full breadth of the range; a corridor off which open three cellars, all vaulted; a first floor with Dining Room or Hall and a second storey above; a stair tower which projects from the residential block with the main entrance opening into a vestibule and having a chamber below the stair, variously described as a "guard room" or "porters' cubby" depending on the size. At Muchalls the private chamber and the laird's room are housed in the wing but otherwise the similarity between the two plans is unmistakable and both conform to the classic leiper plan.

Another leiper feature is the diagonal walls across the south-west re-entrant angle containing the entrance and the north-west re-entrant angle which is an enlargement of an earlier stair in the same position. (Fig.14.10) Similar diagonals are to be seen at Drum and the lesser-known Tilquhillie near Banchory, both Leiper works.

Fig. 14.10 Corner detail, Muchalls. 1999 (Bailey)

The west and south sides are enclosed by a truncated barmkin wall with a gateway flanked by shot holes which are circular within but divided externally into three orifices to centre, left and right, so termed "triple-splayed shot-holes", suitable for a small hand gun and identical to Tolquhoun, the first notable feature and very characteristic Leiper trade-mark.

That the north wing contains the early nucleus immediately west of what is now the main block, is shown by the great thickness of the kitchen's north-west wall where the vast seventeenth century fireplace has been built against an earlier gable, which accounts for its being to one side instead of straight ahead in the north gable as would normally be the case. As I already suspected in 1977, this was largely confirmed by the evidence discovered in the early 1990s.

Burnett

When Alexander Burnett of Leys acquired the property in 1606 from Francis Hay, 9th Earl of Errol, he lived in the old castle where he died in 1619, shortly after having begun his new home. It seems clear that he commissioned the same mason who had been at work on the new south range of Drum Castle for Alexander Irvine, Burnett's Deeside neighbour to the east.(19) Not only does the ground plan echo Tolquhoun but some details also point to the near-contemporary work at Drum. Vaulting being deemed desirable for sound-, smell-, and fire-proofing, the new-style groined vaulting as used at Drum was chosen here because it allowed more head room and storage space against the walls. It is improbable that the aesthetic effect was considered for these purely domestic regions; that is a later conceit.(20) Whilst the new walls could receive such vaulting during construction, the insertion of new vaults below the old hall required the two new corbels and the projecting piers from which to subtend the groins as were discovered in 1992. (21)

It was to be Alexander's son Sir Thomas Burnett, 1st baronet and 13th laird of Leys, who was to finish the new Muchalls, so it must have been his decision to include turrets as symbols of his baronial status and enliven the otherwise typically plain leiper-type elevations. This is paralleled at Lickleyhead near Insch which is leiper plan but where the angle turrets have been identified as being additions by one of the Bell school. (22) The present roof line is the result of Lord Robertson's alterations in the nineteenth century which included the removal of the garret storey and, it seems, the upper storeys of the turrets, which accounts for the relatively low elevations we see today.

The Interior

Moving from the technicalities of past history and rising above the complexities of ground floor plans, it is in the interior that the magnificence of the Muchalls of the Burnetts emerges. What in an earlier age, as at Crathes, would have been a soaring stone-vaulted hall is here the long low flat ceiling of the hall or banqueting room on the first floor of the east wing. This is the greatest glory of the building. The splendid heraldic ceiling which was finished in 1624, displays the coats of arms of the associated families of Hamilton, Dunfermline, Lauderdale, Forbes, Arbuthnott, Gordon and, of course, Burnett.

There are medallions (Fig.14.11) in high relief, patterned ribs and pendant "knops" for lamps forming a spectacle which has been regarded as the finest of its kind in the country. At the north gable is a chimney piece surmounted by four caryatids between which is the gilded and painted Royal Arms of Scotland. (Fig. 12.33) Off the hall is the dining room and beyond that a study, again superbly plastered and medallioned with heraldic chimney pieces. [23], (Fig. 12.30)

Fig. 14.11 Ceiling Medallion, Muchalls Great Hall. 1999 (Bailey)

It was not always peaceful of course. In 1639 the Royalist Lord Aboyne raised a force and camped at Muchalls. The following day, the opposing Covenanters arrived and rifled the house but the almost new fabric survived. It was Sir Thomas who, on his appointment as Sheriff of Kincardineshire, had the barony of Leys transferred to that county in 1646 and created the anomaly of Crathes Castle and the adjoining town of Banchory, although north of the river Dee, no longer being in Aberdeenshire. When he died in 1653 the property was leased to Robert Burnett of Cowtoun as tutor and guardian to the heir, the grandson of Sir Thomas, who was a minor. There was a confused period until Alexander, 2nd baronet, bested his guardian and settled in with his wife who is said to have borne him twenty-one children. He died in 1666 and was succeeded by Thomas Burnett, 3rd baronet, who died heavily in debt in 1714 which led to Alexander, the 4th baronet, selling the property to Thomas Fullerton of Gallery, near Montrose, for £6,730. It must have been in his possession when the Hanoverians arrived in 1746 and destroyed the Episcopalian chapel in the aftermath of Culloden. Mr. Fullerton in turn sold it to Aberdeen Town Council in 1750 and in 1800 the Council sold it on to Mr. Silver of Netherley, a property on the road to Maryculter on Deeside, for £20,000, so making a profit of £12,000.

In 1844 the barony of Muchalls was acquired by the Trustees of Dr. Milne's Bequest when Mr. Silver sold "the greater portion of the barony" for £48,000. The Trustees made great improvements to the property until selling it to Aberdeen Educational Trust, now the Aberdeen Endowments Trust, for £62,500. Despite the ever increasing value of the lands and strange though it may seem today, the castle had declined to a semi-ruinous condition, saved only by its stone roof and solid walls. A succession of absentee owners had taken its toll until the Educational Trust was partially fortunate with its first tenant, Lord Robertson of Forteviot, sometime MP for Bute and later one of the thirteen Lords of Session, the judges of the Scottish Court of Session. He preserved and cleaned the interior but was also responsible for the insertion of plate glass windows and the ill-designed eastern extension, both typical late nineteenth century touches.

The happier modern phase began in 1954 when Mr. Maurice Simpson and his wife Geraldine bought the castle marking the beginning of an ongoing cherishing. They had it re-harled but were obliged to replace the original stone roof with the present slates as the weight was proving too much for the roof timbers. This was a task which taxed the skill of the slater, Mr. David Dinnie, a grandson of the famous athlete, especially the conical roofs of the angle turrets. (24) For the next thirty-six years Mr. and Mrs. Simpson, latterly Mrs. Simpson on her own, made the castle available to the public on Sundays and Tuesdays during the summer months whilst adding a wealth of furnishings and curios, until, in 1990, the castle changed hands when Mrs. Simpson sold it to Mrs. Nicol Cormack. This proved to be a most happy arrangement as, to Mrs. Simpson's delight, Mrs Cormack brought her flair for decoration to bear on the entire building. (25) But change was in the air once again as Mrs. Cormack, seeking a fresh challenge, put the property on the market in 1996. It was valued at over half a million pounds and was sold in 1999 to an American couple.

It can only be hoped that the new owners will be as appreciative as the immediately previous owners have been and that they will be as assiduous in preserving this perfect gem of Scottish castellar architecture which has suffered, but also enjoyed, so much.

Muchalls – Notes and References

(1) see I. B. D. Bryce, in this volume.

(2) (The late) Mr. Maurice Simpson and Mrs. Geraldine Simpson; Mrs. Nicol Glenda Cormack.

(3) C. Graham, "Magnificence of Muchalls", Historic Homes Series, in *Press* *and* *Journal*, (29 April 1961); Graham, "Muchalls wins battle of the Dyke", in *Press and Journal*, (11 December 1971).

(4) I. B. D. Bryce, "Castle of the Month : Muchalls", in *Leopard* magazine, 24, (July/August 1977).

(5) Lord Saltoun, *The Frasers of Philorth*, I, 108.

(6) J. Mackintosh, *Historic Earls and Earldoms of Scotland*, 232-4, (Aberdeen 1898). In 1953 the late Diana Denyse Hay, 23rd Countess of Erroll and 27th Hereditary Lord High Constable of Scotland, exercised her rights when Queen Elizabeth was present at a Coronation service in St. Giles Kirk, Edinburgh. The office of Earl Marischal was not revived after the Keiths forfeited their lands and office as Jacobites.

(7) D. MacGibbon & T. Ross, *The Castellated and Domestic Architecture of Scotland* II, 370, Fig. 817, (1887).

(8) C. Graham, "Magnificence of Muchalls", N. Tranter, *The Fortified House in Scotland*, IV, 167.

(9) S. Forman, "Muchalls Castle", in *Scottish Field*, 40, (March 1956).

(10) R. Nicholson, *Scotland*: *The Later Middle Ages*, 482, (1974, Edinburgh).

(11) J. B. Paul, *The Scots Peerage*, II , 267.

(12) A. A. M. Duncan (ed.), *Scotland from the earliest times to 1603*, 231-2. (1977)

(13) I. B. D. Bryce, "Muchalls, Kincardineshire: A late fifteenth century artillery castle" (unpub MS, 18 August 1995; revised edition 3 March 1996). Following a visit by the Castle Studies Group on 13 April 1997, Mr Geoffrey Stell observed that Mr. Bryce had presented "a plausible theory" and that a copy of his paper should be lodged with the Royal Commission on the Ancient and Historical Monuments of Scotland. This has since been done, 25 April 1997.

(14) J. Zeune, “The Long Pause - A Reconsideration of Scottish Castle-Building c1480-1560”, Lehrstuhl fur Archaologie des Mittelalters und der Fruhen Neuziet, Fakultat fur Geistes - und Geowissenschaften, Universitat Bamberg (1984), 1; J. Zeune, “Perfecting the Tower House, Part I: The L-plan Tower-House”, in *Fortress* No. 10, 30, (April 1991); J. Zeune, "Perfecting the Tower House, Part II: The Z-plan Tower House", in *Fortress* No 11, (November 1991) [These last two papers are a reduced version of his doctoral dissertation “Der schottische Burgenbau vom 15 bis zum 17 Jahrundert”, presented to the Otto-Friedrich University, Bamberg, 1987. For the tower-house see I. B. D. Bryce, "Esslemont Castle", in *Leopard*, No. 26, 8-10 (Feb 1977).

(15) I. B. D. Bryce, *A Chronology of the Castles of Scotland 1100 -1685*, 10, 14, 42, 43, 73, 74, 79. (forthcoming 2000)

(16) W. D. Simpson, "The Excavation of Esslemont Castle, Aberdeen-shire", in *Proceedings of the Society of Antiquaries of Scotand* LXXVIII 1943-44, 100-05.

(17) Zeune, "The L-Plan Tower-House", 29.

(18) I. B. D. Bryce, "The Leiper Theory", (in preparation).

(19) It should be noted that in I. B. D. Bryce, "The House of Drum: A Critical Reappraisal" (unpub MS, 1988, 1993) H. G. Slade’s hypothesis that the south range of Drum was designed by a mason of the Bell school. (Slade, "The Tower and House of Drum, Aberdeenshire", in *Proceedings of Society of Antiquaries of Scotland,* 115, 297-356, (1985), is rejected. I believe it to have been more probably by a member of the "leiper" school.

(20) By the same token, the decision by the late H. Q. F. Irvine of Drum to strip the plaster from the lobby of Drum and return it to bare stone and since maintained by the National Trust for Scotland, though much praised in the 1960s, would have appalled the original lairds who had no desire to live within naked stone.

(21) When the 12th century Crusader castle of Belmont was excavated (1986-8) it was found that the east side of the court was built over at a later stage, with a pair of groin-vaults supported on rectangular piers. Dr Denys Pringle, "Crusader Castles: The First Generation", in *Fortress* No. 1, 22 (May 1989).

(22) The possibility that the angle turrets were formerly two storeys in height argues that a Bell mason was responsible. See H. Gordon Slade, "Lickleyhead Castle, Aberdeenshire: a laird's house with alterations by John Bell *c* 1626", *Proceedings of Society of Antiquaries of Scotland*, 106, 170, (1974-5).

(23) In the 1950s a plaster medallion in the stair fell and was smashed to pieces. The fragments were entrusted to a young man in Aberdeen who successfully reconstructed it. Yet this same brilliant craftsman had been laboriously taught to sign his own name whilst doing his obligatory national service with the army. A modern example of the illiterate craftsman.

(23) In 1960 the Simpsons invited Mr. Dinnie and his family to view the finished work of which he was so proud. I was present at that celebration of completion, my first visit to the castle, on Sunday 17th June 1960 with Mr. and Mrs. Dinnie and their four daughters, one of whom was a friend of mine.

(24) Sue Tranter, "Castle of my Dreams", in *Scottish Field*, 21-3, (September 1993).

Figure 14.8 is from a painting by Mrs Irene Pratt, Aberdeen, one of a series of drawings of north-east castles she was commissioned to execute some years ago, and used here with her kind permission.

OTHER BURNETT CASTLES and HOUSES

Whilst Crathes must be regarded as the chief house of the Burnetts of Leys and Muchalls as their dower house, there are fifteen other castles and houses which have been associated with the name of Burnett, however briefly. They are arranged in alphabetical order within their respective counties, thus *Aberdeenshire:* Cobairdy, Crichie, Elrick, Kemnay House, Old Kendal, Skene House, Tillycairn Castle; *Banffshire*: Ardmeallie; *Kincardineshire*: Fasque, Glenbervie House, Monboddo House; *Peebles-shire*: Barns Tower, Castlehill Tower, Woodhousehill; *Roxburghshire*: Fairnington House.

Inevitably there will be some repetition of details of the family as dealt with elsewhere in this volume but no building should be considered in a purely stone and lime context. A bibliography of works consulted is given at the end, with an abbreviated list after each entry.

Aberdeenshire

Cobairdy

Of the castle of the Murrays and later the Burnetts, there is no surviving trace, the stones having been used to build the present mansion of about 1855-60 in its estate 4 miles north-east of Huntly. The earliest Murray of *Culbardy* is Patrick who witnessed a deed in 1414. In 1567 James Murray, 6th laird of Cobairdy, and his brother Alexander obtained remission for their part in the battle of Corrichie (1562) when they had sided with Huntly against Mary, Queen of Scots. The 7th laird was Alexander whose two sons were summoned before the Privy Council for hurting and wounding Gilbert Leslie in 1613, but the next laird of Cobairdy is Alexander Burnett, in 1633, whose name appears again in 1641 when Alexander Burnett of *Colbairdie* is granted sasine (possession) of the Kirktown and Lands of Aboyne. By 1650 it is Sir John Baird, eldest son of Baird of Auchmedden, who is *of Cowbairdie* so the Burnett connection was short-lived.

Temple, *Thanage of Fermartyn*, 219-220; Bogdan & Bryce, no. C/49/3; Shepherd, *Gordon*, 35; Salter, *Grampian and Angus*, 104; Coventry, *Scottish Castles*, 108; Bryce, *Chronology*, 34, 77.

Crichie

The late eighteenth century planned village of Stuartfield lies just south of Old Deer, commemorating Captain John Stuart of Dens and Crichie, who arrived in the area in 1695. Just south of the village is "the House of Denns alias Little Crichie" which had been built by Captain Stuart in 1715, perhaps intended as a staging post for the Old Pretender from Peterhead harbour, 10 miles to the north-east. It is usually said that Stuart bought the lands from William Keith, 9th and penultimate Earl Marischal, in 1709, but the family tradition is that the price was for "15 armed men on horseback for a minimum of three months" as the Captain and the Marischal were close friends and ardent Jacobites. Certainly in 1732 Stuart of Crichie was included in a list of the lesser barons of Aberdeenshire. In the nineteenth century the first house was demolished so the present Crichie House is a rebuilding on the same site, but too plain to warrant mention in McKean, *Banff & Buchan*. Following the marriage of Theodosia Stuart to John Burnett, younger of Daleladyes and a cadet of Leys, their son, also John, added Stuart to his name and founded Stuartfield in 1789. The family remain on the estate with Geordie Burnett-Stuart of Crichie, and his French wife, Patricia, very much a serious farmer.

Tranter, *Eastern Counties*, 138; Bogdan & Bryce, no. B/26/7; Grant, *The Stuarts*, 25-26; McKean, *Banff & Buchan*, 90-91.

Elrick

Described as "crisp, if a little bland" this is a late eighteenth century house but the drum-shaped doocot (dovecote) in the grounds perhaps indicates that there had been an earlier house or even modest castle. Certainly the property of "Elrig", in Newmachar parish, is on record in 1492 when the Flemyng family were in possession. They were followed by Inneses of Innermarkie, Hamiltons and Hervies and it is not until 1662 that John Burnett, burgess of Aberdeen and merchant, is involved when, after a complex process of exchanges and mortgages, he finally got possession of Elrick, confirmed by a royal charter in 1663. There followed eleven Burnett lairds of Elrick, the high number being due to the succession frequently passing from brother to brother before moving to the next generation. There were still Burnetts in possession in the late nineteenth century. Curiously Tranter has it as an old estate of the Strachans which came to a branch of the Burnett family in the mid-seventeenth century by marriage.

Temple, *Thanage of Fermartyn*, 295-299; Tranter, *Eastern Counties*, 135; Shepherd, *Gordon*, 218.

Kemnay House

Worthy of third place after Crathes and Muchalls in the hierarchy of extant Burnett-owned castles is Kemnay House, five and a half miles south-west of Inverurie. In the absence of plans or any detailed survey the early history of this complex mansion is difficult to ascertain. There has been a persistent belief that it has a fifteenth century nucleus but later writers maintain the tall L-plan tower-house is of the early seventeenth century. It is believed probable that there was an earlier castle or house nearby as listed in Bogdan and Bryce. When the property was owned by William Douglas of Glenbervie, who became 9th Earl of Angus in 1588, there must have been a significant structure on the site but it is a later owner, Sir Thomas Crombie, who is credited with the tower-house. Alexander Crombie sold out to Alexander Strachan, 7th laird of Glenkindie, on Strathdon but both he and his son died in 1675 to leave the grandson as laird of both Glenkindie and Kemnay. He in turn sold Kemnay to Sir George Nicholson, a lawyer and later Lord of Session as Lord Kemnay, who re-sold the lands in 1688 to Thomas Burnett, second son of James Burnett of Craigmyle, a younger branch of Burnett of Leys. It was Thomas who extended the wings and added the distinctive "Dutch" gable. Further additions were made in the nineteenth century but the house was semi-derelict in 1964 when

Mrs. Susan Milton (née Burnett) returned from South Africa and successfully undertook the task of refurbishing her ancestral home where she still lives.

Graham, "Kemnay"; Tranter, *Fortified House*, IV, 57-58; Bogdan & Bryce, nos. C/59/1, 2; Shepherd, *Gordon*, 138-9; Salter, *Grampian and Angus*, 71; Coventry, *Scottish Castles*, 192; Bryce, *Chronology*, 39, 79.

Old Kendal / Ardiherauld

Nothing remains of Ardiherauld Castle, (not even the precise site is known) near Old Kendal Farm, 4 miles east of Inverurie. Tranter has Gilbert Burnet (note the single "t"), ultimately Bishop of Salisbury, as a scion of this house, although he was born in Edinburgh. Robert Burnett, later Lord Crimond, purchased the small estate of Kendal, Montkegie, which his son Gilbert inherited.

Tranter, *Eastern Counties*, 96; Bogdan & Bryce, no.C/58/7; Coventry, *Scottish Castles*, 236; Bryce, *Chronology*, 28, 76; Bailey, this vol., 41.

Skene House

The lands of Skene, some 10 miles west of Aberdeen, were erected into a barony by King Robert Bruce in 1317 with Robert de Skene as the first of the line. In the late fourteenth or early fifteenth centuries, a tower house was erected, at that period consisting of a cellar with hall above and sleeping chamber over that, all vaulted with stone. The Skenes of Skene remained lairds and lived in their tower and adjacent "low thatch houses" until about 1680 when, following the death of John Skene, 15th laird of Skene, his widow, Jean Burnett, daughter of Alexander Burnett of Leys, embarked on a remarkable scheme of improvement. The vaults were removed and timber floors and roof put in their place and a large addition built alongside. Perhaps having three sons and four daughters Lady Skene felt the need for more space and sophistication. The old tower is now enclosed in the north wing whilst Jean Burnett's wing is the centre block. The house was further enlarged by a south wing dated about 1745 and it was all substantially remodelled and further enlarged for the Duke of Fife in 1847-50, the 28th and last Skene of Skene having died in 1827.

Tranter, *Eastern Counties*, 155; Bogdan & Bryce, no. C/76/3; Shepherd, *Gordon*, 165; Salter, *Grampian and Angus*, 97; Coventry, *Scottish Castles*, 258; Bryce, *Chronology*, 7.

Tillycairn Castle

Whilst Coventry is correct in identifying this castle, five and a half miles south-west of Kemnay, as having been a Burnett possession, Slade is notably brief and uninformative, only observing that some time after the Lumsdens' demise in 1672 it was held by Thomas Burnett of Sauchen. Descendants of Forbes of Tolquhoun seem to have maintained a longer connection. Ruinous by 1772, it was bought in 1973 and between 1980 and 1984 was handsomely restored by David Lumsden, 19th laird of Cushnie so a family descendant. It is now in other ownership once again.

MacGibbon & Ross, *Cas Dom Arch Scot*, III, 601; Tranter, *Fortified House*, IV, 82; Slade, "Tillycairn", 499; Bogdan & Bryce, no. C/42/4; anon 1989, 41; Shepherd, *Gordon,* 151; Salter, *Grampian and Angus*, 13, 14, 20, 98; Coventry, *Scottish Castles*, 272; Bryce, *Chronology*, 22, 23, 30, 75, 77.

Banffshire

Ardmeallie

On a terraced site overlooking the valley of the Deveron in Marnoch parish, the existing Georgian house perhaps dates from about 1740 but with an updated south facade added about 1825. It probably lies on or near the site of the earlier residence, referred to in 1726 as the home of a branch of the Gordons who owned Ardmeallie during the seventeenth and eighteenth centuries. The first of the Gordons of Ardmeallie, James, who died before 1708, was third son of George Gordon, 4th of Cocklarachie. His elder son Peter was a noted Whig, unlike his brother, nephew and brother-in-law, all of whom seem to have been Jacobites. The Burnett connection does not begin until the 1920s when the Burnett-Stuarts moved in. The present laird, brought up at Ardmeallie, returned from England in 1990 and, with his wife, continued his late mother's work on the gardens.

Temple, *Thanage of Fermartyn*, 278; Tayler, *Cess Roll*, 169-170; Tayler, *Valuation*, 310; Tranter, *North-East*, 55; Allan and Baxter, 30-32; Macaulay, *Classical House*, 104, 106-7; Bogdan & Bryce, no. B/26/7; McKean, *Banff & Buchan*, 54.

Kincardineshire

Glenbervie House

The architectural history of the castle which underlies Glenbervie House was not discovered until 1949 when the Aberdeen scholar, W. Douglas Simpson made his first visit and realised that what had until then been regarded as a large Victorian mansion was actually a fortification of at least the fifteenth century period. Located 7 miles south-west of Stonehaven, its predecessor governed the southern end of the Cryne Corse Pass, one of the great south-north routes over the hills from The Mearns (Kincardineshire) to Deeside (Aberdeenshire), the route chosen by Edward I of England in his invasion of 1296. In 1468 an heiress brought it into the Douglas family who remained lairds until 1675 when the 3rd Douglas baronet of Glenbervie sold the property to Robert Burnett of Leys. The Burnetts remained until selling the property in 1721to Nicholson of Mergie, whose descendants still live there.

Simpson, "Glenbervie", 255-261; Tranter, *Fortified House*, IV, 159-160; Bogdan & Bryce, no. D/100/1; Salter, *Grampian and Angus*, 9, 137; Coventry, *Scottish Castles*, 168; Bryce, *Chronology*, 9, 14, 73, 74.

Monboddo House

Now the centrepiece of a rural housing estate built in the 1980s, 4 miles north of Laurencekirk, Monboddo is a simple oblong mansion of the seventeenth century, enlivened by two angle turrets. A later mansion was added, which would have been when the older house was somewhat altered, but this has since been demolished. As a dated heraldic panel asserts, it was the home of Robert Irvine (or Ervine) and his wife Jane Douglas in 1635. The judge, pioneer, anthropologist and eccentric, James Burnett, was born here in 1714. He was called to the bar and raised to the bench as Lord Monboddo, anticipated Darwin in anthropology and entertained Dr. Samuel Johnson in 1773. He was a highly respected judge despite his bizarre views on some subjects.

Tranter, *Fortified House*, IV, 166-167; anon 1979, 39; Bogdan & Bryce, no. D/98/6; Goring, *Dictionary*, 318; Salter, *Grampian and Angus*, 20, 149; Coventry, *Scottish Castles*, 222; Bryce, *Chronology*, 44, 80.

Fasque

The House of Fasque might seem out of place in this sequence of Burnett houses as the large, if somewhat austere, mansion is invariably associated with only two family names - the Ramsays, lairds of Balmain from at least 1510 and the Gladstones, which family acquired the estate and mansion, now called Fasque, in 1829. Although never mentioned, it was actually a Burnett who commissioned the present house. Alexander Burnett was the second son of Sir Thomas Burnett, 6th baronet of Leys and Catherine Ramsay, sister of the laird of Balmain, whose seat was at the old Fasque. Born in 1757 and married in 1782 to Elizabeth Bannerman, co-heiress of Elsick, he succeeded his maternal uncle, Sir Alexander Ramsay, 6th Baronet of Balmain, who died without direct heirs, and assumed the name and arms of Ramsay. He was created a Baronet of the United Kingdom as Sir Alexander Ramsay of Balmain in 1806. Two years later he demolished the old house of Balmain on the Fasque estate and commissioned the great new house with its polygonal angle towers, entrance hall and butterfly stair. The architect is not known but both the date 1808-09 and the style point to John Paterson who rose from being clerk of works to Robert Adam to practise as an architect in his own right. Sadly, the £30,000 cost of this exercise led to the bankruptcy of Burnett-Ramsay with resultant sale of the house and lands to the wealthy, Edinburgh born, Liverpool merchant, Sir John Gladstone in 1829. Perhaps it was because this action appalled the Ramsays and affronted the Burnetts that the Burnett name is never associated with the Ramsay-Gladstone property.

Tranter, *Eastern Counties*, 325; Macaulay, *Gothic Revival*, 185; Bogdan & Bryce, no. D/96/4; Salter, *Grampian & Angus*, 158; Coventry, *Scottish Castles*, 155; Eileen Bailey.

Peebles-shire

Barns Tower

This fifteenth century tower-house is three and a half miles south-west of Peebles, and is a fairly typical example of its period. Three storeys and a garret in height, it has a barrel-vaulted cellar, hall, and bedroom floor but the garret is now within a much-altered parapet and new gables and roof. The Burnets of Burnetland were known in the parish of Manor in the fourteenth century and the tower has the initials *"W B . M S"* for William Burnet and his wife Margaret Stewart of Traquair on the lintel of the first floor window. He was a notable character in the late sixteenth and early seventeenth centuries. The date *"1498"* over the entrance appears to be a later addition. A well-preserved feature is the original iron yett still hanging at the trance. The tower was abandoned when Barns Manor was built in 1773.

MacGibbon & Ross, *Cas Dom Arch Scot*, III, 414; Tranter, *Fort House Scot*, I, 122; Salter, *Lothian and Borders*, 17, 95; Coventry, *Scottish Castles*, 68; Bryce, *Chronology*, 14, 26, 49, 51.

Castlehill Tower or Castle Hill of Manor

This tower-house appears to have been built in the late fifteenth century by the Lowis family who had been in Manor early in that century. In 1557 a Margaret Lowyss held half the lands of Burnetland and John Lowis of Maner (Manor) was heir of Thomas of Maner in 1607. In the seventeenth century it passed to the Veitch family, thence to Bailie of Jerviswood and in the eighteenth century from them to the Earl of March from whom it was purchased by James Burnet of Barns. In a list of furnishings in 1555 it is interesting to note *and hart horn hinand (hanging) in the hall* so reminiscent of the Horn of Leys at Crathes. The last listed owner was Tweedie of Quarter who acquired it in 1838 and abandoned it shortly after. About 1880 it was repaired as a ruin, which it remains, with only the east wall standing to just above the level of the loft above the hall and capped with cement. It is four and a half miles south west of Peebles.

MacGibbon & Ross, *Cas Dom Arch Scot*, III, 416; Black, *Surnames*, 442; Salter, *Lothian and the Borders*, 10, 98; Coventry, *Scottish Castles*, 104; Bryce, *Chronology*, 17, 19, 49, 50.

Roxburghshire

Fairnington House

In the former county of Roxburghshire, three and a half miles north of Jedburgh, this is a deceptive building. It was originally a free-standing sixteenth century tower-house, probably built by a Hepburn, Earl of Bothwell, which family acquired the property in the late fifteenth century. It should be noted, however, that a William de Farningdon of Roxburgh rendered homage to Edward I of England in 1296 and is believed to be one of the Border Burnett family. It is thought to have been this tower which was burned in 1554 when a raiding party crossed the Border from Wark Castle. It has since been much altered by enlargement of its windows and the addition of later dormers whilst the large lower wing of the seventeenth century converted the tower into an L-plan laird's house. It was a barony of the Burnet or Burnard family in the twelfth century but by 1581 it was in the hands of King James VI who granted it to the Stewart, Earl of Bothwell. The wing appears to have been built after 1647 by a new owner, George Rutherford who would also have carried out the alterations to the original tower. An eighteenth century Rutherford laird carried out considerable improvements to the estate.

Black, *Surnames*, 118; Tranter, *Fortified House*, I, 138-9; Salter, *Lothian and the Borders*, 140; Coventry, *Scottish Castles*, 154; Bryce, *Chronology*, 35, 45, 53, 54.

Woodhousehill

Nothing remains of the tower near Barns, 3 miles south-west of Peebles. It passed from the family of Inglis to the Hoppringles in 1522 until, in the late sixteenth century, it was possessed by the Burnetts of Barns after which nothing is known of its history and it appears to have been eventually abandoned.

Salter, *Lothian and the Borders*, 126; Coventry, *Scottish Castles*, 284.

Bibliography

Allan, S., & Baxter, C., "Gardening down by the Deveron", in *Leopard* No. 180, (June 1993).
anon 1979, (Monboddo Castle estate advertising feature), in *Leopard* No. 49, (May 1979).
anon 1989, (Tillycairn Castle for sale), in *Leopard*, No. 138, (April 1989).
Bailey E.A., personal communication (2000)
Black, G. F., *The Surnames of Scotland*, (1946).
Bogdan, N. Q. & Bryce, I. B. D., *A Compendium of the Castles, Manors and 'Town Houses' of Scotland, Grampian Region, Banff & Buchan District; Gordon District*, (in preparation 1988). [Note: the reference letters and numbers refer to the District, Parish and sequence within the latter. Only "B" (Banff and Buchan) has manuscript textual material.]
Bryce, I. B. D., *A Chronology of the Castles of Scotland 1100-1685* (forthcoming)
Coventry, M, *The Castles of Scotland*, (1995).
Goring, R., (ed.), *Chambers Scottish Biographical Dictionary* (1992).
Graham, C., "Another 500 for Kemnay", in *(Aberdeen) Press & Journal*, I-II, (7 June 1969),.
Grant, D., "The Jacobite Connection: The Stuarts of Den and Crichie", in *Leopard*, No. 109, (May 1985).
Macaulay, J., *The Classical Country House in Scotland 1660-1800,*(1987).
MacGibbon, D. & Ross, T., *The Castellated and Domestic Architecture of Scotland*, Vol. III, (1889).
McKean, C., *Banff & Buchan: An Illustrated Architectural Guide* (1990).
Salter, M., *The Castles of Lothian and the Borders*, (1994).
Salter, M., *The Castles of Grampian and Angus* (1995).
Shepherd, I., *Gordon: An Illustrated Architectural Guide* (1994).
Simpson, W. D., "Glenbervie and its Castle", in *Proceedings of the Society of Antiquaries of Scotland.*

Tayler, A., & H., *The Jacobite Cess Roll for the County of Aberdeen in 1715.* (1932).
Tayler, A., & H., *The Valuation Roll of the County of Aberdeen for the Year 1667,* (1933).
Temple, Rev., W., *The Thanage of Fermartyn*, (1894).
Tranter, N., *The Eastern Counties: Aberdeenshire, Angus and Kincardineshire,* (1972).
Tranter, N., *The North-East: the Shires of Banff, Moray, Nairn, with Easter Inverness and Easter Ross,* (1974).

NOMENCLATURE

It was disappointing to see the old canard – that a Scottish 'palace' is restricted to association with a royal residence – being repeated in Architectural Heritage Society of Scotland *Magazine*, Summer 1998, No. 7, p. 4. The anonymous writer opens the discussion of the refurbishment of Culross Palace with the comment that "Although James VI was a guest of Sir George on several occasions, the house was never a royal residence, making the term palace therefore a misnomer".

In fact the use of the term 'palace' in Scotland has nothing at all to do with royalty, but is directly derived from the Latin *palatium* – a hall, later used as a Scottish legal term signifying a major residence. At the royal palaces of Edinburgh, Linlithgow, Stirling and Falkland their Great Halls played an essential part in the court ceremonial but such formal chambers were not confined to royal residences nor the term palace. Every bishop dwelt in his palace, sometimes a large courtyard building with angle towers. A friend has recently assembled a list of sixty-four sites which can be defined as episcopal palaces and the residences of modern bishops are still known as '"the bishop's palace", regardless of location and architectural style.

W. Mackay Mackenzie, in his chapter on "Castles and Towers" in George Scott-Moncrieff, *The Stones of Scotland*, 62-3 (1931), put it thus:

> "The most notable example is Linlithgow Palace, which bit by bit was converted from a structure of towers and walls into what we now see as a palace in the full sense of the term, a quadrangle of uniform horizontal building enclosing a court or, as it was described in the seventeenth century, ' a palace built castle-wise'. But every palace did not reach this consummation, nor was it defective in not doing so. It was the style of the building that warranted the name"

He goes on to discuss the Palace of Fyvie, the Palace of Fetteresso or *Fetteressaeum palatium* and observes that Fife was "another district specially noted for the number of its palaces. A later addition there was the house at Culross still bearing the name of Palace, though properly that described it more aptly at an earlier stage".

There is the palace block at Dunnottar, a self-contained unit with kitchen, cellars, dining room and private apartments. In his paper on Drumminor Castle, *Proceedings of Society of Antiquaries of Scotland,* vol. 99, 154 (1966-7), H. Gordon Slade describes the surviving block as a "mid-fifteenth century palace house" to distinguish it from the L-plan tower house which orginally stood adjacent. The same writer discusses the use of the terms "tower-house" and "palace-house" under Midmar Castle in *Proceedings of Society of Antiquaries of Scotland,* vol.113, 599, (1983) and comments on this other area of confusion where the " practice is so widespread and so ingrained in architectural writing that it is difficult to challenge it with any very lively hope of success".

Whilst disagreeing with Professor Charles Mckean's rejection of the term "fortified house", I accept his use of the term "palace" regarding Boyne in his *Banff & Buchan: An Illustrated Architectural Guide*, 39 (1990), although by a curious irony perhaps his other favourite word *chateau* would be equally apposite to describe this notably French-inspired house. So why is Tolquhoun never described as a palace despite being composed of a main block, three surrounding ranges, twin-towered entrance and two flanking towers, a palace if ever was one?

Amongst all the vagaries of taste and fashion it should be known and understood by all connected with our native architecture that, regardless of the building being a dwelling of king, bishop, lord, laird or merchant, the Scots, being a logical race, always understood that the palatial nomenclature, like the more homely "Place", was derived from the great hall and is not in any way another misnomer.

(I.B.D. Bryce, 1998, published in Architectural Heritage Society of Scotland Magazine, no. 8, 9, (Summer 1999).

15

THE LEYS ESTATE AT 2000

James C. A. Burnett of Leys

The following account is of the Leys Estate as it exists in 2000 with reference to some of the changes that it has suffered or enjoyed during the last century. Because of the lack of available information about activities and events during the earlier part of the 1900s, most comment relates to the later part of the period.

I have also included a few personal recollections of the time after I came to live at Crathes in 1965, or earlier, when we used to spend our holidays here. Sadly, there is an absence of records largely resulting from the fire in 1966 when much of the castle was destroyed. However, I do have some previously unrecorded accounts that have been handed down by members of the family who are no longer with us.

*****

The impact of the political and economic affairs of the twentieth century has resulted in a marked increase in estate activity and change during the past 50 years. Two world wars, capricious and potentially punitive taxation policies, public attitudes towards the ownership of land and the development of the oil industry have been foremost in influencing changes at Crathes. Included in these was the gift to the nation of the castle and gardens together with an onerous endowment which included a substantial part of the estate. This must have been the most significant event in our Burnett history since the day of the original grant of land from King Robert the Bruce in 1323.

It was in 1952 that my grandfather, Sir James Burnett of Leys, the 13th baronet and 25th laird, decided to transfer the ownership of the castle and gardens to the National Trust for Scotland. He had suffered the loss of both of his sons and, with no heir to the baronetcy and being without the means to maintain the castle and the gardens, this appeared to be the only suitable course of action available to him. After 1952, my family continued to reside within the castle at the pleasure of the National Trust until the Queen Anne and Victorian wings were severely damaged by fire in 1966. Although the Trust and I agreed plans to reconstruct the affected parts of the castle to accommodate our family, it was eventually decided that we should build a new home, to be called the House of Crathes, on a nine acre site of Trust land nearby. Here we could enjoy privacy and permanent security of tenure. The site is convenient for both the Trust and ourselves and included in the lease is the house that was formerly known as The Butler's Cottage and now as Woodbine Cottage. A family friend, Michael Thompson, and Schomberg Scott representing the National Trust, designed the new House of Crathes. A prominent local building company, Alexander Hall, completed it in 1973.

Fig. 15.1 House of Crathes. 1999 (Bailey)

We undertook the building of the House of Crathes with the National Trust contributing the surplus of the insurance payment that resulted from the fire. However, during the planning of the house, a problem emerged when it was discovered that my grandfather had excluded the contents of the Castle when he transferred the ownership to the Trust twenty years earlier. On the assumption that this was an oversight either on his part or on that of the Trust, I agreed to transfer to the Trust all of the Castle contents that were relevant and important to earlier family occupation, thereby enhancing the presentation of the property to visitors. Included in that transfer, and now on display in the Long Gallery, is the Register of Barony Court 1621-1709, a record of the enforcement of the authority of the laird of the day.

> "It records mainly pecuniary offences but others include civil and criminal offences such as 'stricking and dinging', 'hurting, wounding and bluid-shedding', 'comitting ane ryatt', 'being ane unlawfu' and infamous man', 'pick-locking ane house', 'steiling of

> fruit', and 'braking dound dykis of parkis and woodis'. Penalties included fines, imprisonment and consignment to the stocks, as well as less conventional punishment such as 'banischment from the lairds landis', 'escetting of hail guidis to the laird' and 'pulling down the hous of the offender'. The Barony Court also recorded and enforced statutes and edicts such as the defence of the lands against the Highlandmen (tenants were to be at an appointed spot bearing the laird's guns within three hours) and going to the service of the camp (1640). Tenant farming was no joke at times. Any more serious crimes were probably dealt with by the Sheriff Court at the Shire Capital, Stonehaven."
> (Gordon Walkden, *About Banchory*,1987)

The new arrangement may be mutually satisfactory for both the Trust and the family, but it has inevitably diminished the association of the family with the Castle and removed the link that usually exists between great houses and accompanying estates to which there is generally a mutually complementary relationship. When they are separated, and especially when one or the other loses a long-standing family association, an important element of integrity disappears regardless of the consequent benefits.

Such changes of land ownership were not restricted to Crathes alone. Earlier in Deeside than even the Gordons, the Burnetts are probably the only family that has continued to reside on their original Deeside estates since the fourteenth century. Neighbouring lands were gifted to Irwin of Drum at about the same time as those of Leys were bestowed upon Alexander de Burnard.

> "The hereditary office of Kings Forester had been given to William de Irwin in February 1323 for loyal service to King Robert the Bruce. It was discovered that the office of forester had earlier been given to Alexander de Burnard and, by way of compensation for this oversight, he was given a new charter when he received the lands of Killenachclerach and Easter and Wester Cardneys in March 1323."
> (FentonWyness, *Royal Valley*)

Ownership of most of the local estates has changed during the twentieth century. The Drum estate was sold in 1976 following the death of Henry Quentin Forbes Irvine, the 24th laird, after the National Trust for Scotland had assumed ownership of the Castle and policies in 1975 following an earlier bequest. Curiously, these two neighbouring families had lived alongside each other for over 600 years with neither great friendship nor serious altercation and without association in marriage. Perhaps a lesson could be learnt from such a record.

The nearby estates of Banchory Lodge, Blackhall, Inchmarlo, Sluie, Craigmyle, Glassel and Kerloch, have either been sold in their entirety or broken up. So also have Durris, renowned for its great contribution to the social life of Deeside before the war, and Raemoir, which was purchased by the Pearson family who have acquired many local estates to supplement their principal seat at Dunecht. In 1997, much of the neighbouring estate of Park was sold and that of The Knappach in 1998. The Douglases have left their lands of Tilquhillie with its 1576 castle, where they had lived since 1479, albeit with a short break in the nineteenth century. As with the Burnetts, the Douglas family of Tilquhillie had produced a Bishop of Salisbury.

The owners of these properties were not alone in such disposition. My grandfather sold the Trustach lands that became the estates of Woodend (1946) and Cairnton (1947), both renowned for their salmon fishing, and part of the Hill of Fare (1950). He also feued to the Forestry Commission substantial areas of land close to Banchory (1952).

Cairnton became well known for its fishing largely due to the occupancy and input of Arthur Wood of Glassel who fished at Cairnton for many years from 1913, leasing the property from 1919 until 1934 and who made great contributions to the knowledge of salmon fishing. He demolished the existing house and the replacement was completed on the opening day of the 1920 fishing season. An expert fisherman himself, there is a note from him in the estate records stating that, in 1915, he caught 265 salmon at Cairnton to his own (single-handed) rod during the season including 121 caught during the last 13 days.

Fig. 15.2 Old Cairnton House – now demolished (photograph from Crathes Archives)

The endowment that accompanied the gift to the National Trust included the policies surrounding the castle and extending to 582 acres, farms at Brathens to the north-west of Banchory and all the estate feu superiorities in order to provide an income to assist in the maintenance of the castle and the gardens. The Trust was given an option to accept the farms of Collonach and Rashenlochy in the parish of Drumoak, but the financial windfall resulting from the otherwise disastrous gale of 1953, when most of the estate woodland suffered severe windthrow, allowed the Trust to forego this entitlement.

As a consequence of Sir James's death, Nethermills Farm at Crathes (1957) and the earlier mentioned farms in the parish of Drumoak were sold to finance death duties, as were the fishing beats of Lower Crathes (1955) and Kineskie (1953) beside the Banchory golf course. The farms of Tillybrake (1962) and New Banchory (1959) on the eastern edge of Banchory were later disponed with the proceeds totalling £5,400. It was not foreseen at the time, but this land was shortly to provide for the principal expansion of Banchory. In 1967, it was decided to sell the uppermost part of the remaining fishings, the Station Pool, which now lay alongside the extended town.

In a more remote form, the original Leys estates had been further reduced by the sale of the Burnett Ramsay-owned Banchory Lodge estate which included a substantial part of Banchory although primarily located to the south of the River Dee.

> "That the northern county boundary of Kincardineshire follows the River Dee, except where it includes a large part of the Lands of Leys, often arouses curiosity. Sir Thomas Burnett of Leys, the 1st baronet and 13th laird, inherited the Barony of Muchalls in Kincardineshire and obtained, by Act of Parliament in 1646, the transfer of the Barony of Leys to be in that county."

The monument on Scolty was erected in 1839 as a memorial to General Sir William Burnett of Banchory Lodge, son of the 7th baronet of Leys, and 'a man of culture and letters with a wide knowledge of literature, farming and forestry'. The estate had been left to his nephew William Burnett Ramsay and passed down until sold by a descendant, Thomas Bentinck, in 1949. At the time of the sale the land amounted to 1911 acres. Prior to the construction of the bridge over the Dee at Banchory, the river was crossed by ferry at the Cobleheugh Inn, which is now the site of the Banchory Lodge Hotel and which was part of that estate. In preparation for her retirement, my mother Rohays purchased Castleairey, a small house overlooking the High Street in Banchory, one of the oldest houses in the town and one of the properties included in the Banchory Lodge estate sale. The particulars of the sale in 1949 described it as "well known to the Banchory residents as originally built for the local doctor and much mystery has been attached to the legend of the Green Lady who is reputed to still haunt the house". I moved to Castleairey from the castle following the fire of 1966 and, with my wife Fiona, continued to live there until the completion of the House of Crathes in 1972. Castleairey is now largely hidden from public view by development. We never encountered the ghost during our stay there.

Following the death of my grandfather in 1953, the estate rested in the ownership of Trustees until I inherited it in 1966 at the age of 25. I changed my surname by deed poll from that of my father, Henry Cecil, to Burnett of Leys to accord with my grandfather's wish that the name of Burnett would continue, as it had since the fourteenth century, with whoever lived at Crathes. I am sometimes asked why he wished this for me and not for my elder brother. My explanation is that there was the possibility that my elder brother might have inherited my paternal uncle's peerage and would have been required to maintain the surname of Cecil as the family name of the Barons Amherst of Hackney. It so happened that there have been sufficient male successors to that barony for such a possibility now to be remote. There may be a few to whom the existence here of the illustrious name of Cecil may be of interest. It is because the barony, with its former name of Tyssen-Amherst, devolved upon the marriage of my great-grandmother, the eldest daughter of the 1st baron, to Lord William Cecil, the third son of the 3rd Marquis of Exeter.

There then followed something of a reversal of the above trend of the diminution of the size of the estate. I decided that I wished to farm on my own account and took occupancy of the farm of Uppermills in 1965. At that time, the possibility of other farms becoming available seemed somewhat remote. With the help of the proceeds from the sale of the Station Pool and some of the insurance monies from those contents of the castle which were lost in the fire, I purchased the farms of Drumyocher and Old Cake in the parish of Arbuthnott and that of Broomfield in the parish of Drumoak and formerly part of the Drum Estate. It was not long before we sold them to finance a rationalisation of an expanding but arguably unsuccessful agricultural enterprise. This included the acquisition of several of the farms of the former Craigmyle Estate near Torphins some of which are recorded as having previously been in the ownership of my family as early as 1605 and later in 1813. They now comprise a unit of over 950 acres. In 1997, some small areas of land at Kilduthie at the southern edge of the Hill of Fare which had been sold in 1952 by my grandfather to the Forestry Commission, were repurchased as commercial woodland.

In 1983, through an increasingly complex estate ownership structure, the major part of the neighbouring Inchmarlo estate was acquired. Inchmarlo had been owned by Alexander Bowhill, an eminent Edinburgh stockbroker who, as trustee for the Leys estate between 1953 and 1966, was largely responsible for its rescue from its serious financial position on my grandfather's death. The Inchmarlo estate was purchased with the minority interest remaining in the ownership of Alexander Bowhill's grandsons. Part of the estate was then sold and the remainder is today within the estate control and is managed as described later.

At 2000, ownership of the Leys estate is spread between myself, my wife Fiona, our eldest son Alexander and two family trusts, one of which, the Banchory Trust, was established in 1987 to preserve a major portion of the estate. The land at Torphins passed to the other, the Fordie Trust, in 1997. The remaining part of the Inchmarlo Estate is owned by the family-controlled Inchmarlo Land Co. Ltd. The boundaries of the Lands of Leys in both 1900 and 2000, together with some detail of ownership, are depicted on the map in the Appendix to this chapter. The trustees for the properties that are held in trust in 2000 are members of two neighbouring estate-owning families, Angus Farquharson of Finzean and Angus Pelham Burn, who, with his wife, owned the neighbouring estate of Knappach until 1998.

Until 1972, the estate was managed by a resident factor from an office close to the Castle. The last resident factor, William Russell Birnie, was assisted in his role by his wife as clerkess. Not relevant here but worthy of record is that Mabel Birnie was an accomplished singer and on one occasion in 1947 sang a duet with the later famous Kenneth McKellar in the Banchory East Church. On Mr. Birnie's retirement, the office relocated to St. Nicholas House in Banchory, the former schoolhouse opposite the East Church, and from where the estate management was then undertaken by a part-time agent. An increasing volume of estate interests and activities necessitated the expansion of the business into the adjacent former schoolmaster's house, St Machar. The Banchory office provided facilities which have enabled the creation of several small local businesses. These included the Deeside Piper, a free newspaper for the valley, which I founded with Lord Aboyne, a member of the newspaper-owning Kemsley family and a retired publisher, Stanley Maxton. It was transferred to the ownership of the Angus County Press in 1984 since when it has become a more commercial and professional newspaper covering a large area of the north-east of Scotland.

The estate factor is generally a major contributor to the wellbeing of an estate and in this Crathes has proved to be no exception. The resident factor's role may be more understandable if the reader should peruse the report of the celebration of the jubilee of the factor, Mr. Davidson, in Appendix 1. Whatever else one can obtain from this account, it must be a masterpiece of appreciation and courtesy. Amongst Mr. Davidson's prominent successors was Mr. J. F. C. Dunbar, whose austerity and sense of fair play earned him deserved respect. It is reported that on one occasion, he severely rebuked a prospective farm tenant for calling on him during his evening meal with a request for the relevant tenancy. The consequence of this outburst led to the caller suggesting in no uncertain terms to 'J. F. C.' that he could keep his farm. Despite any offence which may have been caused at the time, the caller was later offered the tenancy which he accepted.

In 1984, due to the greater responsibilities attached to land ownership, the management of the estate was entrusted to Strutt and Parker, a national firm of land managers and estate agents. This firm now leases most of the office building which itself was substantially increased in 1993 in order to accommodate its rapidly growing business. This development reflects the increasing necessity of all but the largest estates to remodel their management and activities in accordance with economies of scale, the wide range of obligatory compliance and the many changes affecting land ownership and occupancy.

AGRICULTURE

The soil having been formed chiefly by the decomposition of granite rocks, and no loamy deposits having been made by the streams of the district is almost everywhere light, and not naturally fertile. In most places it is not sufficiently retentive of moisture, but in some a ferruginous indurated subsoil prevents both the deflux of water, and the roots of plants and trees from finding sufficient nourishment and depth. In some of the low grounds a spongy moss, mixed with gravel, and bearing a coarse grassy, presents a surface of little value, and difficult to improve, while an inadequate drainage renders others swampy for a great part of the year, or subjects them to frequent injuries from floods. No plants, however, decidedly indicative of a very poor or very inferior soil are observed to prevail.

(Rev. William Anderson, *Statistical Account of Banchory-Ternan. The New Statistical Account,* October 1842)

At 2000, the Crathes estate, excluding Fordie and Inchmarlo, consists of 19 agricultural holdings. Records show that the same land in 1900 consisted of 165 farms and crofts. Comparisons can be drawn from the number and size of properties with land attached to them although both sets of figures exclude moorland on the Hill of Fare and land at Trustach (Woodend and Cairnton), all of which have since been sold.

	1900	2000
Less than 1 acre	30	0
1-9 acres	49	1
10-49 acres	43	2
49-100 acres	19	3
over 100 acres	24	13

The total areas of the estate in 1900 were:

Arable	3926
Roads, etc.	156
Moss	335
Planting	1938
Pasture	4616
Total	10973 acres

Although there has been no accurate measurement of the estate from the current Ordnance Survey maps, the productive areas, excluding lad at Fordie and Inchmarlo, at 2000 amount to the following:

Farmland	1635.46 ha	4039.5 acres
Forestry	625.36 ha	1544.0 acres

During the last century, the nature of farms has changed as a result of more efficient husbandry and changing economic conditions. These advances led to the modernisation or conversion of many of the estate farm buildings as was frequently the case with farms in the north east of Scotland. The principal improvement to the average farm during this time was the construction of a roof over the midden, which was most commonly situated between the wings of the steading, to form a substantial cattle court. Other than such building alterations and the replacement of stackyards with dutch barns, the landscape would have differed little from 1900. Most of the land which it was possible to drain had been so improved in the nineteenth century, although there is nothing to suggest that my forebears were amongst the first of the 'improvers'. With government encouragement, a number of the stone dykes that form field boundaries were removed in the 1960s to create larger and more efficient fields. This policy has since been rescinded.

Fig. 15.3 WoodendBarnTheatre - a typical improved steading. 2000 (Bailey)

> The state of agriculture is in general much the same as it has been in the memory of man, more grain of the common kind, oats and bere, is raised than is consumed in the parish, but the export of grain is not great. It is believed that there is much less now raised than was 50 or 60 years ago, as the stocking rate of farms is greatly diminished, particularly the number of oxen employed in tillage. Potatoes, of which every occupier of land raises some, would seem to be the only real improvement. Of turnips, sown grass or enclosed fields, the specimens hitherto exhibited are poor indeed. Of near 90 farmers of one kind or other, out of whom pay £50 pounds sterling and upwards, most of them less than £20, and many of whom less than £10 - there are not above six or seven who can be said to have attempted improvement. Mr. Baxter of Glassel, Sir Robert Burnett, and Mr. Russell have done and are doing much in this respect, but examples set by proprietors, of enclosing and dressing fields, appear not to be minded by ordinary farmers, who from ability and the short duration of their leases, are not disposed, nor can be expected, to imitiate. If ever this part of the country is improved, it must be by the heritors themselves, or by their pitching on farmers of enterprise and means, and affording such the requisite encouragement. In this way much might be accomplished at a small expense to the landholders, if accompanied with leases of at least two nineteen years, the conversion of mill multers, and other services, enforcing winter herding, and fixing proper plans for enclosing and cropping. (Statistical account of the parish of Banchory-Ternan, or Tarnan, June 1791)

There were tenants on the estate whose prominence in the farming community did not go unnoticed. John Cooper was the occupier of Candiglirach until he replaced his brother's tenancy at the Ley. He was a progressive farmer and at Candiglirach there were wintered in 1907 over 120 two-year-old cattle, a remarkable number for the day. Not necessarily the tidiest of farmers, he was a man of great energy and each year 100 loads of peat were gathered from the Red Moss to drive the steam engine which powered the mill at the farm. The granite chimney required for this engine remains today and is understood to be the only one of its type in the north-east which is circular. Cooper was a great employer and was heard to remark that he would give his men his pet peacock to pluck on the day when he could no longer give them a job. The peacock survived.

Recorded is an occasion in the Banchory Mart when Cooper, a man of impressive stature, met another prominent tenant of similar corpulence and between whom there was little friendship, John Adam of the Bush Farm. Cooper had a very noticeable squint and was attempting to pull open the mart door whilst Adam was trying to enter the building by pulling the same door in the opposite direction. When the door was eventually opened and the two adversaries collided, Cooper accosted Adam. "Why dinna ye look far yer gan?" to which Adam responded "Why dinna ye ging far yer lookin? ".

The Red Moss itself is an area of interest. Much peat was cut by the tenants and I am assured that the one week in which this chore was annually carried out was the hardest week's work of the year. The peat was not of the highest quality, and described as foggy instead of black and liable to leave much ash. The estate employed a moss grieve the last of whose daughter, Agnes Laing, died in the 1970s while living in the now derelict croft beside the moss where her father was employed. The last load of peat was probably taken by David Humble, until recently the tenant of the Ley Farm, for his neighbour Fred Duncan of Woodend Farm in 1945.

In the 1930s every farm would have had a mill most of which were driven by two or four horses. There were several water driven mill wheels including those at Kilduthie, Hattonburn, and Greendams. Of note, there was a concrete silage tower at Harestone. The silage was tramped by a horse which, when the tower was full and objective accomplished, was shot and thrown from the top.

The wars of the last century did not leave the estate unaffected. Before the Great War, two good friends John Humble of Dowalty and George Patterson of the Hirn were sitting on a dyke at the crossroads at the top of Baldarroch Brae (known at that time as The Toll), with little to do to pass the time of day. They decided that they should occupy their time more usefully and that they would join the army. They enrolled in The Terriers very shortly before war was declared in 1914. Both went to serve in France but only Patterson returned.

Although there was a home farm close to the castle and the area recorded in 1900 was 589 acres of which 183 were arable and 389 woodland, I have no records of any in-hand farming practice and the arable area has long formed part of Harestone Farm, for much of the past century farmed by the factor. Notwithstanding, all farms were tenanted until 1965 when Uppermills of Crathes was taken in hand, thereby initiating a substantial farming enterprise. A government scheme in the 1960s encouraged farm amalgamation by means of grants to assist in the works necessary to create larger and more efficient units. It also offered compensation payments to outgoing occupiers and it appeared mutually beneficial for both the landlord and many older tenants of smaller farms to participate in this scheme. For seemingly good reason at the time, these were taken in-hand under a family partnership. These farms included Uppermills, Bohill, Craigton, Todholes, Glashmore, Quiddiesmill, Greendams, Myrebird, Dowalty, Coy, Old Mill of Hirn, Drumfrennie, Wickerinn, Druggam and Milton, and later North Hirn, South Hirn and Kilduthie. (see folded MAP in appendix to this chapter)

The business expanded as described above and at its peak occupied about 2,500 acres with a beef herd of over 450 cows. The business included the tenancies of Catterloch and Cairniewhin on the neighbouring Raemoir estate and was supplemented by 350 acres at Drumyocher at Fordoun in The Mearns in the late 1960s which was replaced eventually by 956 acres at Fordie (1972-1997).

All units were operated as mixed stock and arable holdings. After 1983, when the in-hand acreage was reduced, the farming enterprise consisted of two farm's. Fordie was predominately a stock farm with a maximum herd of over 300 beef breeding cows. On the other, South Hirn, on 405 acres (164 hectares), we principally produce barley for malting and seed potatoes for Montrose Potatoes Ltd., a marketing group of which estate membership has existed since its formation in 1971 and which is now based at a large store near Fettercairn. Both Fordie and South Hirn farms had at some time included substantial organic enterprises. These were initiated in anticipation of government support but terminated when this failed to materialise and without which they could not be sustained.

Fordie was itself tenanted in 1997 and the South Hirn group remains the sole in-hand unit in 2000. However, in retrospect, although the decision to take in hand so much land proved to be unwise, the associated improvements that were carried out as a result were to be of considerable benefit when they were later tenanted.

Employment in the farm business ranged from 17 full time staff at the peak of its activities to a single man, Ken Smith, with the current low input operation at South Hirn. Since 1968, the farms have enjoyed the services of a well-equipped machine shop at Upper Mills although the operation of this was transferred in 1986 to the estate building company, Banchory Contractors Ltd. (see this Chapter).

There were good reasons for the reversal in the policy of farming much of the estate land myself. Costs had risen disproportionately to the value of produce and increasing compliance created its own problems including some which were never envisaged. On one occasion some 60 of our newly weaned calves escaped from Uppermills. Some of them were eventually caught the following day in fields on Durris after stampeding over the fields of Baldarroch and then through the river. Regardless, such a substantial involvement in farming may be viewed as an error of judgment that might have been avoided if Robertson's 1842 agricultural survey had been considered.

HOUSES

There's Crathes with its stately towers,
Inchmarlo with its leafy bowers,
Raemoir, Tilquhillie, Hattonburn,
Baldarroch and the Mill o' Hirn,
Twixt Scolty and the Hill of Fare.

In 2000, the Estate includes 65 non-agricultural dwellings. However, the number of houses on the estate has decreased since 1900 but the greatest rate of decrease was between 1968 and 1988 (Appendix III). The principal reason for these sales was to finance the agricultural enterprise, the purchase of other property, taxation resulting from the formation of the Trusts which help secure the preservation of the estate in the face of heavy taxation, also to offset some unsuccessful business enterprises and improvements to the property. Political uncertainty and the possibly limited life of the currently buoyant local economy supported the decisions to sell certain houses instead of improving them for letting. Moreover, the continuing exodus from the land resulted in many of them becoming obsolete for the purposes for which they were originally built. There is also always an increasing expectancy as to the standards of let houses and it was usually considered that investment in this type of property was not regarded as a priority for limited funds. This has led to a policy of giving consideration to complete replacement of substandard houses to accord with modern specifications. The Neuk and the Neuk Farmhouse are the first examples of this policy.

In contrast to the position a several decades ago, fewer houses are lived in by the locally employed. Although we endeavour to accommodate those who do work in the area and give appropriate priority to those who have a connection with the estate, a large number of tenants commute to places of work outwith the immediate vicinity. Their employment is affected by fluctuations within the oil industry and consequently the turnover is relatively great.

When I returned to live at Crathes in 1965, there were about 50 houses without internal bathrooms. This had been rectified by the mid-seventies, but the architectural merit of many of these improvements prompted the introduction of Estate Design Guidelines and eventually a more comprehensive Estate Charter. The objective of the guidelines was to encourage ourselves and purchasers of estate property to maintain buildings with an appropriately traditional appearance. It is flattering that these guidelines were adopted a few years later by the local authority in seeking similar objectives for other areas within the county and were considered worthy of preservation. The Charter was commissioned in 1997 to set down the parameters whereby the estate should be managed by following generations. The subjects initially covered in the Charter are those of Landscape, Access, Woodland, Conservation and Development.

The estate has several residences of significance. These include Hattonburn, a former inn and the only three-storey house on the estate. It was modernised as a home for my mother Rohays (Lady Boyd-Rochfort), after she was widowed in 1983.

Fig.15.4 Hattonburn. 1999 (Bailey)

Another major reconstruction was the earlier mentioned Woodbine Cottage close to the House of Crathes.

Fig 15.5 Woodbine Cottage, Crathes. 1999 (Bailey)

Fig. 15.6 Neuk Smiddy (from a Burnett family photograph)

Fig. 15.7 Dower House - formerly the Neuk Smiddy (Bailey)

The Dower House, initially known as Leys Cottage, was converted by my grandmother's sister, Elizabeth Carr, from the former Neuk Smiddy(Fig.15.6) in the 1960's.

Fig.15.8 Thistleycrook. 1999 (Bailey)

Other than the House of Crathes, the most important house on the estate is now Thistleycrook on the former Craigmyle estate which is now know by us as Fordie after its principal farm.

It was considered that the size of the property warranted a significant house and the magnificence of the site prompted the conversion of the Thistleycrook steading in 1997 to a house which Fiona and I regard as a future home for our younger son, Victor. The architect for the work was Ben Tindall of Edinburgh. Of interest in the house are two fireplaces which were acquired from Muchalls Castle in 1996. The building of this sixteenth century castle near Stonehaven had been attributed to Alexander Burnett, the 12th laird, who completed the construction of castle at Crathes and had also been the owner of much of the land at Craigmyle. The fireplaces had been installed at Muchalls after being removed from Craigmyle House during its partial demolition earlier in the 20th century.

The most significant farmhouse on the estate is at Harestone Farm. For many years it had been the home of the resident factor and was seriously damaged by fire in 1984. This accident may have been more than a coincidence since there have been several fires during recent years on that sector of the estate albeit all with clear explanations as to the causes. In addition to those at Harestone and the castle, fires have ruined or seriously damaged Myrebird Croft House, Coy Croft and Baldarroch Cottage. This is the cottar house of the farm of the same name and which is known for its legendary 'De'il' which caused great alarm in 1838 as described in William Walker's humorous verse.

> Afore the fire folk couldna' sit for fear,
> For peats and clods cam bunging ben the flear;
> The parson cam' and gained the house wi' prayer,
> But still the clods were thuddin' here and there.
> The spoons an' dishes, knives and forks,
> They frisk'd aboot as light as corks:
> An' cups an' ladles joined the dancin',
> An' thro' the house they a' gaed prancin'.

The source of the trouble was seemingly identified, if somewhat arbitrarily, as a young servant girl who was presumably dismissed from her employment.

Since 1970 there has been a tendency property use to diversify from the traditional industries of agriculture and forestry. Several houses and farm steadings that had become redundant, or surplus to requirement as a result of the changing pattern of agriculture, were converted for residential use and sold. Others such as the Mill of Hirn (now a recording Studio), Milton of Crathes (Visitor and Craft

Centre) and Woodend (Community Arts Centre), were leased for more varied use. James Scott Skinner, one of Scotland's famed fiddlers, was born in Banchory and was brother- in -law to the tenant of the Mill of Hirn in 1843. He was inspired by the Mill to write one of his best known pieces, the strathspey 'The Miller of Hirn.' The Mill was tenanted until 1977 after which time it was operated by Norman Duncan before being converted to its present use.

Lad cam' ye doun by Feugh's green howe,
The Feugh that rins through Crathes, O?
Heard ye a fiddler dirl a bow,
Wi something like a pathos, O?
Weel, gin he meet wi' your applause,
I brawly can discern, O,
The dusty-robed fiddler was
"The Miller o' the Hirn," O.

Hoch, hey, the Hirn, O!
The water clatter Hirn, O,
There's few can play a reel wi' him,
"The Miller of the Hirn", O.

A jolly, sonsie, pawky chiel!
Wi' sense, and lots of siller, O,
As e'er turned on a water wheel,
Is Hirn's mealy Miller, O.

Wi' fusslin' lips an' smirkin' e'e,
He ne'er was kent to girn, O,
Oor real auld Deeside school is he,
"The Miller o' the Hirn", O.

Hoch, hey, the Hirn, O!
The happy, sappy Hirn, O,
There's few can fiddle a fling wi' him,
"The Miller of the Hirn", O.

The Miller's mankind's best o' frien's.
Be't nobles, beaux, or bumpkins, O,
In barley meal, ait, pease and beans,
An flour, for pies an pumkins, O,
He never slacks, but fills the pock,
An' blythesome bears the birn, O,
An nane mair blythe than that auld cock,
"The Miller of the Hirn," O.

Hoch, hey, the Hirn, O!
The "heesie-weesie" Hirn, O,
We'll "Drone" nae mair sin' we hae got
"The Miller o' the Hirn," O.

(Extract from the works of "La Teste".)

Fig. 15.9 The Mill of Hirn. 2000 (Bailey)

Fig. 15.10(a) Milton of Crathes. 2000 (Bailey)

Fig. 15.10(b) Milton of Crathes. 2000 (Bailey)

Fig.15.10(c) Milton of Crathes. 2000 (Bailey)

Several farms, some with redefined boundaries, have been rented specifically for equestrian activities with an added objective of eventually establishing a network of riding routes over the estate in accord with a policy of accepting the increasing demand for access to the countryside. Whilst appreciating the necessity to protect the interests of the occupiers of land in respect of agriculture, forestry and sporting pursuits, we are continually seeking to accommodate such requirements.

Acquisition of two shops in Dee Street in Banchory in the 1960s added to the variety of estate property interests. These were purchased together with an antiques business but were later leased to a sporting agency, *MacSport*, the creation of which involved the estate and in which we retained an interest. The current occupancies for the buildings include the local headquarters of the Scottish Liberal Party for its representatives at the United Kingdom and Scottish Parliaments and a take-away food business.

There had been industry on the estate at the end of the nineteenth century in the form of the granite quarries at Craigton. These have long been redundant although the quarrymen's cottages nearby provide heavily demanded one- and two-bedroom accommodation. The three quarries are impressive although the two smaller ones were recently sold as part of an agreement to repurchase some areas of woodland at Kilduthie which earlier had been sold to the Forestry Commission. The area is of added attraction because of the nearby Burn of Corrichie on the south side of the Hill of Fare (or Fair) where the army of Mary Queen of Scots soundly defeated the Gordons under the Earl of Huntly in the fierce battle of the 28th of October 1562.

Murn ye heighlands, and murn ye leighlands
I trow ye hae meikle need;
For thi bonny burn o' Corrichie
Has run this day wi' bleid.

(Forbes, The Battle of Corrichie, *Ruddiman's Weekly Magazine*,1772)

The quarries produced an attractive pink granite which was used for many local buildings including the West Church in Banchory. If there is any near equivalent industry to the activity of quarrying, it may be the landfill tip that is being operated by the estate building firm, Banchory Contractors, near the Hirn. The increasing necessity for compliance in the management of all waste material has led to the development of this area for both disposal and recycling.

Fig. 15.11 (above) Craigton Quarries. 2000 (Bailey)

Fig.15.12 (below) Craigton Cottages. 2000 (Bailey)

Quiddiesmill was a woollen mill and would have probably employed about a dozen workers. The remains of the settlement, where many of them would have lived at a little distance to the north-east of Quiddiesmill, are still visible. Quiddiesmill Steading was sold in 1981 to some American kinsmen who converted it into a house.

At 2000, members of the family own property outwith the Leys estate. Houses in Moore Street and Clareville Street in Central London are owned by my wife, Fiona. Alexander, our eldest son, has a house in Furness Road in Fulham. Our daughter Eliza has a flat in Munster Road in Fulham and is amongst the beneficiaries of the Donside estate of Ardhuncart which had been purchased by my father-in-law, Colonel Harold Phillips, in 1952. For a number of reasons, we have built a house on a farm in southern Spain.

FORESTRY

> *Jock, when ye hae naething else to do, ye may be sticking in a tree; it will be growing, Jock, when ye're sleeping.*
> (Sir Walter Scott, *The Heart of Midlothian.*)

Although forestry is, or is intended to be, for the most part a commercial enterprise, few if any estates shrink from planting trees that will provide no return and which only future generations will enjoy. I would like to think that our estate is no exception in this respect.

In the absence of any clear records of forestry in 1900, the following accounts may give some indication as to the forestry on the estate in the preceding century. Although this account may have failed to address some of the problems that confront afforestation today, timber was clearly a more suitable form of land use than agriculture for much of the estate.

> "The Leys Estate, the property of Sir Robert Burnett, Bart., comprehends in this parish about 9000 acres. Of these, Sir Robert himself has about about 120 acres in his own hand, completely enclosed, and in full cultivation around the mansion. He has also. upwards of 2000 acres in plantation, the greater part of which is full grown beautiful firwood, chiefly in the neighbourhood of the house, and on a detached property about six miles to the west. He is still continuing to plant on different parts of his lands. And when once the hill of Frustach (sic), (six miles up the river) is fully planted, which at the rate of operation is now going on, must be . in a year or two, there will be 2500 English acres on this property in plantation.

But the great mass of the property is still in the ancient style of farming, and it is probable will long continue so. For wherever land is to require, as much of it does here, from thirty to forty pounds sterling an acre, to give it a semblance suitable to modern husbandry, I should think that the best way to manage it would be to make much of what is already in tillage, and to plant the rest with wood. Indeed forest timber thrives here admirably well. It requires little else to produce a plantation of firs, but to enclose the land and to keep out cattle. The young trees spring from the seed blown from the adjoining woods, or from that which is carried by the crows. Even the holly trees seem indigenous to the soil, and would if permitted, soon fill the ground. (Source: Robertson, G. *Agricultural Survey of Kincardineshire*, 1810)

"The existing plantations are very extensive, being equal to more than five-sixths of the arable, and to more than one-fourth of the whole surface. They consist chiefly of pine and larch, with patches of birch, and belts of oak, beech, ash and some ornamental trees. The greater part was planted during the last seventy years, and only about one third of the whole is nearly ready for the market. The soil, especially on the heights near the river, is generally well adapted for oak and other hardwoods. Larch is found, however, to give way after twenty or thirty years on certain dry and thin soils, and to become diseased in the heart. Pines grow most profitably in the hollows and towards the base of the hills, while, at some intermediate places, birch is found readily to thrive. More attention is now given than formerly to adapt the trees to the locality in which thev are planted, and, owing to the decreasing value of fir timber, and the quality in this district about to be brought into the market at once, the proportion of hard-wood is greatly on the increase. More than 290,000 larches and 66,000 oaks have been planted on the estate of Leys alone, within the last three years".
(Source: Anderson, Rev. William, *Statistical Account of Banchory-Ternan. The New Statistical Account*, (October 1842))

Returns to the Board of Agriculture in 1916 recorded that the estate had 2,468 acres of Scots pine, 12 acres of European larch and 69 acres of Norway spruce, plus 380 acres of mixed conifers and hardwoods over the whole Leys estate. No doubt there is much nineteenth century estate-grown timber still in use on the estate in one form or another. One example, which is less mundane than some, is a display cabinet created from a distressed wardrobe and currently in use in the Milton Gallery. Its origin is recorded within the piece of furniture and also in the notes of an anonymous lady member of the family.

"A large beech tree growing near the bottom of the front lawn between the lime avenues was blown down in 1848. A wardrobe in the house has in it the following inscription:-
Made for Miss Burnett out of a big beech tree at Crathes Castle planted in 1705 blown over in a hurricane in 1848.
Dimensions of the tree:- girth at base 22 feet: girth 13 feet from the ground 20 feet: whole height from ground 82 feet: spread of branches 100 feet: diameter of ten arms each 5 feet circumference. Made by James Allen & Co. Aberdeen 1850."

Several lime trees were felled in 1996 alongside the North Deeside Road near the Milton. Some of these were converted into panelling for the principal room at Thistleycrook, but at the time of writing, it remains awaiting installation.

At 2000, the area of the estate under recognised forestry is 590 hectares at Crathes and 35 hectares at Fordie. The most intensive planting was between 1954 and 1964 as a consequence of government incentives to enable the country to achieve greater self-sufficiency in timber following two wars, and the great gale on the last day of January 1953. No single event can have had such an impact on the estate landscape and it had a significant effect on my ailing grandfather. The estate forests were devastated with 750 acres of blown timber, an enormous area in comparison with nearby estates of Castle Fraser (200 acres), Learney (250 acres) and Dunecht (500 acres). During the following period, when trustees owned the estate, planting was considered the most prudent form of reinvestment for any surplus estate income. Tree planting was facilitated by the arrival in 1953 of the disease myxomatosis which decimated the rabbit population.

A larger proportion of earlier planting had been of Scots pine, but later the more popular Sitka spruce was introduced as a higher yielding species. Small plantations were usually established for sporting purposes but mostly only with government incentives. The average size of most of the forestry compartments has now become increasingly uneconomical and at the year 2000 the woodland falls into the two categories of more commercially viable plantations and smaller woodlands that are managed with the emphasis on amenity and conservation. The Estate Charter now dictates the inclusion of planting of shrubs and broadleaf trees around all new plantings and this should have a pronounced effect on the landscape towards the end of the twenty-first century. A similar policy had clearly been implemented early in the century since maturing beech trees surround. We should have recognised the merits of such a policy. Forestry management over the last few decades has been unplanned and lacking in policy and efficiency. This is partly as a result of the planting of a large number of small areas of land with the consequent disincentive to maintain them. With government encouragement and assistance, we established a number of solely coniferous shelter-belts which, after a few years, do little towards the enhancement of wildlife.

Until the 1970s the forestry staff consisted of up to five employees. This was reduced before 2000 to a single person, James Forbes, and the more economical policy of the use of contractors or casual employment for most woodland operations has been adopted. Before 1952, when the castle was gifted to the National Trust for Scotland, there had been a sawmill operating at the Home Farm steading. This was then transferred to the Milton and eventually closed down when the forestry department became based at Upper Mills and work reduced to round-post production.

Timber for home use in 1900 is recorded as having a value of £93/12/7d. and wood sold from the sawmill as £1/1/6d. (e.g. "Cutting 1 larch tree into a cart for Mr. Jolie of Neuk 2/- and William More, Hill of Coy, for cutting 250 ft. bords wood 2/6"). Timber sales towards the end of the 1990s are predominately from thinnings. The average output from the woodlands for the three years to 1999 was 4389 tonnes in addition to timber used for home consumption.

Poems are made by fools like me.
But only God can make a tree.
I think that I shall never see
A poem as lovely as a tree.
(Joyce Kilmer, *Trees, 1914*)

FISHING

With the lunch break came my turn for the downstream Boat Pool with which I fell head over heels in love as soon as I laid eyes on it. Instinctively I knew I was gazing at the pool of my dreams. The undulating "broken" water merged into tail glides what were backed by "apron" pools which every now and then were flailed by gale-like winds, but even a hurricane blowing couldn't have destroyed my sixth sense conviction that this was my lucky pool and that this was my lucky day too.
(*Rod & Line*, October 1973)

Although of relatively less importance than in 1900, fishing remains a prominent estate enterprise. In 1900 the fishings included those of Woodend, Cairnton, Kineskie, Lower Crathes and the Station Pool in addition to the home water. The remaining home beat in 2000 consists of a 2.5 mile stretch of the left bank between Milton of Crathes and Banchory and is owned by the trustees of the Banchory Trust.

Other than the home water, the fishing was mainly let for most of the century and not necessarily without problems.

"Dear Sir.
Having received information from several people that Mr. Horn's servant was in the practice of fishing on the water opposite the haugh below the Wood of

> Trustach, I, some time ago, went down for the express purpose of warning him off the said water which, I particularly understand to be that, which, by my own new lease, I have the exclusive right of fishing over.
>
> When I told the servant that he had no right to fish there, he replied that the water he was on was included in his master's tack and that I could not prevent him and that further, I had no business to fish there without his master's leave. This I was persuaded was not the case which I told the man and most firmly believe myself."
>
> "It is impossible for a moment to suppose that I could ever have agreed (as I have done), to pay an excessive grassum and high rent upon any other account than that of my fondness of fishing and it is equally impossible that I should ever have consented to my exclusion from the only good fishing water I possessed in the lease; ...I request the favour of an answer by the Bearer.
>
> Mrs. Burnett joins me in offering the best respects to Lady Burnett and the family at Crathes. I remain, Dear Sir, Your most obedient humble servant. John Burnett."
> (from letter in Crathes archive)

> In the Spring of 1937 there was the biggest spate since 1829. A new hut at Woodend disappeared. The water was inside the hut at the Floating Bank and the sawmiller's family had to be rescued from their house at the Crathes Sawmill. The approach to Crathes bridge, north bank, was washed away.
> (from Estate fishing book in Crathes archive.)

At 2000, the fishing is available for let for most of the season and for a maximum of 4 rods. Prior to 1980, there was a full time ghillie, Bob Watt, who had been in this position for 35 years. Sadly he died the day following a celebration to mark his retirement.

There is little evidence that the river has undergone great change during the last hundred years although there are two places which have been identified during recent years as where "it is worth having a cast". These small pools have been eponymously named after their identifiers, Bob Watt and his successor, the late Roddy Thomson.

There is a cycle of salmon runs resulting in a change in the pattern of catches over the century. Earlier this century there had been a significant autumn run which disappeared only to return during recent years. Salmon catches have declined since the 1960s for a variety of reasons not least being the arrival of disease UDN that depleted the stocks on most European rivers in the 1970's. A reminder of changed times is to compare an exceptional single day's catch of 29 salmon on 4 February 1978 with the season's catch of 61 salmon and grilse in 1999. Frequently the combined catches for the various estate beats exceeded 1000 salmon and in 1931 the total was was 1954 salmon and 147 sea trout (Cairnton 827,

Woodend 609, Kineskie and Lower Crathes 355 and the Home Water 163). At the other extreme, the fishing book states that 1929 was the worse seaon on record on the home beat with a total bag of 30 salmon - and 51 goosanders! Practices of catch and release, a restriction to fly-fishing and the delay of a month at the opening of the season have been implemented in order to assist with the arrest of this decline. In 1999 salmon fry were planted in the Coy Burn for the first time for several decades and plans are under consideration for substantial improvements to allow this tributary of the Dee to be a significant salmon nursery again. In 2000 the estate is providing fishing tuition to satisfy an assumed demand.

GAME

"He yaf nat of that text a pulled hen
That seith that hunters ben nat hooly men"
(Geoffrey Chaucer, *Canterbury Tales.*)

Game conservation and shooting has for long been an important ingredient of the estate way of life. Both quantity of game and the quality of habitat have declined during the latter part of the century. Unsympathetic agricultural practices, coniferous planting with disregard of wildlife habitat, increased predation, disturbance and the reduction in the number of gamekeepers have all contributed to this decline. Poaching has hitherto not seriously affected the management of game and there have been few occasions where the police have been involved. Reaction to poaching today might not be as it was in the days of Sir James Horn Burnett.

> "The kindheartedness of Sir James was proverbial. The moors and policies had for some time been infested with poachers, and although Sir James was by no means hard on these marauders, yet as fires had occurred, he, as a Justice of the Peace, could not consistently allow such offences to go unpunished. One night his keepers succeeded in making a capture and marched their man up to the castle. Sir James was informed of the presence of the culprit, and descended in all the wrath of offended justice to rate the prisoner. He poured forth on the poacher's devoted head a good round scolding, characterising poaching in terms of strongest obloquy, and leaving the offender trembling for his fate at the hands of so stern a judge. In returning to his own room, however, Sir James met the housekeeper, and said, - "There's a man in the Justice-room, been on the hills a' nich, ye might see that he gets a guid warm breakfast, puir chiel."
> ("Saturday in Crathes Woods", in *Aberdeen Journal*, 16 January 1894)

There are no records that any shooting was rented out before the early 1970s. Since then, shooting has been let with an increasing lack of success due to the difficulties in producing the quality and quantity of sport that is now demanded. After 1985 it was decided to lease parts of the estate to syndicates, to concentrate more on rough shooting and, more recently,to reduce permanent employment to that of a part-time gamekeeper, Brian Sim, whose responsibilities include those of the ghillie. This is in effect an amalgamation of these two associated departments and reflects continuing changes in rural employment.

In 1950, the estate employed 4 gamekeepers and two rabbit trappers. 1997 saw the retirement of the last full time gamekeeper on the estate, Frank Dey, who had been employed at Crathes since 1953. Shooting in the castle policies continued at the Trust's pleasure on a reducing scale until its termination was agreed in 1990 due to the increasing public use of the Trust grounds. A sporting lease of land, earlier feued to the Forestry Commission north of Banchory, remains in 2000 but no shooting activity is carried out in this area.

The table below provides some detail of game killed on the estate. The reduction in the partridge numbers is particularly noticeable. Myxomatosis dramatically reduced the rabbit population and temporarily increased that of brown hares. This situation reversed as rabbits became increasingly immune to the disease. In 1952, four gamekeepers and two trappers killed a total of over 32,000 rabbits although there is no accurate comparison for recent years. A few pheasants were at one time reared on the old tennis court in what is now the Guide Field to the south of the walled garden. After the Second World War, there were a number of areas where grouse could be shot but these had nearly all been planted by the mid-1960s. Substantial planting on the southern face of the Hill of Fare moorland and changes to agricultural practice that previously attracted grouse down to neighbouring farm land have contributed to this reduction. In 2000 there are probably no grouse on the estate and the remains of the peat grouse butts on the Red Moss, the only area in which any grouse are now likely to be found, are barely visible. Earlier grouse records would have also included those shot on the area of the Hill of Fare which was then part of the estate.

> "Shooting Hut on the Hill of Fare - This was built about 1897. The stone for it and also for the bridge made at the same time over the Burn of Corrichie were quarried on the spot by men from the Craigton Quarry then a going concern. James Fraser, gamekeeper did the woodwork, Smith of Birkenbaud the thatching and a Banchory mason the building. A bottle enclosing a coin and scribbled names of the workers was built into the East (?) gable.
> Before the building of this hut a rough shelter, the remains of which can be seen South East of the bridge was used by watchers on the Hill."
> (from notes of anon Lady)

The Hill of Fare was an area of the estate which was not without its own problems.

> "The Deeside moorland fire in Aberdeenshire with six estates now in its zone is still causing serious anxiety....Hundreds of people are engaged in fighting the flames and preventing them spreading to valuable woods....Many are wearing masks to protect them against the suffocating smoke....The ten mile fire frontage is about is about fifteen miles from Aberdeen where yesterday the air was redolent with the smell of burning peat....Holiday makers in their hundreds, including women, are giving active assistance to stop the progress of the flames."
> (*The Times*, July 1921)

The last occasion on which a capercailzie was shot on the Crathes estate was in 1970 since when there has been a estate-imposed ban. However, for several years during the 1970s, woodland close to Fordie on the western part of the Hill of Fare was rented from the neighbouring Raemoir estate and where a small number of these magnificent birds were shot. Commercial roe-stalking has been carried out on the estate since 1974. In 1990, in the interests of landscape improvement, wildlife conservation and shooting, several ponds at Crathes and Fordie were created although some of these have yet to be used for that purpose. This may account for the increase in the numbers of wildfowl that have been shot in recent years.

10 year average shooting bags

	1895-1904	1989-1998
Grouse	132	nil
Black game	1	nil
Partridge	237	4
Pheasant	296	562
Woodcock	15	7
Snipe	5	13
Wild fowl	10	101
Pigeon	129	22
Plover	0.5	nil
Brown hare	73	2
Blue hare	78	nil

In the absence of accurate information, the numbers of rabbits killed has not been included. It can be concluded from these comparisons that there has been a serious reduction in the population of grey partridges. Modern agriculture is undoubtedly the largest contributor to this demise. Pheasant comparisons have little meaning since the numbers may reflect the numbers of birds that were reared and of which there is no record. The absence of blue hares results from the sale of the area of the Hill of Fare and golden plover now enjoy protection. The number of pigeon shot are, as in the case of the rabbits, largely unrecorded. To control numbers, many young crows were shot before the 1970's when subsidised bullets were distributed by the government for that purpose. Grey squirrels were first seen in the 1970s and ospreys are now frequent visitors to the riverbank. A large colony of black-headed gulls used to nest on the Loch of Leys, but either because of the plunder of their eggs or the changing level of the loch, they have departed during the last twenty years.

One introduction to the scene of game and vermin control is that of fox-hunting, despite the uncertain future of this pursuit. The Grampian Foxhounds were founded in 1997 by Richard Holman Baird, a descendent of the Earl of Kintore who owned the last pack in the north-east of Scotland. The hounds have visited the estate several times and have made a valuable contribution to fox control.

To accord with the changing responsibilities of the management of land and to assist in fulfilling the objectives of the Estate Charter, it is intended to employ a fulltime ranger in 2000.

RECREATION and ESTATE DEVELOPMENT

Increased means and increased leisure are the two civilizers of man.
(Benjamin Disraeli, "*The Times*", 4 April 1872.)

The most noticeable changes of the twentieth century for the locality have resulted from Aberdeen's development as an important oil capital, the consequent expansion of Banchory and the mobility of employment. These have in themselves resulted in development of the estate in a manner that was not envisaged, although something on a similar scale was embarked upon at the very end of the nineteenth century. In 1886, Sir Robert Burnett developed the Burnett Park and donated it to the community. He also proposed substantial feuing plans for land on the edges of Banchory at Corsee, Arbeadie and Kineskie. The latter two were abandoned for some reason and Kineskie was later gifted by Sir Thomas Burnett in 1905 to become the Banchory Golf Course. It is reported that, when he opened the course with the use of a club which is now displayed in the club-house, his erring tee-shot hit the local minister.

Few can deny that the Burnett Park must be one of the more attractive in the country. Until the inaugural cricket match in June 1889, the Banchory Cricket

> Club had held matches at the Market Hillock to the east of the town. This was less than ideal and has been described as 'a quite remarkable pitch, hemmed in on one side by a series of wooden sheds that made cricket a novelty, and accurate placing between them an essential to success.' Wild hits were well fielded by the huts and sometimes a luckv catch was made off a roof.' It was a distinctly popular pitch with Aberdeen teams perhaps less for its uniqueness as a cricket pitch than for the close proximity of the sheds which furnished shelter and refreshment of the old-time hilarious variety!'
> When the Burnett Park was eventually available, problems did not cease. There were in 1873 as many as four cricket teams in Banchory which at that time had a population of over 3,000. When the Banchory Cricket Club assumed sole occupancy of the new park, protests resulted in a extremely stormy public meeting (there was a lot of 'hooting, groaning and stamping of feet') which ended in a scene of indescribable confusion...
> (Timothy Wilkinson , *A History of the Banchory Cricket Club*, 1987)

Sir Robert, who was an advocate of recreational activity and a pioneer of jogging in this country, was undoubtedly satisfied with the creation of the Burnett Park. He had even more adventurous intentions for the area to include a hotel and a railway siding to serve it but these plans never materialised. The park has been somewhat urbanised during the last few years with improvements to facilitate the use of motor cars and with the provision of a large new pavilion. It has always been of much benefit to the community although it was ploughed up and planted with corn during the war. Similar use for potato growing was also made of the Banchory Golf Course on what was Kineskie Farm. Of relevance, but surprising, is that Sir Robert Burnett, when he created the Burnett Park, made an agreement with the householders and inhabitants of Banchory that they would refrain from walking on the riverside walk alongside what was to become the golf course. Although the wording of the agreement is recorded, the document is conveniently lost. The connection between the two areas also appeared when facilities for croquet, tennis and bowls were established on the east end of Kineskie Farm because the Burnett Park was too remote from the centre of the town! The Burnett Park is now the home of the Banchory Tennis Club.

The estate has been indirectly involved in the expansion of Banchory throughout the nineteenth and twentieth centuries by facilitating development of infrastructure, housing and industry. Notable examples of these have been the turnpike road from Banchory to Aberdeen (1806), the Deeside railway (1853), the construction of the aqueducts to Aberdeen (1864 and 1924) and the Invercannie water works (1923). Of these the railway was probably the most significant both by its introduction and its removal. Of interest are the conditions under which it was constructed in the first place.

> "Judgement was given on Tuesday in the House of Lords in the appeal at the instance of Sir Robert Burnett of Crathes against the decision of the Court of

> Session refusing him declarator against the Great North of Scotland Railway Company, binding them under the terms of a feu charter to stop all passenger trains at Crathes Station, including "the Queen's messenger" and Sunday Post Office trains, as well as the Saturday afternoon excursion trains. Both the Lord Ordinary and the Second Division of the Court of Session had decided against Sir Robert; but yesterday the Lord Chancellor and his colleagues unanimously sustained the appeal, reversed the judgement of the Courts below, and found the railway company liable in costs". (*Aberdeen Weekly Journal*, 28 February 1890)

Today there is a proposal to reopen a section of the former Deeside Line as a visitor attraction. The proposal is that it should be run from Milton to Banchory and, as I write, the first sections of line have been donated and have already been delivered.

> I tell this tale, which is strictly true
> Just by way of convincing you
> How very little, since things were made,
> Things have altered in the building trade

The decision to involve the estate more directly in local development was initiated in 1971. The high cost of operating a small joiner's shop at Candieshill and an increasing estate need for a wider range of building services led to the establishment, in 1973, of the Estate Works Department. It later became the construction company, Banchory Contractors Ltd., and subsequently the Bancon group of companies, with an increasingly diverse range of interests. The group has been responsible for many local developments including housing near the Tor na Coille Hotel, Forestside, Shepherds Court, Highfield, the former Crathes Station and the site of the former slaughterhouse at Tillybrake. The latter was constructed on land purchased from the estate and for which fat cattle from the estate farming enterprise had been the very first customers! The land had been feued to the Aberdeen and Northern Marts Co-operative in 1968 for £6,300 but it required £1.3 million to repurchase it in 1994 after it had been decided to close the slaughter house.

This business permits many estate works to be carried out by what is regarded as an estate enterprise. The ability to do this is possible because of the larger volume of work undertaken by the company outwith the property. Under the stewardship of Frank Garden, it has grown from the antiquated joiner's shop of 1973 to an integrated business employing a full-time staff of over 100. In 2000, the group, under its parent company Bancon Developments, embraces Brown Brothers (Aberdeen), a plumbing and electrical business in Aberdeen, the Banchory House and Garden Centre and the Inchmarlo Land Company. The principal departments of the building company, Banchory Contractors, specialise in the production of timber-framed buildings and property maintenance in addition to more substantial contracts and developments. The Bancon group has also played a significant role in the more recent stages of the development of Inchmarlo House as one of the premier Continuing Care Communities in the country.

However the most important and significant achievement of this enterprise in relation to the estate has been development in Banchory and more especially on the Hill of Banchory. By 2000, plans to build 200 houses have been approved by Aberdeenshire Council and are in the course of construction on that site which had been identified as the area where the community wishes to see expansion of the town. In addition to providing a large number of affordable houses, current plans for the area include a school, a business park, a business centre and a sizeable social and recreational centre to benefit the community. There is also a substantial development in the initial stages of construction at nearby Upper Lochton. If the Hill of Banchory area develops its potential as has been identified in accordance with the wishes of the Local Authority and the Community and, if an involvement in some of the developments on that site is retained, it will become an important new interest for the estate.

It is an agreed policy that both the group and the estate become increasingly integrated with the community and fulfil expected responsibilities. Where they are involved in local developments or in the provision of facilities that are of public benefit, it seems appropriate that they display their shared signature which incorporates the principal features of the Burnett Coat of Arms being a horn and holly leaves.

Fig. 15.13 Bancon company logo.

Between 1960 and the end of the century, an involvement has been created in several businesses. Two small shopping enterprises in Aberdeen were short lived but the two shops purchased in Dee Street in Banchory have proved useful additions to the estate portfolio. A diversification from the business of more usual construction services took place in 1984 in the form of an office furniture systems business, Prime Space Design Ltd. The company provided the Scottish agency for the products of Steelcase Strafor, one of the world's largest office furniture systems manufacturers. Disappointingly, after three years of encouraging trading and rapid growth, the company had to be placed into administration with the onset of the recession in 1987 and it was later sold. The same economic downturn resulted in the disposal of the 50% interest in the Tor Na Coille Hotel in Banchory. This hotel, originally built at a cost of £1000 on land feued from the estate in 1873, was purchased in partnership with local businessman and estate tenant of many years at Harestone Farm, Harry Barclay. The ownership of the hotel led to the establishment on the premises of the Deeside Indoor Sporting Club and the Banchory Squash Club both of which continue to flourish.

By 2000, there are wide-ranging examples of estate involvement in recreational activities. These include the football pitches at St. Ternan's Park at the Milton and the Crathes Primary School. An agreement with the Local Authority for use of the former Deeside railway line between Banchory and Crathes resulted in the establishment of the first stretch of the proposed Deeside Way. The Inchmarlo golf course was created in 1997 to complement the golf driving range that had been developed on the adjacent tenanted land in 1995. To this complex is currently being added by the tenant an 18-hole championship course. In 1987, The Inchmarlo Land Company granted a long lease on a field close to the Burnett Park for use as an athletics field and named the Alexander Park. We would like to think that this park will grow to be as attractive as its neighbour. At times when attitudes in sport are somewhat different to those of yesteryear, we have attached a slogan to the Alexander Park, *Sole Virtute,* with the wish that anyone participating in any activity on the field will do so in the spirit for which sport was intended.

Other activities on the estate include a "Skirmish" site (a popular 'paintball warfare' pastime), at Druggam. I would like to think that my few years as a Kincardineshire county councillor was not entirely without achievement inasmuch as I managed to persuade my fellow councillors to retain ground for a playing field on the former New Banchory Farm at Silverbank when approval for housing was granted on that land in 1973. It was purchased from the owners for the then princely sum of £35,000 and although use of it may not have been justified at the time, it is undoubtedly essential to the needs of today.

In 1980, as an enthusiastic but highly unsuccessful piper, I was involved in the foundation of the Banchory and District Pipe Band whose members wear the Burnett of Leys tartan.[(Fig.12.45)] My interest was encouraged because one of the best known personalities and tutors in the piping world, the late Bessie Brown, lived locally near the Loch of Leys. Whether it was because of our common interests in matters other than piping or her recognition of my deficiency in the skill necessary to achieve an acceptable standard, time actually spent on tuition decreased as lessons progressed. The band flourished throughout the 1980s and in 1990 it achieved notable success by reaching a play-off in its grade in the World Pipe Band Championships.

The estate has never been lacking in its responsibilities towards education. The Reid and Burnett School, which had been established by Lady Burnett in Banchory in 1750 was closed in 1911. It provided education for girls and a few small boys teaching Latin, English, writing and arithmetic and in particular 'sewing and good manners',

> "June 26th 1878. Commenced the bigger boys to darning on sewing days. I think it is highly important to boys.
>
> 1889. Too much has been attempted with a staff of no special strength. The ordinary and essential branches have suffered. The style of answering should be improved, simultaneous shouting should be abolished. A handful of children do all the answering in the class and the rest know next to nothing."
> (from School Inspectors' reports.)

The school at Glashmore in the parish of Drumoak was closed in 1938. John Ross, whose father moved from Craigton to Todholes and who now lives at Hoghillock, was amongst the 80 pupils who attended it at the start of the century.

The Hill of Banchory development that is mentioned above was initiated as a result of that location being identified by the Local Authority as the preferred site for a new school campus for the town. It has since been agreed that the construction of the school will be an integral part of that development and may for the most part be provided by the estate.

THE CASTLE and THE GARDENS

> *There is a story of a Persian prince who was fond of appearing in the street with his dress sparkling with costly gems. One day an aged beggar came bowing before the prince saying "I thank your highness for your jewels." The prince looked at the beggar haughtily and said, "What mean you? I have given you no jewels". "Pardon me," replied the beggar. "You have shown them to me, I have gazed on their charms and enjoyed their beauty.*
> ("Saturday in Crathes Woods", *Aberdeen Journal,* 16 January 1894)

Any account of the Leys Estate would be incomplete without reference to the family association with its former home and in particular the changes to the castle and gardens during the past century or so.

Shortly before 1900, there had been a substantial addition to the Castle.

"An east wing was built on to the house in 1894-5. In doing this the billiard room and another small room at one time a library but latterly used as a Turkish bath were knocked into one, a small jutting out part of the house which gave access to the garden by a short stair removed and a dairy which stood further to the North demolished to make room for the new addition. In place of the entrance to the garden which had been done away with another provided by means of a turret stair leading down from a new room, the Schoolroom.

The architects were Messrs. Brown and Watt, Aberdeen. Total cost including new lavatory accommodation afterwards added outside and in the addition – £2876. Outlay on furnishing the new wing - £453. Electric Light was installed over the house and outside offices in 1900. Metal tubing was substituted for the wood casing in 1928. In 1907 the horse-course for working the old threshing mill of the home farm was converted into a garage.

During 1926-7 following the death of Sir Thomas certain improvements, decorative work and structural alterations were carried out at Crathes by the wife of the new laird in his absence.

No architect was employed, the factor J. C. F. Dunbar acting in that capacity.

In 1927 the East Bay of the porch was thrown into the hall, the West bay connected with the passage passing the servant's hall and the porch re-roofed. A glass inner front door was also added. Three small girders were put in to support the increased span of the entrance hall roof."

(from anon Lady's notes)

At a meeting of the Glasgow Architectural Association on January 5th 1897, Mr W. J. Blane summed up his paper entitled 'Some Scotch Houses' placing the following four buildings and their characteristic in the following order of merit:- Crathes, dignity with beauty of detail; Castle Fraser, beauty of detail with dignity; Midmar, dignity without beauty of detail-, Craigievar, beauty of detail without dignity. After a short discussion the lecturer was awarded the usual vote of thanks.

(Source: *The British Architect*, (15 January 1897))

Fig.15.14 Crathes Castle – an early 20th century view (courtesy RCAHMS)

Fig. 15.15 Crathes Castle – an early 21st century view (Bailey)

My grandparents effected considerable alterations to the tower although they were relatively cosmetic in relation to those carried out by Sir Robert (11th baronet 1876-1894). He had been largely responsible for the refurbishment and furnishing of the castle and much of it failed to accord with their tastes. The walls of the Tower Room, which was also at some time the dining room, had been covered in heavily embossed leather (Fig.15.17) which my grandparents removed to reveal the impressive stonework beneath although it has since been plastered to reproduce the original wall finish.

Fig. 15.16 (above) The Tower Room before refurbishment (courtesy RCAHMS)
Fig. 15.17 (below) The Tower Room with revealed stonework (Crathes archive)

There were no further major changes to the building until the reconstruction by the National Trust after the fire of 1966. This resulted in the Queen Anne wing being reduced to from four to two storeys. The fire, which originated in the fireplace in the drawing room at the junction of the eighteenth century addition and the Victorian addition, spread rapidly towards the tower and was halted from further progress by the heavy door leading to the Green Lady's room. In the aftermath of the fire, we came upon an outdated instruction as to procedures which should have been adopted in such an event. The instruction stated that the safety of the Horn of Leys was paramount. The second priority was to ensure the safety of some of the earliest charters which may have been on public display. Third in order of priority was to make sure that Lady Burnett was alive and well! The author of this instruction was not identified.

The other great impact on this part of the estate during the first half of the century resulted from the development of the garden by my grandparents, Sir James and Lady Burnett, from around 1926. Although there had been already a very fine garden at Crathes since before 1640,

> "Crathes - near Aberdeen. Sir Robert Burnett, Bart. An excellent kitchen-garden in the old style, with magnificent holly hedges. abundance of prolific fruit, and venerable exotic shrubs."
> (Loudon, John Claudius. *Encyclopaedia of Gardening*. 1825)

they undertook intensive planting to create one of the greatest gardens in the land.

> "So skilfully have the alterations and improvements been carried out under the present excellent and intelligent management of Sir James and Lady Burnett, that the gardens....have in aspect and sentiment remained in accordance with the whole atmosphere of the place."
> (Taylor,1937)

The above and the following are probably sufficient to give the reader an overall view of this achievement.

> "First I think it is important for me to put Crathes Gardens into perspective in relation to other gardens in the country. The fame which Crathes enjoys rests upon two very great assets - the remarkable collection of plants found there and the excellence of design.
>
> The first may not be surprising when one considers that Sir James was essentially a plantsman who avidly collected any plant which had a rarity or curiosity value, as well as better forms of plants which had a generally more accepted value as good garden subjects. The period in which Sir James was gathering his collection (1900 -1930), was at a good time when Britain was rich with what was available through plant collectors and the many new hybrids which were then being offered by nurserymen. Fortunately the plant collection at Crathes was well maintained

during the war and is now considered the most important in Scotland, excluding that the Royal Botanic Garden, Edinburgh and certainly ranks very high among the private collections found in Britain.

The design of the garden owes much to the incredible flair which Lady Burnett had for this aspect of garden art. Although one knows that the assistance of several experts has helped to form the garden at Crathes, the coordinating hand and mind were undoubtedly those of Lady Burnett. There are few people whose work can seriously be compared with that of Gertrude Jekyll but Lady Burnett is considered by various authorities to be amongst those who can. As one might expect, her already great ability increased over the years and some people who have had close association with Crathes and Lady Burnett feel that in the Colour Garden the best of her natural ability and acquired taste is expressed very forcibly, a point of view which from my own short acquaintance with Lady Burnett I would wholly agree."
(J. E. Robson. *Crathes Castle Gardens (the Colour Garden memo)*, 20 July 1967)

The quality of the garden was reflected in the wide variety of rare plants, trees and shrubs which my grandparents acquired from around the world. My grandfather, a lover of trees, established a small pinetum to the north of the castle in 1940. However, if he saw it today, he would be the first to acknowledge that it was somewhat short of being successful. His interest in trees was such that they chose to send my mother to school at Westonbirt in Gloucester – adjacent to the world renown Arbotetum! Their mark was made in diverse ways. Amongst the more permanent alterations was to move the Doocot from a location near the home farm buildings to its present position at the southeast corner of the garden; an operation which my grandmother insisted had been carried out at no expense to the estate. The fact that it employed considerable time of many estate staff appeared to her to be irrelevant to the argument. Any such extravagance changed to parsimony after the death of my grandfather on the discovery of a severely embarrassed estate. A heavy smoker, her choice moved to Woodbine cigarettes and the fag ends were retained for reconstitution for further alleged enjoyment. Unused mustard was always returned to the pot and we grandchildren were occasionally treated to 'Coca Cola' - but only in sherry glasses. Maybe it is unfortunate that such prudence does not exist today. Her caution over financial matters during her widowhood might be compared with the prudence displayed by her mother in law during her courtship and illustrated by a relevant poem from the archive.

The Idol's (?) reply
Oh Tommy dear - and can it be,
That you have fallen in love with me.
My arrows sure have sped more true,
Then I surmised - or even you.

The only point that puzzles me,
Is what my income is to be,

The flame of love may boil the pot,
But where's the mutton to be got?

Yet spite of this, I'm sending now,
To deck with orange flowers my brow,
Then let me know without delay,
When you can fix the happy day.

February 14th 1859 (to Thomas Burnett)

Although there were undoubtedly changes within the castle during the first part of the century, its use during the Second World War as a military convalescent home saw the end of the family occupancy of the tower for other than special occasions. Until that time it was used regularly and it would seem appropriate to mention here that the Green Lady's room was one where the occupants never managed to enjoy a good night's sleep. Many anecdotal and probably apocryphal stories are told about this legend, but it may be that they are based on more than fantasy. Sir Alexander, the 4th baronet, a simple and kind-hearted man, suffered from what was locally called a "boodie fear", a dread of ghosts. A hundred years after his death, a child's skeleton was found in that room beneath the hearth during its removal. Allardyce's *Family of Burnett of Leys* records that "the room has the reputation of being haunted by the apparition of a lady dressed in green, with a child in her arms, but as she has not appeared within the memory of the present generation, no inducement can be held out to the Society of Psychical Research to pay it a visit".

Following the transfer to The National Trust for Scotland, an apartment at the north end of the Victorian Wing was created for the Trust representative. After the fire of 1966, plans were drawn to rebuild to accommodate both the needs of the family and the National Trust. However, the growing number of visitors and the aesthetics of building a 'new' addition to the castle, led to the decision to construct the House of Crathes.

Between 1952 and 1966(the date of the fire), the family enjoyed occupancy of a large portion of the castle at the National Trust's pleasure. We retained the shooting in the policies, and many of the farm buildings and any cottages that were occupied by estate employees. The last of these was resumed in 1984. We enjoyed the use of the gardens and its produce much as we did beforehand. We revived, for our private use, the wild garden on the west drive and which eventually became known as Caroline's garden. Once there used to be an attractive summerhouse above the rocks overlooking this garden, but at some time vandals pushed it off the top. This is not a problem of today alone.

> "The gardens and grounds are exceedingly well kept, and their beauty is much enhanced by the broad, old hedges. Formerly it was a privilege, much taken of by the public generally to visit the gardens and grounds of Crathes, but owing to the vandalism of the visitors, the proprietor had to withdraw the privilege."
> (Anon., "Banchory and Round About" *The Northern Figaro*", Third Issue, 1897)

In the early days of the National Trust's ownership, the family played an unofficial but influential role in much of the decision making at Crathes. Several properties enjoyed the involvement of a 'godmother' who would act as a representative member of the associated family in the absence of an appropriate family member. Shortly before this system of family involvement came to an end, my wife Fiona was invited to be the godmother for Crathes. However, the dramatic increase in visitor numbers and the changing economic circumstances surrounding the management of any such property, encouraged the surrender of many of these facilities and privileges. It can be argued that such changes, albeit understandably necessary, have unavoidably affected the relationship between the family and the Trust as it existed at the time of the gift.

> "...that the family associations and traditions and the whole atmosphere and character of the place should remain unchanged. The essential quality of a Country House, under the ownership of the Trust, is that it is lived in and that it is a home. We want therefore to steer the delicate path between the privacy and intimacy of the family home and the accessibility of a place of public resort.
>
> And now Crathes belongs to the Trust! But please let there be no sadness that it no longer belongs to the Burnetts of Leys: it is only in the Valuation Roll and sundry legal documents that their ownership has ceased. In name and fame, in reputation and substance, it still remains, and may it ever remain, their place, and they remain its lairds."
> (Chairman, The National Trust for Scotland, 1952)

Fig. 15.18 Plaque in Crathes Gardens. 2000 (Bailey)

Before 1960, our visits to Crathes were usually in April and August and so may not have provided us with a full picture of life at Crathes. However, changes in the property itself are evident. In the building that now houses the National Trust shop and Ranger's office, there were garages, the gun-room, the estate office, the former stables and, in the 1950s, an unsuccessful estate enterprise of a deep-litter chicken business. As children, we were provided with adventurous opportunities by these buildings. They were seldom locked and contained for our enjoyment a variety of interests including swords, pistols and other items of military hardware some of which now adorn the castle walls. There was even a very large gin trap which we were led to believe was an old man-trap!

Within the castle, life was such that it is easy now to understand the serious situation in which the estate found itself on my grandfather's death. There appeared to be no shortage of permanent and temporary staff although the number had been somewhat reduced since the war. When Sir Thomas was alive, the castle staff consisted of a butler, a footman, a parlour maid, 3 housemaids, a hall boy, a cook, a kitchen maid, a scullery maid, 2 laundresses and 2 ladies maids. This was in addition to the estate employees which included 6 gardeners, 6 foresters, 6 gamekeepers, a coachman and doubtless a team to maintain the property and operate the joiner's shop. Nevertheless, life may have been dull by later comparisons. Sir Thomas and Lady Burnett did not entertain much but every year they took a house in Charles Street in London and went often to the theatre. They never 'brought out' their daughter Ethel and it was their eldest son, my great uncle Edwin, who took her to her first dance when she was 32!

After the war, there were two chauffeurs, one of whom also drove the estate lorry and who went twice a day to the Crathes Emporium to deliver and collect mail and 'messages'. The other was my grandfather's army batman, James Christie, who had heroically saved his life during the Great War.

"IN THE FIGHTING LINE.

INTERESTING SIDELIGHTS

Gordon Highlander's heroism.

A Gordon Highlander who had just returned from Ypres wounded has a thrilling tale to tell. Too modest to give his name, he passes over his own achievements under fire which he describes as terrible in the extreme, to relate the gallant exploits of one of his comrades, one of the most thrilling which the war has yielded. On Saturday, October 31, the Gordons had been fighting with all their old-time valour during the greater part of the day against fearful, almost overwhelming odds. Indeed, at one time it was feared that defeat had overtaken them, but they hurled the Germans, defeated and dismayed, back into the trenches. Night fell and the victors,

> who had paid a heavy toll, retired on their own position. A Company, under the command of Captain Burnett of Crathes, bore the brunt of the fighting, and as the survivors were reaching their own trenches, Captain Burnett's servant observed that he was missing. Back over the battlefield he made his way to the spot where he last saw his master. Not until he had traversed almost three quarters of a mile, right up to within a stonethrow of the enemy trenches, was he successful in finding the wounded officer. Captain Burnett, who had been severely hit, observed the figure of the searcher against the skyline and thinking that it was possibly a friend, sounded a familiar call on his whistle. In a moment his faithful henchman was by his side, while from the German trenches nearby came a fusillade of bullets. Picking up the captain and getting him on to his back, the rescuer with all possible speed, made for the British lines amid a shower of lead. If the outward journey was hazardous, the home trek was doubly perilous, but in a marvellously short time the rescue was accomplished. When within a few yards of his goal the highlander observed a small group of soldiers, and knowing they were friends, he approached them with his burden - the captain was by that time becoming faint through loss of blood - and asked for a drink. His surprise can be imagined when he had discovered that he had accosted the Brigadier and his staff. It is almost needless to say that his request was not long in being granted. Captain Burnett, who is now in hospital in Dublin, is making a satisfactory recovery, and bv his side is his faithful servant, who at the risk of his own life snatched him from the jaws of death.
> (*The Times*, 1914)

Despite an indulgence that may have made him unsuitable to be a chauffeur, even in those days, he remained in his employment until his retirement some thirty years later. I have been told that my grandmother preferred to be driven by Christie when he was drunk than by my grandfather when he was sober!

The kitchen was spacious and inconvenient. All food, and whatever was required to accompany it, had to be raised by hoist to the dining room which, during the 1950's, was adjacent to the tower and on the first floor. The use of certain rooms seemed to change with frequency and this room, which no longer exists, has variably been the billiard room and a drawing room. The billiard table was at some time moved to what was known as the smoking room, a large room that lay alongside the garden in the Victorian wing. Latterly it was taken to a room on the fourth floor of the Queen Anne wing from where it must have rapidly returned to ground floor level again on the ill-fated night in January 1966.

It was probably 1953 or later before there was more than one telephone in the castle. This was situated in the 'telephone room' adjacent to the smoking room. The recipient of any call, if he or she happened to be outside and even at the furthest point of the garden, was summoned by a large grey megaphone that stood in the hall - a system of communication that often must have taken all of ten minutes to achieve its objective.

Personal memories of life before 1953 are few. On several occasions we accompanied our grandparents in judging the estate garden competition. This ceased long ago but the trophy continues as that for the local rural primary school football competition. Visits to Aberdeen's fish market and the railway station were regular features of our holidays. In the summer we were taken in a small boat alongside the coast south of Stonehaven to fish for mackerel. This was invariably disastrous with the unequal angling success accompanied by seasickness. The Aboyne and Braemar Gatherings were regulars on the summer programme. There was also a regular call on the Boys Brigade camp in the then eponymously named field to the south of the Castle where seemingly huge numbers of members gathered each summer.

The Crathes gardens were open on two or three occasions each year in aid of the Nursing Association. We grandchildren were permitted to commandeer a small area of the garden from which we could sell garden produce, (the fruit and vegetables were then grown in the main garden). For this visitors were obliged to pay a one penny supplement to their earlier charge in order to obtain entry. The castle was always filled with flowers from the garden, which my grandmother was proficient in arranging. The aroma, accompanied by that of Turkish cigarettes, is one that could not fail to be appreciated.

We were taught to shoot and fish at an early age. Fishing was endured with the lesser enthusiasm of the two. We only learnt much later that efforts to encourage us included the addition by the ghillie of small fish under the pretence that he was changing the fly!

Until the fire of 1966, there was no second access to the first floor and Trust visitors, who were far less numerous than today, reached the ground floor by means of our private staircase. Since opening days were then according to season, certain days of the week and sometimes afternoons only, this was no great intrusion. One of the benefits to come from the fire was the ability to build improved reception and better access to the first floor of the tower.

The army, and especially the Gordon Highlanders which my grandfather commanded, had been his life and reminders of it, especially in the form of family losses, were never far away. He was badly wounded in the Boer War and the Great War. He had one heel shot away and was also left with a permanently bent left arm. He spoke with great rapidity and was know to most of his closest friends as Maxim after the machine gun of the same name. I understand this to be a characteristic that has been passed to later generations. He never went to Staff College but still achieved the rank of Major General. He had a strong dislike of staff officers as he thought that they should be fighting with their men.

"**Lieutenant Burnett.of the 2nd Gordons**.
Lieutenant J. L. G. Burnett of the 2nd Battalion Gordon Highlanders, who has been mentioned in Lord Kitchener's latest dispatch,...has been specially commended for his coolness and resource on the occasion of a train being derailed and attacked on Pietersburg line on August 10th."
(*The Scotsman*.)

He was an excellent Scottish country dancer and when he commanded the 2nd Battalion, all subalterns were required to pass a strict test before they were allowed to partake in any highland dancing on any social occasion. His ability to play the drum was something that became almost an obsession in which he frequently found enjoyment either with drumsticks that always lay on his desk or with knives at the dining table!

"Lady Burnett of Leys struck an original note when she declared open the new public hall at Crathes. The building, in the erection of which she has played a conspicuous and generous part, has been provided at a cost of £1100....Sir James Burnett was a notable contributor to the musical programme that was carried through after the opening. He is an expert with the drum, and his solos delighted the audience."
(Aberdeen *Press and Journal*, 15 November 1929)

My grandfather was interested in the unusual. During the war there used to be monthly film shows at the Castle and on one occasion the absence of my grandfather and one of the tenants, Mr Humble, did not go unnoticed by my grandmother. When she demanded to know the reason for their absence from what may have been an understandably avoidable film, she was told that it was their business and not hers. The reason was that Mr Humble, unbeknown to many, had constructed his own air-raid shelter on his farm and the curiosity of my grandfather required to be satisfied.

His other great interests were gardening and railways. There were few more knowledgeable when it came to railway timetables and it was with great satisfaction that he could take you from one side of Europe to the opposite side of Asia. Bradshaw's Railway Directory was his favourite bedside reading material. He knew it so well that he never bothered to look up the times of the trains before a journey - and timetables did change! But it was the army that was his great interest.

He was also noted for his affinity to women and at one time was unofficially engaged to several ladies. He betrothed his eventual wife after meeting her while serving in India, but this did not prevent him from making a similar offer to a lady with whom he had an affair on the train back to Scotland with resulting litigation for breach of promise!

BYDAND

**To the memory of the Gordon Highlanders
who have fought and died for
freedom in Singapore.**

DEAR WARRIORS from our keeps and crofts and glens
And from our Silver City by the sea,
Rest calmly in that sun-scorched land
Where duty called you. Once so free,
You girt the sword - that freedom
Now imperilled might be ours.
You chose the path of glory, and,
Mustering all resistance, made your epic stand:
Bydand - Standfast - Bydand!

Perchance no silken flag will bear the name
Of your last Honour, so that we,
In homes where you were nurtured, loved, and learnt the fame
Of past supremacy on land and sea,
May live in peace.
Still, graven deeper than on flat or stone
In every heart in every northern home
Is writ in tears, how in a distant land
You fought, Imperial Brothers, Glorious Band:
Bydand - Standfast - Bydand!

Dear Warriors, we who live to bear the pain
Of your great sacrifice must shoulder
Now fresh burdens. Once again
Effort renewed, and since of high endeavour
Pride is born, proud of your fame
We, by blood and sweat and toil and tears,
Will raise an epitaph for future years
For children yet unborn in freedom's land,
Memorial to your last, most glorious stand:
Bydand - Standfast - Bydand!
(Sybil Burnett of Leys, 16 February 1942)

Within the castle and adjacent to the long gallery, there is a room that is now kept furnished by the family and which provides evidence of the continuing association with Crathes of the family, its branches and its kinsmen. Here, there is exhibition of today's family in the widest sense and an insight into current Burnett activities that are not promoted elsewhere in the Castle. There are, however, several articles on loan which are displayed in the Castle including a gold and ivory walking stick, my grandfather's medals and the Barony Court Register in addition to the Horn of Leys.

Fig.15.19 Charles Tyrrell, Chairman of the NTS with, seated, Fiona and James Burnett and their son Victor at the opening of the Family Room. June 1989. (Jim Henderson. AMPA, ARPS)

Apart from the family room and the permanent arrangement over the House of Crathes site which is leased for all time to the successive members of the family, there is one area within the policies which remains in my family's ownership. This is the family cemetery that was created in 1898. It occupies a delightful location a few hundred yards south of the castle. The last person to be laid to rest there was my mother. Also buried there is my grandfather's bulldog, 'Junior'. When he commanded the 51st Highland Division, he commuted daily to his office in Perth in his open Humber Snipe car, with one of his favourite cigars, and his bulldog sitting on the seat beside him!

My grandfather never recovered from the shock of losing both his sons. The elder, Sandy, committed suicide at Oxford. He was a talented artist and wrote many imaginative and skilfully illustrated letters, to his family, which were sadly lost in the fire of 1966. Roger was killed in Germany 1945 in an action which several of his fellow soldiers who were present have told me should have earned him a

Victoria Cross. I knew neither my uncle nor my father who was killed in 1942. Curiously, the first time that I ever saw a moving picture of either was on a television programme in 1997 in which was replayed an old film taken by one of the patients at the Castle when it was a hospital during the war.

My grandfather's brother, later Sir Edwin the 14th baronet, spent the latter part of his life in a hotel in Ballater with his sister Ethel. Both were excessively thrifty and our frequent visits to see them were both unpopular and unrewarded.

A moving reminder of life at the Castle and one which embraced much of its history, took place in 1992. From an idea originating after a visit of Burnetts to Crathes, there developed a community play, *Tensions in Trust*. Written by Professor John Hargreaves, participation in the event was widespread amongst the local community and resulted in the adoption of the rehearsal location, Woodend Barn, as a permanent home for the newly formed community arts association. The play commenced with the re-enactment of Sir James Burnet's funeral procession passing by the front of the Castle much as it did forty years earlier *en route* to the cemetery. The cast represented the family and servants and the audience the followers. Within the principal performance of this reproduction of the event and which took place in a marquee in front of the castle, was provided a history of Crathes and the Burnett family as enacted by the 'servants'. It was a comprehensive and summary reflection of a long and often illustrious history and opened a fresh chapter for the estate.

In comparison with 1900, we recognise there is now a substantial difference in the roles and responsibilities of estate ownership towards those whose lives it affects. Over the years we have enjoyed many celebrations of events associated with the estate. One of the most recent of these was at the House of Crathes in July 1994 to mark Alexander's 21st birthday. It took the form of a small drinks party for the tenants and employees and, in its relatively humble form, reflected the relevance of the estate to the family at 2000. I hope that these pages will explain more fully the background to that relevance and the context in which it occurs. Appendix 1, a report on a complimentary dinner for the factor in 1908, provides as good a representation as can be found of life on the Estate some 100 years earlier. Such changes from that day may have resulted from the gift to the nation of the castle and gardens and the consequent loss of identity of the estate as a complete entity with a more permanent community. However it is more likely to be the transfer of many obligations from the landowner to the individual or to the state which has reduced the authority and importance of estates such as ours. It has also been the shrinking world with its more mobile population that has led to the diminution of the community. This trend has accompanied the closure of the Deeside railway line and Crathes Station in 1966 and the Crathes Shop and Post Office in 1997. Happily the Crathes village hall, which was built in 1929, continues to thrive. The support of the community and the improvements which it has recently undergone are not unique to its history.

> *"Following tea, served in a large marquee on the lawn, the company were entertained by a gymnastic display by a team from the Aberdeen Depot Gordon Highlanders at which the music was provided by the Gordon Highlanders Pipe Band...Crathes Public Hall was the scene of the evening's celebrations. A small body of enthusiastic workers had transferred the hall into a place of charm and beauty. Lit by the Colar system of gas lighting which is being introduced with such success in the north-east, the hall presented a charming spectacle."*
> ("Report on Celebrations at Crathes for Rohays Burnett's coming of age," (Aberdeen) *Press and Journal*, 1 September 1937).

The hall has also been home for the activities of the Crathes branch of the Women's Rural Institute which was founded in 1927. For two years until the Crathes Hall was built, the members met at the Castle. It was proposed that the new hall should be somewhere near the Crathes School and it was the protests of the villagers and the residents of lower Crathes that persuaded its relocation to its present and more suitable site.

Also surviving and flourishing in a world in which the economies of scale appear to direct our lives, is the Crathes Primary School albeit not with a wholly local roll. The school role reduced in the 1970s to a pupil number which suggested that closure, or the sale of the schoolhouse, might have been a possibility. It was the conditions attached to the title given by the estate that influenced the retention of the schoolhouse which recently has been barely sufficient to cater for the number of pupils who now attend. Such influence may shortly disappear with the imminence of land reform.

LOOKING FORWARD

Changing circumstances should not alter our overall objectives towards the future of the estate. There will be changes in land use, occupancy and activity that it is prudent to address and there will be increases or decreases in the estate which it may seem necessary to consider. However, it must remain the prime objective that family ownership of the Lands of Leys shall continue and for successive members of the family to reside at Crathes. To such a vision must be attached some caution and although political interference, public demands and economic necessity must influence the direction and nature of future ownership, it is still essential for those objectives to be maintained.

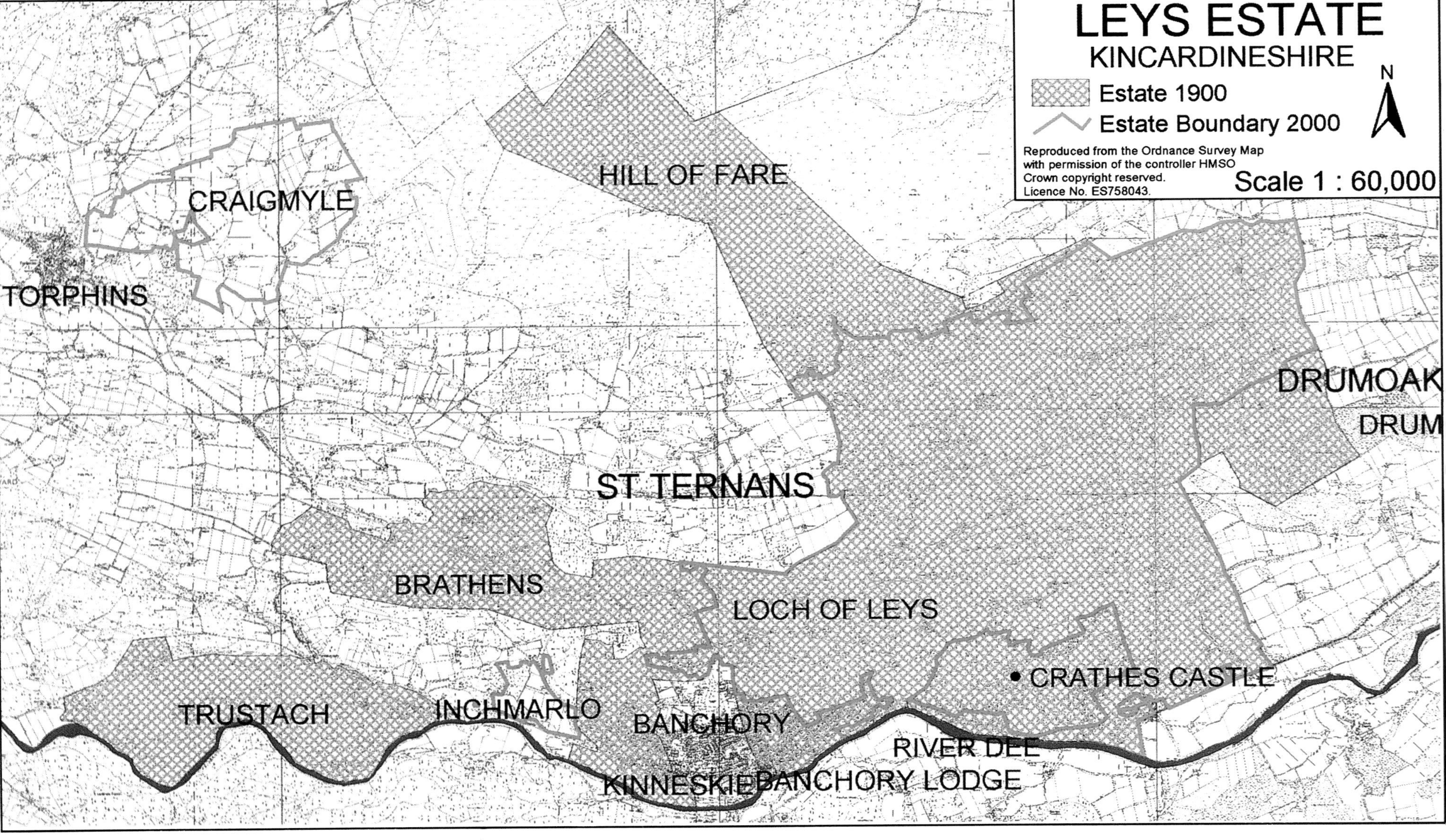
LEYS ESTATE
KINCARDINESHIRE
N
Estate 1900
Estate Boundary 2000
Reproduced from the Ordnance Survey Map
with permission of the controller HMSO
Crown copyright reserved.
Licence No. ES758043.
Scale 1 : 60,000
HILL OF FARE
CRAIGMYLE
TORPHINS
DRUMOAK
DRUM
ST TERNANS
BRATHENS
LOCH OF LEYS
CRATHES CASTLE
TRUSTACH
INCHMARLO
BANCHORY
RIVER DEE
KINNESKIE
BANCHORY LODGE

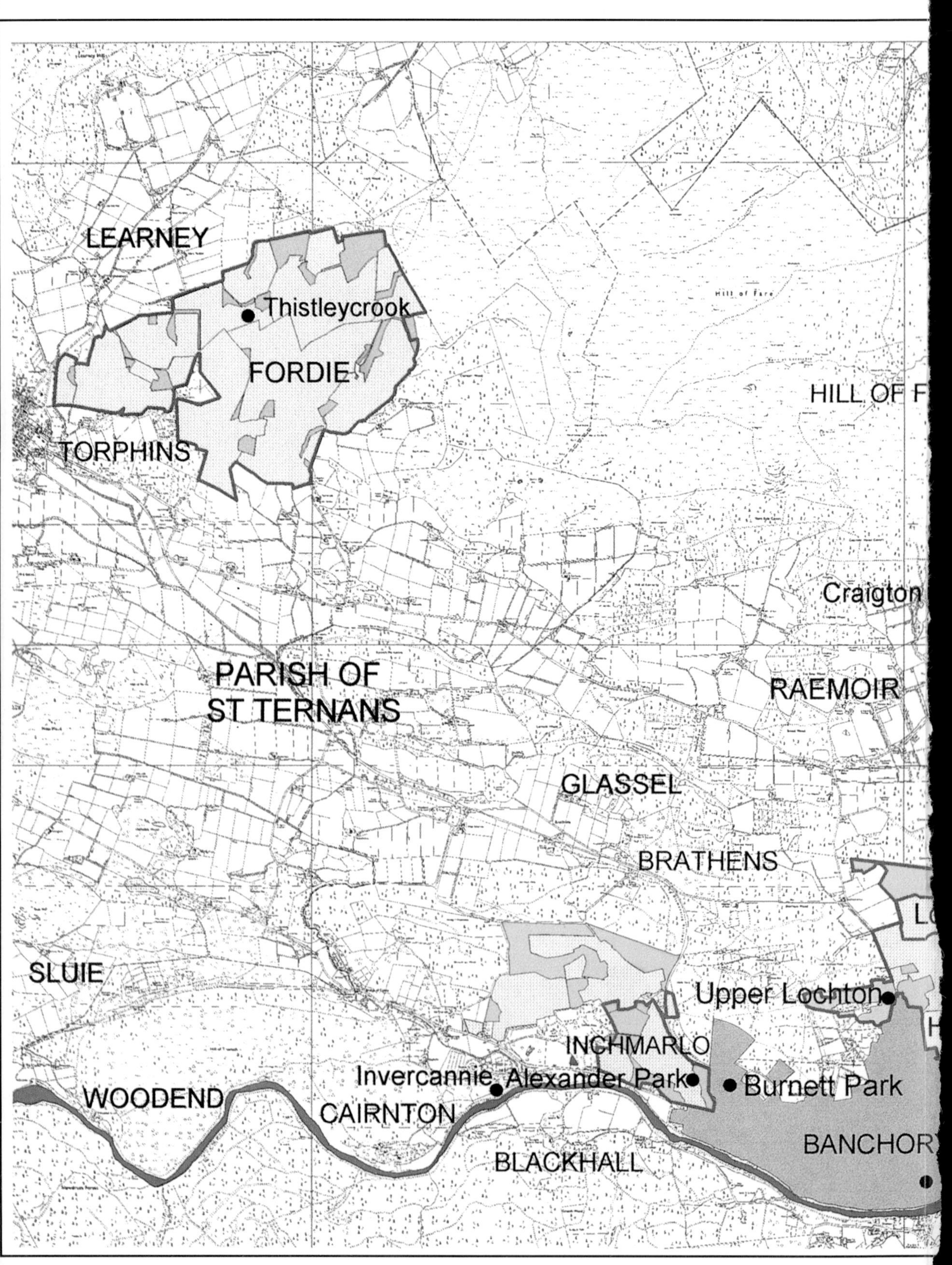

LEARNEY
Thistleycrook
FORDIE
TORPHINS
Hill of Fare
HILL OF F
Craigton
PARISH OF
ST TERNANS
RAEMOIR
GLASSEL
BRATHENS
SLUIE
Upper Lochton
INCHMARLO
Invercannie
Alexander Park
Burnett Park
WOODEND
CAIRNTON
BLACKHALL
BANCHORY

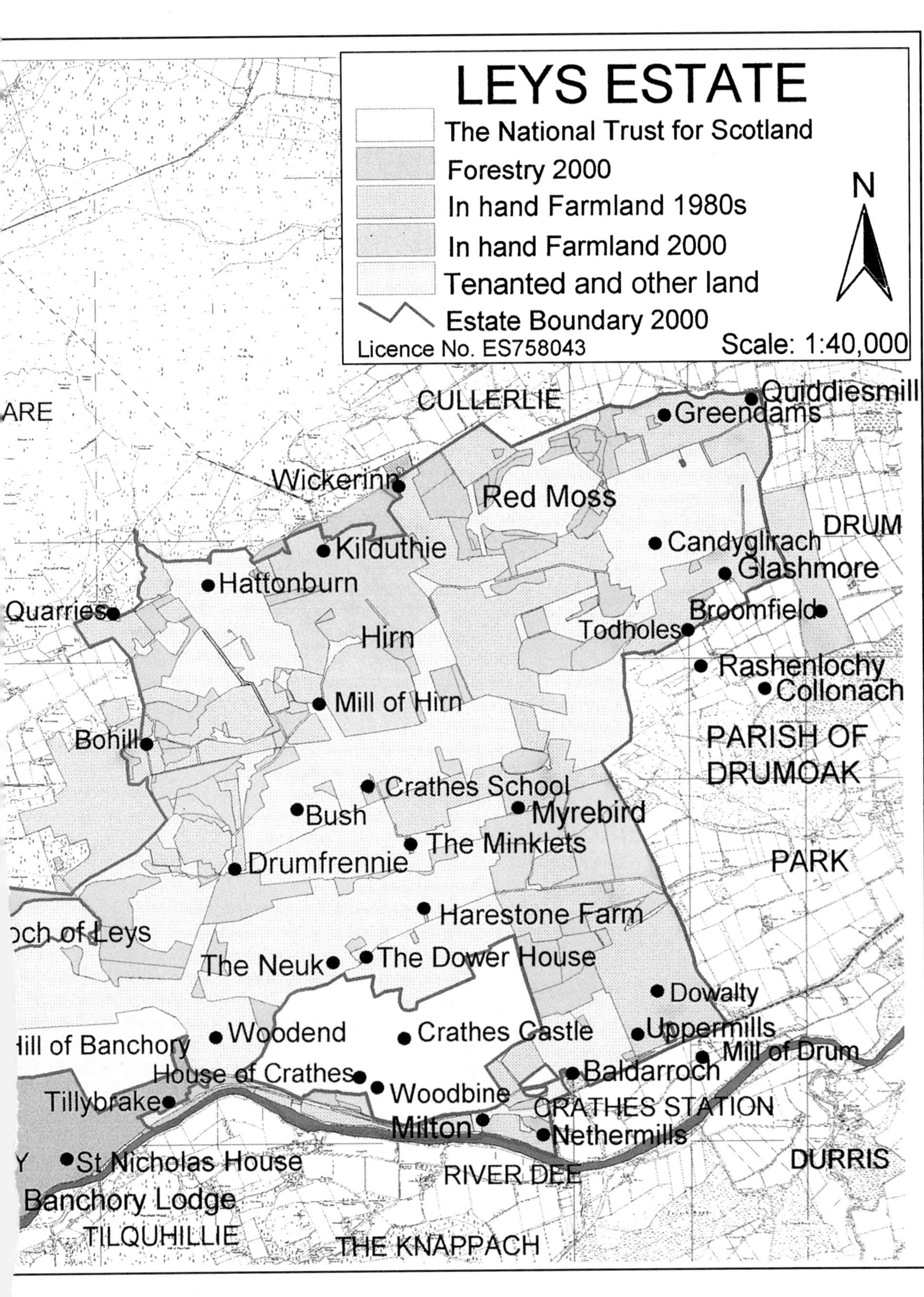
LEYS ESTATE
The National Trust for Scotland
Forestry 2000
In hand Farmland 1980s
In hand Farmland 2000
Tenanted and other land
Estate Boundary 2000
Licence No. ES758043
Scale: 1:40,000
N
CULLERLIE
Quiddiesmill
Greendams
Wickerinn
Red Moss
DRUM
Candyglirach
Glashmore
Kilduthie
Hattonburn
Quarries
Broomfield
Todholes
Hirn
Rashenlochy
Collonach
Mill of Hirn
Bohill
PARISH OF
DRUMOAK
Crathes School
Myrebird
Bush
The Minklets
Drumfrennie
PARK
Harestone Farm
The Neuk
The Dower House
Dowalty
Woodend
Crathes Castle
Uppermills
Mill of Drum
House of Crathes
Baldarroch
Tillybrake
Woodbine
CRATHES STATION
Milton
Nethermills
St Nicholas House
RIVER DEE
DURRIS
Banchory Lodge
TILQUHILLIE
THE KNAPPACH

Leys Estate - Appendix 1

Honour to Mr Davidson - Factor Crathes

The Aberdeen Free Press **- Friday February 2, 1906**

Complimentary Dinner and Presentation

Interesting Speeches

A very interesting event took place in the Town Hall, Banchory, yesterday afternoon, the occasion being a complimentary dinner and presentation to Mr John Davidson on the occasion of the celebration of his jubilee as factor on the estate of Crathes. Mr Davidson's hosts were the tenants and feuars on the Estate and other friends, who, during those many years, have found in him one who, while conserving the interests of his employers, extended to them, as an upright and honest man of business, every consideration, which they at all times appreciated. During his residence in the district also, Mr Davidson took an active part in public affairs, and in this connection he did much for the general welfare of the community. Mr Davidson's personal qualifications, too, gained for him the respect and esteem of a wide circle of friends, and in honouring him they also took the opportunity of honouring Mrs and Miss Davidson, who have alike shared with Mr Davidson in their regard. In addition to entertaining him to dinner, Mr Davidson was presented with an handsome silver salver with suitable inscription whilst he was also the recipient on behalf of Mrs Davidson of a beautiful gold brooch, and on behalf of Miss Davidson of a gold bracelet of chaste design. The dinner was attended by a very representative company, numbering close on 200.

The chair was occupied by Mr William Adam, Bush, who was supported to his right by Mr John Davidson, the guest of the afternoon; Mr W Mitchell, Auchnagathie; Mr A. Ledingham, S.S.C.; John Gordon, Banker; Dr Cran, Banchory; Mr Braid, factor, (Durris) and on the left by Mr G. J. Walker of Portlethen; Mr A. Dewar, Factor, Fasque and Glen Dye; Mr Ledingham, (Messrs Williams & Sons, Aberdeen); Mr A. T. MacRobert, Aberdeen Lime Company; Reverend James Hall and Mr Joseph Merson, Solicitor. The croupiers were Mr Charles Hunter, Uppermills; Mr James Cushnie, Collanach; and Mr James Hunter, Montague. The company also included:- Mr Merson, Windsor Place, Banchory; Councillor Todd, Aberdeen; Messrs McNicol, Drumfrennie; Andersons, Hattonburn; Anderson, Kilduthie; Thomson, South Hirn; Taylor, North Hirn; Thomson, Oldmill; Anderson, Rashenlochie; Reith, Glashmore; Forbes, Greendams; Pratt, Quiddiesmill; Ross, Todholes; Jolly, Neuk; Cooper, Leys; Leask, Drumshalloch; Donald, Lochton; Hunter, Uppermills; Todd, Nethermills; Hunter, New Banchory; Littlejohn, Craigton; Wilson, Brathens; Coutts, Brathens; Davidson, Pitenkerrie., Duncart, Invercannie; Dr Brand, Banchory; Mr Mitchell, Caimton; Captain Reid, Durris; Messrs Thorn, Quithel; Jamieson, Nether Balfour; Adam, Burn of Bennie; Scott, Burn of Bennie; Munro, Silver Stripe Sawmills; Baillie Ross, Banchory; Messrs Tough, Forester; Davidson, Beltwood; Johnston, Commission Agent; Calder, Barehillock; Davie, Wellhead; Adams, Nether Anguston; Wilson, Builder Banchory; Webster, Dubston; Thom, Ennochie; Gibb, Northern Agricultural Company; Low Commercial Company; W. Adams Jnr, Bush; The Reverend Charles Mackie, Drumoak; Messrs Duff Oaklea; Pirie, Blackhall; Ross, Letterbeg; McLaren,

Banker, Torphins; Shand, Sunnyside; A. Johnston, Cults; Fraser, Invercannie; James Taylor, Tour; etc.

An excellent dinner was purveyed by Mr A Williams, Burnett Arms Hotel, and was served at tastefully laid out tables. After dinner the Chairman proposed the usual loyal toasts, which were cordially received. Mr James Hunter gave the "Imperial Forces", and Major Gordon, Banchory, in reply, noted that it was well remembered when the volunteers in Banchory were started. Mr Davidson was one of the first to come forward for enrolment - (applause) that was in February 1860 - 46 years ago. Mr Davidson was a most enthusiastic volunteer, and continued so for 10 or 12 years; and rose the rank of colour sergeant before he left, and was one of the best shots in the company - (applause). He (Major Gordon) had much pleasure in being there that day to do honour to Mr Davidson who had been his friend during the past 50 years. It delighted him (Major Gordon) to see Mr Davidson there amongst so many good friends - (applause).

The Chairman then intimated apologies for absence from Provost McHardy, Banchory; Mr Ross, Easter Beltie; Mr John Thom, Smithfield, London; and Mr J Bruce, "Free Press", Aberdeen; all of whom joined in expressing congratulations to Mr Davidson on that interesting occasion.

The Presentation Ceremony

The Chairman, proceeding, said: - I have now great pleasure in rising to proceed with the most important part of the business of the afternoon - my only regret being that I am not better qualified to do justice to it. As you are all aware, we are met today to do honour to and congratulate our guest, Mr Davidson, on the long period he has so faithfully discharged his duties on the Crathes Estate and to express the wish that he may be long spared to occupy the position he has so ably filled in the past - (applause). This matter has been spoken of for some time, and took practical shape when a few of us met and decided to go on the lines we have done. That we had a popular cause and we were right in our decision is already evident, I think, by the hearty response to our appeal by tenants, feuars, and friends alike, and if more evidence were wanted this splendid gathering today bears witness to the high esteem in which Mr Davidson is held - (applause). 50 years ago, Mr Davidson, after having gained experience at Mains of Portlethen with the late Mr Walker, and also under the late Mr Porter at the Home Farm of Monymusk - two of the most agriculturists of their time - took over the management of the Crathes Estate in succession to his father, who was held in high esteem by the community, and whose place was a difficult one to fill (applause). The conspicuous level headedness, however, which, has characterised Mr Davidson throughout the long period I have mentioned soon made it apparent, though still a young man, he was a fit successor to a worthy father (applause).

During the long period of Mr Davidson's management there have been many changes at Crathes. He has served under four lairds, and has been well acquainted with all the ups and downs affecting agricultural life during that period. He has seen agriculture at its highest and also at a very low ebb, and I think it speaks volumes for his management as well as for the genuine interest the proprietors of Crathes have taken in the well being of their tenants, that there are so many of the same families on the Estate that were at the beginning of that time (applause). No doubt most of the heads of the families are gone, but their places have been filled either by their sons or representatives - except in very few cases. Mr Davidson, a successful, practical farmer himself, and having a thorough knowledge of all the difficulties farmers have to contend with, has been able by his sound judgement and kindly advice, to so arrange matters that very little friction - if any - has every arisen between

proprietor and tenant, and we, as tenants on Crathes, have undoubtedly to thank Mr Davidson to a great extent for the prosperity we enjoy and the kind relations that exist between our laird and ourselves (applause). I am sure we could not find one more courteous and obliging to deal with than he is and we can always depend upon him giving a fair representation to the laird (applause). I cannot carry my recollections back to the time when Mr Davidson came to Crathes, and probably only a few here can do so, but so far as I can remember, 1 have always considered that Mr Davidson had at heart the welfare of all cases on the Estate, and that he was steadily in his unassuming and unobstructive fashion, seeking to improve our condition, and that he was at the same time acting fairly towards our landlord, who he represents. If we consider how difficult it is for one in his position to retain the confidence of both landlord and tenant and that he has done so for so long a time, we cannot help admiring the tact and ability which has enabled him to do it, and which he has at all times displayed. Beside the marked ability Mr Davidson has shown as acting between tenant and proprietor he has been always able to take a practical hold of all necessary improvements on the estate and in every department of estate work. Notwithstanding the many private duties Mr Davidson has had to attend, and although of rather a retiring disposition he has taken to no mean part of the public work of this parish (applause). He has been an Elder of the parish church for as long as I can remember and taken an active part in all Church work the Kirk Session recognising that a short time ago by presenting him with his portrait on his retirement from acting as Treasurer. Until the passing of the local government Act for Scotland he was an active member of the Local Boards of this parish. He was a member of the first school's Board and had much to do 'with the shaping of the educational affairs of this parish and he has for many years given valuable service to agriculture in this district as secretary of the Deeside Agricultural Association (applause). Mr Davidson also has always been ready to extend his kindly help to those in need, and it redounds to his credit that he has not done so in a manner calculated to bring him fame, but he has been content to enjoy the secret pleasure of his generous acts (applause). In private life, Mr Davidson is a genuine and open hearted friend, and whether in his own house, where Mrs Davidson makes a most admirable hostess or in that of his neighbour's house, his genial personality never fails to make itself felt (applause). In order that Mr Davidson may carry away a most lasting and tangible expression of our esteem and regard than this entertainment can give the tenantry, feuars, and other friends have had an opportunity of subscribing for the small gifts which are before me; and the Response has been a most hearty one and from all classes. I have then, Mr Davidson, in name of the tenantry, feuars, and friends, to ask your acceptance of this piece of plate for yourself and also of this brooch for your good lady, and this bangle for Miss Davidson and I trust you may find them useful and above all that you may long spared to look upon them as at least of some acknowledge of the high esteem and respect in which you and your family are held in Crathes and district (applause). The Chairman then read the inscription on the silver salver as follows:- "Presented to Mr John Davidson, Factor, Crathes, from the tenantry and feuars of the Estate of Leys and other friends at a dinner held in his honour in the Town Hall, Banchory, to commemorate 50 years' service with the Burnetts of Leys - 1865-1905 – 1st February 1906" (applause).
The Chairman continuing, said - and now, gentlemen, I ask you to rise and drink to the continued health, happiness and prosperity of our guests and his fireside (loud applause).

The toast was enthusiastically pledged, the company singing "For he's a jolly good fellow".

Mr Davidson's Reply:

Mr Davidson, who was received with cheers, said - Mr Adam and Gentlemen, ever since I heard of your intention of honouring me in this fashion I have felt that when it came to the point, I would have the utmost difficulty in thanking you all adequately, by word of mouth, but I am sure you will all grant me your kindest indulgence (applause). You can quite understand that, when a man has come to my time of life, and more especially when he has had very little practice in speaking in public, he does not feel at all sure of himself, and dreads the ordeal. On that account, and on that account only, I have looked forward to this day with fear and trembling. Mark you, I have appreciated this honour in my heart of hearts, the very fullest extent from the first day I heard of it, and if I have seemed at all reluctant to receive this great honour from your hands, you must understand that it was entirely due to a feeling of nervousness that I should be able to stand up before you - such a large and representative gathering of my friends and neighbours - some of you very old friends indeed - and in my reply to anything like justice to the kindly feelings and sentiments which you have shown this day towards me and mine, all which have led to you honouring me in such a generous and totally unexpected fashion. The heart is sometimes too full for words and I have very great difficult in expressing what I feel at this time. That I appreciate to the fullest the honour you have done me goes without saying. I should have been quite pleased to take your goodwill for granted, for during the long period I have acted as factor at Crathes I have experienced nothing but the greatest kindness from you all.

At the same time he would be a strange person who did not feel a glow of pride when honoured as you have honoured me. I am proud of the honour but I cannot help feeling that it is too great; that I am not worthy of it - (no! no!). Naturally, however, it gives me the greatest of pleasure to know that you feel so kindly disposed towards me. My work as factor has been, as I have practically said already, on the whole very pleasant, remarkably free from anything of the disagreeable nature sometimes associated with a factor's duties. His life is not always a happy one. Coming in between the proprietor and the tenant he has to act frequently as a buffer and suffers accordingly. Of course I have had difficulties too - everybody will have as long as men are men - but I conscientiously say that they have been very few (applause). At the same time I do not wish to take all the credit for that. It is not so very difficult to get on with tenants, if the proprietor is a generous, fairminded man - a gentleman in the truest sense. In that respect 1 have been very fortunate. I have served three proprietors in Crathes - Sir James, Sir Robert and Sir Thomas, all men deserving of the greatest respect. It is a good sign in favour of the proprietor when you find farms held in the same families from generation to generation, and we have a good many like that in Crathes (applause). It has always been the policy of the baronets of Leys to keep a good tenant and his family on the Estate if possible (applause). Curiously enough my father, whose tenure of office lasted 33 years, also served under three proprietors at Crathes - Sir Robert, Sir Thomas and Sir Alexander - so that Crathes has been served 6 proprietors during the last 83 years (applause). During the last half century great changes have taken place, both on the Estate and in the district - the railway on Deeside as elsewhere, has worked wonders. Banchory, from a few scattered houses has grown out of "a' *kennin'*. But some of you can tell that story better than I can. I must conclude these rambling remarks and in doing so allow me once again to say "Thank you, but "Thank you from the bottom of my heart, both on behalf of my wife, my daughter and myself, for the kindly goodwill and generous appreciation you have shown towards us this day, and for those valuable and beautiful gifts, the tangible expressions of that goodwill, with which you have presented us. I sometimes think my wife feels and appreciates the honour you have done me even more, if that be possible than I do myself. Although I have reached my jubilee I may still have the pleasure of going out and in amongst you for some little time yet; but, in the nature of things, that time can't be long. In any case, I trust that the kindly relations that have existed between us in the past will continue to the end (great applause).

The Lord of The Manor

Mr John Cooper, Leys, gave "Sir Thomas Burnett Bart. of Leys, Lady Burnett and Family." It was now 37 years ago he said, since the tenants on the Estate of Leys, met as they did that afternoon to pledge the health of the Burnetts of Leys. That was on the 2nd February 1869, when Sir James Horne Burnett was entertained by his tenantry. That did not seem a very long period to look back upon, but only 6 or 7 gentlemen were present that afternoon who were there on that occasion. There were every so many descendents of those who were present at that time, but many had gone over to the majority. After referring to the ancestry of the Burnetts of Leys, whose connection with the North of Scotland and Deeside dated back to the time of Robert the Bruce, Mr Cooper went on to say that Sir Thomas Burnett, the present proprietor of Leys, entered the army early in life and attained the rank of Colonel before he retired. He succeeded to the Estates on the death of his brother, Sir Robert, in 1894. Since that time Sir Thomas has lived a very busy life. He took a very close and warm interest in the management of his estates, and was held in the highest esteem and respect by his tenantry (applause). He had on several occasions granted abatement of rent unsolicited, it being his wish to share with his tenants in the most unostentatious manner in the depression which overcame agriculture (applause). Sir Thomas was a keen sportsman, but the very opposite of a game preserver, although very much against destruction by unauthorised persons (laughter). Sir Thomas took a very active and intelligent interest in all public work. In fact in every department of public life he was willing to serve. At present he was Chairman of all the public boards in the parish; he was convener of the County of Kincardine and Vice-Lord Lieutenant of the County. He was also a director of several large and important commercial undertakings. He was a typical country gentleman, and there were few, if any, in the North of Scotland who were more highly respected. He was gentleman of sterling worth and ability (applause). Lady Burnett took a very kindly interest in everything that pertained to the welfare of the tenants. No-one was made more welcome than Lady Burnett when she called on them. She had always taken a practical interest in agriculture, as shown by the substantial encouragement she had given the dairy product at the Show of the Deeside Agricultural Association (applause). In the domestic circle Lady Burnett was the pattern of loving and capable administration. Miss Burnett was a young lady of most amiable and kind disposition, greatly beloved by all who knew her, a student and admirer of Deeside in its various seasons. Lieutenant Burnett, yr., of Leys, had chosen the army as his profession, and was at present serving with his regiment in India. He saw a good deal of active life in the South African war, and maintained the reputation of his family by so distinguishing himself that he was mentioned in dispatches for his heroic conduct. He was a young gentleman of a most active, bright and cheerful disposition. They hoped it would be a very long time before he was called to the baronetcy, and that his experience and training would equip him to follow in the worthy footsteps of his ancestors. Lieutenant Edmond (sic) had also taken to the army and, likewise, with his brother, was serving with his regiment in India. He was a gentleman of a very quiet and modest disposition and a keen sportsman. They were always very pleased to have those gallant officers with them during their furlough, and he was sure he expressed all their wishes when he hoped that they might long be spared to maintain the name and fame of the Burnetts of Leys (applause).

Letter from Sir Thomas Burnett

The Chairman read the following letter of date 16th January from Sir Thomas Burnett of Crathes who is at present on a visit to Egypt.

Dear Mr Adam, I much regret that my absence from this country will prevent me from being present at the dinner which the friends and neighbours of my old friend Mr John Davidson of Harestone propose to give him as a mark of their esteem and regard. I need hardly assure you that I am in complete sympathy with the kindly feelings which has prompted you to do honour to one who has been so long and intimately connected with my family and the Estate of Leys. Mr Davidson has served under four lairds of Leys, and it is in great measure due to his high character and his honesty of purpose with his dealings with the tenants on the Estate that the relations between Landlord and tenant have been of such a friendly and harmonious character. Although I cannot be with you on 1st February , I will drink the health of my old friend and his kind hosts in a bumper of the nearest approach to "the wine of Scotland" which the country can produce. I wish you a successful and happy gathering (applause).

The Tenants and Feuars

Mr George J. Walker proposed the health of "the tenants and feuars of the Estate of Leys" and, in doing so, said he had been more or less associated in business with the Estate of Leys and the tenantry for a good many years, and during that time they had shown a considerable amount of enterprise. Drainage and improvement of land, fencing, and so forth, always got considerable attention from them, and they had always been supported in those improvements by having good landlords - landlords who were ever ready to appreciate and to encourage them in their efforts. You might also say that the tenants on the Estates had had the benefit of the advice of their good friend Mr Davidson and he was sure one and all would say that it was given ungrudgingly and with the best results (applause). It was a notable feature in the tenantry of Leys, and it had been remarked upon there already, that a very large number of the tenants were descendants of their forefathers. There were several families on the Estate that he could mention whose fathers, grandfathers, and great grandfathers had been on the Estate before them. That spoke volumes for the tenant and landlord also. He did not know a property where this obtained to such an extent as on the Estate of Leys. Therefore it gave him a very great pleasure indeed to wish the tenants and feuars on the Estate of Leys every comfort that this world could give them, prosperity in their undertakings, and long life to them (applause). As to the feuars, he had not come so much in contact with them but everyone coming there 40 years ago and seeing the village of Banchory and the development which had taken place in the interval, but be struck with the energy and push and enlightenment of the feuar - those gentlemen who had planted down their money to improve the village and who deserved the highest credit for what they had done. Before he would sit down, he wished to say that he had had the utmost pleasure in being there to join them in doing honour to his old friend Mr Davidson (applause). Mr Davidson's friendship with him was not of yesterday's date. In 1846 - exactly 60 years ago - Mr Davidson and he first became acquainted, and they had been friends ever since (applause). They would thus pardon him for referring to the pleasure it gave him to be there to see the honour done to Mr Davidson. In giving this toast he wished to couple with it the name of Charles Hunter, who was a representative of a family - perhaps one of the oldest connected with the Leys Estate in existence. He would also mention as a feuar the name of Mr George Merson, who, he believed, was the oldest living feuar on the Estate of Leys.

Mr Charles Hunter, in responding on behalf of the tenants said Mr Walker, as Valuator on the Estate, was pre-eminently qualified to propose this toast. Mr Walker had referred to the good qualities of the tenants, but he had gracefully refrained from referring to their shortcomings. If the tenants were worthy of all the praise that Mr Walker had given them the question arose as Artemus Ward put it, "why this thusness!". The reason was not far to seek. It had already been referred to by Mr

Davidson and Mr Walker, that they sat under a splendid landlord. More than that they had sat under a succession of landlords. Mr Walker had referred to the length of time which some of them had had the privilege of being on the Crathes Estate. His family dated back to 130 years ago, and he thought there were tenants on the Estate who could claim still longer connection (applause). He thought on the Crathes Estate they were as well off as the farmers in Ireland. They had got practically fixity of tenure, fair rents and freedom of cultivation (applause). It was not in his province to say anything about Mr Davidson but he would say, in passing, that they had never felt or heard any angry word from Mr Davidson. In Sir Thomas Burnett, as a landlord, he thought the tenants were highly favoured, and also that in Mr Ledingham they had a gentleman who gave good and wise counsel and had the welfare of the tenants at heart. As valuator for so many years on the Crathes Estate, he thought Mr Walker had always endeavoured to put on a fair rent. They hardly ever heard of any rents or farms being raised - there was once exception, that of his (Mr Hunter's) own - (laughter). Perhaps Mr Walker had given him his deserts. He did not think Mr Walker could have anticipated that there could be anything in the nature of the agricultural rates relief to make it up, and speaking on that subject lead him to say that he had heard a lot of bosh spoken when any legislation was brought about for the good of the tenants, and that it simply went into the pockets of the proprietors. That, he thought, was sheer rubbish, because he did not know of a farm on Deeside where relief was granted where they had been any enhanced rent, but on the contrary, he could point to many where there had been reductions. With all the privileges and advantages, the tenants on the Estate of Crathes had had it seemed to him peculiar that he did not know a single instance where a farmer had been able to retire with anything in the nature of a competency. It was simply due, he thought, to the great importation of foreign produce of all kinds, to preferential rates, and to Free Trade (laughter). With the assistance and encouragement they got from their proprietor and the words of encouragement they had got from Mr Walker, he was sure he spoke the sentiments of everyone on the Estate that they would all put their shoulder to the wheel to throw still more energy into their business so as to break up the fertility of the soil to the highest maximum, and that they would, like Mark Tapley, "try to be jolly even under adverse circumstances" (laughter and applause). Mr Hunter then returned thanks for the enthusiastic reception with which the toast had been received (applause).

Mr Mearns on behalf of the feuars, also replied to the toast. He said it was 39 years ago that he took off his first feu on the Estate of Crathes. As far as the factor and the feuars were concerned they had little to do together. He had worked on the Estate of Crathes as a slater for more than 40 years under Mr Davidson with the very greatest of pleasure. He had always found him very anxious that everything should be done straight with every man - both with employer and employed (applause). It afforded him the greatest pleasure to have an opportunity of saying so on that occasion. He had found Mr Davidson as an employer a judicious man who deserves the respect of everybody who had been accustomed to do business with him (applause).

Mr A T MacRobert Aberdeen, proposed the "Town and Trade of Banchory", and in doing so, referred to the prosperous condition that the town now found itself in, referring particularly to the briskness of the building trade.

Baillie Ross, in the absence through indisposition of Provost McHardy, suitably replied.

The Agricultural Industry

Mr Joseph Merson proceeded the toast of "Agricultural" and, in doing so, said it was usual on such occasions to refer to the depressed condition of agriculture, that he would like to refer them to an address given by Mr Duthie of Collynie last Saturday at a farm in the Garioch at one of the demonstrations in connection with the Agricultural College. The prevailing note in that address was wise and stimulating and Mr Duthie showed that he had faith in agriculture and faith in the possibilities of achieving success in agriculture in the future by proper and well directed efforts. They all agreed with Mr Hunter that the farmer's life was not a path of roses, and they all hoped that the near future may have better times in store for the agricultural industry (applause).

Mr W A Mitchell, Auchnagathie, in reply, said, he wished at the outset to say how gratified he was at being a guest at that Extra-ordinary meeting and demonstration. He had frequently had the honour of partaking of the hospitality of Banchory, but such an ovation as that seldom occurred, and he held it a great privilege to be there as a guest, and an honour to be asked to take part in the proceedings (applause). In offering a reply to the toast of agriculture he felt that it was a little difficult to do so without a tear in the eye (a laugh). Those of them that could look back to the first 20 or 25 years of Mr Davidson's office under the Burnett family, and remembered the prosperity of agriculture then as it affected both the proprietor and tenant, he thought they could look back to those times with feelings of regret that there was very little prospect of such prosperity occurring again. For the past quarter of a century they all knew very well that such a thing as agricultural prosperity had been almost an unknown quantity. With perhaps not a few adverse climatic seasons, with the constant introduction of all sorts of agricultural produce, with the rise in the cost of labour and its attendant requirements, and on account of their long lease systems by which they had not a corresponding fall on their rents, he thought that the living of the farmer had been almost a state of existence. They had difficulty in getting a remedy. There was very little immediate prospect of an improvement in the state of matters, for they saw a steady yearly increase of imports of all kinds of agricultural produce, which signified the diminution of prices, and they must also count up the high cost of living in all classes of the community; in fact, it had come to such a position that hardly any spirited young man who was not bound to it by family ties would remain and make agriculture his profession. Then the question arose - What about rural depopulation? He thought there was very sufficient reasons for this rural depopulation. But where was the remedy to be found? Perhaps there was a way out of it. The first essential in meeting the difficulty was that everyone should make an effort to keep the first quality of livestock, even down to poultry. He thought it was found from experience that the best quality was quite as easily - perhaps more easily - kept, than an inferior quality and they found a readier and better market. An essential to sow only the best seeds, and to use the best quality of manures, and those suitable for various qualities of soil on their farms. Above all those, there was not the slightest doubt that the strictest economy in management was one of the prime essentials towards success. There was some who thought the admission of Canadian live cattle would cure all their ills, but that was very questionable. Although it would be most advantageous to some, it would undoubtedly be injurious to others - (hear, hear and applause). Another thing now was that probably they were to have the forces of the air utilised in favour of agriculture (laughter). He would not venture an opinion on that, but it was afraid that the forces of the air would be found in the future as in the past somewhat volatile and not very much to be depended on (applause). This was a depressing subject, and he suggested that they should leave it, and say "be gone, dull care!" and let them give attention to enjoying themselves on that auspicious occasion (applause).

The toast of "The Clergy" was ably proposed by Mr James Cushnie; and Reverend James Hall, in reply, also joined in expressing personal appreciation of Mr Davidson's worth. Mr Davidson, he said, truly deserved that public recognition for long and faithful service on the lands of Leys, and for his worth and lovableness as a man, they esteemed him very highly as a parishioner, as a neighbour, and as a friend (applause). They were there that day from all points of the compass and he was sure that one and all of them were of opinion that their good friend Mr Davidson deserved all the kindness that could be shown to him. (applause).

Mr James Anderson gave the toast of "Law". Mr Alexander Ledingham BSc in reply said, He had now had the honour and pleasure of being legal assistant and adviser to Sir Thomas Burnett in the management of his estate for 15 years. It had been to him a light and agreeable task. The leading thought which had been in his mind that afternoon was that during those years he had never been asked to do a harsh thing, or even to say a sharp word to any tenant or crofter (applause). He did not know whether that came more from the kindly consideration of the laird or the sagacity and moderation of his adviser, Mr Walker, or the fair dealing of Mr Davidson, or whether it was from the high quality of the tenants themselves, but he believed that was a unique thing in the management of a great estate. He hoped those relations might long continue between the laird and the tenantry and the crofters, and there was every reason to believe they would. Personally he very cordially joined in the appreciation of his old friend, Mr Davidson, with whom he had had most happy and pleasant contact during all those years. (applause). When a man had lived more than 50 years active life in one neighbourhood, he could get no higher honour than such as was given him on that occasion when his neighbours and friends, and those people who had been associated with him, met to say, "you are an honest, true man, and we respect you". They all hoped Mr Davidson might still live for years to enjoy the friendship and respect they had shown him that night (applause).

Other toasts were "Education", proposed by Mr James Hunter, and replied to by Mr Thomas Menzies; "Friends from a distance", proposed by Baillie Ross and responded to by Mr James Taylor, Toux. The health of the Chairman was cordially pledged, on the call of Mr James Thomson.

During the afternoon the toast list was interspersed with songs. Mr Scott Hunter presiding at the piano. The proceedings which were admirably arranged by Mr John Cooper, Leys, were throughout most enthusiastic and successful.

It may be mentioned that the silver salver was supplied by Mr George Duff, Watchmaker and Jeweller, Netherkirkgate, Aberdeen, whilst Messrs James Hardy & Co, Aberdeen, supplied the brooch and bracelet.

In the evening a ball was held in the hall, which was largely attended and proved most enjoyable. The music was supplied by Mr Robertson's band.

Leys Estate - Appendix II

Burnett Items and Articles with Burnett Heraldry

During the past few years, a small number of 'Burnett' items have been added to our collection at Crathes. These include a few copies of the Spalding edition of 'The Family of Burnett of Leys'.

Earlier mentioned is the Burnett of Barns heraldic display which now hangs in the family room in the Castle. I have managed to acquire a few early editions of some of the works of Bishop Gilbert Burnett and these are also displayed in that room.

Majorie Hutton, a descendant of James Burnett, Lord Monboddo, gave me several items associated with her brilliant and eccentric ancestor. Include were his 'bullet' teapot and plate tea tray as well as his crown Derby china inkstand albeit without the top.

Geordie Burnett-Stuart of Crichie found and has given to me a famille rose biscuit armorial plate which would have been part of the service made in China and commissioned by his ancestor, John Burnett of Countesswells or Dens who made his fortune in Aberdeen as a linen merchant. Since this able and philanthropic eighteenth century businessman gave away two-thirds of everything he owned, it is of little surprise that almost none of it remains in family hands.

I was offered and decided to acquire a jug which had been presented by Thomas Burnett, Younger of Leys, to his political agent *"as a mark of the high sense Mr Burnett entertains of the zeal and ability with which Mr Christian discharged the duties of Mr Burnett's principal agent in his contest in 1832 for the Representation of Kincardineshire in the first Reform Parliament".* The jug also describes the details of the contest. *"At the First Election under the Reform Act the Candidates for the Representation in Parliament of the County of Kincardineshire were Major General the Honorable Hugh Arbuthnott the Representative in several Parliaments under the former system and an opponent of the Act and Thomas Burnett, Esquire Younger of Leys under many and great disadvantages. 269 electors voted for Mr Burnett and endeavoured, though for the time unsuccessfully, to vindicate the Independence of Kincardineshire. 388 electors voted for General Arbuthnott".*

Many family pictures were destroyed by fire in 1966. One of these was of my great grandfather, Sir Thomas Burnett, and of which the artist had made a copy for Loadt Burnett's family, the Cumyns of Rattray. The late Phillip Cumyn generously commissioned a copy of this for me by the artist Anna Zinkeisen.

When Aberdeenshire County Council vacated their buildings in Union Terrace in the 1970s, two large portraits of Thomas Burnett of Monboddo 1773-1854, who was County Clerk of Aberdeenshire for many years and his son who was Clerk of Supply were offered to the nearest members of the subjects' families. Since closer relations decided that they were unable to hang these very substantial pictures, I accepted them. Thomas Burnett was a founding partner of Burnett and Reid, Solicitors in Aberdeen and I have lent the pictures to that firm to grace their offices. Not far away, in the Northern and university Club hang two full-length portraits of George III and his Queen Charlotte by Sir Joshua Reynolds. These were moved from the castle in the nineteenth century but there is no record in either camp as to whether they were a gift or on loan. It was earlier assumed that the paintings were by Allam Ramsay but in 1976 the club secretary told me that they had been advised that they were painted by Sir Joshua Reynolds.

I might include here two 'estate' acquisitions. I acquired a copy of Scott Skinner's *'Miller of Hirn'* original fiddle music and Alexander was presented with the original Crathes Station platform sign, on his twenty fifth birthday, by his godfather, Angus Pelham Burn.

In addition to the above, a few family items (mostly now competition trophies) have been moved to more useful homes but remain within family ownership. These include a large silver vase for Banchory Squash Club, a large silver cup and a large amorial salver for the Deesider Indoor Sporting Club and a salver at the Inchmarlo Golf Club. The former estate gardens contest trophy is now competed for annually on the football field by the local primary schools.

Leys Estate - Appendix III

Extract from Leys Esate – Acquisitions 1900 - 2000

1967 Shops in Dee Street
Broomfield Farm
1971 Fordie, Cormoir and Braeside Farms
Meikle Maldron Farm
1971 Mains of Craigmyle Farm
1971 Former Deeside Railway Line
Inchmarlo Estate
Pitcullen Farm
Thistleycrook Farm
1994 Berry Hill and Kilduthie Woodlands
1997 Ambleside House, Silverbank
Former Auction Mart, Silverbank

Extract from Leys Estate – Dispositions 1900 – 2000

1900 Land at Corsee for Nordrach-on-Dee Sanitorium (Glen O' Dee)
1905 Land at Kineskie for Banchory Golf Course
1911 Land at Kineskie for Banchory Drill Hall
1921 Land at Inchmarlo Road for War Memorial
1923 Land for Invercannie Water Treatment Works
1925 Land for Churchyard
1929 Land for Crathes Public Hall
1946 Woodend Estate
1947 Cairnton Estate
1948 Land for Silverbank Sawmill
Land at Silverbank for Kincardine Auction Mart
1950 Moorland at Hill of Fare
1952 Woodland at Brathens and Hill of Fare
Crathes Castle, Policies and Farms at Brathens
1952 Land at Silverbank for new Sewage Works
1953 Mills of Drum
Kineskie Fishings
Land at Silverbank for Council Housing
1955 Lower Crathes Fishings
1957 Nethermills Farm
1959 New Banchory Farm
1962 Tillybrake Farm
1967 Station Pool Fishings

1968	Hattonburn Croft House
1969	Land at Tillybrake for new Slaughterhouse
1970	Loanhead Smithy
1973	Bush Croft House
1974	Quiddiesmill Croft House
1975	Deeview Cottage
1976	Lochhead Cottage
	Upper Lochton
1977	Harestone Cottage
	Wellhead Croft House
1978	Barehillock Croft House
	Broomfield Farm
	Hattonburn Lodge
	Todholes Farmhouse
1979	Land for housing at Tillybrake
	Craigton Farmhouse
1980	Greendams Farmhouse
	Myrebird Farmhouse
	East Coy Croft House
	Harestone Cottage
1981	Craigton Farm Steading
	Quiddiesmill Farm Steading
	Drumfrennie Cottage South
	Burn of Bennie House
1984	West Burnside of Coy Croft House
	Little Minklets Cottage
	East Burnside of Coy
1985	Little Minklets Farm Steading
	Neuk Croft Cottage
1986	Dowalty Farmhouse and Steading
	Burn of Bennie Croft
	Wickerinn Farmhouse
1987	Drumshalloch Croft House
	Hirn Smithy Cottage
	Upper Lochton Cottage
1988	Ley Croft House
1989	Land for Council Housing, Burnett Terrace
1990	Coy Farm Steading
1991	Wickerinn Farm Steading
	North Hirn Farm Steading
1992	Crathes Station ground
	Milton Cottage

1999 North Hirn Farmhouse
North Candiglirach Steading

Leys Estate - Appendix IV

Valuation Roll of the County of Kincardine						
Properties of Sir Thomas Burnett						
Whitsunday 1900 to Whitsunday 1901						
	*	Annual Value				
	**	Feu Duty or Ground Annual				
Description of Subject		Tenant (Occupier if other than Tenant)	Yearly rent or Annual Value			
Estate of Leys						
Crathes Castle, Gardens, and Offices		Proprietor		160	0	0
Home Farm and House		do		171	10	0
Policies		do		20	0	0
Woodlands and Muir		do		184	0	0
Shootings		do		25	0	0
Market Customs		The Stonehaven Auction Co		1	0	0
Forester's House and Croft		Proprietor (James McGregor)	*	7	0	0
Overseer's, House and Croft, Neuk Croft		Jas. Rennie, Postman & Crofter		13	0	0
Gamekeeper's House and Croft		Proprietor (James Fraser)	*	10	0	0
Shootings, Low Ground (part of)		Thos Turner Farley, Cairton		25	0	0
Grouse Moor and remainder of Low Ground Shootings		Proprietor		120	0	0
Woodend House and Garden		Mrs Harriet Leslie		97	0	0
Farm and House of Hattonburn		Mrs Isabella & John Anderson		178	19	10
Do. Craigtown		Samuel Ross, Farmer		75	4	2
Do. Invercanny		Reps of Alex Duncan, do		51	0	0
Do. Newmill and part of Myrebird		Wm Adam Bush		60	15	6
Do. Bush and Minklets		William Adam, Farmer		183	0	0
Do. Pittenkerrie		William Davidson, Do		137	1	2

Subject		Tenant or Occupier				
Do. Coy		James Coutts, do		67	7	0
Do. Loch-head		Alexander McNicol, do		50	10	0
Farm and House, Upper Brathens		Miss Margaret Davidson, Farmer		81	5	0
Do. Lochton of Leys		George Donald, Sen., and Wm Donald, Joint tenants		80	0	0
Do. New Banchory		George Hunter, Farmer		52	16	0
Do. Bohill		George Donald, Jun., Farmer		32	0	0
Do. Upper Mills, Crathes		Charles Hunter, Farmer		48	0	9
Do. Upper Mills, Crathes		do.(James Ligertwood, Grieve)	*	4	0	0
Do. Oldmill of Hirn		Wm Thomson, Farmer		73	0	0
House, Oldmill of Hirn		do(John Thomson Labourer)		2	0	0
Do. Do.		do. Vacant		0	0	0
Do. Hirn		Proprietor(William Caird,Gamekeeper)	*	5	0	0
Farm and House, Drugham		Robert Leighton, Farmer		60	15	0
Do. Baldarroch		James Leighton, do.		84	5	0
Do. Drumshalloch		James Leask, do		46	1	0
Do. Myrebird		William Paterson, do		30	4	0
Do. Kilduthie		James Anderson, do		158	17	6
House, Mill, & Croft, Meal Mill of Hirn		Peter Massie, Miller & Crofter		24	0	0
Farm and House of Dowalty		William Humble, Farmer		73	10	9
Do. Tillybrake		Joseph Strachan, Flesher		55	0	0
Do.Birkenbaud and Mill of Crathes		Miss Isabella Philip, Farmer		63	11	6
Farm and House of Upper Leys and part of Burdshillock		William Jolly, Farmer		77	4	6
Croft and House, Broomshillock		John Park, Crofter		10	13	0
Farm and House, Candieshill		Charles Gilbert, Farmer		30	0	0
Do. Ley and Burdshillock		John Cooper, Farmer		132	7	0
Faru, Kineskie (part of)		John&Jas Berry, Hotelkeepers		6	0	0
Farm and House, North Pittenkerrie		James Ross, Farmer		43	1	0
Do. North Leys		John Davidson, Factor		159	17	5
Do. Drumfrenny		Alex. McNicol, Jnr, Farmer		70	16	0
Do. North Hirn		Mrs Mary Taylor, do.		83	10	0
Croft and House, Neuk		William Tough, Crofter		18	0	0
Farm and House of Wicker Inn		James Thomson, Farmer		45	5	0
Quarry, Hill of Fare		do.		200	0	0
House at Craigton Quarry		William Barclay, Quarrier		5	0	0
do. do.		James Leighton, do.		5	0	0
do. do.		George Begg, do.		5	0	0
do. do.		John Lawie, Engine Driver		5	0	0
do. do.		James Cooper, Quarrier		5	0	0

Subject		Tenant or Occupier				
do. do.		John F. Thomson, do		4	0	0
do. do.		Alexander clark, Labourer		5	0	0
do. do.		James Ross, do		4	0	0
do. do.		William Grant, do		5	0	0
do. do.		William Blackhall, do		4	0	0
do. do.		Alex. Clark, Engine Driver		5	0	0
do. do.		William Mackie, Quarrier		5	0	0
do. do.		John Reid, Blacksmith		5	0	0
Farm and House, Nether Mills of Drum		Adam Todd, Farmer		123	10	0
Do. South Hirn		James Thomson, do		173	14	0
Do. Woodend		David Murray, do		65	10	0
Do. Woodend of Trustack		William Leask, do		25	10	0
Do. West Brathens, and ……………………..part of Nether Brathens		Reps. Of William Wilson, do.		85	15	0
Saw and Turning Mills, Invercanny		Mrs Mary Gertrude Duncan, Wood Merchant		23	0	0
Meal Mill and House, do.		do.		18	0	0
House at Mills of do		do. (Geo Fyfe, Sawmiller)		5	0	0
do. Do		do. (Charles Fowler, Carter)		4	0	0
House and Garden, Trustack		George Tough, Forester		4	15	0
Land, Silverbank		Alex. & George Paterson, Wood Merchants, Glasgow		24	0	0
Croft and House, Silverbank		John Ewen, Market Gardener(Harry Shand, Farm Servant)	**	25	0	0
Do. and Smithy, Neuk		Robert W Duncan, Blacksmith		15		0
Farm and House, Nether Minklets		Mrs Calder Duncan, Farmer		60	5	0
Croft and House, Brucklebog		Cumming, Birnie, Crofter		11	3	
Do. Lochton		William Marr, do		3	0	0
Do. Hill of Trustack		Mrs Agnes Yeoman, do		8	3	0
Do. Craigtown		Farquharson Hadden, do		8	2	0
Do. Bridgefoot of Invercanny		Mrs Mary Gertrude Duncan, Invercanny(James Hay,Crofter)		12	10	0
Do. Brucklebog		Thomas Skene, Crofter		22	3	0
Do. Do		David Adam, do		18	5	2
Do. Drumfrennie		Francis Tough, do		10	13	0
Do. Hill of Coy		John Gordon, do		11	0	0
Do. Easter Myrebird		James McRobbie, do		11	10	0
Do. Craigtown		John Littlejohn, do		21	0	0
Do. Gallowhillock		John Duncan, do		18	10	0
Do. East Brathens		William Ewen, do		9	2	0
Do. Lochton		John Leighton, do		21	0	11
Do. Burnside of Coy		Reps.ofGeorge Masson, Crofter		18	10	0

Subject		Tenant or Occupier				
Do. East Burnside of Coy		William Moir, Crofter		15	3	0
Do. Hill of Trustack		Donald Grant, do		4	1	0
Do. Cairnton		William Mitchell, do		23	0	0
Do. Newton of Leys		James McIntosh, do		13	18	0
House and Yard, Hill of Coy		Alex Middleton, Labourer		4	0	0
Do. Do		Francis Lawson, do		4	2	0
Croft and House of Loch-head		Thos Carnie, Quarrier&Crofter		7	3	0
Do. Lochton		James Thomson, Carpenter		14	10	0
Do. Do		John Ross, Crofter		14	17	6
Do. Do		Thomas Tough, do		10	6	6
Do. Do		Robert Fraser, do		10	2	2
Do. Do		John Gibson, do		4	11	6
Do. Do		Reps of Alex.Carnie, do		4	1	3
Do. Do		David Scott, do		12	6	0
Strachan's Croft and House		William Donald, do		10	0	0
Croft and House, Birkenbaud		William Smith, do		16	10	0
Do. Hill of Trustack		Alex Durward, do		8	10	0
Do. Clayholes		Thos T. Farley, Cairnton		10	2	0
Do. Burn of Benny		Francis Lindsay, Crofter		31	16	8
Do. Do		William Leighton's Reps		10	2	0
Do. Myrebird		Mrs Tough, Crofter		6	12	0
Do. Pantick		Reps. Of John Ross, Crofter		10	3	0
Do. Hill of Coy		James Fraser, Crofter		12	11	6
Do. Drumshalloch		William Calder, Crofter		13	0	0
Do. Hattonburn		Robert Adam, do		7	8	0
Do. Bush		John Paterson, do		7	1	2
Do. Brathens		Alexander Stephenson, do		6	12	0
Do. Kilduthie		John Tough, do		1	11	0
Do. Hill of Trustack		James Collie, do		5	4	0
House and Shop, Drumfrenny		Mrs Jane Burnett, Merchant		5	2	0
Do and Croft, Brucklebog		William Smith, Crofter		5	1	6
Do and Do, Broomhillock		William Donald, Labourer		4	0	9
Do and Do, Burdshillock		George Gibson, Crofter		4	1	6
Do and Do, Leightwood		Reps.of Wm.Lawie, Labourer		3	0	9
Do and Garden, do		Francis Gibson, do		6	0	0
House, Hill of Trustack		Occupier: Ruinous		0		
Do Clayhills and Invercanny		James Fiddes, Crofter		5	6	6
Do Pittenkerrie		Robert Esson, Labourer		4	1	6
Do do		William Fraser, Surfaceman		4	1	6
Do Lightwood		John Littlejohn Jun., Clerk		6	0	0
Do St Duthie		Alex. Thomson, Quarryman		5	0	0
Do Newbrae		Mrs Isabella Philip		1	0	0
Do New Banchory		Isaac Wright, Labourer		2	1	0

Subject		Tenant or Occupier				
Do Crathes		Proprietor(Robert Bartlett, Coachman)	*	4	0	0
Croft and House, Crathes		Miss Annabella Smith, Grocer		4	19	0
House, Smithy and Croft, Hirn		Edward Gill, Blacksmith		13	0	0
House and Yard, Trustack		Alexander Morrison, Tailor		7	3	0
Sand Pit at Crathes Station		Great N of Scotland Railway		32	3	0
Do Silverstripe		George Wilson, Builder		12	0	0
Shootings, Cairnton and Trustack		Thomas T Farley, Cairnton Cottage		39	0	0
Spring Salmon Fishings, Kineskie		Proprietor		8	0	0
Do Do Lower Crathes		Dr Lawson, Corsee, Banchory		50	0	0
Autumn Salmon Fishings, do		Col. E. Villiers, 44 Lennox Gardens, London		80	0	0
Autumn Salmon Fishings, do		Proprietor		80	0	0
Do Kineskie and Crathes(part of)		James Hunter, Kirkton		35	0	0
Fishings, Invercanny		T.Turner Farley, Wartnaby Hall, Melton-Mowbray		100	0	0
Do Cairnton		do. Do.		150	0	0
Cairnton Cottage, Garden and Land		do. Do.		100	0	0
Fishings, Woodend		Richard Woodlay, Burrows		220	0	0
House, Crathes		Proprietor (Alex Gilbert Grieve)	*	4	0	0
Do. East Lodge		Proprietor (John Milne Woodman)	*	4	0	0
Do.		Proprietor (James Birse, Sawmiller)	*	4	0	0
Do.		Proprietor (John Fraser, Gardener)	*	4	0	0
Do. West Lodge		Proprietor (George Jolly, Labourer)				
House on Farm of Hattonburn		Miss Isabella&John Anderson				
		(John Rettie, Cattleman)	*	2	10	0
Do. Do.		Miss Isabella&John Anderson				
		(Alex Peters, Farm Serv.)	*	3	0	0
Do. Craigtown		Samuel Ross				
		(James Mitchell Quarry Worker)	*	5	0	0
Do. Newmill		William Adam(Wm Low, Farm Grieve)	*	4	10	0
Do. Myrebird		William Adam(Alex.Harrow, Labourer)	*	4	10	0
Do. Minklets		William Adam(Mrs Margaret Davidson)	*	4	0	0
Do. Bush		William Adam(Wm Keillor,Cattleman)	*	4	0	0
Do. Minklets		William Adam(John Webster, do)	*	4	0	0
Do. Do.		Wm Adam (Charles Geddes, Horseman)		4	0	0
Do. Pittenkerrie, Glassel		Wm Davidson(Jno Cruickshank,Farm Serv)		4	0	0
Do. Upper Brathens, do		Miss Margaret Davidson				

Subject		Tenant or Occupier				
		(John Archibald Farm Servant)	*	4	0	0
Do. Do		Miss Margaret Davidson				
		(Robert Taylor, Quarrier)	*	4	0	0
Do. Baldarrock, by Crathes		James Leighton				
		(AlexShaw, Farm Servant)	*	2	10	0
Do. East Baldarroch		James Leighton				
		(Mrs Ross(Widow))	*	4	0	0
House of Birkenbaud, Crathes		Miss Isabella Philip				
		(Alex Calder,Postman)	*	5	0	0
Do. Mill of Crathes		Miss Isabella Philip(Vacant)		3	0	0
House on Farm of Ley		John Cooper(Alex Clark, Grieve)		4	0	0
do. do do		John Cooper				
		(Wm.Brown Farm Servant)		4	0	0
House, Harestone		John Davidson, Factor				
		(Wm Davidson, Grieve)		4	0	0
do		John Davidson, Factor				
		(Wm Ewen,Farm Servant)		4	0	0
House on Farm of Wicker Inn, Banchory		James Thomson				
		(Geo.Henderson, Contractor)		4	0	0
Do. Do		James Thomson(vacant)		2	10	0
Do. Do		James Thomson				
		(Jas CG Thomson, Farm Servant)		4	0	0
Do. Nether Mills of Drum , Crathes		Adam Todd				
		(James Duguid, Farm Servant)		4	0	0
Do. Do		Adam Todd				
		(Don.Murchison, Gardener)		4	0	0
House, Netherton of Brathens		William Wilson(vacant)		4	0	0
House at Mills of Invercanny		Mrs Mary Gertrude Duncan(vacant)		5	10	0
Do. Do		Mrs Mary Gertrude Duncan				
		(Hugh McCondach, Farm Servant)		4	0	0
Do. Do		Mrs Mary Gertrude Duncan				
		(Robrt Hall, Carter)		5	0	0
House, Clayholes		Thomas T Farley				
		(David Rae, Gardener)		5	0	0
do. Do.		Thomas T Farley (vacant)		3	0	0
do. Brathens		Thomas T Farley				
		(Robert Milne, Gamekeeper)		5	0	0
do. Trustack		Alexander Morrison, Tailor				
		(Mrs Isabella Milne, Gamekeeper)		3	0	0
do. Dowalty, Crathes		William Humble,				
		(Alex. Paul, Farm Servant)		3	0	0
do. Tillybrake		Joseph Strachan				

Subject		Tenant or Occupier				
		(George Paul, Farm Servant)		3	0	0
Woodlands		Proprietor		15	0	0
Land, part of Farm of New Banchory		George Hunter, Farmer		40	0	0
Do do. Tillybrake		Joseph Strachan, Butcher		5	0	0
Land and House, Farm of Kineskie		John&James Berry, Hotel-keepers		88	5	0
Land at Mavisbank		James M. Tracey		1	0	0
Do Banchory		George Hunter, Farmer		8	11	0
House, Townhead		Wm Mackie, Blacksmith		8	2	6
Old Schoolhouse, St Machar Cottage		Miss Mary Wm McDonald		15	8	6
Cottage and Garden, Old School		Mrs Jane Young		13	8	6
House, Tillybrake Cottage		Wm Tough, Sawmiller		4	0	0
do. Do.		George Niven, Labourer		4	0	0
do. Do.		Amos Murison, do		4	0	0
do. Do.		Robert Aitken, Shoemaker		4	0	0
do. Do.		William Howes, Labourer		6	10	0
do. Do.		George R Mason		6	10	0
Spring Salmon Fishings, Kineskie		R. Upton, Faskell		42	0	0
House on Farm of Kineskie		James Berry, Jun				
		(Jas Taylor, Farm Grieve)	*	10	0	0

Leys Estate - Appendix V

Leys Estate Tenants
January 1st 2000

LEYS ESTATE

NAME	TENANT or OCCUPIER
FARMS	
Hattonburn	Hattonburn Farm Partnership (Mr I McDonald)
Glashmore	Glashmore Farm Partnership per I & A Beaton
GRAZINGS	
Upper Lochton	Upper Lochton (Vacant)
	Mr L Poskitt
	Mrs Linda Easton
	Mr A H Dickson
	Drumfrennie F P per J Adams
Old Mill of Hirn	Drumfrennie FP per J Adams
Woodfield	Ms J Canning
Crathes	Mr A Hutcheon

Old Mill Of Hirn	In-hand
HOUSES	
South Hirn F/H (J&F)	Mr & Mrs Hoyle
Bohill F/H	Mr George Howitt
Quiddiesmill F/H	Mr R McKay
No 2 S. Hirn Cottage	Mr J Stewart
Woodbine	Mr and Mrs Ron Warren
Old Mill of Hirn	Mr O'Brien and Ms E Gerber
Hattonburn F/H	Mr A Warne
No 1 South Hirn Cottage	Mr Maxwell
Kilduthie F/H	Mr and Mrs Bath
Hogshillock F/H	Mr J Ross
No 2 Kilduthie Cottage	John Irvine
Upper Lochton Croft	Miss J Crawford
No 1 Kilduthie Cottage	K Smith (Crathes Farms)
Lochton Cottage	Robin Baxter
North Hirn F/H	advertised for sale
The Neuk	renovation
OTHERS	
Uppermills Shed	Banchory Contractors Ltd
Garage Stances	Mr D Black
(Burnett Terrace)	Mr R Cranna
	Mrs Beaton
	Ms K Gillanders
	Mr W Murray
	Mr M Robertson
	Mr W Hay
Old Slaughterhouse Store	Mr J Merchant
Shootings	PEW Syndicate
	Uppermills (A Brown)
Minklets Yard	Banchory Contrctors Ltd
Minklets	Banchory Contrctors Ltd
Milton Football Pitch	St Ternan Football Club
No 5 Dee Street	Mrs S Watt
No 3 Dee Street	Mr Cruickshank
Mill of Hirn (Studio)	Mr M Allen
Craigton Quarries	-
Hirn Tip	Banchory Contractors Ltd
St Nicholas House	Strutt and Parker
	Bancon Developments Ltd

BANCHORY TRUST

FARMS

Baldarroch (House & Bldgs)	Mrs Maguire
Brucklebog Croft	Mr G Carnie
Candyglirach Farm	Mr E Jaffray & Son
Harestone Farm	Mr N Barclay
Wickerinn F.P. (J&F)	Wickerin FP (M Steel)
Bohill & Catterloch F.P. (J&F)	Catterloch FP per AM Allardyce
Kilduthie Steading	Wickerinn FP
Greendams Grazing	Mr & Mrs G Ross

HOUSES

West Brucklebog	Mr R Gray
No 1 Tillybrake Cottage	renovation
No 2 Tillybrake Cottage	Frank Dey
No 3 Tillybrake Cottage	Mr I Scott
No 4 Tillybrake Cottage	Mr W Davey
No 2 Pantoch Cottage	Mrs Sim
No 3 Pantoch Cottage	Mr Robert Lawrie
East Birkenbaud	Mr K Hennesey
No 5 Craigton Cottage	Mr Anderson
Kashentroch	Mr B Warren
Glashmore F/H	Mr and Mrs Isaac
Dower House	Vallourec Oil & Gas (Co Mr & Mrs Lancry)
East Brucklebog	Mr G McCormack
No 9 Craigton Cottage	Mr Farquhar and Miss Scott
No 8 Craigton Cottage	Miss E Samuels
No 7 Craigton Cottage	Miss I Mackie
No 6 Craigton Cottage	Miss S Hochscheid
No 4 Craigton Cottage	Mr M Burns
No 3 Craigton Cottage	Mr D Shaw
No 2 Craigton Cottage	Mr and Mrs Crowhurst
No 1 Craigton Cottage	Miss J Leatham
Coy F/H	Mr W Kelly
Candieshill Cottage	Mr W McKenzie
Baldarroch Cottage	Banchory Contractors Ltd
Broomhillock	Mr K Baikie
Brucklebog Croft	Banchory Contractors Ltd
Druggam F/H	Mr N Mathewson
Lightwood Cottage	Llewellyn Ryland Ltd c/o Mr Crawford Keir
Mid Coy	Banchory Contractors Ltd
Milton F/H	Capital C Catering
Minklets F/H	Mrs S Archibald
No 1 Pantoch	Leys Estate (Jim Forbes)
Hirn Cottage	Vacant
West Craigton Cottage	Banchory Contractors Ltd
Birkenbaud	(Brian Sim)
Candyglirach Croft	Dr G Polhill

OTHERS

Milton Restaurant	Capital C Catering
Milton Shop	Atholl Countrywear
Milton Studio	Mrs C Wright
Milton Sawmill and Bothy	Miss K Clark
Druggam Recording Studio	Hold the Frame (c/o M Allen)
East Bruckelbog Studio	Mrs L Hislop
Candieshill Store	Leys Estate
Druggam Steading Store	W Young
Skirmish	Mr E Brooks
Garage Stance	Mr B Hay

AJA BURNETT

FARMS

Uppermills F.P. (J&F)	Uppermills FP (Mr A Beaton)
Burn o' Bennie	Fiona Terry & Murray Reid (grazing)
	Fiona Terry & Murray Reid (house/steading)
	A Coutts
	C McIntosh
	M Tasker
	G Peter
Bush & Newmills	A Cruickshank
Drumshalloch	Mrs A Mackintosh
Lochton of Leys	Mr A Coutts
The Neuk/Ley/Part Woodend	R & R Adams
Bush Croft Fields	Mr A McIntosh
Woodend Farmland	Mr R Adams
Drumfrennie F.P. (J&F)	Drumfrennie FP per J Adams

GRAZINGS

Bush Grazings	Vacant

HOUSES

St Duthac Cottage	Mr A Robb
Uppermills Cottage	Mr W Adams
Lochton of Leys Cottage	Banchory Contractors Ltd
Drumfrennie Croft Cottage	Mr C Gordon
Lilac Cottage	Mr A Strachan
N. Drumfrennie Cottage	Mr D M Davidson
Ley Farm Cottage	Messrs Reeves

Woodend F/H	Miss S Hargreaves
Bush F/H	Mr and Mrs Theodore Ripoll
Ambleside	Ms Angela Kellas
Bush Cottage	Paul Cruickshank

OTHERS

Ambleside	Robert Wiseman & Son Ltd
Garage Stance	Mr Meany
Crathes School Football Ground	GRC Aberdeenshire Council
Woodend Steading (Barn)	WAA (Rent waived)
Bush Farm Steading	Part Vacant

<u>FORDIE TRUST</u>

FARMS

Fordie Farm	C Wilson
Pitcullen Store	CIBA Agriculture
Shooting	Torphins Syndicate (J Turnbull)

HOUSES

Thistleycrook	Mr and Mrs Drysdale
Thistleycrook Cottage	Pamela Garden
Cormoir (Fordie Trust)	Mr A Menzies

16

BURNETT BURIAL PLACES

Eileen A. Bailey

People will not look forward to posterity who never look backward to their ancestors (Edmund Burke, 1790)

Fig. 16.1 A corner of the Burnett family burial ground, Crathes Castle. 2000 (Bailey)

All churchyards and memorial inscriptions are liable to become victims of the ravages of time and the elements and sadly sometimes also by the destructive hand or neglect of man. It is important, therefore, that at least the location of identifiable memorial inscriptions is noted at the year 2000 lest they do not survive. Some of the burial places have been visited and photographed for the Burnett archive. It should be remembered that the only indication of some burials will be an entry in a church record and of others there will be no surviving record. The location of individual burial places has, where possible, been included within the text of the genealogy chapters. The following are included for general guidance.

BURNETT OF BARNS AND FARNINGTON

The burial place of many of the Burnetts of Burnetland and Barns was at the parish church of Manor.

BURNETT OF ARDROSS

The effigy of a knight in armour in the parish church of Kilconquhar, Fife, is said to record the resting place of John Burnett of Ardross.

BURNETT OF LEYS

There is a burial place known as the 'Crathes enclosure' in the churchyard of St. Ternan, Banchory.

There is a private family burial ground at Crathes, close to the House of Crathes. (Fig.16.1)

The main burial place of Burnetts of Leys was the churchyard of St. Nicholas in Aberdeen.

BURNETT OF KEMNAY

The burial place of a number of the Burnetts of Kemnay is in the churchyard of the parish church of Kemnay.

BURNETT OF CRIMOND

Bishop Gilbert Burnett and his son Thomas Burnett were buried in the vault of St. James's Church, Clerkenwell, London.

BURNETT OF MONBODDO

The churchyard of the parish church of Fordoun contains the main burial place of the Burnetts of Monboddo. Lord Monboddo and his daughter Elizabeth/Eliza Burnett are buried in the churchyard of Greyfriars in Edinburgh in the burial lair of Lord Grant of Elchies.

BURNETT OF ELRICK

The family burial place of the early members of this family was the old burial ground, formerly known as Monycabock, Newmachar where no inscriptions are now visible. John Burnet, 1st of Elrick and his two wives were buried within the church of St. Nicholas, Aberdeen. The carved gravestone (Fig.7.1) was, by 1890, lying in the churchyard close to the burial place of John Burnett of Elrick who died in 1748 and whose marble memorial stone was set into the wall.

BURNETT OF SHEDDOCKSLEY

The memorial inscription of Andrew Burnett of Sheddocksley is now located in the floor of St. Mary's Aisle of St. Nicholas Church, Aberdeen but was formerly behind the pulpit of the church. After a fire in 1874 it was removed from the church to the churchyard before being placed in its current position.

BURNETT OF KIRKHILL

The memorial inscription of Alexander Burnett, 1st Laird of Kirkhill, is on the Burnett stone in St. Mary's Aisle of St. Nicholas Church, Aberdeen. This stone also records the death of his wife, his father Thomas Burnett and of Andrew Burnett of Sheddocksley.

BURNETT-STUART

Some memorial inscriptions of members of the Burnett-Stuart family are to be found in the cemetery of Old Deer.

BURNETT-RAMSAY

In St. Ternan churchyard, Banchory, there were several memorial inscriptions of Burnett-Ramsays which were noted by Rev.Charles Rogers in his *Monuments and Memorial Inscriptions of Scotland* published in 1872. These murals were set into the east end of the north wall of the old churchyard.

INNES

Margaret Anne (Irvine) Innes, daughter-in-law of Thomas Innes of Learney and Helen Christian Burnett, was buried at Echt Churchyard.
Some of the Innes of Learney family including Thomas Innes, his wife Helen Christian Burnett and Thomas Innes, Lord Lyon, are buried at Kincardine O' Neil churchyard.

CUMINE

A number of the Cumine family who are linked through marriage to Burnetts are buried at Rattray, near Peterhead. Some Cumines and Burnetts are buried at Old Machar, Aberdeen.

LUMSDEN

Several of the Lumsden family, of Belhelvie Lodge, are buried in a family enclosure at the churchyard at Belhelvie.

Memorial inscriptions in many of the churchyards in Aberdeenshire have been recorded and published in booklets by Aberdeen and North-east Scotland Family History Society. The Scottish Genealogy Society has published, as one book, the recorded pre-1855 memorial inscriptions in the churchyards of Kincardineshire.

INDEX

A

Abbey
  Battle 1
  of Arbroath 32
  of Melrose 33
Abbey of Arbroath 36
Abbey of Melrose 7
Abbot of Arbroath 36
  Bernard 32
Aberdee 42
Aberdeen
  Bishop of 12
Aberdeen Educational Trust 256
Aberdeen Endowments Trust 256
Aberdeenshire26, 28, 52, 65, 67, 77, 82, 83, 90, 92, 93, 103, 106, 107, 112, 113, 114, 116, 118, 125, 126, 133, 146, 147, 164, 167, 187, 197, 233, 237, 245, 248, 250, 251, 252, 253, 255, 258, 259, 260, 264, 268, 299, 303, 331, 344, 348
Aberdein
  Alexander 62
  Robert 62, 63
Aberdein of Cairnbulg
  Alexander 60, 62
Aberdein of Garvocklea
  Francis 124
Aberdein or Burnett
  Annie 124
Aberdon 42
Aboyne Gathering 315
Abraham of London 42
Adam
  John, in Bush Farm 280
Aedie
  George 132
AGRICULTURE
  on Leys Estate 277
Aitken
  Rev. John 59
Alexander
  Violet 20
Alexander I 225
  King 6
Alexander II 225
Alexander of Hawkes Bay
  Alexander 20
Alexander or Burnett
  Elizabeth 20
Alexander Park 304
Allardyce
  James 100
Allardyce of Allardyce
  John 47
Alrichsey 3
Amherst of Hackney
  Lady 80
Anderson
  Rev. William 277
Anderson of Hallyards
  William 21
Angevin 7
Anglo Saxons 2
Anglo-Saxon 1, 7
Angus
  Earl of 49, 154
aqueducts 301
Arbeadie 64, 300
Arbroath Abbey 32
Arbuthnot
  Katherine 188
  Robert 90
ARBUTHNOT MUSEUM 202
Arbuthnot of Pitcarlies
  Robert 38
  Robert, 1st of Fiddes 44
Arbuthnot of that Ilk
  Sir Robert 38
Arbuthnot or Burnett
  Helen 46, 90
  Jean 49

Katherine 44
Margaret 59
Arbuthnot or Gordon
Jean 49
Arbuthnott
Arms of 255
Gen. Hugh 65
Archbishop
Burnett 11
Archbishop of Glasgow 12
Archbishop of the Picts 228
Archbishop Sharp *See* Sharp, Archbishop
Ardhuncart 292
Ardiherauld Castle 262
Ardmeallie 259
Ardross
Fife 23
Argentina 105
Ariel 65
Arlesey 3
Armenian 167
Armorial
Balfour of Denmiln 177
Centlemen's Arms 177
Dunvegan 177
Forman Lyon Office 177
Forman of Luthrie 177
Hamilton 177
Hector le Breton 177
Lindsay of the Mount 177
Lindsay Secundus 177
Mrs C.M. Kerr 177
Queen Mary's Roll 177
Seton 177
The Hague Roll 177
Workman 177
Armorial de Berry 177
Armorial de Gelré 177
Armorial de l'Europe 177
Armorials 177
Arms
Burgh of Banchory 202
Arms of Burnett and Dalrymple 183
Arms of Burnett and Hamilton 178
Arran
Earls of 37
Arras 74
Artesian 7
Arthur
James, of Montgomerie 150
artifacts
from Loch of Leys 229
Atholl
1st Marquis 13
Auchindoun
Castle 237
Auldearn 62, 98
Auquhorthies 89

B

Bailie of Jerviswood 266
Baillie of Hillis
James 10
Baillie of Jerviswood
George 47
Baillie of Lamington 17
Baillie or Burnet
Helen 10
Baillie or Burnett
Jean 17
Baillie or Sandilands
Isabella 139
Baird of Auchmedden 260
Balbithan House 100
Balcarres House 186
Baldarroch Brae 280
Baldarroch Cottage 286, 342
Balglassy 23
Balmain
Alice H. 172
Charlotte A. 171
Gen. James G. 171
Helen I. 171
James H.F. 172
Louis F. 172
Marion M. 171
Mary Jane 171
Millicent 172
Balneaves or Garden
Katherine 115
Baltrop
Capt. Adrian B. 163
Banchory and District Pipe Band 304
Banchory Contractors Ltd 281, 302
Banchory Cricket Club 301
Banchory Golf Course 300
Banchory House and Garden Centre 302
Banchory Lodge 64, 157, 272, 274
Banchory Squash Cl 304
Banchory Tennis Club. 301
Banchory Trust 295
Bancon Developments 302
Bannerman
Alex. of Frendraught 140
Anna 140
Charles, of Crimondgate 140
James, Professor 99
Margaret 140
Mordaunt 140

Patrick 140
Pof. Alex, 6th Bart of Elsick 140
Sir Alex., 4th. Bart. Elsick 63
Sir Alex., 4th. Bart. of Elsick 155
Sir Alexander, 30
Thomas 140
Bannerman or Burnett
Elizabeth 63
Bannerman or Burnett-Ramsay
Elizabeth 155
Barclay
Rev .Adam 48
Barclay or Burnett
Jean 52, 166
Barnard(e) 2
Barnes or Burnett
Cecilia M. 125
Barns
in Peebleshire 8
Barns Manor 265
Barns Tower 8, 259, 265
Baron of Kilduthie 182
Baron of Leys 36
Baronetcy of Nova Scotia 180
Barons Amherst of Hackney 275
Barony
of Balmain 154
of Broughton 8
of Cringeltie 14
of Farningdoun 7
Barony Court Register 318
Barony of Leys 180, 182
Barstow
Charles Murray 161
Battle Abbey 1
Battle of Arras 74
Battle of Bannockburn 32
Battle of Corrichie 260
Battle of Culloden 60
Battle of Durham 23
Battle of Harlaw 248
Battle of Hastings 1
Battle of Justicemills 41
Battle of Loudoun Hill 32
Battle of Neville's Cross 23
Battle of Pinkie 28, 37, 38, 89, 128
Battle of Preston 13
Battle of Prestonpans 60
Battle of Steinkerke 16
Battle of Ypres 73
Baxter of Glassel 279
Baxter or Burnett
Sabrina 54
Bayard
Simonis 34
Beattie
George, Montrose 61
Belhelvie
Churchyard 348
Belhelvie Lodge 136, 348
Bell family
Master masons 242
Bell or Burnett
Sybil Maud 104
Bellamy
Eliza 104
Bellamy or Taylor
Robyn 104
Bellanridge 17
Benachtie 47
Benbecula 228
Bentick
Thomas 157
Beornheard 3
Bernard
Abbot of Arbroath 32
Bernard or Lees
Mary 125
Bernard(e) 2
Bernie or Boyd-Rochfort
Lina 82
Beston 4
Billingsby Dight or Ramsay
Bessie 163
Birch
Margaret E.A. 115
Mariana 115
Rev. Charles E. 115
Birnie
William Russell 276
Bishop Gilbert Burnett 346
Bishop Kennedy 12
Bishop of Aberdeen 12, 34
William Elphinstone 237
Bishop of Baieux 1
Bishop of Brechin 16
Bishop of Glasgow 7
Bishop of Salisbury 54, 94, 262, 273
Black
John, of Bordeaux 152
Prof. Joseph 152
Black or Burnett
Isobel 152
Blackbutts 247
Blackhall 46, 272
Adam 39
Alexander, heir to Blackhall 39
James 39
William 39
William, 1st of Finnersie 39
Blackhall of Barra
Alexander 39

Blackness 238
Blake or Burnett
  Gilbert 95
Bogdan
  Nicholas Quentin 107
  Robert Andrew 107
Bogdan(ovitch)
  Dr. Andrew 107
Bohill 281
Bombay 124
Bond of Allegiance 40
Bonnington 16, 18, 22
Bork
  June Baldwin 43
Boscumbe 4
Boswell
  James, Lyon Depute 183
Bourchier or Burnett
  Harriet 114
Bournemouth 168
Bower
  William, Abbot of Inchcolm 32
Bowhill
  Alexander 275
Boyd-Rochfort
  Arthur Roger 82
  Cecil Charles, Capt. 81
  Rohays 283
  Sir Cecil 81
Braemar Gathering 315
Braintree 44, 45
Brathens 274
Brazil 19, 102
Bremner or Innes
  Jane 115
Brickenden
  Richard, of Inkpen 98
Brickenden or Burnett
  Elizabeth 98
Brickenden or Lamont
  Elizabeth 98
Bridge of Muchalls 247
Brittany
  Duchy of 6
Broughton
  Barony of 8
Brown
  Enest de S. H. 163
  Hon. William 95
  John, Burgess 11
Brown of Newton 19
Brown or Burnet
  Marion 11
Brown or Burnett
  Marjory Chalmers 19
Brown,
  Bessie, Piping Tutor 304
Bruce of Blairhall
  Robert 93
brun 2
Brussels 16, 177
Buchan or Innes
  Lady Lucy 116
Buckinghamshire 115
built-up islands 227
Burch or Burnett
  Emily Julia 103
Burgh of Banchory
  Arms of 202
Burn of Corrichie 290
Burnard 7
  Alexander 3, 26, 31, 225
  Alexander, of Leys 36
  Geoffrey 7
  Gilbert 4
  John 7
  John of Ardross 23
  John, Clavigero 35
  John, laird of Ardross 23
  Margaret,wife of Roger Yr. 4
  Odo 4
  of Burnetland and Barns 8
  Ralph 7
  Richard 4, 7
  Richard of Farningdoun 4, 7
  Richard, of Farningdoun 177
  Robert 4
  Robert, Deputy Sheriff 35
  Roger 4
  Roger of Farningdoun 7
  Roger, of Farningdoun 31
  Roger, son of 4
  Roger, son of Roger 4
  Simon, son of Alexander 34
  Stephen 4
  Walter 7
  William 4
  William, son of Simon 35
Burnard of Ardross 23
Burnards
  of Bedfordshire 4
  of Bedfordshire 7
  of Farningdoun 7
  of Wiltshire 4
Burnards of Farningdoun 23
Burnards of Wiltshire 7
Burnet
  Aaron 44
  Agnes 148
  Alex., Bishop of Aberdeen. 12
  Alexander 37, 45
  Alexander , heir of Carlops 13

Alexander ,of Craigour 128
Alexander, 1st of Carlops 13
Alexander, heir to Leys 36, 37, 44
Alexander, of Braintree 45
Alexander, Rev. 11
Alexander, Yr., of Leys 49
Alexandfer, of Kynneskie 38
Andrew 36, 38
Andrew of Cowcardie 38
Andrew, Dr. 55
Anne, wife of Lord Elphinston 12
Archbishop 11
Archibald 13, 38
Captain Alexander 14
Captain James 10
Christian 38
Dan 44
David 15
Duncan, Rector of Methlick 37
Elizabeth 11, 150
Gavin 9
Gavin, WS 15
George 148
Isobel 9, 15
James 15, 38
James of Manner 11
James, in Cardney 38
James, of Countesswells 149
Jane 45
Janet 11
Jean 150
Joel 44
Johannes 36
John 8, 38, 44, 45, 147
John of Burnetland 8
John of Stanepath 10
John of Woodhouse 9
John, 1st of Elrick 347
John, Fiar of Barns 10
John, merchant 147
John. heir to Leys 38
John. of Leys 36
Katharine 148
Lilias 13
Lot 44
Malcolm Valentine 137
Margaret 13
Marie 11
Marion 9
Mary 45
Matthias 44
Montgomery 15
Mordecai 44
of Burnetland and Barns 8
Peter 150
Rev. James 11
Robert 34, 37, 45, 59, 148, 150
Robert jnr, WS 15
Robert Jnr., Dr. 11
Robert, Dr. 11
Robert, of Little Ormiston 14
Robert, the "divine" 44
Robert,Advocate 14
Robert,nephew of Archbishop 12
Simon 37
Sir William of Cringltie 14
Theodosius 148
Thomas 9, 38, 44
Thomas, 1st of Kemnay 97
Thomas, Dr. 44
Thomas, of Slowy 38
Thomas, of Wooddalling 45
Thomas, Rector of Methlick 38
Thomas, Servitour 15
Willelmus 35
William 15
William ,heir of Barns 9
William of Barns 8, 9, 10
William of Kailzie 10
William, heir of Barns 9
William, heir of John 9
William, heir of William 9
William, Hoolet of Barns 10
William, of Sauchen 51
William, of Slowy 38
William, WS 15
BURNET
Alex., Archbishop of Glasgow 192
Alexander, Merchant in Aberdeen. 194
Alexander, of Craigmyll 193
Andrew, of Warristoune 193
Dr. Thomas 193
James, of Sketchocksley 194
John, of Daleladies 194
Robert, Procurator Fiscal 193
Robert, WS 192
Thomas, of Inneleith 192
William, of Barnes 192
Burnet of Barns
James 266
Burnet of Burnetland 178
Burnet of Elrick
John 98
Burnet of Farningdoun
Roger 27
Burnet of Glenbervie
Thomas 47
Burnet of Leys 178
Sir Thomas 179
Burnet or Arbuthnot
Isabel 38
Burnet or Blackhall

Agnes 39
Burnet or Burnett
Agnes 49
Bessie 51
Jean 59
Burnet or Collins
Lois 44
Burnet or Craigmyle
Isobel 39
Burnet or Cumyn
Christian 37
Jean 51
Burnet or Douglas
Helen 11
Burnet or Fithian
Miriam 44
Pricilla 44
Burnet or Forbes
Isobel 39
Jean 51
Burnet or Leaming
Hester 44
Burnet or Lockhart
Margaret 11
Burnet or Mackenzie
Mary 13
Burnet or Melville
Anne 13
Burnet or Naysmith
Agnes 14
Burnet or Rutherford
Janet 9
Burnet or Sandilands
Agnes 9
Burnet or Scot
Christian 14
Burnet or Skene
Elizabeth 39
Janet 38
Burnet or Storer
Anna Amelia 166
Burnet or Templer
Frances 45
burnet plant 7
Burnet River 19
Burnets
of Farningdoun 7
Burnets of Burnetland 265
Burnets of Farningdon 27
Burnett
"Bonnie John" 152
Abigail Scott 20
Adam 145, 153
Admiral, Sir Robert L. 106
Agnas 152
Agnes 16, 18, 54, 130, 135, 138
Air Chief Marshall Charles 105
Alex. Donald 105
Alex. Edwin 66
Alex. George, 6th of Kemnay 101
Alexander46, 51, 53, 62, 63, 92, 97, 113, 128, 129, 130, 131, 133, 135, 138, 139, 143, 153, 166, 169, 187
Alexander D.G. 102
Alexander Edwin 67
Alexander F. 137
Alexander George, heir to Kemnay 100
Alexander J. 105
Alexander J. Amherst 80
Alexander of Monboddo 58
Alexander, of Kirkhill 41
Alexander, 1st of Kirkhill 43, 137
Alexander, 4th of Kemnay 99
Alexander, 9th Bart. 64
Alexander, 9th laird of Leys 240
Alexander, heir of Leys 59
Alexander, heir to Craigmyle 89, 91
Alexander, heir to Kemnay 98
Alexander, heir to Leys 40, 45, 49
Alexander, heir to Monboddo 111
Alexander, heir to Sheddocksley 142
Alexander, of Cobairdy 260
Alexander, of Countesswells 143
Alexander, of Craigmyle 46, 90, 97
Alexander, of Craigour 130
Alexander, of Kemnay 144
Alexandra Smith 108
Alexanmder, 1st of Kirkhill 347
Allen 174
Amy V.Carson 101
Andreas 142
Andrew53, 58, 128, 133, 134, 135, 136, 138, 145
Andrew jnr.,Dr. 54
Andrew of Sheddocksley 40, 347
Andrew William 54
Andrew, Dr. 54
Andrew, merchant 130
Andrew, of East Camphill 130
Andrew, of Elrick 133
Andrew, of Sheddocksley 142
Andrew, Surgeon 54
Andrew, WS 97
Andro 128, 143
Androw 131
Anna 18, 91, 98, 139
Anne 19, 62, 98, 129
Anthony 145
Archibald 51
Archibald C. 22
Arms of 255
Arthur 102, 113, 121, 124

Arthur Coffin 123
Arthur Moubray, heir to Kemnay 103
Athole 149
Barbara 169
Bethia 92
Bishop Gilbert 54
Bridget 106
Callum 145
Cameron 105
Capt. George 135
Capt. George H.M. 137
Capt. Peter, of Elrick 137
Captain William 16
Carol 105
Catherine 54, 131, 136, 152
Catriona 145
Charles 18, 53, 145
Charles J.F. 149
Charles John 100
Charles John, Major. 20
Charles Spearman 65
Charles Stuart 103
Charles, Advocate 60
Charles, of VA 43
Charlotte 149
Christen 131
Christian 20, 50, 99
Christian C.L. 22
Christian Catherine 21
Christiane 128
Christina Leslie 97, 100
Christopher F. 105
Clementina 19
Cristen 43
David 136, 138, 139
David A.F. 105
Davyhd 43
Dawn 105
Denys 145
Diana 106
Donald Rodber 137
Dr. Andrew 111
Duncan,Dr. 45
Ebenezer Erskine 102
Eleanor S. 22
Eliza Amelia 80
Elizabeth50, 54, 58, 59, 62, 98, 99, 102, 113, 130, 153
Elizabeth Boscawen 149
Elizabeth G. 172
Elizabeth Mary 105, 125
Elizabeth Rohays M. 80
Elizabeth/Eliza 122
Elspet 43, 131
Emma 145
Erskine William 101
Ethel 67
Florence 105
Frances Mary Stuart 102
Francis 54, 115, 136
Francis F. 149
Fullarton C. 22
Geils 138
Gen. Sir William 274
General William 64
George3, 7, 47, 54, 90, 99, 119, 132, 138, 152, 169
George Irvine Leslie 145
George, 3rd of Elrick 133
George, 3rd of Kemnay 98
George, heir to Kemnay 98
George, Lord Lyon 100, 144, 176
George, of Kemnay 62, 63
George, of Wester Slowie 58
Georgina 124
Gilbert 94, 95
Gilbert, Advocate 93
Gilbert, Bishop 93
Gilbert, Professor 45
Haylie 145
Hazel 106
Helen 62, 90, 98, 123, 134, 166
Helen. 65
Henrietta P. 149
Henry 114
Henry Martyn 100, 102
Ian 102
Ian A. Kendall 101
Isaac 153
Isobel 130, 143, 153
Isobell 42, 131
Issobell 43, 152
James20, 55, 61, 92, 97, 113, 115, 122, 129, 133, 145, 148, 152
James Charles, Surveyor 19
James Cumine 123
James Gilbert 171
James Horn, 10th Bart. 65
James L.G. 67
James Lauderdale 67, 182
James Ludwick 149
James Malcolm 125
James of Barns, Captain 20
James of Craigmyle 27
James of Shetchocksley 41
James Shank 124
James, 1st of Monboddo 90
James, 1st of Monboddo 111
James, 2nd of Monboddo 111, 112
James, Capt. 59
James, heir to Barns 17, 18
James, heir to Monboddo 112

James, of Craigmyle 46, 62, 89
James, of Dantzig 130
James, of Lagavin 111
James, of Monboddo 46
James, of Sheddocksley 143
James, WS 20
James,of Countesswells 144
James. heir to Barns 19
Jane 17, 18
Janet 18, 19, 53, 133
Jean 18, 50, 51, 52, 54, 58, 62, 119, 130
Jeane 128, 174
Joan 104
John18, 40, 50, 54, 60, 90, 106, 113, 114, 124, 133, 134, 135, 136, 138, 149, 152, 174
John A. 20
John Alex., 7th of Kemnay 103
John Alexander 20
John Alexander, heir to Kemnay 101
John George 100
John George, 7th of Powis 144
John Hamilton 21
John jnr, of Virginia 43
John of Daladies 147
John Stewart 22
John, heir to Daladies 152
John, 1st of Elrick 130, 173
John, 2nd of Elrick 132
John, 5th of Kemnay 99
John, 7th of Powis 100
John, Advocate 113
John, heir to Kemnay 99
John, in Glenwrath 17
John, of Ardross & Currie 346
John, of Colpnay & Elrick 131
John, of Daladies 151
John, of Elrick 135, 347
John, Scots Factor 47
John,. of Elrick 29
John,yr of Camphill 129
John. 1st of Elrick 128
John. heir to Leys 40
John. of Daladies 30
John.,of Daladies 40
Johne 131
Johnne 142
Johnne, merchant 42
Joseph 153
Joseph M.E. 166
Kate 116
Kate Egan F. 21
Katherine 40, 54, 62, 65, 128, 129, 152, 169
Kathleen Elizabeth 101
Lamont(female) 99
Letitia Wilkins 101
Lettie Muriel 103
Lewis 61
Lillian May 124
Lt. Col. Joseph, of Gadgirth 153
Lynn Hall 22
Maitland James 21
Malcolm S.L. 145
Margaret16, 45, 50, 54, 90, 97, 113, 114, 129, 130, 138, 139
Margret 43
Marianne 114, 149
Marjorie 135
Marjory 20, 113
Mary 50, 52, 54, 62, 64, 94, 98, 130, 133, 135, 140, 169
Mary Bertha 67
Mary Erskine 100
Mary Jane 149
Mesdie 174
Montgomery 22
Moubray 105
Nesta 106
Newell, of Kyllachie 114
Nicholas 54
Nicola Mary 105
Nigel M.F. 105
Obadiah 47
Octavious Winslow 102
Olive Kendall 101
Pamela 145
Patrick 133, 138, 174
Patrick Graham 20
Paul Alexander 105
Penelope S. 149
Peter 114, 136, 137, 153
Peter, of Elrick 137
Phoebe, of VA 43
Rachel 51, 58, 97
Rachell 131, 152
Rev. Alexander 52
Rev. John 53
Rev. Robert 52
Rev. Willliam, Brooklyn 166
Robert43, 47, 54, 56, 58, 61, 63, 64, 65, 92, 97, 129, 132, 133, 134, 138, 139, 145, 153, 168, 172, 174
Robert C. 105
Robert Lee, Captain 20
Robert Lindsay 106
Robert of Lethenty 173
Robert, 4th of Elrick 133
Robert, 5th Bart. 62
Robert, Advocate 51
Robert, heir of Sauchen 52
Robert, in Poland 130
Robert, Lord Crimond 14, 28, 38
Robert, Montrose 50

Robert, of Cowtoun 46, 61, 90, 255
Robert, of Crimond 92
Robert, of Elrick 135
Robert, of Glenbervie 49
Robert, of Kair & Ballandro 111
Robert, of Lethenty 30
Robert, of Muchalls 58
Robert, of Sauchen 52
Robert, WS 170
Rodber W.S. 137
Roger William Odo 79
Sam 145
Samuel 153
Sandra M. 105
Sandy 318
Sarah 54
Sarah, of VA 43
Sir Thomas 46
Sir Alex. E., 14th Bart. 82
Sir Alex., 2nd Bart. 111
Sir Alex., 9th. Bart. 65
Sir Alexander of Leys 98
Sir Alexander, 2nd Bart 55
Sir Alexander, 2nd Bart. 155
Sir Alexander, 4th Bart. 61
Sir Alexander, of Craigmyle 91
Sir Edwin, 14th Bart. of Leys 319
Sir James & Lady 309
Sir James H., 10th Bart. 65
Sir James Horn 117, 229, 297
Sir James Horn, 10th. Bart. 160
Sir James L.G., 13th Bart. 67
Sir Robert, 11th. Bart. 66
Sir Robert, 5th Bart. 62
Sir Robert, 7th Bart. 64
Sir Robert, 7th. Bart. 166
Sir Thomas 95
Sir Thomas, 12th Bart. 67
Sir Thomas, 1st Bart. 48, 143
Sir Thomas, 1st. Bart. 27
Sir Thomas, 3rd Bart. 58
Sir Thomas, 3rd Bart. of Leys 255
Sir Thomas, 3rd. Bart 56
Sir Thomas, 6th Bart. 63, 154, 166
Sir Thomas, 8th Bart. 65
Sir Thomas, Physician 92
Stuart Alexander 102
Stuart Moubray 100
Susan Leitia, heiress to Kemnay 107
thomas 63
Thomas43, 49, 51, 58, 59, 62, 91, 95, 115, 117, 129, 130, 133, 138, 139, 140
Thomas , of VA 43
Thomas A. F. 105
Thomas A.F. 105
Thomas Gilbert A. 79
Thomas L. Forbes 105
Thomas L.F. 105
Thomas of Craigmyle 46
Thomas of Glenbervie 49
Thomas Y.C. 22
Thomas, 12th Bart. 66
Thomas, 1st of Kemnay 28, 90
Thomas, 2nd of Kemnay 98
Thomas, 2nd of Kirkhill 138
Thomas, 3rd of Krkhill 139
Thomas, 6th Bart. 47, 59
Thomas, 6th. Bart. 90
Thomas, 8th Bart. 64
Thomas, Dr. 14, 92
Thomas, heir to Kemnay 97
Thomas, heir to Kirkhill 138
Thomas, heir to Leys 46
Thomas, merchant 40, 42, 137
Thomas, of Camphill 129
Thomas, of Chigwell 94
Thomas, of Clerkseat 49
Thomas, of Kemnay 46
Thomas, of Kepplestone 114
Thomas, of Pilrig 57
Thomas, of Sauchen 51, 263
Untong 150
Victor Cecil Tobias 80
Violet 18, 19
Walter 16
Wiliam Kendall 102
William16, 18, 20, 50, 51, 52, 54, 55, 58, 90, 95, 113, 128, 129, 130, 135, 136, 166, 169, 170, 172
William ,of Balfour 56
William Arthur 125
William Farquharson 115
William Kendall 101
William of Barns 15
William of Camphill 128
William of Craigour 27
William, Advocate 112
William, Colonial Secretary 19
William, Commander RN 64
William, Factor 166, 173
William, Governor of New York 94
William, heir to Camphill 129, 130
William, in Glenwrath 17
William, Lt. Col. 21
William, of Burnetland, NSW 20
William, of Camphill 89, 130
William, of Craigour 89
William, of Criggie 47, 59, 63
William, of Tillihaikie 128
William, of West Camphill 130
BURNETT
Alexander, Aberdeen, 184

Alexander, of Craigmyle 184
Andrew, of Wariston 184
Arthur Moubray, 8th of Kemnay 107
Cameron Beleau 199
Charles J., Ross Herald 185
Charles John 197
Charles John, Ross Herald of Arms 198
David, of Dalston 200
Dr. Thomas 185
George, Lord Lyon 185
George, Lord Lyon King of Arms 195
George, Lyon Depute 194
James Cumine, 5th of Monboddo 124
James M., 7th of Monboddo 125
James Shank. 6th of Monboddo 125
James, of Sheddocksley 184
James, 3rd of Monboddo 120
John Cameron 198
John Cameron, Oklahoma 185
John McIntyre 198
John, of Dalladies 184
Joihn, of Balelack 201
Patrick Britton 199
Robert, Aberdeen. 184
Robert, WS 184
Sir Brian Kenyon 200
Sir Robert Burnett, of Morden Hall 199
Thomas of Wood-dalling 199
Thomas, of Inverleith 184
Thomas, Woodalling 184
William T. Bridgeford 197
William T.B. 185
William, of Barns 184
Burnett Arms 187
Burnett Coat of Arms 303
Burnett heraldry 186
Burnett of Countesswells & Kepplestone 29
Burnett of Cowtoun
Robert 131
Burnett of Craigmyle 27
Alexander 55
Sir Alexander 28
Thomas 27
Burnett of Crimond 28
Burnett of Durris
Andrew 133
Burnett of Elrick 29
Burnett of Kemnay 28
BURNETT OF KEMNAY
Susan Letitia, Baroness of Kemnay 197
Burnett of Kirkhill 30
Thomas 112
BURNETT OF LEES
Sir Thomas, 1st Bart. of Nova Scotia 192
Burnett of Lethenty 30
Burnett of Leys
Alexander 27, 254
James C. A. 26
James C.A. 182
new Achievement 181
Robert 264
Sir Robert, 7th. Bart 183
Sir Thomas 187
Sir Thomas, 1st Bart. 180
Sir Thomas, 3rd. Bart. 181
undifferenced Arms 182
BURNETT OF LEYS
James Comyn Amherst, Baron of Kilduthie196, 197
Sir Thomas, 8th Bart. of Nova Scotia 194
Burnett of Leys tart 203
Burnett of Leys tartan 182, 304
Hunting version 203
Burnett of Monboddo 28
Eliza 346
Burnett of Powis 30
Burnett or Aberdein
Mary 62
Burnett or Aitken
Margaret 59
Burnett or Allardyce
Helen 47, 61
Burnett or Anderson
Annie E.B. 21
Burnett or Arbuthnot
Jean 47, 90
Burnett or Balmain
Jane Farquhar 171
Burnett or Bannerman
Helen 99
Margaret 140
Burnett or Barron
Helen 55
Burnett or Beattie
Elizabeth 61
Burnett or Birch
Marianne 115
Burnett or Boyd-Rochfort
Rohays 81
Burnett or Brown
Mary 95
Burnett or Burnet
Agnes 47
Anne 55
Burnett or Burnett
Agnes 90
Bessie 133
Catherine 124
Elisabeth 27
Elizabeth 46
Helen 47, 61, 62, 90, 98
Jean 47, 91, 97

Margaret 58, 111
William, of Criggie 90
Burnett or Byres
Margaret 152
Burnett or Calder
Katherine 55
Burnett or Cant
Anne 55
Burnett or Carnegie
Jean 111
Mary 59
Burnett or Cheyne
Christian 16
Isabel 47
Burnett or Chisholm
Helen 17
Burnett or Christie
Penelope 116
Burnett or Crawford
Helen 93
Burnett or Crearer
Katherine 104
Burnett or Cruickshank
Janet Ann Eliz. 21
Burnett or Cumine
Elizabeth Williamson 117
Harriet Hay 116, 121
Burnett or Cumyn
Janet 48
Burnett or Davidson
Hope 135
Burnett or Donaldson
Hope 135
Burnett or Douglas
Elizabeth 55
Burnett or Dunbar
Jean 62, 98
Burnett or Dundas
Alison 17
Helen 93
Burnett or Erskine
Margaret 91
Burnett or Farquharson
Isabel 91
Mary 129
Burnett or Findlater
Christian 143
Burnett or Forbes
Catherine 64
Margaret 40
Mary 47, 90
Burnett or Foster
Maysie 145
Burnett or Fraser
Helen 59
Burnett or Fullerton
Elizabeth 55
Burnett or Gardiner
Joan 19
Burnett or Garioch
Elizabeth 112
Burnett or Gordon
Anne 55, 91
Elizabeth 91
Katherine 50, 51
Burnett or Grant
Anne Rebecca 113
Burnett or Halyburton
Anna 93
Burnett or Hamilton
Elizabeth 51
Burnett or Hart
Mary Isabella 166
Burnett or Hicks
Jean Muriel M. 108
Burnett or Hine
Amelia 170
Burnett or Holloway
Alice Christina 100
Burnett or Hutton
Marjorie E. 124
Burnett or Innes
Barbara 47
Helen Amy 123
Helen C. 115
Helen Christian 347
Burnett or Irvine
Irene D.M. 106
Burnett or Joyce
Ellen L. 171
Burnett or Keith
Janet 45
Nicholas(female) 130
Burnett or Kennedy
Margaret 55
Burnett or Ker
Bessie 143
Burnett or la Forge
Catherine H. 173
Burnett or Lauder
Jean 61
Burnett or Lees
Cecilia D.M. 125
Burnett or Lillie
Mary Gascoigne 149
Burnett or Low
Dorothy 106
Burnett or Lumsden
Hay 136
Burnett or Lunan
Jean 55
Burnett or Maitland

Katherine 47
Margaret 91
Burnett or Marquis
Anne 167
Burnett or Martin
Margaret 53
Burnett or McCracken
Lilias 20
Burnett or McGie
Christian 16
Burnett or McLennan
Elizabeth 168
Burnett or McLeod
Margaret 136
Burnett or McRobert
Beatrice 133
Burnett or McTavish
Helen 167
BURNETT or Milton
Susan L., 9th of Kemnay 108
Burnett or Mitchell
Mary 95
Burnett or Mitchelson
Anna 16
Burnett or Moir
Marjorie 138
Burnett or Montgomerie
Isabel 174
Burnett or Mowatt
Marjory 134
Burnett or Murray
Margaret 18
Burnett or Naughton
Marie 16
Burnett or Nicholson
Agnes 90
Eliza Jane 123
Burnett or North
Roberta Dundas 113
Burnett or Ogilvie
Alexander 58
Margaret 61
Violet A.D. 21
Burnett or Oliver
Jane 169
Burnett or Orphoot
Edith C.S. 21
Burnett or Paton
Eliza Deborah 118
Burnett or Ramsay
Alexander 155
Margaret 65
Burnett or Rennie
Agnes 168
Burnett or Robertson
Elizabeth 17
Euphemia 93
Burnett or Sandilands
Clementina 139
Marjorie 29, 143
Burnett or Scott
Katherine 53
Burnett or Seton
Katherine 61
Burnett or Shank
Elizabeth 57
Mary 57
Burnett or Skene
Elizabeth 45
Janet 48
Jean 50, 262
Burnett or Skilbeck
Anthea 145
Burnett or Stark
Amelia 102
Burnett or Steele
Margaret 112
Burnett or Stewart
Henrietta 16
Victoria M. Rohays 105
Burnett or Stratton
Ann 104
Burnett or Swann
Sybil 104
Burnett or Symmer
Mariot 48
Burnett or Taylor
Catherine 169
Elizabeth Bannerman 66
Jean 170
Mary 119
Burnett or Thom
Margaret M. 172
Burnett or Turnbull
Marjorie 152
Burnett or Twopenny
Eliz. Deborah 113
Burnett or West
Elizabeth 95
Burnett or Williamson
Helen, heiress to Monboddo 121
Burnett or Wright
Mary Bertha V. 124
Burnett or Wyse
Margaret 112
Burnett or Young
Violet 19
Burnett Park 300
Burnett Ramsay 274
William 156, 157, 274
Burnett Room
armorial devices 183

Burnett -Stuart
  Rev. John 148
Burnett tartan 203
BURNETT(Williamson)
  James Burnett, 4th of Monboddo 123
Burnett,
  Sir Robert 292
burnette 2
Burnett Ramsay
  Alexander, heir to Balmain 156
  David 156
  Thomas 156
Burnett Williamson
  Arthur 121
  Grace 122
  Helen 122
  Henrietta 122
  James Burnett 121
  John 121
  Margaret 122
Burnett Williamson or Cumine
  Elizabeth 121
Burnett-Ramsay 29, 347
  Ina Margaret 157
  Katherine Jane 157
  Thomas 157
Burnett-Ramsay or Bentick
  Annie Elizabeth 157
Burnett-Ramsay or Robinson-Douglas
  Frances Mary 157
Burnetts
  of Inverleith 38
  of Warriston 38
Burnetts of Burnetland 346
Burnetts of Kemnay 346
BURNETTS OF KINCHYLE 166
Burnetts of Leys 202, 346
BURNETTS OF LEYS 31
Burnetts of Monboddo 346
Burnett-Stuart 29, 147, 347
  Adrian J.A. Capt. 151
  Amy F.M. 149
  Augustina 148
  Cerise Marie 151
  Eustace R. 150
  Eustace Robertson 148
  Francis, WS 151
  Gen. Sir John T. 150
  Geordie, of Crichie 260
  George Eustace, of Ardmeallie 151
  Gilbert Robertson 151
  John 148
  Joseph 151
  Julia I.M. 151
  Lilias Mary 149
  Rev Theodosius 148
  Theodosius 148
  Thomas 151
BURNETT-STUART
  Gen. Sir John T., of Crichie 195
  John Theodosius, of Crichie 185
  Joseph, of Ardmeallie 195
  Thomas 196
Burnett-Stuart or Arthur
  Elizabeth 150
Burnett-Stuart or Slessor
  Kathron Lilias 151
Burnett-Stuarts 263
Burns
  Robert 122
Burton
  Harriet Hay 119
Bute
  Earls of 20
Byres of Kincraigie
  Robert 152
Byres or Pearson
  Margaret 97

C

Cairniewhin 281
Cairn-na-Mounth Pass 239
Cairnton 273, 295
Cairo, 73
Calder
  Robert 55
Calsayseat 144
Camp Kettles 230
Campfield House 67
Camphill 128
Campvere 47, 134
Candieshill 302
canoe
  from Loch of Leys 230
Canon of Aberdeen 37
Cant
  Rev. Andrew 55
capercailzie 299
Cardney 33
Carlops 92
  Alexander Burnet of 13
Carmichael or Whiteford
  Ann 16
Carnegie
  Alexander 60
  David 60
  Elizabeth 60
  George, of Charleton 60
  Henry 60

James, 3rd Bart. 60
John 60
Sir David, 1st. Bart. of Pitarrow 111
Sir John, 2nd Bart of Pitarrow 59
Sir Robert 154
Carnegie or Aberdein
Helen 60
Carnegie or Ramsay
Catherine 154
Carnegie or Scott
Margaret 60
Carnegie or Tailor
Jean 60
Carnousis 35
Carr
John 161
Carruber's Close 19
Carruthers or Menzies
Janet 11
Carson or Burnett
Margaretta M. 101
Carter or Burnett
Jane Ashe 123
Cartwright or Burnett
Mary 105
Cassillis
John, 6th Earl of 94
Castle Fraser 232, 233, 237, 294
Castle of Crathes 48
Castle of Leys 33, 227
Castle of Leys 225
Castleairey 274
Castlehill Tower 27, 259
Catterloch 281
Caverhill 8, 9
George 8
Marion 8
Cecil 275
Anoushka H. Amherst 81
Arthur N. Amherst 81
Benjamin D. Amherst 81
David Henry Amherst 81
Henry David 80
Henry Kerr A. 80
Jake H. R. Amherst 81
James Edward 82
Jemima Rohays Amherst 81
John Strongbow Amherst 80
Katrina H. Amherst 81
Michael J.Amherst 80
Miranda E. Rohays 80
Richard S. Amherst 80
Rupert L. Amherst 81
Sapphire Rose 81
Cecil or Burnett of Leys
James Comyn Amherst 80
Celdraton 3
Cennomanian 7
Chalmers of Cults
Alexander 38
Chalmers or Burnet
Elspeth 38
Janet/Jenis 38
Marjorie 38
Chalvertoun 3
Chamberlain
of Earl of Southesk 10
Chancellor of Scotland 32, 187
William Elphinstone 237
Chancellor of Shieldhill
Robert 17
Chancellor or Burnet
Jean 17
CHANCERY
of Order of St. John in Scotland 202
Chaplain to the Rolls 94
Charleston, SC 54
Charters
of Waltham Abbey 4
Chartulary
of St. Neot's 3
Cheldreton 4
Cheyne
James 16
James of Arnage 47
Rev. Robert 16
Cheyne or Hay
Jean 16
chimney
granite 279
Chipp
Agnes M. 172
Alice W. 172
Amelia M. 172
Anna G. 172
Charles W. 172
Elizabeth Burnett 172
Katherine Burnett 172
Warren 172
Warren S. 172
Chipp or Burnett
Julia Maria 171
Chirnside 57
Chisholm
Robert 17
Cholderton 3
Christie
James, Chauffeur 313
Maj. Napier T. 116
Mary Harriet 116
Napier T. 116
Penelope 116

Private James 73
Christie of Durn
James 116
churchyards 345
Clan Burnett Incorporated 182
Clark
James. merchant 139
John Moir 167
Clerk Register 31
Clerkenwell 96
Clerkship of the Principality 16
Cluny 52
Cobairdy 259
Cochrane
Rupert 159
Cochrane or Ramsay
Isabella 159
Cockburn of Yardheads
James 15
Cockburn or Burnet
Elizabeth 15
Codford 3
coinage
of King David I 6
Coldingham 11
Cole or Stratton
Lucy 105
Collector of Cess 17, 139
Columbia 117
Commissary of Aberdeen 38
Commissioner of Supply 11, 13, 15, 90
Commssioner of Supply 63
Convention of Estates 14
Cooper
John, in Candiglirach 279
Cooper or Burnet
Mary 44
Cooper or Dundas
Helen 10
Corbett or Cecil
Hon. Fiona E.C. 81
Cornage 27
Corsar or Burnett
Helen Morton 105
Corsee 300
Cotford 4
Countess of Kincardine 93
Janet Robertson 93
Countesswells 143
Coupar or Gordon
Agnes 52
Coutts of Cluny
William 55
Coutts or Burnett
Elizabeth 55
Coutts or Ramsay
Elizabeth 55, 155
Covenanter 46, 49
Covenanters 51
Cowdray House 1
Cowie 248
Cowie Mounth Pass 247
Cowie or Causey Mounth 247
Coy 281
Craigievar 53
Craigievar Castle 186, 232
Craigmyle 272
Craigmyle Estate 275
Craigmyle House 286
Craigmyle of that Ilk 28, 89
Craigston
Castle 242
Craigton 281
Crailing 9
crannog33, 34, 225, 226, 227, 228, 229, 238, 240, 241
Crannog 36
crannogs
Irish 229
Cranstoun
Sir John 10
Cranstoun of that Ilk 10
Cranstoun of the Ilk
William 9
Crathes
Castle 233
Crathes Castle 34, 46, 178, 225, 230, 235
CRATHES CASTLE 202
Crathes enclosure 346
Crathes Gardens 309
Crathes Hall 320
Crathes Primary Sch 320
Crathes Station 319
Craven county 54
Crawford or Ramsay
Julia C. 161
Crearer
Alison Sybil 104
James 104
Crearer or Roper
Helen 104
Crichie29, 39, 147, 150, 151, 195, 201, 259, 260, 267, 330
Crichie House 260
Crimond 47
Cringeltie 14
Barony of 14
Cringltie House 14
Cromarty
Earl of 12
Crombie
Sir Thomas 261

Cromwell
Oliver 101
Crosmier or Burnett
Frances 148
Crossmichael 52
Crozier Smith or Burnett
Sybil Aird 79
Cruickshank
Henrietta Hay 21
James Burnett 21
James R. Lee 21
Rev. James 21
Cruickshank of Stracathro
Patrick 156, 159
Cruickshank or Ramsay
Jane 156
Margaret 159
Cruickshank or Scott
Elizabeth 53
Cruickshank or Smith
Christian 21
Cryne Corse Pass 264
Cumberland 2
Cumine 348
Adam 117
Alan 117
Alexander 117, 122
Alice 118
Charles 122
Elizabeth 117, 121
George 122
George J.G.G., of Rattray 117
George Lewis 117
George Louis 117
Harriet 117
Isabel 118
James 117, 121
Jane 121
Mary 122
Peter 118
Philip Arthur, of Rattray 118
Robin 117
Sylvia Hay K. 117
Thomas, heir to Rattray 117
William 121
William Adam 117
Cumine of Pithullie
William 121
Cumine of Rattray
Adam 121
James 116
Cumine or Burnett
Mary Eliz. 67
Mary Elizabeth 117
Cumyn of Altyre
Robert 51
Cumyn of Culter
Alexander 45
Sir Alex. 48
William 37
Currie
Midlothian 23
Curtis or Burnett
Guillemina 137
Curzon
Marquis 232

D

d'Eu
William 3, 4
Dakota 105
Daladies 29, 30, 40, 147, 150, 151, 152, 195, 196, 201
Dalkeith 19, 20
Dalrymple
Margaret 183
Dalrymple-Elphinstone
Gen. Robert Horn 64
Darwin 120
Sir Francis 111
David I
King 6
Davidson
Mr John, Factor 321
Davidson of Inchmarlo
Duncan 157
Davidson of Midmar
James 135
Davidson or Burnett-Ramsay
Anne 157
de Bienfaite
Richard 4
de Farningdon
William 266
de Hay
William 248
de Hem
Jacque 45
de Hem or Burnett
Judith 45
de la Rue or Burnett
Germaine 125
de Laverne or Burnett-Stuart
Patricia 151
de Ow
William 3
de Saussure or Burnett
Elizabeth 54
Dean of Canterbury

Dr. George Stanhope 94
Dean of Edinburgh
Edward Ramsay 159
Declaration of Arbroath 33
decoration
heraldic 183
Deeside3, 64, 78, 225, 232, 238, 239, 240, 247, 254, 255, 264, 272, 276, 287, 294, 299, 301, 302, 304, 319, 323, 324, 325, 327, 332
Deeside Piper 276
defence 226
Delhi Durbar 73
Demerara 20, 21, 22
Demidoff or Burnett
? Mary Ann 137
Dens & Crichie 147
Deriche or Burnett
Sarah 45
Dey
Frank, Gamekeeper 298
Dinnie
David 256
Dishington
William of 23
Dissington
John, of Ardrosse 23
Dissingtoun
Sir William de 23
Dochfour Estates 167
Dogflat 9
Dollarburn 9
Dominica 148
Donaldson
Prof. Alexander 135
Doomsday Book 2, 3
Douglas of Baads
James 11
Douglas of Glenbervie 261
Sir Robert 49
Sir William 89
Douglas of Muirhousedykes
James 11
Douglas of Tilliwhilly
Sir Robert 55
Douglas or Burnett
Margaret 49, 56
Douglas or Irvine
Elizabeth 111
Douglas or Nicholson
Katherine 50
Dowalty 281
Dower House 285
Draiw or Burnett
Elizabeth 105
Dresden 100
Druggam 281
Drum27, 31, 33, 35, 36, 38, 48, 64, 97, 107, 142, 225, 233, 239, 240, 245, 253, 254, 258, 272, 275, 332, 336, 339
Forest of 31
Drumfrennie, 281
Druminnor
Castle 237
Drumoak 274
Drumyoche 281
Duchess of Hamilton
Anne 93
Duchy (of Normandy) 7
Dudley-Bateman or Cumine
Isabel 117
Dufftown 137
Duke of Fife 262
Duke William 1
Dunbar
Bishop Gavin 144
Mr. J.F.C. 276
Dunbar of Boath
Alexander 62, 98
Dunbar or Burnett
Elizabeth 50
Duncan
Andrew 118
Fred, in Woodend Farm 280
Norman 287
Duncan of Rosemount
David 66, 160
Duncan or Westrop
Elspeth Mary 118
Dundas
John 10
Dundas of Blair
George 10
Dundas of that Ilk
George 11
Dundas or Burnet
Christian 11
Dunech 294
Dunfermline
Alexander Seton, 1st Earl 187
Arms of 255
Earl of 56
Dunfermline Palace
Constable of 187
Dunkirk
Governor of 11
Dunnottar
Castle 236
Durris 272
Dyce of Disblair
James 99
Dyce or Burnett
Janet 99

E

Earl of Bothwell 8, 266
Earl of Buchan 250
Earl of Dunfermline 187
Earl of Erroll 248
Earl of Huntly 290
Earl of Lauderdale 188
Earl of Traquair 11
Earlshill 250
Easter Camphill 28
Eastmeadow
 of Farningdoun 7
Easton or Burnett
 Margaret 56
Echt Churchyard. 347
Eddeworth 4
Edinburgh 51
Edinburgh Castle 186
Edinburgh Regiment 13
Edward I of England 264
Egeria 65
Eglinton 174
Electress Sophia in Hanover 98
Elibank
 Patrick, 3rd Lord 12
Elita 4
Elizabethtown 44
Elphinston
 Alexander, 7th Lord 12
Elphinstone or Burnett
 Margaret Dalrymple 64
Elphinstone or Dalrymple
 Mary, of Logie 64
Elrick 28
Elrick, 259
English College of Arms 176
Entwisle or Ramsay
 Ellen Matilda 162
Episcopal Records
 of Glasgow 7
Episcopalian chapel 250, 255
Erroll
 Earl of 46
Erskine
 Nicholas(female) 92
 William 91
Erskine of Drum 38
Erskine of Pittodrie
 Sir Thomas 91
Esslemont
 Castle 236
Esslemont Castle 251
Estate Charter 283, 294
ESTATE DEVELOPMENT
 of Leys Estate 300
ewer
 bronze 230

F

Fairnington 7
Fairnington House 266
Fairnington House. 259
Falconer or Ramsay
 Elizabeth of Glenfarquhar 155
Family cemetery
 at Crathes Castle 318
Family History Society
 Aberdeen & North-east Scotland 348
Farewell to the 92nd 76
Farningdoun 4, 7, 8, 23, 31, 32, 177
 Barony of 7
Farnington 7
Farquharson
 Donald 50, 129
Farquharson of Finzean
 Angus 276
Farquharson of Monaltries
 Alexander 91
Farquharson or Burnett
 Elizabeth 121
Fasque 65, 154, 155, 156, 160, 259, 264, 321
Fedderate
 Castle 237
Ferguson of Pitfour
 James 147
feudal land system 6
Fichner
 Gerhardt 107
Fichner Irvine
 Tobias Alexander 107
Findlater
 Alexander 143
 Bessie 143
 John 143
 Margaret 143
Findlay
 Mary 17
FISHING
 on Leys Estate 295
Fitzgerald or Burnett
 Eve Diana 106
Flanders 7, 10, 16, 34, 64
Fleming of Kilconquhar
 George 12
Fleming or Burnett
 Elizabeth 12
Fleming or Smith

Jean 12
Flemington Tower 23
Flemish 6, 7, 34, 177
Flemish weavers 34
Forbes
"Blind" John 39
"Bluebonnet" 39
Alex., 2nd of Echt 36
Alexander 39
Arms of 255
Arthur 40
Arthur, of Echt 47
Isobel 39
James 294
John , 3rd Bart. 51
John, 6th. Lord 40
Robert, of Finnersie 40
Sir Arthur, 4th Bart. of Craigievar 134
Thomas of Knockquharne 40
Thomas, of Knockwharn 48
William 39
Forbes Gordon of Rayne
Arthur 101
Forbes of Sonnahinny
John 39
Forbes of Brux 40
Forbes of Corsindae
Alexander 47
Forbes of Corsinday
Alexander 90
Forbes of Craigievar
Sir William 112
Forbes of Echt
Arthur 40
Elizabeth 188
Robert 47
Forbes of Monymusk
Sir William 51
Forbes of Pitsligo 39
John 90
Forbes of Schivas
Alexander 64
Forbes of Sheils
Charles 133
Forbes of Tolquhoun 263
Forbes of Waterton
Jean 91
Forbes or Burnet
Elizabeth 36
Marjorie 40
Forbes or Burnett
Anna 174
Elizabeth 112
Isobel 111
Forbes or Cumine
Mary 122
Forbes or Leith
Marjory 39
Forbes or Rickart
Janet 51
Fordie 277
Fordoun 228
Forest of Drum 27
Forest of Kintore 31
FORESTRY
on Leys Estate 292
Forestry management 294
fortified house 269
Foster
Denys 145
Foster or Paice
Rosemary 145
Foys or Burnet
Jane 44
France1, 2, 35, 46, 47, 74, 81, 92, 93, 94, 101, 103, 137, 185, 187, 280
Fraser
Alexander, 1st of Powis 99, 144
Alexander, Regent 144
Capt. Hugh 144
Christian, heiress of Powis 99
William, Advocate 59
Fraser of Cluny
Sir Alexander 33
Fraser of Corntoun
Alexander 248
Fraser of Findrack 59
Fraser of Inverallochy
Sir Simon 51
Fraser or Burnett
Christian 90
Fraser or Mackenzie
Anne 13
Frederick the Great 99
Freedom Lands 142
French 7
Friendville 170
Fuller or Burnett
Maraval 22
Fullerton
Thomas 61, 255
Fullerton of Kinnaber 55
Fullerton-Lindsay-Carnegie or Ramsay
Susan 159
Fyvie Castle 187, 232

G

Gallica or Cecil
Vanessa W. 81

GAME
on Leys Estate 297
Garde or Williamson
Olivia 118
Garden
Frank 302
Garden of Troup
Francis 136
Peter 115
Garden or Burnett
Mary 115
Gardiner
Agnes 19
George, Comptroller-General 19
James Burnett 19
Gardyne or Burnet
Janet 37
Gardynes were of that Ilk 37
Garioch of Kinstair
George 112
Garthbeg 167
Gellatly or Moir
Janet 19
Genealogy Society
Scottish 348
General Pultney's Regiment 14
Germanic 2, 3
Gibbon or Taylor
Mary 169
Gibson
Alison 10
Christina Ker 107
John Ker 107
Roger Ker 107
Gibson or Dundas
Alison 10
Gifford I
Walter 4
Gight
Castle 237
Gillanders or Burnett
Anne 166
Gladstone
Sir John 156, 265
Thomas 156
William Ewart 156
Glamis
John, Lord 40
Glamis Castle 186, 187
Glasgow
Archbishop of 12
Glashmore 281
School at 305
Glassel 272, 273, 279, 338
Glenbervie House 259, 263
Glencairn
Earl of 12
Glenfarquhar 36
Glenlyon 115
Glenrath 17
goosanders 297
Gordon
Alexander 52
Arms of 255
Charles 91
George, 4th of Cocklarachie 263
James, of Rothiemay 42
Ludovic 52
Rev Dr. John, of St.Paul's 55
Rev. Thomas 52
Rev.Thomas 52
William 52
Gordon Highlander 313
Gordon Highlanders67, 68, 69, 70, 71, 73, 74, 75, 76, 77, 78, 116, 161, 182, 315, 316, 317, 320
Gordon of Fechil
John 152
Gordon of Glenbuchat
Patrick 49
Gordon of Hilton
Dr. James 98
Gordon of Lesmoir
Alexander 46
Katherine 189, 241
Gordon of Pitlurg
Robert 51
Gordon of Straloch
Robert 51
Sir Robert 52
Gordon or Black
Isobel, of Hallhead 152
Gordon or Blackhall
Katherine 39
Gordon or Burnett
Charlotte S. 101
Charlotte S. Forbes 103
Katherine 45, 152
Gordon or Forbes
Isobel 39
Gordon or Lumsden
Catherine 129
Gordons of Ardmeallie 263
Gothenburg 60
Govan of Cardrona
John 9
Graham of Morphie
Sir Robert 47
Grampian Foxhounds 300
granite quarries
at Craigton 290
Grant
Lord Patrick 123

Grant of Dalvey
Sir Ludwick 144
Grant of Grant or Hutton
Jacqueline P. 125
Grant of Redcastle
Alexander 113
Grant or Burnet
Elizabeth 149
Grant or Burnett
Elizabeth 144
Gray or Stuart
Agnes 147
Great Hall (Crathes) 179
Great Malvern 101
Green Lady 275
Greendams 280, 281
Gregorie
James 132
Professor James 132
Gregorie or Forbes
Janet 132
Gregorie or Thomson
Helen 132
GREYFRIARS KIRK 201
grouse 298
Guestrow 41
Gunn or Burnett
Maureen 105
Guthrie of Breda
Sir John 129
Guthrie or Burnett
Anne 129

H

Haigh or Ramsay
Octavia 163
Hall
Anne Margaret 167
Isabella M.C. 167
John Robert 167
Halyburton of Pitcur
James 93
Hamilton
Arms of 255
Janet 188, 240
John, 2nd Marquess 188
Robert, Canon of Aberdeen 37
William, Writer 51
Hamilton Arms 179
Hamilton of Sanquhar 187
Hamilton or Burnet
Janet 37
Haneslawe 3
Hanoverians 250, 255
hares
brown 298
Harestone Farm 280, 286, 304, 342
Hargreaves
Prof. John 319
Hargreaves or Burnett
Florence Emma 102
Hart
Capt. Edward 166
Hartwell or Burnett
Aida Maria W. 137
Hastings 1, 2
Hattonburn280, 282, 283, 321, 333, 334, 337, 338, 340, 341
Hay
Alexander, WS 16
Christian 10
Francis, 9th Earl of Errol 254
Lt. Gen. Sir R.J. 162
Hay of Belton
Admiral 162
Hay of Locharret and Yester 9
Hay or Burnet
Isobel 9
Margaret 13
Hay or Govan
Isobel 9
Hay, 2nd Lord Yester
John 10
Hayes
Sir Henry 149
Hayes or Burnett
Penelope 149
HEICS 65, 114, 124
Henry I *See* King Henry I
King 6
heraldic panels (Crathes) 178
heraldry 176
friendship 189
personal 189
probative 189
royal 189
Heralds' Visitation
of Norfolk 44
Heriot or Burnet
Margaret 14
Hicks
Capt. Ronald C. 108
Robert Moubray 108
Simon 108
Highland Chiefs 181
Hill of Banchory 303
Hill of Fare 225
Hilton or Ramsay
Mary 162

Hine
Amelia Burnett 171
Elizabeth Jane 171
Frederick 171
Henry 171
James 171
James Balmain 171
John Burnett 171
Margaret 171
Rev. Henry 170
Robert Burnett 171
William 171
Holland 19, 47, 93, 120, 129, 134, 177, 179
Home Farm
Sawmill 294
Home of Wedderburn
William Foreman 160
Home or Ramsay
Georgina Hay 160
Hopkins or Burnett
Elizabeth O. 172
Horn of Leys 27, 190, 234, 266, 309
Horsfall or Burnett-Stuart
Elizabeth 148
House of Burnett 182
House of Crathes 189, 271
House of Leys 176
House of Newe 39
HOUSES
on Leys Estate 282
Howes or Cecil
Joanna 81
Howieson or Burnett
Marjorie 29, 131
Hughes or Cecil
Elizabeth Clare 80
Humble
David, in Ley Farm 280
John, in Dowalty 280
Huntingdon
Earldom of 6
Huntly
Castle 236
Earl of 28
Hutchison or Ramsay
Mabel 163
Hutton
Malcolm U.L. 125
Ronald S.L. 124

I

Inchmarlo124, 272, 275, 276, 277, 278, 282, 304, 331, 332
Inchmarlo Land Company 302
Ingles
William of Murditoun 9
Ingles of Mannerhead
John 11
Ingles or Burnet
Marion 11
Inglis
Marion/Mariota 8
William of Murdiston 8
Inglis or Baillie
Catherine 10
Ingram of Newburgh.
John 125
Ingram or Burnett
Gladys 125
Innes
Alexander 123
Capt. William 116
Helen C., of Cromney 116
Lt. Col. Francis Newell 116
Margaret Anne 347
Thomas 116
Thomas, Lord Lyon 116, 347
William Disney 123
Innes of Balveny.
Robert 47
Innes of Learney 347
Thomas 115
Innes of Pethenick
Alexander 48
Innes of Raemoir
Alexander 123
William 115
Innes or Ramsay
Anne 161
Inquest of land-holdings 2
Invercannie water works 301
Irish crannogs 229
Irvin
Alexander de 31
Irvine
David Howard 107
Hugh Ramsay Innes 107
William of 31
Irvine of Barra
Francis C. Q 107
Quentin Hugh Innes 107
Irvine of Drum
Francis 107
Irvine of Monboddo
Capt. Robert 111
Robert 28
Irvine or Bogdan
Mary D. Forbes 107
Irvine or Burnett

Catherine S.H. 100
Elizabeth 28, 111
Sarah H. 145
Irvine or Fichner
Susan Mary 107
Irvine or Gibson
Jean C.C. 107
Irvine or Innes
Margaret Anne 116
Irvine or Ramsay
Margaret, of Monboddo 155
Isle of Man 149
Ivechurch
Rector of 11

J

Jacobean
tower-houses 233
Jacobite13, 18, 56, 61, 82, 84, 112, 120, 133, 138, 146, 147, 152, 201, 267, 268
Jacobites 263
Jamaica 162
James
Henry 6
Jameson
Andrew, master mason 131
George, Portrait Painter 29, 131
Jameson or Burnett
Mary 29, 131
Jamesone
George 55
Jedburgh 7, 11, 13, 266
Andrew Ker, 1st Lord 13
Johnson
Dr. Samuel 264
Johnston
John 42
Lucretia 42
Sir John, 4th Bart of Caskieben 133
Johnston of that Ilk
John 92
Johnston or Burnett
Margaret 42, 137
Marjorie 133
Rachel 28, 92
Johnstone
Rev. James 137
Jones or Cumine
Emmeline 117
Joyce
Louisa Jane 171
Mary Augusta 171
Wilhelmina M. 171
William Willis 171
Willis Burnett 171

K

Katherine 187
Keeper of the Great Seal 12
Keeper of the Royal Forest 27
Keith
Thomas 130
Keith of Auquhorsk
Gilbert 45
Keith of Bruxie
George 134
Keith or Burnett
Elizabeth 134
Georgina 124
Margaret 129
Kellie Castle 186
Kemnay 259
Kemnay House 261
Kemney
Baron Janos 119
Kendal 47, 92, 93
Kendall or Burnett
Letitia Amelia 101
Kennedy of Kermucks
John 55
Kennedy or Burnett
Lady Margaret 94
Margaret 102
Kent 11
Ker
Isobel 143
Rev. Alexander 143
Kerloch 272
Kerr or Hay
Katherine 10
Kilconquhar 23, 346
Kildrummy 240
Kilduthie 280, 281
Killenachclerach 33
Kincardine O' Neil 240
Kincardine O' Neil churchyard 347
Kinchyle 53, 166
Kineskie 274, 300
Kineskie Farm 301
King Alexander III 7, 34
King Charles I 11, 15, 183
King Charles II 11, 15, 92, 94
King David 34
I 6
King David I 6, 7, 34
King David II 23, 34

King Edward 7
King George I 112
King George IV 181
King James III 36, 154
King James IV 7
King James V 37
King James VI 38, 241
King James VIII 58
King Malcolm IV 6
King or Ramsay
  Kate 162
King Richard II 7
King Robert I 23, 26, 31
King Robert the Bruce 32
King William 2
King William of Orange 94, 147
King William the Lion 34
King-Emperor, George V 73
Kinnaird or Sandilands
  Anna 139
Kirkhill30, 41, 43, 99, 112, 137, 138, 139, 140, 347
Kirkton of Skene 91
Kirkwood of Pilrig
  Rachel 56
Knapp or Burnett
  Mary Louisa 166
Kyllachie 115

L

la Forge
  Amelia J. 173
Lady Bonnington 16
Lady Evlick 57
Ladysmith 69
Lagavin 28
Laing or Burnett
  Morag 105
Lake dwellings 227
Lambert
  Rev. Bruges 161
Lambert or Burnett-Stuart
  Carlotta J. 150
Lamont
  Dr. George 98
Lands of Leys 276, 320
Langham
  Geoffrey 107
  Philip 107
  Seymour 107
Larkins or Burnett
  Mary C. 22
Lauder 11, 61, 154
Lauder of Bellmouth
  Sir Robert 61
Lauderdale
  Arms of 255
  John Maitland, 1st Earl 188
Laurencekirk 112
Laye
  Major Francis F. 159
leaf device 4
Learney 294
Lechtoun or Burnet
  Agnes 37
Lee of Greenock
  Robert 20
Lee or Burnett
  Christian Catherine 20
Lees
  Admiral, Dennis M. 125
  David Brian 125
  Jeremy M. 125
  Rodney Burnett 125
Leicester or Irvine
  Eve Molly 107
Leighton of Usan 37
Leighton or Burnett
  Helen 173
Leiper
  Thomas, Master mason 253
Leith of Newlands
  William 39
Lennoxlove Castle 186
Leopard
  Magazine 252
Leslie
  Isabella 144
  John, of Powis 144
  William de 35
Leslie or Blackhall
  Grissel 39
Leslie or Burnett
  Anna 138
  Christian 30, 99
  Elspeth 129
Leys Bursaries 51
Leys crannog 227
Leys Estate 270
Lichtoun or Burnett
  Katherine 128, 130
Lickleyhead
  Castle 254
Lighton or Burnett
  Helen 166
Lillie
  Rev. John 149
Lindsay of Covington
  Martha 17

Liverpool 13, 171
Lloyd
  Martha Anne 101
Loch of Banchory 33, 36, 225, 237
Loch of Leys 225, 300
Lochtoun
  of Leys 34
Lockhart
  James , WS 11
London 35, 36
Lord Aboyne 255, 276
Lord Arbuthnot 55
Lord Bothwell 154
Lord Crimond 47, 92, 262
Lord Fyvie 187
Lord Grant of Elchies 346
Lord Kemnay 97
Lord Lyon King of Arms 176, 191
Lord Lyon of Arms 100
Lord Monboddo 46, 58, 112, 120, 123, 264, 346
Lord of Errol 248
Lord Panmure
  William Maule 161
Lord Patrick Grant 123
Lord Robertson of Forteviot 256
Lord Saltoun 166
Lord Southhall
  Alexander Pearson 51
Lord Warriston 92
Los Angeles 66
Louterell Psalter 230
Lovat
  Hugh, 10th Lord 13
Low
  Walter 106
Low Countries 2
Low or Grove
  Diana 106
L-plan tower house 269
Lumsden 348
  Clementina J. 137
  Col. Thomas, of Belhelvie 136
  David, 19th of Cushnie 263
  Elizabeth 41
  Harry Burnett 136
  Harry, 15th of Cushney 129
  Harry, Advocate 136
  Hugh David 137
  Sir Peter Stark 137
  Thomas 136
  William 136
Lumsden of Clova
  Robert 38
Lumsden of Cushnie
  John 40
Lumsden or Burnett
  Elizabeth 40
  Jean 129
Lumsden or Chalmers
  Jean/Jenis 38
Lumsden or Johnstone
  Helen Garden 137
Lunan
  John 55
Lyon or Forbes
  Elizabeth 40

M

Mackenzie
  Alexander, Fraser of Fraserdale 13
  Craig 81
  Elizabeth 13
  George 13
  John 13
Mackenzie of Coull
  Sir John 12
Mackenzie of Prestonhall
  Roderick 13
Mackenzie of Rosehaugh 178
Magicienne 65
Mair or Burnett
  Roberta 145
Maitland
  Alexander 23
  John 14
  Sir Charles 91
Maitland of Auchincreve
  Robert 47
Maltman
  Adam 58
Manor
  Church of 8
  parish of 8
MARISCHAL COLLEGE 201
Marquis
  Alex. Burnett 167
  George 167
Marquis of Exeter 275
Marquis or Clark
  Isabella 167
Marquis or Hall
  Ann Burnett 167
Marsham or Burnett
  Jane 45
Martin
  Alexander 53
  Andrew 53
  Christina 104
  James 53, 104

Robert 53
Stewart James 104
Thomas 53
Martin or Burnett-Stuart
Mary Campbell 151
Martineque 152
Mary Queen of Scots 37, 290
Mary, Queen of Scots 260
Matilda 4
wife of King David I 6
Maule of Glaster
William 92
Maule of Panmure
Robert 92
Maule or Burnett
Beatrix 92
Maule or Ramsay
Elizabeth 161
Maxwell or Burnett
Barbara 135
Mayville
Stevenston 21, 22
McCracken
Lilias de Crez 20
McCraken
Frank de Crez 20
McDonnell or Burnett
Margaret 20
McGie
Rev. William 16
McGillivray or McTavish
Ann 167
McLennan
Alexander E. 168
Annie 169
Duncan 168
McLeod
Archibald Norman 136
McNiven
Lance Corporal 72
McRobert
Elizabeth 133
James 133
McTavish
Alex. Burnett 167
Anne 167
Archibald 167
Catherine 168
Duncan 167
Elizabeth 168
George 168
Helen Mary 167
Josephine 168
Margaret 168
Robert 167
William Burnett 167
McVeagh or Lumsden
Catherine 136
medallions
at Muchalls Great Hall 255
Melrose
Abbey of 4
Melrose Abbey 33. *See* Abbey of Melrose
Melville of Monimail
John, Lord 13
Melville or Burnet
Elizabeth 38
memorial insc 345
Memorial inscriptions 348
Menzies of Culterallers 11
Menzies of that Ilk
Robert 91
Menzies of Weem 13
Menzies or Burnet
Grizzel 11
Menzies or Somerville
Grizzel 11
Midmar 47
Castle 242
military convalescent home
at Crathes Castle 311
Mill of Hirn 286, 288, 335, 340, 341
Millar
James, Coppersmith 56
Mills
Rev. Barton 161
Mills of Drum 240
Mills or Burnet
Phebe 44
Milton
Alice 108
Caroline 108
Frederick James 108
John 26
Timothy J.F. 108
Milton Gallery 293
Milton of Crathes 286, 295
Milton or Smith
Letitia I. 108
Milton, 281
Minchiner or Ramsay
Susan 161
Mitchell
David 95
James 95
Mary 95
Sir Andrew, of Thainston 99
Mitchelson of Middleton 16
Elizabeth 17
Moir
James, Regent 138
Moir of Stoneywood

James 140
Moir or Burnett
Agnes 138
Janet 19
Moirs of Leckie 19
Monboddo 111, 264
Monboddo House 259
Moncreiffe
Dame Jean 187
Sir Ian, Kintyre Pursuivant 176
Moncrieff of that Ilk
Sir John 51
Moncrieff or Burnett
Jean 51
Moncur or Burnett
Jane 27
Monmouth Co 174
Monterey CA 171
Montgomerie
Alexander 174
Anna 174, 175
Elizabeth 174, 175
Hugh 174
James 174
Jane 175
John 174
Mary 174
Robert 174
Sarah 174
William 174, 175
William, of Eglinton 174
Montreal 136
Montrose 48, 142
Marquis of 12
Monycabock 133
Mortimer or Burnett
Jean 46, 90
Mowatt
Andrew 134
George 134
Helen 134
Isobel 134
James 134
Janet 134
John 134
Mowatt or Peter
Marjory 134
Mowatt or Stuart
Margaret 134
Muchalls46, 48, 49, 56, 58, 59, 61, 89, 90, 97, 180, 185, 186, 187, 188, 189, 240, 246, 247, 248, 249, 250, 251, 252, 253, 254, 255, 256, 257, 259, 261, 274, 286
Muchalls Castle 186
Murless
Sir Charles F.N. 81
Murless or Cecil
Julia 81
Murphy or Burnett
Matilda J. 67
Murray
Alexander of Elibank 12
Amelia 13
Anna 12
Elizabeth 12
James, of Cobairdy 260
James. Lord 91
Patrick, 3rd Lord Elibank 12
Rev. Alexander J. 157
Violet 17
Murray
Mary 12
Murray of Glenrath
John 17
Murray of Polmaise
George 18
Murray of Stanhope
Sir David 17
Murray or Burnet
Margaret 11
Murray or Mackenzie
Helen 12
Muses Room
Crathes Castle 243
Myrebird 281

N

Nairne or Wyse
Margaret 112
Naismith
James 14
Napier or Nicholson
Elizabel I. 123
Nasmith
James 93
Nasmith of Posso
Sir Michael 93
Nasmyth of Posso
James 14
National Trust for Scotland 82, 232, 270
National Trust of Scotland 183
Naughton
Andrew 16
Rev. Andrew 16
Naysmith
James, Baronet of Nova Scotia 14
James,heir to Posso 14
Naysmith of Posso and Dawyck
Sir James 14

Nelson or Burnett-Stuart
  Nina 150
Neot's
  St.3
Ness Castle 167
Nether Crailing 9, 10
Netherlands 34
Nethermills Farm 274
Neuk Smiddy 285
New Jersey 47, 174
New Zealand 20, 115, 125, 149, 150
Newmarket 81
Nicholson
  Arthur B., WS 123
  Edward, Advocate 123
  James Badenoch 123
  Sir George 261
  Sir George, Lord Kemnay 28
  Sir William, of Kemnay 50
  William,of Glenbervie 50
Nicholson of Glenbervie
  Sir William 47
Nicholson of Glenbervie.
  Sir William 90
Nicholson of Mergie 264
Norman 7
Norman Conquest 7
Norman French 1
Normandy
  Duchy of 6
Normans 1
North Carolina 22
North Hirn 281
Northumbria 6
  Earl of 6
Nova Scotia 154
  Baronet of 48

O

Odo
  Bishop of Baieux 1
Ogden or Burnett
  Mary 166
Ogilvie
  John Burnett 21
  John, Ynr. of Inneshewan 21
Ogilvie of Kempcarne
  John 58
Ogilvie of Melros
  James 61
Old Deer 347
Old Kendal 259, 262
Old Machar, Aberdeen 348
Old Mill of Hirn 281
Oliver
  Alex. Burnett 169
  Duncan S. 169
  Robert Stuart 169
Olympitis or Paton
  Irene 118
Orkney
  Earl of 23
Orpheus 115
Orphoot
  Burnett Napier 21
  Thomas H. 21
Osborne or Burnet
  Elizabeth 44
Over Glack 9

P

Pack-Beresford
  Henry 104
Paice
  Robert Tasker 145
Pakistan 72
Palace of Holyroodhouse
  Keeper of 187
Park of Drum 31
partridge 298
  grey 299
Paterson or Burnett
  Anne Rebecca 114
  Deborah 113
Paterson or Sandilands
  Catherine 144
Paton
  Elizabeth Bertha 119
  Emanuel 119
  George 118
  John 119
  William Roger 118
Paton of Grandholm
  George 152
  John 118
  Katherine 29
Paton or Burnett
  Katherine 147, 152
Paton or Garde
  Ida Margaret H. 118
Paton or Kemney
  Augusta 119
Paton or Robinson
  Sarah Matilda 118
Paton or Sinclair
  Mary Louisa 118

Patterson
George, of the Hirn 280
Paxman
Lucy 105
Oliver 105
Rebecca 105
Richard 105
Payne or Cecil
Natalie 81
Pearson
Alexander, Lord Southhall 51
John 97
Pearson or Burnett
Katherine 51
Margaret 28, 97
Pelham Burn
Angus 276
Perman & Hynd 107
Peter
Rev Dr. Alexander 134
Pheasant 299
pheasants 298
Philip or Fleming
Margaret 12
Philips or Burnett
Fiona Mercedes 80
Picard 7
Pietersburg 70, 71, 72
Pike or Burnett
Abby 172
Pinkie House 186
Seton Room 187
pipe banner 181
Pitcairn or Burnett
Constance 128, 130
Isabella Morison 136
Pitmedden 28, 61, 89, 91
plasterers
English 186
plasterwork
heraldic 186
Pledge
Rev. Ebenezer 102
Pledge or Burnett
Anna Maria 102
plover
golden 300
Poland 128, 129, 130, 138
Polson
Rev. William 53
Port Ewen 170
Porteous
George, herald painter 57
Powis 144
Powis House 145
Presenter of Signatures 18
Prussia 152
Public Register
of all Arms etc in Scotland 191
Purves of that Ilk
Sir William 59
Purves or Burnett
Anne 59

Q

Quaker 30
Quakers 173
Queen Anne 92
Queen Mary's Roll 177
Quiddiesmill 281, 292, 321, 333, 341

R

Raemoir 225, 272
Ralph Burnard 7
Ramsay
Agnes M.A. 159
Alex. Burnett 163
Alex. P.O. 161
Alexander 159, 160, 161
Alexander E. , heir to Balmain 162
Alexander H. 163
Alexander W. 163
Arthur 163
Arthur D. 159
Bertin 162
Capt. Fox Maule 161
Capt. John 162
Capt. Robert 159
Caroline E. 162
Catherine 160
Catherine Forbes 157
Constance A. 163
David of Balmain 56
David, of Balmain 154
Edith P. 159
Edward Bannerman 159
Edward L. 159
Edwin Hewgill 160
Elizabeth Maule 161
Ellen 159, 162
Ellen G. 163
Enid E. 163
Ethel 162
Evelyn 162
Fanny jane 161
Florence A. 163
Frances 160

Francis 160
Francis F. 161
George Dalhousie, CB 161
Gilbert I. 163
Hallie 162
Hector A. 162
Helen 159, 160
Herbert 163
Herbert W.A. 163
Hilda 162
Hugh E. 162
Hugh F. Ramsay 162
Isabella 160
John 154
John R. 162
Lt. Col. Marmaduke 161
Maj. Gen/ Edward B. 161
Marmaduke 159, 161
Marmaduke F. 159
Mary 160
Nina Mary 159
Nora Mabel 163
Norman 162
Nowell B. 162
of Balmain 29
Olive 162
Patricia 161
Patricia T. 163
Rhoda B. 162
Robert 159
Robert C. 159
Sir Alex, Bart of Balmain 63
Sir Alex. E., 4th. Bart. of Balmain 163
Sir Alexander, 2nd Bart of Balmain 160
Sir Alexander, 3rd bart. of Balmain 162
Sir Alexander, 6th. Bart of Balmain 163
Sir Alexander, of Balmain 155
Sir Charles, of Balmain, MP 155
Sir David, MP 155
Sir David, of Balmain 155
Sir David, of Balmain, MP 155
Sir Gilbert, of Balmain 154
Sir Herbert, 5th. Bart. of Balmain 163
Sybil 162
Thomas 65, 158
Wilfred 159
William 160
William Admiral (Sir) 160
William Alexander 160
William, of Balmain 154
Ramsay Irvine
Sir Alexander 155
Ramsay of Balmain
Sir Charles 154
Ramsay of Barra or Irvine
Mary Agnes 107
Ramsay or Baltrop
Nora M. 163
Ramsay or Barstow
Elizabeth 161
Ramsay or Brown
Ellen Augusta 163
Ramsay or Burnet
Helen 15
Ramsay or Burnett
Katherine 63, 154
Lauderdale 65, 160
Ramsay or Carr
Elizabeth 161
Ramsay or Duncan
Lauderdale 160
Ramsay or Elliot
Christina 162
Ramsay or Hay
Georgina 162
Ramsay or Lambert
Mary 161
Ramsay or Laye
Elizabeth P. 159
Ramsay or Mills
Elizabeth E. 161
Ramsay or Murray
Elizabeth M. 157
Ramsay or Sparks
Mary 161
Ramsay or Taylor
Elizabeth 160
Ramsay or Thom
Jane 157
Ramsays of Balmain 29, 202
Rappahannock 42
Rashenlochy 274
Rattray 348
Rattray House 67, 82
Ravenscraig
Castle 236
RECREATION
and Leys Estate 300
Red Moss 279
Reddendo 238
Regent Moray 100
Register of Barony Court 271
Reichswald 80
Reid
Peter, merchant 59
Rev. James 51
Reid and Burnett School 305
Reid or Burnet
Catherine 51
Reid or Burnett
Elizabeth 58
Jean 52

Rennie
Agnes Emily 168
Alexander 168
Anne 168
Archibald Hill 168
Catherine A. 168
Charles G. 168
Jane Allan 168
Mary M. 168
William 168
Revolutionary Settlement 13
Rigail or Burnett
Mary 135
Robertson
James, Advocate 93
Robertson of Currie
James 17
Robertson or Burnett-Stuart
Maria 148
Robinson
Kildare 118
Robinson-Douglas
W.D. 157
roe-stalking 299
Roger Burnard 7
Rohays 4, 80, 81, 82, 105, 274, 283, 320
Roheise 4
Roll
of Battle Abbey 1
Roll of Battle Abbey 1
Roman Tripods 230
Roper
Clare 104
Lucy 104
Rose or Burnett
Elspet 172
Ross
John 305
Rotterdam 47, 53
Rout of Aberdeen 46
Rowallan
Thomas, 2nd Baron 81
Roxburgh Castle 23
Roxburghshire 7, 9, 177, 259, 266
Royal Arms of Scotland 178
Royal Forester 33
Royal Museums of Scotland 230
Royal William 65
Russell of Ashiesteel
William 17
Russell or Burnett
Lilias 17
Russell or Ramsay
Jane 160
Russian Imperial Court 103
Rutherford
General 11
George 266
Hugh 7
Rutherford of Hunthill
John 13
Rutherford of Kidheuch
Adam 9
Rutherford or Burnet
Isobel 13
Rydall or Burnett
Mary 145

S

Sahardi or Cecil
Jenine 81
Salem 95
salmon 34, 273, 296
Salmon 296
Saltoun
parish of 96
Sandilands
John 46
John of Bold 9
John, Provost 144
Margaret 139
Robert, Advocate 139
Sandilands of Cotton
James 29
Sandilands of Countesswells
John 90
Sandilands of Craibstone
James 144
John 139
Sandilands or Douglas
Jean 11
Sandys or Ramsay
Jane Maria 162
Sangford
Frances Sarah 102
Saplinbrae, Old Deer 103, 106, 107
Saratoga 64
Sauchieburn 238
Saxon thegns 2
Scharnhorst 106
Schoolhill 41, 131
Scolty 274
Scot of Bonnington
Simon 10
Scot of Eskdale
Sir Robert 14
Scot of Hundleshope
John 14
Scot or Burnet

Margaret 10
Scot or Burnett
Maria 94
Scotichronicon 32
Scots of Thirlstane 11
Scott
David 53
David, of Achath 53
James, of Achath 53
William 53
Scott of Thirlestane
Sir Robert 14
Scott or Burnett
Elaine 105
Scott or Polson
Catherine 53
Scott Skinner
James 287
Scottish 'black-house' 227
Scottish Genealogy Society 348
Scottish 'palace' 268
Scottish Royal Arms 185
seal
of Odo Burnard 7
seal impressions 177
seals
of Odo Burnard 4
of Roger Burnard 4
SEAVIEW HOUSE 202
Servitour to his Majestie 15
Seton of Meldrum
William 92
Seton of Pitmedden
Sir William 61
Shanghai 76
Shank
Alexander, of Castlerigg 57
Elizabeth 57
Henry 58
Martin 58
Rev. Alexander 57
Rev. Martin 57
Rev. William 57
Thomas 57
Shank of Castlerigg
Henry 57
Shank or Thomson
Jean 57
Shank or Walker
Margaret 57
Sheahan or Stratton
Teresa 104
Sheddocksley 49, 142, 152
Sheriff of Haddington 113
Sheriff of Peebles 8
Sheriff of Peeblesshire 14
Sheriffmuir 112, 133
Shetchocksley
James Burnett of 41
Shethocksley 40
Shiprow 41, 135
Shirrefs
Rev. James 170
Shirrefs or Burnett
Amelia 170
Shone or Cecil
Nellie 81
Silver of Netherley 255
Sim
Brian, Gamekeeper 298
Sinclair
Hon. Charles Home 118
Sinclair or Duncan
Effie Helen 118
Sinclair or Holman
Mary Esme 118
Skene
Alexander 38, 50
Andrew 50
Catren 50
George 50
Gilbert 39
James 48, 50
John 50
John. 15th of Skene 262
Margret 50
Rev. George 53
Robert 39
Thomas, Lt. 50
William 39
Skene House 50, 259
Skene of Raemoir
James 38
Skene of Skene
Alexander 48
John 50
Skene or Barclay
Janet 48
Skene or Burnett
Agnes 53
Margaret 142
Skene or Farquharson
Jean 50
Skene or Garioch
Margaret 48
Skene or Innes
Jean 48
Skene or Skene
Margaret 48
Skene or Tytler
Barbara 50
Skenes of Skene 262

Skilbeck
  Edward 145
  Henry 145
  Richard 145
  Virginia 145
Slessor
  Brig. Henry Cotesworth 151
Slessor or Burnett-Stuart
  John George 151
Sluie 272
Smith
  Calum 108
  Rev James, of Eddlestone 12
  Rev. James 21
Solemn League and Covenant 92
Somerville of Gladstanes
  William 11
Sourlands 9
South Africa 68, 69, 72, 108, 157, 191, 262
South Carolina 54
South Hirn 281
Southampton, NY 44
Spain 18, 50, 292
Spalding Club 67
Sparks
  John 161
Spearman
  Charles 65
Spearman or Burnett
  Caroline M. 65
Speed
  Col. Henry A. 107
Speed or Burnett
  Muriel 107
Spitz Kop 69
squirrels
  grey 300
ST ANDREW'S
  Episcopal Cathedral 201
St Gorgone's
  Kirk of Manor 9
St Neots 4
ST NICHOLAS KIRK 201
St. Andrews 12
St. Columba 32, 228
St. James's Church, Clerkenwell 346
St. Neot's 4
St. Nicholas
  Aberdeen 346
St. Nicholas House 276
St. Palladius 228
St. Salvador's College 12
St. Ternan 228
St. Ternan churchyard 347
St. Ternan's Park 304
Stacey or Montgomerie
  Sarah 174
Stanhope or Burnett
  Maria 94
Stark
  Rev. James 102
Steele
  Alexander 112
Steele or Burnett
  Margaret 153
Steil
  Magdalen 112
  Margarat 112
Steinkerke
  Battle of 16
Stewart
  Charles 106
  Edward 106
  James Michael 105
  John, WS 16
  Michael 105
  Thomas 106
Stewart of Shillinglaw
  James 10
Stewart of Traquair
  Margaret 265
  Sir John 10, 14
Stewart or Burnet
  Margaret 10
Stewart Royal Arms 186
Stewart, 2nd Baron of Traquair
  Sir William 10
Stobo 14, 92, 93
Stonehaven 247
Storer
  Edward 166
Strachan 155
  Rev. Andrew 38
Strachan or Burnet
  Christian 38
Strachan or Burnett
  Margaret 134, 135
Strathauchin or Skene
  Elizabeth 39
Stratton
  Finella 105
  Humphrey 104
  Isabella 105
  John 104
  Rosalind 105
Stratton or Bellamy
  Jane 104
Stratton or Paxman
  Diana 105
Stravinsky
  Igor 1
Stuart

Capt. John, 1st of Crichie 147
James 147
John 134
Marjory 134
Mary 134
Stuart of Dunearn 100
Charles 100
Stuart of Inchbreck
Prof. John 134
Stuart or Burnett
Alison 100, 144
Mary 100
Theadosia 29
Theodosia 147, 152
Stuart or Ferguson
Anna 147
Stuart/Stewart
Col. James 147
Stuartfield 147, 260
Svinos or Paton
Cocostaki 119
Swann
Charles 104
Gilbert 104
Marcus 104
Martha 104
Swann or Martin
Ann 104
Symmer of Balyordie
George 48
Symon Burnard 34

T

Tailor of Kirktonhill
Robert 60
tartan 181
Tasmania 149
Taylor
Alexander 170
Catherine 169, 170
Elizabeth 169
Ellen 169
George John Pitt 66
Helen 170
Henry 160
James 170
Jane 170
John 104
John, Advocate 113
Joseph 170
Mary 170
Robert 169, 170
William 169, 170
Taylor or Burnett
Margaret 113
Templer
Rev. Thomas 45
Tennyson 225
Teviotdale 10
The Family Room 183
The Hague Roll 179
The House of Crathes 185
The Knappach 273
The Old Pretender 112
Thirlestane Castle 186, 188
Thistleycrook 190, 285, 286, 294, 332, 344
Thom
Alexander 158
Alexander, of Ceylon 172
Dr. Alexander 157
Maj. William S. 172
William Ramsay 158
Thomas & Newell Burnett 114
Thomson
Rev. William 57
Roddy, Ghillie 296
Tiger and Sphinx 76, 78
Tilliecorthie 139
Tillihaikie 27, 28, 46, 89, 97, 128, 130
Tillybrake 274
Tillycairn 51, 259
Tilquhillie 273
Toasch or Burnett
Isabel 131
Todholes 281
Tolquhoun
Castle 240
Tolquhoun Castle 253
Tonley 152
Tor Na Coille Hotel 303
Tower or Burnett
Elizabeth 136
Tower Room
at Crathes Castle 308
Treasurer of Annuities 16
Treasurer of the Temporalities 16
Treasurer-Clerk 15
Treasurer-Clerk of Scotland 8, 13
Treaty of Berwick 23
Tunbridge Wells 98
Turnbull of Stracathro 30, 151
Patrick 152
Turnbull or Burnett
Agnes 30, 40, 151
Turner of Turnerhall
Robert 139
Turner or Burnett
Margaret 139
turnpike road 301

Tutor of Leys
  Robert Burnett 29, 58, 90
tweed
  of Leys estate 203
Twopenny
  Col. Edward 113
Tytler
  John 50

U

Uppermill 281
Urquhart
  James 173
Urquhart of Meldrum
  Adam 173
Urquhart,
  Patrick 173
Usan House 82

V

Valeries
  St.1
Van Horn
  Abraham 95
Van Horn or Burnett
  Mary 95
Veitch
  Sibilla 8
Veitch of Dawyck
  John 18
Veitch or Burnet
  Elizabeth 9
Veitch or Burnett
  Anna 18
Veitch or Murray
  Christian 18
Vernon, BC 102
Virginia 42
Viscount Arbuthnot 59

W

Wachopes/Wauchopes 225
Wakefield 138
Walchop
  John of 33
Walchope
  Allan 225
  Robert of 225
Walker
  Rev. James 57
Wallis or Burnett
  Kate 137
Waltham
  Abbey of 3, 4. *See* Abbey of Waltham
Warriston
  Lord 38
Washington 64
Watt
  Bob, Ghillie 296
Wemyss 53
Wemyss and March
  Earl of 82
West
  Richard 95
  Richard, Lord Chancellor 95
West Church
  Banchory 290
West or Williams
  Mary 95
Wester Kailzie 10
Westmoreland 2
Whigham & Vernon 66
White Room
  Crathes Castle 243
Whiteford
  Dr. Walter 16
Whiteford or Burnet
  Christian 16
Whitney or Ramsay
  Isabel E. 163
Wickerinn 281
Wilday of British Guiana
  Charles 21
Wilday or Burnett
  Elizabeth 21
wildfowl 299
William & Thomas Burnett 112
William III 92
William the Conqueror 1, 2, 3
William the Lion 6
Williamson
  Kirkpatrick 121
Wishart of Logie
  James 15
Wishart of Pitarrow 51
Wood of Glassel
  Arthur 273
Wood or Burnett
  Helen 45
Woodbine Co 283
Woodbine Cottage 271
Woodend149, 273, 277, 279, 280, 287, 295, 296, 297, 319, 332, 334, 336, 338, 343, 344
Woodend Cottage 149

Woodhousehill 259, 267
Wright
  Charles 124
  Charles F., Barrister 124
  James 124
  Stewart 124
  Violet G.L. 124
Wyse
  Alexander, of Thornton 112
Wyse of Lunan
  David 112

Y

Yarmouth 35
Young of Auldbar
  Peter 91
Young of Rosetta
  Dr. Thomas 19
Young or Burnett
  Nicholas(female) 91